BETWEEN TWO HOMELANDS

publication of this volume
is made possible by
Jewish Federation of Greater Hartford
within one homeland

BETWEEN TWO HOMELANDS

Letters across the Borders of Nazi Germany

Edited by Hedda Kalshoven

Translated from the Dutch by Hester Velmans
and from the German by Peter Fritzsche
Preface by Peter Fritzsche

University of Illinois Press
Urbana, Chicago, and Springfield

The publisher gratefully acknowledges the support of the
Dutch Foundation for Literature for the translation.

Ik denk zoveel aanjullie: Een briefwisseling tussen Nederland
en Duitsland, 1920–1949 © 1990 by Hedda Kalshoven-Brester
Originally published by Uitgeverij Contact, Amsterdam (1991)
English edition © 2014 by the Board of Trustees
of the University of Illinois
All rights reserved
Manufactured in the United States of America
1 2 3 4 5 C P 5 4 3 2 1

∞ This book is printed on acid-free paper.

Library of Congress Control Number: 2014937797
ISBN 978-0-252-03830-3 (hardcover)
ISBN 978-0-252-07985-6 (paperback)
ISBN 978-0-252-09617-4 (e-book)

CONTENTS

PREFACE

Peter Fritzsche

The letters and diary entries that follow have profound things to say about the most brutal regime in the twentieth century. They are an indispensable source for understanding the Nazis. They shed light on the lives of individuals who lived in new, unexpected, and often terrifying times. A series of unlikely circumstances have made these sources available to contemporary readers.

One hundred years have passed since the youngest Germans who voted freely for the Nazis were born. In the meantime, more has been written about Adolf Hitler and his supporters, about the National Socialist movement they built up, about the world war the Nazis set in motion in 1939, and about the murder of the Jews they planned and implemented than about almost any other topic in history. To this day, we continue to fold this succession of terrible events over and over again. Indeed, in his book *The Writing of the Disaster*, the French philosopher Maurice Blanchot refers to the Holocaust and, behind it, the strong-armed movement of perpetrators, the mute responses of observers, and the bewilderment and final silence of victims, as "the *absolute* event of history," when "all history took fire," when "the movement of Meaning was swallowed up." This "utter-burn" of events—the word choice indicates the difficulty of description—is indelible but also datable.[1] It originated in the most destructive war in modern history and still gives the present day its shape. It was 21 April 1944, when, from her Jewish family's hideout in the "Secret Annexe" on Amsterdam's Prinsengracht, Anne Frank remarked on "the eighteenth birthday of Her Royal Highness Princess Elizabeth of York," that is, Queen Elizabeth of the United Kingdom, who to this day is very much our contemporary.[2] The events seize us, but what historians do not agree on is their meaning: the reasons why the Nazis garnered so much support among German citizens before the seizure of power in 1933 or the evolving nature of that support in the Third Reich and through the war years. Scholars continue to debate the extent to which Germans were fundamentally attracted to the revolutionary and specifically racial aspects of National Socialism and the extent to which Germans approved of the persecution of their Jewish neighbors. Was Nazism a meaningful part of people's lives, or did Germans approach the regime in a more opportunistic, adaptive manner, and in what ways did citizens feel terrorized or ebullient as they participated in the course of events? Questions about the racial mindedness of ordinary Germans in the Third Reich and thus about the political malleability of lives in the twentieth century persist. Nazism poses fundamental questions about how people act as political beings—how they converge to make ideological commitments, how they respond to crisis and catastrophe, and how they understand power, entitlement, and injustice. The disasters of war and revolution in the twentieth century also indicate how little people actually see and how attenuated is their capacity for empathy. The events remind us that experience is always warped by expectation. For all these reasons, the attempt to understand the phenomenon of Nazism remains a compelling task.

We can't go back and interview Germans in the 1930s or 1940s about the Nazis or about the violence they saw around them or the complicity they might have shared. But thanks to an extraordinary cache of one family's letters and diaries that encompass the entire period from the end of World War I to the aftermath of World War II we can come close to hearing the discussions and debates that a handful of people had about the rise and the rule of the Nazis. We can take some provisional measure of how politics and war embedded themselves in everyday life. The German Gebenslebens and the Dutch Bresters trade impressions of Hitler, tell jokes on Jews, prepare racial passports, and worry about their men in the war. What has now come to be understood as the Holocaust is just visible on the margins, evident in a remark about the murder of Jews in Kiev and in a few diary notations about "Eddy," a Jew in hiding. The letters and diaries create a convoluted, but quite open space in which we gain sight of the members of one German-Dutch family moving about, creating intimacy, keeping distance, and trying to understand on-rushing events. We can make some sense of the small, but consequential ways in which they made history, although perhaps not quite as they wished. This astonishing set of "ego documents" introduces readers in an unprecedented way to real fleshed-out protagonists in the precarious setting of revolution, war, and genocide.

The spaciousness of the overall testimony is the result of several highly unusual factors. In the first place, the letters pull together a group of correspondents over four generations, extending down to Hedda Kalshoven (born Brester), the editor of this collection, who belongs to the last generation to have experienced and remembered World War II. The principal cast includes the great-grandmother, Minna von Alten (1859–1940), her daughter Elisabeth (1883–1937) and Elisabeth's husband, Karl Gebensleben (1871–1936), and their two children, Irmgard or "Immo" (1906–1993)—Hedda's mother—and Eberhard (1910–1944), Hedda's uncle, who was killed in the war. The correspondents also include a cousin, Minna von Alten's other granddaughter, Ursula Meier (1912–1986), Irmgard's husband August Brester (1900–1984), and her father-in-law Jan (1860–1934), as well as friends of Immo and Eberhard, particularly Carl-Heinz Zeitler, an outspoken opponent of the Nazis. The second reason for the spaciousness of testimony is the long time period during which the correspondents communicated: this selection of letters begins in 1920 and ends in 1949, from Immo's first trip to Holland after the First World War to her first return visit to Germany after the second. It is rare for a collection of letters, augmented by diary entries, to stretch across such a long time period. But the main reason for the spaciousness of testimony is that the correspondence crossed the boundary of Germany and Holland. After Immo married August Brester in 1929, she made for herself a new home in the Netherlands. The separation from her German family created contrasts between old and new, between the nationalist milieu in which Immo had grown up and the more liberal surroundings to which she moved. Immo and her mother, especially, tried to explain themselves to each other, a commitment that generated much more commentary about political events than is usually the case in family letters. What is extraordinary about this set of documents is the deliberate interest in explaining motives, particularly about National Socialism, which Elisabeth venerated. The difference in perspective sharpened when Germany invaded Holland in 1940 because Immo was forced to regard her own brother, Eberhard, an officer in the Wehrmacht, as one of the invaders of her new home. However, feelings of mutual affection and the desire for contact, especially after the birth of Immo's four children in the 1930s, constantly brought the German and the Dutch sides of the family together. The correspondence in this volume is thus shaped both by geographical and political difference and by personal intimacy. The deaths of Immo's parents in 1936 and 1937 and of her grandmother in 1940 also bound Immo and her brother more closely together despite their different perspectives on the war. The value of these documents is so great because they bring to voice a fairly large number of people across a long time period who are inclined by the circumstances of emigration and war to draw attention to what divides them as much as what brings them together.

What do they say? And what do we learn about the Nazis and the Third Reich? In the letters, the first reference to the Nazis or to Hitler comes immediately after the 14 September 1930 Reichstag elections when the National Socialists received a stunning 18 percent of the vote. It is not clear whether Elisabeth Gebensleben voted for the Nazis, but she remarked on the "fabulous boost" they enjoyed. A year later, Elisabeth clearly appeared as an enthusiastic supporter of the National Socialists; she cheered the party's rallies in Braunschweig, confident that the "national cause is on the march." Even so, she attended a meeting of the right-wing German National People's Party on the eve of presidential elections in March 1932 in which Hitler campaigned against the conservative President Paul von Hindenburg and a number of minor candidates. Indeed, her mother, Minna von Alten, declared her loyalty to the German Nationalist candidate, Theodor Düsterberg, not to Hitler. A preliminary tally on the occasion of a weekend visit to Karl Gebensleben's relatives at the end of the month indicated "12 National Socialists, 4 for Düsterberg, and 1 for Hindenburg," the holdout being Aunt Agnes who had to endure some ribbing as a result. Obviously politics was very much on the mind of family members, who carefully considered their votes in 1932.

Elisabeth's letters celebrated the Nazis as the long wished-for party of national salvation that would finally restore Germany to greatness. She mocked Chancellor Heinrich Brüning in comparison to Hitler. Indeed, the presidential elections in 1932 were a dramatic turning point in the transformation of nationalist politics: Hindenburg's 1925 supporters almost completely deserted him in 1932 to vote for Hitler, while Hindenburg's left-wing opponents in 1925 rallied to the incumbent president seven years later. This almost-total reversal in electoral loyalties indicates how appealingly different the National Socialists appeared to be. They truly drew people to a new political home. At the same time, some family members seemed to sympathize with the Nazis without necessarily casting ballots for Hitler—Minna, for example, and possibly Karl. This makes sense because after 1933, many Germans were happy to live in the Third Reich without being convinced Nazis or card-carrying party members. What this suggests is that the "national cause" was not identical with National Socialism; it mattered and moved people before the Nazis, although the National Socialists became its most prominent representatives. You could happily live in the Third Reich without having to love the Nazis.

The letters confirm how active the Gebenslebens were in the antirepublican "national cause" long before the Nazis appeared on the scene. Elisabeth wept for joy when she heard of Hitler's appointment as chancellor on the afternoon of 30 January 1933, but she herself had prepared the day. Ten years earlier, she described the busy routines of emboldened nationalists. Elisabeth looked out the window of her house in April 1924: "A troop of young people is just passing by, singing 'Swastika on the Flag, with a Black, White, and Red Band.'" Five days later, her thirteen-year-old son, Eberhard, could be seen "out on the street distributing campaign literature for the German Nationalist People's Party." He would later enroll in voluntary labor camps and eventually join the SA, the brownshirted Nazi paramilitary force. A few weeks later, seventeen-year-old Irmgard, a member of the Bismarckjugend, the youth group of the German National People's Party, looked forward to a Sunday flag consecration and to the dance that followed: "Everywhere there is great excitement . . . all the regimental associations are coming, even the riflery clubs." Along with her children, Elisabeth was quite representative of constituents of Weimar Germany's nationalist milieu; she nursed resentments against the Treaty of Versailles, passed along anti-Semitic comments, and expressed relief when her new maid, Frieda, who not surprisingly came from a working-class background, had nothing to do with "dissidents" or "Reds." These are all aspects of the bourgeois, antirepublican, and somewhat chauvinistic world that Immo left when she married and moved to Holland. If Immo's brother and her father came to love the uniforms they acquired, "down to brown britches and black leather gaiters," her future father-in-law, Jan Brester, mocked things military and urged Immo not to "bow to authority" and to "*think for yourself!*" If Elisabeth argued that her nineteen-year-old son ought not "to gain too many foreign impressions," Immo learned Dutch, raved about the international crowds at the 1928 Olympics in Amsterdam, and honeymooned in Chamonix, France. Although Immo was circumspect about disagreeing with her mother, Elisabeth was very clear about where she stood. She hated Bertolt Brecht's *Threepenny Opera* and its jazz music—all the "work of the Jews"—which besmirched the "finest and most pure art" that Braunschweig's court theater had presented in the old days. In a way, the family knew that Immo was gaining "too many foreign impressions" herself; Elisabeth, Karl, and Minna, all three, sent the happily married Dutch exile conservative newspapers from home and felt gratified when they believed Immo was reading them.

If Minna remained loyal to the German Nationalists because they remained loyal to the kaiser and the old prewar Germany, which until the end of her life provided Minna her point of reference, her daughter, Elisabeth, became a wildly enthusiastic supporter of the Nazis. She celebrated their spirit of sacrifice, their dedication and discipline, and especially their numbers. As far as she was concerned they were the only force sufficiently large and determined to resist the Communists, who, she worried in 1932 and 1933, threatened Germany with outright civil war. Although she tired of the many party functions that she, as the wife of Braunschweig's acting mayor, had to attend in 1933, and although she also grew somewhat impatient with party fanatics, she never lost her admiration for Hitler, whose speeches on the radio she made a point of hearing until the end of her life. To her daughter's exasperation, Elisabeth's letters went on and on about Hitler, about the Nazis, and about the new Germany. To explain her obsessiveness, Elisabeth quoted from Matthew, "For out of the abundance of the heart, the mouth speaketh." As for Elisabeth's husband, Karl, he also sported a "huge grin" when he passed on the news of Hitler's appointment as chancellor on the afternoon of 30 January 1933, and he later joined the party and assumed various administrative functions. But Karl was always more "old school," someone who retained feelings of loyalty even to the deposed Social Democratic mayor, Ernst Böhme, under whom he served. Their son, Eberhard, a bit of an intellectual, admired the "idealism" of the Nazis, but wondered if they were not too good to be true. There are "more than 25 opinions" about the Nationalist Socialists and "what they intend to do," he commented in 1932. After 1933, however, most of Eberhard's doubts subsided; like so many other Germans of his age—he was twenty-two when Hitler came to power—he was carried away by the nationalist celebrations and enlisted in the SA. He broke quite conspicuously with his best friend, Carl-Heinz Zeitler, over the issue of the Nazis—apparently they had a huge argument about race and eugenics. For her part, Immo gently, but continuously expressed misgivings about the Nazis before attempting to discontinue overtly political discussions with her mother entirely. Her husband, August, was a firm and unambivalent opponent of the Nazis, just as his father would have been.

When the National Socialists assumed power on 30 January 1933, Elisabeth was not blind to their violence. But the incidence of worrisome incidents was outweighed by the threat the Communists allegedly posed. "Communists" and "the same goes for the Social Democrats," she maintained, "have to undergo a three-year probation in a concentration camp" before their readmittance into German society. The brutal removal of Braunschweig's mayor, Ernst Böhme, in March 1933, was "disgraceful," Elisabeth admitted, but not as bad as what the "Reds" had done to Braunschweig's mayor in 1918. Eberhard, however, commenting on the same incident, noted that the number of "blemishes" was becoming "rather large," a scrupulousness his mother did not share. At one point, Immo stepped out of character and directly confronted her mother—and Elisabeth is the central figure in letters written in the mid-1930s—about the "horrible persecution" of the Jews, just days after the government-sponsored boycott of Jewish businesses on 1 April 1933. To Immo, her mother expressed "compassion" for "*individual misfortune*," but insisted that "world history is bigger than the fate of individuals." In any case, she continued, "Versailles" had taken the "opportunities for life" away from Germans; it was now "completely understandable" for them to fight back on behalf of their "own sons." Elisabeth's reasoning is faulty, nonetheless she argued that German Jews should make up for what the Allies had taken by restricting their representation in the professions to their proportion in the population: "that is one percent"—she believed she knew. The rhetoric in Elisabeth's letter recapitulated the work of becoming a Nazi. Elisabeth Gebensleben confronted Nazi terror, but, after a moment of hesitation, dismissed the evidence as accidental or justified it in the name of German suffering. "Tonight Hitler speaks," she remarked to Immo in closing: "I *definitely* have to hear that" on the radio.

Elisabeth's convictions, Immo's questions, and even Eberhard's doubts suggest how much, at least in the Gebensleben family, the accomplishments and the violence of the Nazis were discussed. The deliberations made Elisabeth firmer on the question of Nazism, but left Immo more horrified. What is clear is that Germans did in fact talk about what was going on. They were neither shy nor ignorant. Many Germans such as Elisabeth wanted very much to believe in the nobility of the Nazis' aims. They observed the world as if they were watching scenes from a Nazi movie, exactly as the party's propagandists would have wished; looking out the windows as she was traveling by train on 1 May 1933, Elisabeth noted the "fir sprigs strung over the streets," the "bouquets of flags, everywhere flags and more flags; processions across the countryside and cheering crowds." Radio broadcasts of the events such as the "Day of Potsdam" on 21 March 1933, when Hitler and Hindenburg stood together as newly united representatives of the new and the old Germany to open the new Reichstag, were also extraordinarily stirring events for German nationalists. On this day, the Gebenslebens ostentatiously displayed the old flag of the Kaiserreich along with the Nazi swastika-emblazoned banner. They were among the majority of Germans who desperately wanted to consume idealized images of a renovated nation; the consumption of domestic unity, social equality, and international recognition was very much part of the experience of Nazism.

True believers also knew that they were engaged in the task of healing the nation by virtue of their volunteer activities. For the enthusiastic Gebenslebens, at least, the Third Reich came with a busy schedule of events. Elisabeth, along with her maid, Frieda, attended meetings of the National Socialist Women's League and enrolled in a fourteen-week course "First Aid in Emergencies." "There is always so much to do," she noted not long after Hitler came to power. Eberhard continued his higher education into the political world of National Socialism in a series of military training camps. "You can imagine," Elisabeth wrote to Immo as Eberhard prepared to leave for Zossen, near Berlin, in September 1933, "the bustle of activity at our house until late at night. Packing up all his things . . . telephoning a doctor. . . . The last things packed, Eberhard left the station with his heavy bags at 7:15 the next morning." His cousin, Ursula Meier, became a leader in the League of German Girls. A wardrobe of uniforms, badges, certificates, and souvenir photographs documented their promotion up the administrative ladder.

Like most other Germans, family members were also obligated to prepare "Aryan" passports, which meant rummaging through papers to prove "Ayran" ancestry at the old family estate in Hedeper. Nazism worked itself into the texture of everyday life very quickly. For young people like Eberhard and, his cousin, Ursula Meier, it also opened horizons, and their grandmother, Minna von Alten, proudly followed their careers; Eberhard eventually became a Regierungsrat at the Ministry of Economics in Berlin.

World War II both confirmed and changed life in the Third Reich. "Brown britches and black leather gaiters," "First Aid in Emergencies," and the military training camp in Zossen demonstrated that the Third Reich was fundamentally constructed on a war footing. It created the homefront long before declaring war. War was both the aim of Nazism's political mobilization and the essence of life. At first, the victories came inexpensively. Writing to her granddaughter, Immo, in Holland, Minna, for one, was cheered by the "Anschluss" with Germany's incorporation of Austria in March 1938 and likewise the "return," as it was put, of Memel to the Reich a year later. In Amersfoort, Immo, on the other hand, was deeply distraught when war loomed over the issue of Czechoslovakia and its German-speaking borderlands in September 1938, though these were thoughts that she confided to her notebooks, not to her grandmother. As for Eberhard, he agreed with the basic aims of the war, the subjugation of Poland in 1939, and the incorporation in some form of Holland into the Reich. Yet, and this is the second point, the extreme violence of the war unsettled him, and he gained new perspectives after visiting his sister's family in German-occupied Holland and after he became engaged to Herta Euling, a so-called Mischling who lived and worked in the Third Reich with one Jewish grandmother listed in her "Aryan" passport.

Almost one-third of all German soldiers who served in the Wehrmacht, about 5.3 million men, were killed in action; Eberhard was one of them. He was among the majority of Wehrmacht casualties who died in the last year of the war when Germany's military defeat was all but certain. Yet initially Eberhard was relatively lucky. As a result of a horse-riding accident in Poland in November 1940, then a minor wound that resulted from being shelled in the foot in Russia in March 1942, and finally a mysterious nervous breakdown that he suffered on Christmas Day 1942, some time after returning to Russia, Eberhard enjoyed long periods of convalescence. As a lawyer he cherished homefront postings in Berlin and Frankfurt an der Oder. Like many soldiers, he treasured his time at home, and, at the same time, he yearned to be in the thick of things at the front. His diaries and letters show that he became increasingly weary of the war, in which his fellow soldiers ended up being "murdered," but the real source of his despondency was his inability to bring his love life with Herta into harmony with his professional life with the Nazis. Toward the end of the war, in the months before his death on 9 September 1944, Eberhard had little confidence in the future, not so much because of the looming defeat of Germany, which he in fact anticipated, but because he could not marry Herta and remain in the party and thus continue his career in the Third Reich.

The beginning of the war was a confirmation of Nazi perspectives on the world, for Eberhard as for so many German soldiers and their relatives. Eberhard took part in the German invasion of Poland (1 September 1939), and he found himself in Bromberg (Bydgoszcz), a town with a sizeable ethnic German minority in early

September 1939. Bromberg was the site of a massacre of German civilians by Polish civilians on 3 September after the withdrawal of the Polish army, an atrocity widely known as "Bloody Sunday." Although Germany's propaganda machine wildly inflated the number of German victims killed in Poland, several hundred civilians were in fact murdered in and around Bromberg. It is likely that Eberhard witnessed the terrible aftermath of the killings. "There wasn't a single village that we marched through where 30–40 Germans were not massacred," he wrote to his grandmother some ten days later: "Some we exhumed, others are still lying in the fields next to the country roads." But Eberhard's estimate of "untold thousands" of victims was off the mark, a product of rumors and Germany's unbalanced fear of *franc tireurs*. Both the shock of what Eberhard had actually witnessed and the casual racial assumptions that he brought along with him to Poland explain his declaration that the massacres "justify *any and all* measures on our part." As it was, in the weeks after Bloody Sunday, the Germans murdered hundreds of Polish residents and every Jew in Bromberg.

Eberhard was not a brutal *Herrenmensch*, but he assumed the swagger of superiority in Poland, a place where he knew that the "real East begins" and where "overall social conditions" were not "good and well" so that the "big picture" of Germany's conquest offered a "step forward." At least for a time, he enjoyed living like an overlord on a local "estate," sent requisitioned delicacies back home to his relatives, and enjoyed laundry service from local Polish women. To his brother-in-law, August Brester, whose anti-Nazi opinions he well knew, he sent a postcard depicting traditional-looking Polish Jews—"Jewish Politicians" read the printed caption. Eberhard's correspondence was so unthinking to suggest that his racial prejudices appeared completely self-evident and unproblematic to him.

Eberhard's relatives in Braunschweig were not so different: they simply assumed that prisoners of war would labor on their farms and that captive nations such as Holland would provide food for their families. Immo must have been appalled to read these early transcriptions of German entitlement. Even so, the letters themselves do not register what must have been the chasm between Immo in occupied Amersfoort and her relatives back home in victorious Braunschweig.

For a time, Germany's war had the feel of a great adventure. The American journalist William Shirer commented after Germany's invasion of Holland, Belgium, and France in May 1940: "It seems funny, but every German soldier carries a camera."[3] Soldiers saw the war as a grand event in which their participation merited souvenir snapshots. On duty at a train station in the provinces, Eberhard watched "soldiers on leave, prisoner transports, ethnic Germans, Hungarian peasant girls in buxom traditional dress," scenes he compared to a "colorful motion picture." Anticipating leaving for Arras in France in the middle of June 1940, less than a year later, Eberhard commented that "another page in the big picture book of the war will be turned." However, the war in Russia, after the German invasion on 22 June 1941, was far grimmer, far less picture worthy. At first, Eberhard found the country "full of mysteries and surprises," and at the beginning of October 1941 he expected that "soon things will come to an end here." He then had the fortune to be posted back to Berlin, where he spent Christmas. However, when he returned to the eastern front in March

1942 he stepped into the last parts of the terrible Winter War in which the Russians had launched their first counteroffensive against the Germans. "What a picture of misery all around us," he wrote about the beleaguered Germans. "Hobbling around in greasy winter vests," Eberhard's comrades "are barely recognizable as soldiers. And they are still on active duty (even with amputated toes)." Moreover, Eberhard and his unit felt increasingly isolated from the high command: "Do they just want to let us bleed without providing us with any support?" he asked. After a number of close calls, he also felt just plain lucky. "Who is watching over me?" he wondered. A few weeks later Eberhard was wounded; for the time being, the worst of his war was behind him.

When he returned to Russia in October 1942 to carry out administrative duties behind the front, the German offensive was already buckling. All around Eberhard, partisans were taking their toll: "Almost every night the Russians sneak out like Indians to capture 1 or 2 prisoners from the infantry," he wrote in his diary: "We seem to be powerless to stop them." "The front steadily melts away," Eberhard added in December. As for the "big picture: Africa *and* the East"—it was "not so good" either. According to Eberhard's "cold calculation, there is no way we can win." Even so, he tried to buck himself up—he wrote at the same time, "a people that endures in belief in itself can be redeemed!" Millions of supporters of the Nazis faced the bitter trade-off between calculation and faith, one that became more difficult as the war grew more protracted. Less than a year later, in September 1943, when confronted with the news that Italy had joined the Allied forces, Eberhard tried hard to stand firm: "I have never felt so close to the Führer as I do now," he confided to his diary.

On numerous occasions, Eberhard showed himself to be a true believer in Nazism: in the ongoing discussions with his anti-Nazi brother-in-law, in his brief in favor of Holland's integration into the "Greater" German Reich, which he wrote and sent to August in winter 1942, and in the countless mental exercises he made to retain faith in Hitler and the war. But Eberhard also gained new perspectives that sowed seeds of doubt of the kind that he had expressed back in 1932 and 1933, although he never assumed the oppositional stance of his former best friend, Zettel.

In December 1939, Eberhard met the love of his life, Herta Euling, a pianist in Berlin who was three years older than he. By early January 1940, Eberhard and Herta were officially a couple; "a new, tender, more wonderful world" had opened for Eberhard. However, Herta had a Jewish grandmother, a fact that, under the 1935 Nuremberg race laws, made her a "Mischling of the second degree." Herta's precarious position in the Third Reich undoubtedly shaped her view of the world, and the couple tried hard to skirt the "shoals of a political argument about the Nazis," as Eberhard once put it in his diary. The entries refer to "complicated discussions" and even "quarrels," although Herta and Eberhard remained together. In the summer of 1940, Eberhard finally confided to his grandmother: "Ohmchen, if only the 25% didn't exist . . . then I would marry her immediately." His family sympathized with his predicament but felt that the "25%" was sufficiently large to endanger his Nazi party membership and, with it, his career. Apparently, Eberhard and Herta put off a final decision. However, at the end of July 1942, Herta became pregnant. This was the summer when the last large-scale home leaves were granted for the millions of soldiers on the eastern front, and many soldiers, like Eberhard, returned to Russia in the summer and fall knowing that they would be fathers. The result was a mini-baby boom at the beginning of 1943, an age cohort that retired from public life only a few years ago.

As an expectant father, Eberhard immediately went to work to prepare a petition to the party court and the Nazi chancellery (Section IIa) to seek permission to marry Herta yet remain in the party, a complicated process that required testimonials and documents from both the party and the Wehrmacht. After substantial delays, and a further appeal, Eberhard's petition was not only rejected in August 1943 but was itself considered grounds for a further investigation into the suitability of Eberhard's party membership. These blockades were the reason for Eberhard's increasingly morose outlook on life, although he seemed to have been spared further political entanglements as long as the war ground on. In the meantime, Herta's baby, a girl, was stillborn on 6 April 1943. Arriving in Berlin shortly thereafter, Eberhard was devastated. He raged against "God's senselessness": "Isn't the murder of a creature in the mother's womb the most outrageous *crime*?" he asked in the middle of World War II.

There were other outrageous crimes about which Eberhard became aware, perhaps because Herta had told him some of the truths regarding the Nazis' persecution of the Jews that he was not—at least judging from the 1939 postcard sent from Poland—necessarily predisposed to hear. Posted in Lemberg (Lwów), the site of gruesome pogroms against the city's Jews in early July 1941, right after the Germans had marched in, Eberhard wrote Immo that there was not only "lots to talk about" but also quite a bit to be "mindful of," a hint, perhaps, of his reaction to the murder of hundreds of innocent civilians. In September 1942, he passed through Kiev, where he had "repeated conversations" about the massacre of Jews at Babi Yar that had occurred a year earlier. He also added details about slave labor battalions in his diary. This entry is the only reference to the Holocaust in the documents. Eberhard's concluding comment is a mixture of self-pity and horror: "Poor, dear Germany will pay for this." This remark, centered as it was on the future of Germany, was not unusual. In some ways, he was mourning the Third Reich. In any case, Eberhard seemed to have growing misgivings about the conduct of the war. In December 1942, he even took up the legal case of an ethnic Russian who had been "stuck into a German uniform and refused to serve." Eberhard's heart was in the right place, but, in the shadow cast by Stalingrad, he remained riveted by the impending collapse of own his future: "Does it even make sense to fight for the rights of a single individual when a general catastrophe is looming?" Eberhard was repeatedly unsettled by pieces of evidence that did not conform to his overall and his enduring commitment to National Socialism. His diary and his relationships with his sister in Holland and with Herta were spaces where he could give voice to bits of doubt. After Eberhard was killed in action in September 1944, Herta averred that he died for the cause in which he believed, but by that time Eberhard no longer was the same confident party member or adventure-loving soldier he had been in 1939 and 1940. Perhaps Eberhard—and the collection of documents veers toward him in the 1940s—is representative of ordinary Germans who were unwilling and unable to get out of Third Reich, but also uncomfortable in its confines.

There were many pathways out of the Third Reich, so many ways to reckon with the past, so many burdens to bear. Eberhard was killed in the war, as was a cousin, Diethelm, and other relatives. Immo's husband, August, participated in the Dutch resistance to the Nazis, and Immo and August hid political refugees in their home, including a Jewish boy, Eddy. The only documentary trace of his nine-month stay are Immo's cryptic notebook entries: "Eddy came . . . Eddy scarlet fever . . . Eddy left." For Immo and her family, liberation by the Allies could not come fast enough in spring 1945. Eberhard's old school friends, Gerhard Nicolai and Zettel, chose to emigrate and leave Germany permanently. For them, 1933 was a caesura that could not be undone. But Immo's friends back in Braunschweig took much longer to confront the advantages they had gained as a result of the Third Reich and the consequences of the war that followed. And most of them confronted those consequences in a self-serving and self-pitying way, something that caused Immo a great deal of unhappiness. The Gebensleben's former maid, Frieda, who had been with Elisabeth and Karl on the day when Hitler was appointed chancellor, is a good example of how many Germans came to see themselves as victims after the war. They made little connection between their actions before 1933 and their lives after 1945. The poignant list prepared by Dorothea X. at the end of December 1946 summarizing the postwar fate of former classmates from the 1920s is a compelling document of the ways in which the Third Reich and the war it launched assembled, dispersed, and then ruined Germans. But general silence about the fate of Europeans in the German war zone persisted for many years. It should be said that two generations later, Immo's daughter, Hedda, found her relatives in Germany very open to the publication of this letter collection.

A final note. Instead of footnotes to explain references and to contextualize the activities of the correspondents, Hedda Kalshoven has written brief explanatory paragraphs interspersed at regular intervals among the letters and diary entries. They are meant as practical guides to the specific content of the next series of documents. And let me add: it has been a great honor to work with Hedda, and I am grateful for the opportunity to have participated in this project. I am most grateful for the support of Willis Regier and the University of Illinois Press. And many, many thanks to my wife, Franziska, and our life.

NOTES

1. Maurice Blanchot, *The Writing of the Disaster*, trans. Ann Smock (Lincoln: University of Nebraska Press, 1986), p. 47.
2. Anne Frank, *The Diary of a Young Girl* (New York: Bantam, 1993), p. 214.
3. William Shirer, *Berlin Diary: The Journal of a Foreign Correspondent, 1934–1941* (New York: Knopf, 1941), p. 413.

IN DER FREMDE

Aus der Heimat hinter den Blitzen rot
Da kommen die Wolken her,
Aber Vater und Mutter sind lange tot,
Es kennt mich dort keiner mehr.
Wie bald, wie bald kommt die stille Zeit,
Da ruhe ich auch, und über mir
Rauschet die schöne Waldeinsamkeit
Und keiner mehr kennt mich auch hier.

IN A FOREIGN LAND

From home behind the lightning red
Come the clouds,
But father and mother are long dead;
No one there knows me any more.
Soon, oh how soon comes the silent time
When I shall rest too, and above me
The forest's beautiful solitude whispers
And no one knows me here either.

JOSEPH VON EICHENDORFF (1788–1857)

INTRODUCTION

On 11 June 1920, a thirteen-year-old girl arrived in the Netherlands on a "war-children transport" ferrying German children to the Netherlands to recuperate from World War I. She got off the train in Utrecht, anxious to see where she would wind up. She suffered from homesickness the first few days, but soon began feeling at home with the family that had taken her in. Her foster parents did their best to make the stay of this girl from Braunschweig into an experience she would never forget. In spite of the contrast with her own home in Germany, or, rather, perhaps because of it, the girl who was to become my mother had already begun to fall in love with the country that, nine years later, would become her own when she married the youngest son of her foster family.

There were salient differences between the family in Utrecht and the one in Braunschweig. My Dutch grandparents were calm, sober people, averse to flamboyance and self-importance. They held strong antimilitaristic views and believed in independent thinking and judgment. It was in that spirit that they had raised their two sons.

My mother, on the other hand, had been raised in an environment that attached great importance to tradition and patriotism and admired everything military. After Germany's defeat in World War I (1914–1918) and the November 1918 revolution, nostalgia for the empire's lost glory, a profound sense of humiliation, and material deprivation had left their mark on her family's mindset.

That background, and her close ties to her parental home, did not prevent her from falling in love with the Netherlands. Upon marrying my father in 1929 and exchanging her German passport for a Dutch one, she threw herself heart and soul into her new life as the wife of a Dutch doctor.

Still, her home country remained an important part of her life. Visits back and forth, and an active correspondence, served to maintain contact with her family. My maternal grandparents and the German uncles and aunts conjured up a different kind of atmosphere, by the language they spoke if nothing else, and on our visits to Braunschweig, we became part of my mother's German world in which she felt so at home. Back in Holland, I didn't pay particular attention to the German side to our family; it was so much taken for granted that I didn't see it as anything special. My father had given us his nationality; we were Dutch.

My interest in that German side wasn't sparked until many years later, when two things happened: first, my decision in 1982 to obtain a degree to teach history, and second, a trip I made with my mother to Berlin in the autumn of the same year. I listened to my mother as she started reminiscing about Germany, most of the memories coming back to her as we strolled along the wide Unter den Linden boulevard in East Berlin. Suddenly she was the little girl again who, when the family lived in the district of Spandau from 1911 to 1915, would skip along holding her father's hand, waiting for the familiar trumpet signal that heralded the arrival of Kaiser Wilhelm II. The two of them would stand waving at him, swept up in the enthusiastic cheers for the brightly colored uniforms, the braiding and the tassels, the spiked helmets and the stamping, pawing horses surrounding him that signified his power.

I gazed at her, and suddenly I realized that my mother came from a world I really did not know at all. There had always been plenty of stories and anecdotes about the family, to be sure, but now, all of a sudden, I beheld her life against a background of parades and imperial might, of World War I putting an end to all that, and of the subsequent developments that were to have such dire consequences. What did I know about the views of her relatives (who were my relatives too, of course), or of her own opinions? What had been their political beliefs?

For the first time I wondered about that German side that I had never thought about before. I wanted, for the first time, to know what it had meant to my mother to have two homelands, what it was like to experience her new country being oppressed by the old one in World War II. All I knew was that it had been "difficult." But just how difficult?

I started thinking about certain incidents that I, the eldest of us four children, could still remember. Like the time we stayed in Northeim, on the farm of my grandmother's cousin. We had arrived right in the middle of the annual harvest festival. The farmhouse entrance hall was decorated with garlands of stalks of wheat, suspended from the ceiling was an intricately woven wreath, and everywhere there were flags: red flags, with a black and white swastika in the center.

That was in 1938. Not long after that, back in the Netherlands, a new boy suddenly turned up in my class who spoke only German. He was given a seat next to me, so that I could fill him in, in his own language. Both of us were dreadfully shy: I probably wasn't much help to him. I had been told something about "escaped" and "Jewish," but I had no idea what that meant, nor did I have any sense that the red swastika flags in Uncle Ernst's gaily decorated front hall had anything to do with it. I also remembered how pale my mother's face had gone on the morning of 10 May 1940, when Germany invaded the Netherlands, as she cried out, "Will my own brother have to fight us now?" We were evacuated from Amersfoort on Pentecost, but my father did not come with us; he had to remain at his post in the hospital. On the way to Haarlem the car was frequently stopped; someone would lean into the window and ask us where we lived, what school we went to; we had to say "Scheveningen," and I noticed that my mother didn't mention her German origins. They asked her, "Where were you born?" to which she answered, mumbling, "My husband in Arnhem," upon which they let us go through.

The word "German," which had always been so ordinary and familiar, suddenly acquired a new, menacing connotation in the years of the Occupation. Contradictions

occasionally arose of which I am conscious only now, many years later. At school, like
my classmates, I tried to sabotage the lessons of the German teacher, a known Nazi
sympathizer, but at home I used the same German language to reply to the letters
covered in stamps, numbers, and light blue censorship marks that were still arriving
from Germany for me and the other members of the family. The disruptions to our
daily life kept multiplying—the constant hunt for food, the air-raid sirens, the groups
of heavily guarded prisoners on their way to the concentration camp on the outskirts
of our town, and the mounting loathing you felt for every German soldier you met.
But whenever Eberhard, my mother's brother, turned up at our house, we'd race to
greet him, and I'd press my face into the same gray-green uniform as the ones those
rotmoffen ("shit Krauts") wore.

One day my father abruptly disappeared, and men came to seal up his office:
the Doctors' Resistance. Occasionally we'd have someone staying with us whom we
weren't supposed to talk about with outsiders. I also have a vivid memory of my
mother clutching the letter announcing that Eberhard was dead; the Jewish boy
hidden in our house at that time to this day remembers bursting into tears when he
saw my mother's grief over her brother's death. Once we were liberated, I joined the
first silent march to the cemetery in honor of the fallen Allied soldiers buried there.
On reaching the graveyard, however, I suddenly turned from the procession to lay my
flowers on the German graves, in a final farewell to Uncle Eberhard.

Those contradictions now began to haunt me. After a while, I tried broaching
the subject of that German element of our family with my mother, and I wanted to
know about her own experiences. I wasn't sure exactly what I was looking for; I was
just groping in the dark. But we barely ever left the old, familiar territory. Actually,
one of the stories that came out of these talks is a good example of the way my
mother's old and new worlds sometimes overlapped.

On her way to school every day, my mother skirts the park of the castle belonging
to the Dukes of Braunschweig, and she likes to press her nose against the fence to watch
the young Princess Friederike, later the Queen of Greece, being pushed around by a
nursemaid in a navy blue perambulator. Right then and there she decides that one day,
when she has children of her own, she too will have a lovely blue pram like that. And so
she does. When in the "hunger winter" of 1944–1945 her adopted country is left almost
completely ransacked and plundered by Germany, and she sends the children to the
soup kitchen to fetch the family's rations of thin rye-gruel or watery turnip soup, it's that
blue pram that is brought down from the attic to transport the food. I wanted to know
about the political situation of her German family. But here, as usual, we didn't get any
further. Our exchanges always began and ended in the same place: the beloved parental
home, the warm relationship between my grandparents and our family, all those
precious memories; there was no room for follow-up questions.

And that was where we left it. Until the day I discovered the letters.

My mother wanted to look something up for me; she walked over to her desk
and took out a bundle of letters, the ones that had brought her the first signs of life

from Germany after the end of the war in May 1945. I asked her to read a few to me (I couldn't decipher the German script), more out of ordinary curiosity than from any expectation that they would contain anything special. And so I found myself all of a sudden plunged into the Germany of the era just after the collapse—the chaos, the upheaval, and the deprivation that reigned during those first few years, complete with the disillusion, the fear of the Russians, and self-pity heedless of what had been done to other countries.

Living history! Now I grew curious about the rest. I knew there were more letters in a trunk upstairs in the attic. And indeed, there I found old shoeboxes and candy boxes bursting with bundles of letters, the dried-out rubber bands stuck to the envelopes. I picked out a pile at random and gave it to my mother. She started reading aloud a letter from 1933, from my German grandmother. An ordinary letter from a mother to her daughter abroad, full of news the daughter would want to hear, as well as anxious advice, expressed longing for the grandchildren, stories about outings to concerts and plays, and so on. My grandmother had a lively writing style, and it was quite absorbing, at times most amusing, to step into the family life of over half a century ago like that.

But the letter turned out not to be so ordinary after all. In writing the letter, my grandmother kept referring to a speech by Hitler that was to be broadcast over the radio that day and about how all day she couldn't think about him without tears in her eyes: this simple man who had been in the trenches during the World War, and who was now the Führer of sixty-five million people; yes, he might even be the Führer of the whole world some day! Her fervent belief in Hitler as Germany's savior and her worship of his "overwhelming personality" impelled her to urge her daughter to read the speech in her German newspaper, and read it at least twice, because he had the answers to so many questions. My grandmother was proud again to be German, and her pen could barely express the passion she felt for the man who made it possible for her to feel that way once more. Her enthusiasm spilled over in page after page.

The other letters contained in that bundle were the same. Listening to my mother reading them out loud, I didn't dare to look up; my cheeks were aflame. So there it was, then! I felt implicated in something I wished to have nothing to do with. And then there was the realization that I had never really wanted to consider this possibility. At the same time, I was hugely fascinated by having this direct contact.

This unexpected revelation, however, only made the subject even more taboo. For my part, I held my tongue, incapable of even mentioning it. My mother found the letters "interesting," and then we went on to discuss the other things they described. It was creepy, but at that moment neither of us was capable of behaving any differently.

My father wasn't alive for this. He passed away in 1984.

I gradually learned to decipher the handwriting of those letters, which numbered over two thousand. I found the letters of my Dutch grandfather, who faithfully kept his foster daughter (as she remained) apprised of what was happening in their circles in Utrecht. My mother's letters to her own parents and grandmother had found their way back to the Netherlands, so that it turned out that we had the complete correspondence. Letters in the old-fashioned, elaborate handwriting of my German great-grandmother, letters from aunts, friends, and acquaintances, letters from my uncle Eberhard's war years—a number of them from Poland, Russia, and France, some hastily scribbled in pencil, the military postcards printed with quotes from Hitler's speeches. It was all there, intact.

The letters made Germany's history in the first half of the twentieth century come alive for me, as it was experienced and recorded by my own family. Not just alive, but so very close to home! Our Dutch family turned out to be intimately tied to something that had seemed very far removed. My own memories of Braunschweig before the war were happy and sunny. Reading the correspondence, however, gave those memories a whole new dimension. I saw myself as a child dwelling in two different worlds, like my mother; my young eyes had taken in the brown-tinted street scenes, I had even taken part in them. In the memoirs of Carola Stern, born in 1925, I read about her being sent to the meetings of the "Hitlerküken" in her new brown dress, wearing a headband with crocheted flowers, I remembered the snapshots of my sister and me in Germany in the 1930s, in which we are wearing the same headbands, and I felt an almost visceral connection.

What kind of people did my mother come from?

The central figure was, without a doubt, my great-grandmother, Minna von Alten-Rauch (Ohmchen), a presence clad in ankle-length black at every family event. Minna Rauch was born in 1859 in Hedeper, a village south of Braunschweig, where her father was a rich farmer. In 1882, she married August von Alten, a farmer's son from Atzum, who was a Justice of the Peace in nearby Salder. Minna's life was not an easy one. Over the years, after the premature death of her husband, she lost three of her four children. Eventually she went to live with her only surviving daughter, Elisabeth (my grandmother), and, later, stayed close by, in the same neighborhood. In 1937 that daughter too died, far away in the Netherlands, in my father's hospital, where he had brought her when the situation became critical. When Ohmchen (my sister and I called her Olla) herself passed away in late 1940, her only grandson was lying in a field hospital in Poland and her granddaughter, who had married a Dutchman, was out of reach on account of the war. The only ones nearby were her brother Otto and the other granddaughter, Ursel. My mother remembered her as a strong woman who always managed to pick up the pieces with renewed courage and had dedicated her life to others. That she too knew doubt and despair is clear from some of her last letters, as is the grief over the loss of her last child.

Elisabeth von Alten was born in 1883 and married Karl Gebensleben, twelve years her senior, in 1906. She loved going out, she painted and wrote poetry. She was intensely involved with what was going on around her and was transported by music, the opera, and theater. She had a conventional upbringing. My grandparents were highly respected in Braunschweig. Thanks to Karl's position in city government, they were involved in almost all of the city's important social events; they were members of various clubs and societies and had a wide circle of friends. Elisabeth was a talented storyteller; I would hang on her lips whenever she launched into one of her stories—told in German of course, but in my memory the two languages are interchangeable. The Dutch grandchildren changed the German "Ohmi" to "Mimi," and that was our name for her ever after. Karl Gebensleben was born in 1871 in Schöppenstedt, where his father, a farmer's son from Uehrde, ran a coopery. Karl studied architecture and railway engineering at Braunschweig's Technical College, largely paying for his studies through tutoring. After passing his engineer's exams he began working as an inspector for the Prussian railways. In 1901 he took a job working for the city of Braunschweig, at the same time becoming a professor at his old college. In 1911 he was made Head of Public Works and councilman of Spandau, near Berlin. Four years later he took on the same post in Braunschweig. Over the course of his long service he was responsible for the municipal swimming pool, the port, and the rail yards, among other things. Near and dear to his heart was the restoration of the old inner city. He often had to travel for work, but he found time for the theater and concerts and for long hikes in the Harz mountains. He was also deputy mayor for a total of eight years. He died in January 1936, on the first day of his retirement.

Their daughter Irmgard, my mother, was born on New Year's Eve 1906; their son Eberhard in 1910. Eberhard was an intelligent boy who graduated from Gymnasium with the highest final exam score in fifty years. He studied law at Kaiser Wilhelm University in Berlin, spending a number of semesters in Grenoble, Freiburg, and Heidelberg. At university he took up horseback riding; horses were to play an important role in his life.

Eberhard was on the whole a cheerful fellow, but he did suffer from spells of depression. His civil service job at the Ministry of Economics (for which you were obliged to belong to the Nazi party) did not last long. In September 1939 he was sent straight to Poland as a member of the Wehrmacht, then in 1940 to France, and back again to Poland. After that he was either on the Russian front, deep in the Ukraine, or in Germany proper. Toward the end of 1943 he was stationed in Normandy. He was killed in September 1944 near Bruges.

The large farm in Hedeper was inherited by Otto Rauch (my great-grandmother's youngest brother) who had the Neue Haus (New House) built there in 1906. The Alte Haus (Old House), the original farmhouse built in 1640, remained the home of the elder sister, Emily, until her death in 1930. Hedeper was the gathering spot for the entire family and played an important role in my mother's childhood memories. The entire property was sold in 1978.

My Dutch grandfather, Jan Brester (1860–1934), had already been retired from his job as post office commissioner for quite a while when my mother made her appearance in the family as a "German war child." I gather he was home much of the time, with a wide range of interests, very outspoken opinions, and a great sense of humor.

My grandmother, Henriette Wurfbain (1865–1933), had studied the piano. After her marriage she stopped giving lessons, but continued to play. Music was an integral part of her sons' life. Both she and my grandfather read a great deal—German,

The New House in Hedeper; at the bottom right is part of the Old House

French, and English as well as Dutch. Her children called her Moes, and she was said to have been a lovely person.

Because of Jan's early retirement, the Bresters were not all that well off. But thanks to an arrangement with good friends of theirs, the boys were able to attend university. Carel, the eldest (1897–1981), studied math and physics, obtained an advanced degree, and became a teacher. August, my father (1900–1984), studied medicine. After his finals, he worked as assistant to A. Hijmans van den Berg, Professor of Internal Medicine at Utrecht, and later, as Senior Resident, went on to train other medical students. In 1935 he was made Senior Medical Officer of Lichtenberg Hospital in Amersfoort. He stayed there until his retirement in 1965. He was a respected and trusted physician, a peace-loving man with a forgiving and accommodating nature.

How I would have liked to ask my father the questions that occurred to me all those years later! But it was too late for that.

Ordinary people writing each other letters. There is no inherent reason to make such private documents public, no matter how interesting the relationships within such a large family might otherwise be. But these people lived through the Third Reich and World War II, the darkest period in Germany's history, and their letters reveal how they navigated that time. Moreover, the correspondence is so complete that it tells a story in itself. It's a story that can be told only in pieces; I was forced to leave much of it out, not only because of the sheer numbers of letters and postcards, hundreds of them, let alone their length (six densely written pages was the norm), but also on account of their content. There was much in there that was valuable, amusing, or precious to me, the daughter. But what would other people care about stories of us as children, about maids, family quarrels, and romantic adventures, about arrangements for reciprocal visits, recipes, sewing instructions, financial affairs, or accounts of illnesses?

Therefore, the choice of which excerpts to include would be determined by the questions I myself had posed at the beginning.

My mother had actually been struck by the differences between these two worlds on her very first visit to the Netherlands, then just minor differences in attitude and habit. It was only shortly after she had left Germany for good that her parents, like millions of other Germans, began to turn to National Socialism, which they saw as an escape from humiliation and despair. From their letters I got to know them much better than had been possible from just the family stories and my own vague recollections. They were humane, upright, and educated people, but they too didn't see what was really happening at the time. The louder they cheered, the more difficult it was for my mother. She was still deeply attached to "home," but in the Netherlands she had encountered a radically opposite viewpoint, and she could no longer understand her parents' enthusiasm. Yet at the same time she did not like to let them or the others down. She sided with my father in his critique of the developments in Nazi Germany, but tried nonetheless to keep the peace between the two families because harmonious family gatherings were more important to her than political wrangling.

I had been unaware of just how torn she had been until I read the letters and was later able to discuss them with her. So it had been difficult for her even before the war.

When Germany invaded the Netherlands in May 1940, my mother immediately took the side of the Dutch and was prepared to join my father in taking big risks to do so. Her parents were no longer living by then, but the sense of being pulled in two opposite directions stayed with her, though now focused squarely on Eberhard. In spite of the deliberate choice she had made, with all its attendant consequences, he still was the brother she loved, and Germany was still the country where her roots lay. It wasn't until I read the letters, and later on discussed them with her, that I began to grasp her inner struggles over all those years.

My mother's story, from the children's transport to the Netherlands in 1920 to the first time she visited Germany again after the war, in 1949, is a good example of how complicated the situation must have been for a Dutch woman of German origin during this particular historical period. To tell that story, I was able to draw on what in my opinion is a unique collection of letters. But that entailed the discovery that almost all of my German relatives had been supporters of Hitler. Was it really necessary to shout it out from the rooftops? Would it be of use to anyone? Was it fair to do this to my mother, at her age? Would I be betraying all those people from my childhood?

Still, on rereading the excerpts in question, I was struck over and over again by that sense of being in direct touch with the past. The letters, especially my grandmother's letters, provided a firsthand look at how people came to be drawn to

National Socialism, engendering the expressions of blind trust and total submission you can see on people's faces in the pictures and films of that era. It had also become clear to me that documentation regarding the appeal of the Nazis had for the most part been destroyed in May 1945, therefore making these documents valuable for their rarity. It was that combination of immediacy and rarity that convinced me that making these letters public was the right thing to do.

My interest in the person of Eberhard played a large part in influencing my selections. I can still recall him quite vividly: in my mind I can hear the strange intonation of his voice when he tried speaking Dutch to us, and his often somewhat wistful smile comes back to me. His letters gave his wartime visits to us in Amersfoort a new dimension that had not occurred to me before. But I'll never know the real truth: what had his eyes seen, in Poland or Russia, when he stood in the doorway of our girls' room, and we raced up to him, jubilant? He is buried on the moors at Lommel just across the Belgian border, among forty thousand other German soldiers. In the last months of the war, there was no mail, so there are hardly any letters from that time. For the sake of continuity, I took advantage of my mother's habit of succinctly jotting down important events in her diary. I also found a few useful entries in my own journal from that time.

The decision to have this book published was not easy. My conviction that documents like these letters shouldn't just vanish again in the end won out over the desire to protect our family's privacy.

I have to thank my mother for allowing me to make that decision; for her, it was even more difficult. Reading the letters was a shock not only for me, but especially for her, since the idea of the past she had formed in her mind over the years had become quite removed from the truth. I don't remember how long our initial silence about what was in the letters lasted, but that silence did get broken in the end. Stirring up and laying bare the past was a heavy burden for her. As we wrestled our way through that lengthy and occasionally painful process, however, that burden gradually began to lift into a sense of liberation for both of us: the past had finally become something we could talk about.

I admire my mother for agreeing in the end to share this story with others. In a similar vein I wish to extend thanks in memory of my father. Although I had to do without his wise counsel, I believe I have handled it the way he would have. Also included in my appreciation are my sister and two brothers. If my mother and I had not had their support during our periods of doubt, this book would not have seen the light of day. They further backed me up with advice and constructive criticism.

Naturally, this correspondence could not have been published without the permission of the various correspondents or their heirs. It was wonderful to see that they were all prepared to give me that permission. Tracking down the letter writers or their next of kin brought us happy reconnections as well as new acquaintanceships. I thank all of them from the bottom of my heart. I can reasonably assume that two of the correspondents, now deceased, whom despite repeated attempts I wasn't able to track down, have no heirs; another has left no trace at all.

Of the many people who helped me assemble the background information for the letter excerpts, I can list just a few. Dr. M. Garzmann and J. Angel, at the Braunschweig Stadtarchiv, allowed me to consult them on many occasions, as did Mr. K.-J. Krause of the *Braunschweiger Zeitung*. Of the agencies that were kind enough to assist me, I would single out the Bundesarchiv (section Militärarchiv), which thanks to the *Feldpost* numbers on Eberhard's missives was able to reconstruct my uncle's approximate whereabouts in the war. Approximate only, since his personal papers went missing after his death in battle. I also commend the Berlin Document Center of the U.S. Mission in Berlin for sending me photocopies of files in their possession. I owe a big thanks to them and everyone else I haven't mentioned here by name.

I am especially grateful to C. J. F. Stuldreher at the Dutch Institute for War Documentation because he strengthened my conviction that I had unearthed an exceptional correspondence. He was generously prepared to guide my mother and myself and to share his wide knowledge with me. My mother and I owe him a great deal for his support.

All these years my family and friends kept having to listen to me talking about the book. I am thinking primarily of my husband, who went through all the ups and downs from close up, and of my children, who, despite their representing the next generation and so being at a greater remove from this history, nevertheless showed a great interest in, and understanding for, my obsession. As far as all the other relatives, friends, and acquaintances, I would like to warmly thank those who offered to read the book either partially or in its entirety and gave me their reactions and comments, as well as those who were willing to hear me speak about it or showed an interest in this project by enquiring about it, for their practical or moral support.

HK (1991)

Two years after the book's initial publication, my mother passed away. She was lauded on all sides for her courage in allowing this correspondence to be published. I am so glad that she was able to hear the praise, after all the inner conflicts that this decision had cost her.

HK (1995)

NOTE TO THE AMERICAN EDITION

In 2006 my German publisher forwarded a letter to me from a German Studies student in Berlin, who told me that several war diaries written by my Uncle Eberhard had come into his possession. He was a collector. It was only by finding a document that had Eberhard's name on it, left in one of the five notebooks, that he had been able to trace me via the internet, since the journals themselves were unattributed.

I was bowled over at this news and remained riveted by this sign from the past for quite a while.

The student offered to email me the text, which he had already transcribed, and one month later, at my invitation, he arrived to deliver the small notebooks in person. It wasn't until I saw Eberhard's handwriting, so familiar to me from his letters, that I really allowed myself to believe it! After a while the student agreed to turn the journals over to me, so that now they are in my possession.

Thanks to this unexpected occurrence, I was given a glimpse, sixty-two years after Eberhard's death, into quite another aspect of his life, the world he would leave behind when he visited us. I now had a number of answers to my original question of "What had his eyes seen?" although the diaries didn't answer all of them, naturally, for one thing because they did not cover the entire war. The first two notebooks cover the period of 20 November 1939 until 11 June 1940; the other three range from 10 March 1942 to 6 November 1943. So, for instance, his entries from Poland and his first deployment to the Russian front are missing. The last ten months in Normandy and the battles of the retreat through Belgium are also lost. They must have existed, however; the recovered journals are clearly part of a continuous sequence.

Just how these five booklets managed to find their way to me in the end will forever remain a mystery. The Berlin student had purchased them two years earlier from an Internet address that appeared no longer to exist. It's strange to think, for that matter, that those journals must already have touched down in our home in Amersfoort once, since they include Eberhard's notations of his impressions when he was with us!

I retranscribed the contents of the diaries, as accurately as possible this time, while trying to find explanations for much of what is mentioned that I had not heard of before. Next I inserted all of his letters, unabridged and in chronological order, including, therefore, those from the intervals lacking diary entries. That combination of letters and diaries occasionally yielded information, since in his letters he would write at length about events that were mentioned in his journals only in passing. And conversely, casual remarks in his letters were given a clearer frame of reference by what he had noted privately.

But of course even in his private musings he doesn't reveal everything; they are merely jottings, since he himself already knows what it's about. For example, "a curious political conversation" doesn't give you any more to go on, while you would so dearly like to find out what it means.

I was occasionally hit with a sense of alienation, of irritation and impatience even; my uncle kept growing more removed from the image of him I had created for myself. I also think that he was far more supportive of Hitler and his war of conquest than I had previously assumed from reading his letters, and that he did not harbor any doubt as to Germany's right to annex the Netherlands.

Eberhard starts each new entry with a notation of his current location, which has made it possible to establish exactly where he was at any given time, at least in the two time frames covered by the diaries.

The letters from the last months of his life contain a tone of increasing despair. To explain his long silence, he writes to his cousin Ursel that "so many things went awry that he had a 'falling out with the world' and simply did not want to write anymore."

My mother once confided to me that she suspected that Eberhard, in the frame of mind he was in, might have volunteered for the dangerous mission that had proved fatal, because he had lost faith in all he had believed in.

In 1990 I wrote the following entry in the guest book of the Soldatenfriedhof in Lommel: "Eberhard, my uncle, you believed in this madness, yet you were a good man." His diaries have given me—even more strongly than before—a consciousness of the tragic waste of his life, one of all those millions of wasted lives.

Excerpts from the recovered diaries are appearing in print for the first time in this American edition.

This is also the place to express my great thanks to Professor Peter Fritzsche of the University of Illinois, who has played such an important role in the realization of this edition. Right from our first contact it was clear that he shared my fascination for these historical documents. Like me, he was of the opinion that this collection should be made accessible to an English-speaking public. Thanks to his enthusiasm and energy the American edition is now there. Our discussions were always animated and interesting. By his expert knowledge he gave me inspiring support and help, for which I am very grateful.

HK (2013)

BETWEEN TWO HOMELANDS

TO HOLLAND (1920–1929)

A large number of Germans opposed the parliamentary democracy of the Weimar Republic, holding it responsible for Germany's defeat in World War I (the "stab-in-the-back legend"). This sense of illegitimacy, deep mistrust of Germany's new Social Democratic rulers, and general resentments against the Treaty of Versailles created conditions in which right-wing nationalism found growing support among all social classes. The Treaty of Versailles dictated limits on the size of the military and required the payment of reparations for the destruction that German armies had caused in northern France and Belgium, and the treaty also sought the extradition of German war criminals, including Kaiser Wilhelm II who had fled to Holland in November 1918. Despite repeated demands, the Dutch refused to extradite him.

In the first difficult years after the war, Dutch families provided vacation homes for thousands of impoverished and malnourished children from Germany, Austria, and Hungary. After Irmgard (generally known as Immo) returned from her stay in the Netherlands, she remained in contact with her host family in Utrecht. In 1921 August Brester traveled to Germany with college friends and took time to visit the Gebensleben family in Braunschweig. The next year, Immo journeyed to Holland for a second time.

Irmgard Gebensleben to her parents Karl and Elisabeth Gebensleben, Utrecht, 13 June 1920

[. . .] The journey went quite well. At one stop, we each received a cup of milk. We were delayed for a long time in Arnhem. All the people at the train station looked at us with curiosity. Some even came into the train and talked to us, but we couldn't understand much because the Dutch language is actually quite different from low German. As a test, I am sending you a page from a calendar to see if you can read it.

In Utrecht, all the kids got off and a man read out our names and led us over to our foster parents. The Bresters are already pretty old, their sons are around twenty years old. We took the streetcar to Willem Barentzstraat. From the outside, the front of the house is pretty drab looking, but in the back there is a balcony, a porch, and a charming little flower garden. At home, we had a warm meal consisting of soup, meat, vegetables, and stewed fruit. Just imagine that in Holland the meals are completely different. In the morning at 8:30 you have coffee and bread, at noon coffee and bread 1 more time, and a warm meal at 5:30. In between, they drink tea nonstop. Frau Brester is always running around holding a "kopje" of tea. Instead of tea, I get milk. Herr Brester says that I have to drink 1 liter of milk a day, later on more. He calls me Irmi or Immi. The others call me Irmgard. Thank God they can speak a little bit of German. [. . .]

Everybody rides bikes in Utrecht. There are only a few people who walk on the streets. There are also not so many motorcycles or cars. Even with all these new sights I am terribly homesick. I just can't stand it sometimes. It is because everything is so strange, and I have to settle in. But my foster parents are awfully nice.

Elisabeth Gebensleben to her daughter Irmgard Gebensleben, Braunschweig, 15 June 1920

[. . .] Hilde [Immo's travel companion] is also homesick, and with that we have arrived at the sore spot of this beautiful trip. I want to confess something to you: I am a little homesick for you too. But we are both quite brave and don't give in to such things for long.

Irmgard Gebensleben to her parents Karl and Elisabeth Gebensleben, Utrecht, 21 June 1920

[. . .] First I will answer your questions. Herr Brester was a senior official at the post office but is now retired. The older son, Carel, is studying mathematics and physics and August is studying medicine. Both of them are awfully funny. During mealtimes, they are always making jokes so that I can barely stop laughing. [. . .]

Irmgard Gebensleben to her parents Karl and Elisabeth Gebensleben, Utrecht, 3 July 1920

[. . .] I went to the city with Herr Brester today. There was a great deal of activity because of the cattle market. Wearing their traditional costumes and accompanied by their animals, farmers converged onto the marketplace from all over. Then we took a look at the cathedral and heard the chiming of the bells. They have a wonderful, unique tone, which put me in quite a festive mood. It is also very interesting to read the prices in the shop windows. For example, a man's suit costs at most 40 gulden, and even that is pretty expensive. [. . .]

Irmgard Gebensleben in Utrecht (2 July 1920)

Elisabeth Gebensleben to Henriette Brester, Zennern, 7 July 1920

From the bottom of my heart, I want to thank you and your husband for all the love that you have shown our Irmgard. Irmgard has been received in your house in such a friendly way. She writes such happy letters and postcards that I wish I could shake your hand and tell you in person how grateful I am. It is wonderful to know how well Irmgard has recuperated. She is very proud to report that she has already gained 6 lbs. In the last years, we frequently worried about her rapid growth spurt. Unfortunately, in Germany we are not in a position to care for our children as we would like. For us it is a question of adjusting to the circumstances.

As the question of handing over the former Kaiser was being discussed, and in spite of threats of the Allies, the Dutch refused to consider doing so, I said to my children "Hats off to the Dutch!" And now I want to say the same thing in light of the Dutch people's readiness to help and care for our German children.

Irmgard has had such wonderful experiences with you. She tells us of the nice walks that she has taken with your husband. The memories that she will bring back to Germany will last a lifetime. For the last several days, we have been spending our summer holiday near Kassel. I would very much like to accompany Irmgard when she returns from Holland and want to ask you to let me know through Irmgard which train she is taking back. [. . .]

Netherlands Commission for Vacationing Children from Germany to Jan Brester, Utrecht, 15 July 1920

Your foster child Irmgard Gebensleben is scheduled to leave for Germany on 20 July. Please make sure that on that day she is ready at 10½ o'clock, in the 3rd class waiting room of Utrecht's Central Station. Each child is allowed to bring along on the journey: 4 kg of foodstuffs, as well as provisions for the voyage.

Jan Brester to his foster daughter Irmgard Gebensleben, Utrecht, 21 September 1920

[. . .] And that is why we haven't written. But don't ever think that we have forgotten our little-big Irmy. That would be impossible! And do you think of us once in a while? But let me continue.

[. . .] After 60 days military service, Carel came back on 20 July. Stupid sergeants taught him all that was good and excellent. For example, how to shoot the person next to you through the eyes and the exact percentage of young men in war who go mad, etc.! An army chaplain also preached many excellent things, but he choked on the words "love of humanity," or maybe they just slipped his mind. In 1921, Carel will continue his training, this time for 75 days in order to become an officer. Hopefully he will then learn how to completely destroy his fellow man! That would be wonderful! That is just about the greatest thing in the world!

Carel says: "How stupid people can be!" [. . .]

August doesn't want to become an officer. He wants to try to heal people rather than kill them. He is one of those simpletons who actually think that is better! He also wants to do it that way because he *himself* desires it and not because this or that one ordered him to do so! Really, how innocent can you be!

[. . .] Do you remember the expedition to Vianen when we took the old horse-drawn tram on the way back and broke out in giggles when the blanket slipped off the horse!

Irmgard Gebensleben to her mother Elisabeth Gebensleben, Utrecht, 17 June 1922

My dear sweet Mutti! This intimate greeting is not to show you that I am homesick. I don't feel that at all here. Just the opposite, I am so happy that I am allowed to be here and be coddled that I want once in a while to share my good luck with you.

Here it is simply—how should I say it?—I just can't find the right words. [. . .]

Yesterday [August] sat for a small examination. He looked very festive when he left the house: pin-striped trousers, a black frock coat, a black necktie, a black bowler, glacé kid gloves, and patent leather shoes. He passed the examination with flying colors. Here he is not so gentle and quiet as he was with us last year. He teases me all day long. He is always telling me that Germany is a Dutch province and the German language a Dutch dialect. How am I supposed to put up with that?! [. . .]

Jan Brester to his foster daughter Irmgard Gebensleben, Utrecht, 25 August 1922

[. . .] Carel is busy training to be an officer. Today he had to commit to memory how many times you're supposed to rap your gun on the ground for a general. Did you guess four times? Wrong! It's just three. He also knows precisely how many times to do it for a colonel, for a major, for a captain, etcetera. Very important! [. . .]

In 1921, the Allies determined the amount that Germany was obligated to pay in reparations according of the Treaty of Versailles. These onerous transfer payments greatly undermined the purchasing power of the German mark, which had already lost value as a result of the costs of the war. In January 1923, after Germany failed to deliver coal as part of reparations, French and Belgian troops occupied the Ruhr. The German government continued to print money in order to help support Ruhr workers who had gone on strike in protest against the invasion. By 3 September 1923, the value of the mark had fallen to such an extent that a single Dutch guilder was worth 4,620,000 reichsmarks; a day later the exchange rate was 5,087,250. At 10:00 A.M. on 2 October a guilder could buy 125,295,000 marks; at 11:00 A.M. it could buy 125,914,000. In early November an American dollar cost 4.2 billion marks. The psychological and political as well as economic effects were catastrophic. The German public blamed—not completely accurately—Versailles while creditors, especially among the middle classes, lost their savings. Debtors, including farmers with mortgages, of course, did better. The mark was stabilized only at the end of November 1923.

In May 1923, the Gebensleben family moved from Kaiser-Wilhelm Strasse to Am Fallerslebertor.

The Bresters in September 1922: Jan Brester, Henriette Brester-Wurf-bain, August Brester, Carel Brester

Jan Brester to Elisabeth Gebensleben, Utrecht, 14 September 1922

Strange times make for strange letters. I have come into 4,000 M. As you know marks are almost worthless here. An example: for 4,000 M à 0,17 I can buy 2 boxes of chocolates à f 3 and get about f 0.60 back.

Do I have your permission to give the 4,000 M to Irmy? But how do I get it to her? Do you think I can just enclose the banknote? I hesitated a long time to ask you, but it would be sheer *nonsense* not to do so. 100 M is still worth something in Germany, or not? Irmy will let me know if I have your permission, although a big thank you (for 2 boxes of chocolates) is *completely* out of the question. A registered letter to Banking house "Mutti" will follow promptly. Fun and treats give a girl an "onderkin" [double chin]. Irmgard will certainly tell you what a "onderkin" is.

ENCLOSED LETTER

Banking house "Mutti": From Friday, 15 September 1922 until 1 June 1923 pay Immo 100 M weekly allowance every Friday. Jan Brester.

Elisabeth Gebensleben to Jan Brester, Braunschweig, 16 September 1922

It is really too bad that you could not see Irmgard's joy when I gave her the enclosed letter. She clapped and sang and didn't know what to do with herself out of happiness. My husband and I thank you most sincerely for your generosity. The idea of "Banking house Mutti" is charming and I will very happily fulfill my responsibilities every Friday. There are many things we have to deny our children, often with a heavy heart. The times are hard and reason has to prevail. And yet one would so much like to indulge them! That is why your dear letter made me so happy: Irmgard can now treat herself to a few pleasures that would otherwise be off limits. I am not just thinking of chocolates and pralines, which she simply adores, but also theater or concert tickets.

Jan Brester to his foster daughter Irmgard Gebensleben, Utrecht, 20 October 1922

To Fräulein Irmgard Gebensleben.

Our firm today received a letter from Göttingen [*where Carel was working on his dissertation*] detailing how very expensive everything is in Germany. Wherefore we have decided posthaste to increase your allowance (as of today). Your banker will redeem the enclosed promissory note.

We have further ordered our representative in Göttingen to send you some postage stamps, since we wish to know *often, everything, always* and *exactly* how you are doing in these difficult times, and whether the abovementioned pocket money is not too hard hit by them.

My firm herewith furthermore sends you a loving kiss.

Jan Brester to his foster daughter Irmgard Gebensleben, Utrecht, 11 November 1922

[. . .] How nice, that you are able to go to dances or the theater once in a while. I was astonished to read that it's a political party that organizes a ball. Politics and poetry don't usually mix, after all. [. . .]

And I should like you to give me a detailed description of the situation in Germany. How much do things cost? Is chocolate still available, and how much does it cost? How much, for instance, do you have to pay for a theater ticket? Is your allowance still sufficient for that sort of thing? You can tell me *everything*, you know that, dear child. [. . .]

Jan Brester to Elisabeth Gebensleben, Utrecht, 5 May 1923

Banking house "Mutti" will soon be empty, so it may be a good time to purchase more marks. We have no way of knowing what you can buy in Germany for, say, 1,500 M. In Holland that amounts to about 15 cents, practically nothing (an eight-minute tram ride!). What do you think about a weekly allowance of 1,500 M? If that's too low, please let me know how much you think is necessary.

Jan Brester to his foster daughter Irmgard Gebensleben, Utrecht, 5 June 1923

My representative in Göttingen has come home with a balance of 23,515 M as well as 50 postage stamps à 300 M., plus one guilder. Since my account books have already been closed, I don't know what else to do with it. Perhaps you can use some of it, for Bach or chocolate. Or to buy a house and open a post office branch "Am Fallerslebertor"! The German mark keeps falling, the prices keep going up!
[. . .] I'll write you a long letter in Dutch soon, so that you won't forget your (foster) mother tongue completely.

**Jan Brester to his foster daughter Irmgard Gebensleben, Utrecht,
3 September 1923**

[. . .] Since I have calculated that your weekly allowance (just 3,000 marks) isn't
nearly enough, I am sending you several million marks more to augment your funds
until 1 October (approximately one million per week). Please write and tell me how
much the guilder is worth in Germany at the moment. [. . .]

Jan Brester to Elisabeth Gebensleben, Utrecht, 2 October 1923

Banking house "Mutti": I was surprised to see that it is 2 October already! I
hardly dare ask you this: would you please pay out the millions from now until the
beginning of 1924 as you see fit? To tell you the truth, distributing several hundred
millions is not something I am used to. (I enclose two guilders—*f* 2.—.)

**Jan Brester to his foster daughter Irmgard Gebensleben, Utrecht,
17 February 1924**

[. . .] Carel is an officer! He now wears a belt around his waist that has a sword
stuck in it. Great! Lucky fellow! From now on, if someone bothers him, he can just
hack him in two. The stars on his collar twinkle like stars in the sky, and of course
the sky and militarism have a great deal in common. He now also has a special
distinction, and a word of honor. Mine is only second-rate. That's wonderful too!
[. . .]

*On 9 November 1923, the Reichswehr and Bavarian police crushed an
insurrection by the National Socialist German Workers' Party (the NSDAP or Nazis),
the so-called Beer Hall Putsch. Adolf Hitler, the party leader, was imprisoned and
the NSDAP banned. With improved economic conditions, better relations among the
former belligerents, and American loans, the fortunes of the Republic seemed at first
to stabilize. But grassroots opposition to the democratic "system" and to Communists
and Social Democrats (somewhat contemptuously known as "Sozis") persisted. Many
citizens refused to accept the black-red-gold flag of the Republic, which had replaced the
black-white-red flag of the Kaiserreich. Nationalist associations such as the Jungdeutsche
Orden, the Bismarckjugend (Bismarck Youth), and especially the veterans' group, the
Stahlhelm (or Steel Helmets), which under the leadership of Franz Seldte claimed nearly
a half million members, flourished in neighborhoods across Germany. If the most
extreme groups such as the Nazis had faded from view, tensions between the Left and
the Right continued to dominate political life so that even the best years of the Republic
were characterized by parliamentary infighting and the growing strength of a more
populist form of right-wing nationalism.*

*In 1924, Immo moved to Kassel to enroll in a boarding school, where she studied
home economics. But the education she received was so poor that she soon left for
Northeim, where Ernst Roever, a cousin of her mother, oversaw a large agricultural
enterprise. Ernst's wife, Margot, was already an early member of the NSDAP, so
Immo joined her relatives when they attended right-wing gatherings of senior officers
and other nationalists, including Paul von Lettow-Vorbeck (1870–1964), the former*

military commander in German East Africa who had already been dismissed from
the Reichswehr for his participation in the right-wing Kapp Putsch in 1920. Irmgard
belonged to the Bismarckjugend, affiliated with the conservative German National
People's Party, to which her father also belonged. Senior party leaders in the Reichstag
included Oskar Hergt (1869–1967) and Fürst Otto von Bismarck (1897–1975), a
grandson of the former imperial chancellor.

Elisabeth Gebensleben to her daughter Irmgard Gebensleben (at a boarding school for home economics in Kassel), Braunschweig, 27 April 1924

[. . .] This afternoon I went to an election rally of the German Nationalists in Brüning's Assembly Hall; it got pretty heated in there.

[. . .] Just now a troop of young people is passing by, singing "Hakenkreuz am Fahnentuch, schwarzweissrotes Band, usw" ["The Swastika is our flag, the black-white-red ribbon"]. Somewhere today, the Jungdeutscher Orden also conducted a nationalist ceremony.

Elisabeth Gebensleben to her daughter Irmgard Gebensleben, Braunschweig, 2 May 1924

[. . .] This afternoon, Eberhard and Zettel [Carl-Heinz Zeitler] were out on the streets handing out campaign literature for the German Nationalist Party. They even went up to the Scherbelberg and they just had a great time taking part. A letter came for you today; it was from the Bismarckjugend, asking you to come to the municipal park on Sunday evening to help with the election. Whoever doesn't come will be cut from the group. Of course, I will write the executive committee first thing tomorrow and explain your absence as well as your inability to appear at meetings for the next six months. [. . .]

Elisabeth Gebensleben to her daughter Irmgard Gebensleben, Braunschweig, 14 June 1924

You got two more letters from Herr Brester? I would just love to know what he thinks about your leaving the Katharinenhaus [the boarding school]. I don't think you will get an invitation until he is clear and certain about what he is going to do. But do remember what I said: you should not travel to Holland again. G. [Gerda] is not even allowed to dance with German-speaking foreigners and you, you want to go to Holland! Now Immo is laughing to herself, thinking: "I know, I know, *but* one way or the other I will get *there*." [. . .]

Irmgard Gebensleben to her mother Elisabeth Gebensleben, Northeim, 2 July 1924

[. . .] as soon as the navy ball is over. Saturday night a student drinking ceremony, Sunday a flag consecration and a ball, and Monday another dance. There is great excitement everywhere, though Uncle Ernst has stage fright. All the veterans' associations are coming, even Northeim's shooting clubs. [. . .]

Jan Brester to his foster daughter Irmgard Gebensleben, Utrecht, 6 July 1924

[. . .] How nice for you, to have the opportunity to hear all those generals and admirals speak. But remember: don't bow to authority, *think for yourself!* Here they say that Lettow-Vorbeck may be a clever man, but that he never had a clue about the colonial situation.

It may be terribly rude of me, having the gall to think that way—but you know we couldn't care less for all that self-serving claptrap. [. . .]

Elisabeth Gebensleben to her daughter Irmgard Gebensleben, Braunschweig, 17 August 1924

[. . .] Yesterday afternoon, Eberhard and I saw the second part of [Fritz Lang's] Nibelungen film, "Kriemhilde's Revenge." [. . .] It was lovely, but actually too gruesome and horrid. Battle scenes "rendered with astonishing creativity" in the words of the newspaper. Eberhard was totally shocked, as was I. Still I liked the first part better; it was sweeter and uplifting. Today it was just frightfulness and gore. But what does shine through all the horror is loyalty, loyalty to Walhalla, loyalty to the king, Kriemhilde's loyalty to Siegfried, and that has a conciliatory effect. Maybe you will somehow still have a chance to see the film.

[. . .] I am sure you are waiting anxiously for letters from Holland. Still, Herr Brester has written you frequently these last weeks. Now there is nothing wrong with a little pause. In any case, Herr Brester himself wrote that he has to finish a "big job." [. . .]

Elisabeth Gebensleben to her daughter Irmgard Gebensleben, Braunschweig, 19 August 1924

[. . .] I actually wanted to write to you last night in which case you would have noticed that I had gone to the "Meistersinger" the day before. I was full of song and sound; I just can't get the melodies of the "Meistersinger" out of my head. The performance was simply marvelous, so beautiful that when I got home at 11:15 with everyone snug in bed, I just cried my heart out. You might find my overly sentimental enthusiasm incredibly foolish, but I was simply overwhelmed. I kept thinking to myself: can there be anything more lovely on this earth! How dumb we are not to cherish this loveliness more and to appreciate the spiritual wealth of the German people each and every day. I had seen the "Meistersinger" some 15 years ago in Leipzig, but of course my memory of it had completely faded. I promise you one thing, as long as you are not here, I will not go to another Wagner opera. I always end up thinking of you; the more sweet and beautiful the music, the sadder I get because my "kindred" spirit is missing. Next winter, Immeken, we will make sure to savor music together. [. . .]

Elisabeth Gebensleben to her daughter Irmgard Gebensleben, Braunschweig, 27 August 1924

[. . .] Eberhard has to perform at the musical evening on 13 September. The Bismarckjugend is planning an elaborate program over several days for its Reich

Youth Day at the end of September. We've already been asked for information about housing. [. . .]

Elisabeth Gebensleben to her daughter Irmgard Gebensleben, Braunschweig, 9 September 1924

[. . .] Eberhard will certainly tell you about the splendid Stahlhelm celebration; I was happy to know that Vati was with you in Northeim.

[. . .] [Frau A.] then spoke of you and that she was happy to know that you were with the *German Nationalists*. "Irmchen danced again and again with the same gentleman, a big blond guy. The two made a wonderful pair." [. . .]

Elisabeth Gebensleben to her daughter Irmgard Gebensleben, Braunschweig, 13 September 1924

[. . .] Yesterday I received a letter that made me *very* happy—a letter from Herr Brester. There is *one* line that I have to share with you, knowing that you will be pleased by it. [. . .] The line goes: "Last year left us with plenty of regrets. Among other things, it was not possible for Irmy to visit us. Hopefully it will work out next spring; we are already looking forward to it." So Immeken *who* was right? But I already told you, even if you do get invited, we won't let go of you. Now you are laughing Immo! You rascal!

[. . .] since I want to be here on Friday, when the Reich Youth Day begins. [. . .] And even if you don't participate, it will be great for you to be here while it takes place. It will be just like when the Stahlhelmers celebrated, and the city will be festively decked out. Several thousand young men and young women from all across Germany will be coming, as will important leaders of the German Nationalists: Prince Otto von Bismarck, Hergt, etc.

Irmgard Gebensleben to her mother Elisabeth Gebensleben, Northeim, 21 September 1924

[. . .] The big harvest festival took place yesterday, or rather today as well since it lasted until 3:00. [. . .] People arrived around 5:00, about 100 in all. Coffee was served in the hall: a wash basin full of coffee and 16 baking trays with apple pie and crumb cake. Thereafter games in the courtyard: sack races, footraces, and climbing with plenty of prizes—for the girls household items, for the boys knives, shaving mirrors, etc. Then a bit of dancing until dinner at 8:30. The carriage sheds served as the dance floor and I did my part. We had roast pork, potato salad, and stewed pears for dessert. You can't imagine the amount of food: they cooked nearly 100 kilos of meat! After dinner, we sat comfortably around the tables while the dancing continued. [. . .]

Jan Brester to his foster daughter Irmgard Gebensleben, Utrecht, 2 November 1924

[. . .] Please write and tell what is happening in Germany. Has life returned to normal? I follow the political situation in the newspapers on a regular basis and it does give me a clear oversight of everything, of course, probably clearer even than one has in Germany, since we are quite neutral here and there is absolutely no reason to present the situation as better or worse than it is. Here in Holland, fortunately, things are much better lately, and people are able to make a living the old-fashioned way again. Everything is getting very expensive here, however.

Irmgard Gebensleben to her parents Karl and Elisabeth Gebensleben, Utrecht, 12 June 1925

[. . .] You can't imagine how sweet the Bresters are and how many wonderful and new things I have once again seen in Holland. [. . .]

So, yesterday and the day before we went to Rotterdam, me, Herr Brester, and August. Your "Döchting" felt very well in the company of three gentlemen. We ate all our meals with Carel, who has two furnished rooms. [. . .] Rotterdam is hugely interesting, a cosmopolitan city with many wharves and a huge harbor. [. . .] Yesterday morning we toured an ocean liner, the *Slamat*, which tomorrow journeys to the East Indies. It was just mammoth, and all the cabins and living quarters make you completely forget that you are on a ship. [. . .]

Please send me a little more money; there are so many nice things to buy over here.

In the mid-1920s, Immo's visits to Holland became more frequent. In March 1927, she passed her final examinations as a pianist. On Christmas Day 1928, she and August Brester got engaged. Their wedding took place in Braunschweig on 3 September 1929.

Irmgard Gebensleben to her brother Eberhard Gebensleben, Utrecht, 21 May 1927

[. . .] Everything is still as it was here in the house. I feel right at home in my old room and the little garden is exactly as tidy and bloomy as it was two years ago. [. . .]

I can still understand Dutch quite well, but it is not always easy to make myself understood. Yesterday I wanted to buy some rubber bands in town, but it took Herr Brester 10 minutes to explain to me that rubber bands are called "elastics" here.

Elisabeth Gebensleben to her daughter Irmgard Gebensleben, Braunschweig, 30 May 1927

Now I don't know whether to scold you or to worry? First of all, I want to remind you that it has been eight days since your last and only letter to Eberhard arrived here and that your darling mother has not received any sign of life from you aside from the penciled note from the train station. Yesterday, Sunday morning, when Ohmchen and I were alone, I counted on a letter from you, my one pleasure of the day. With one chick on the high seas and another abroad, I felt very lonesome. When no mail came, I decided to go with the time-tested "worrying," and then after a few hours, I turned to "scolding," and today I don't know what to feel, I switch back from one to the other. So if you are doing well, take the scolding and if you are not doing well, know that you are always in my thoughts and that I would like to know what my little bunny is doing. [. . .]

Irmgard Gebensleben to her mother Elisabeth Gebensleben, Utrecht, 4 June 1927

[. . .] Well, as far as Herr Brester is concerned, 13 June is only my *theoretical date of departure*. Nobody can believe that I want to leave then. As for myself, I want very, very much to stay one more week here. [. . .]

But I will need a little more money, perhaps 5 gulden, preferably two banknotes of 2½ gulden each, and 5 marks for the return trip.

Minna von Alten to her granddaughter Irmgard Gebensleben, Braunschweig, 6 June 1927

[. . .] to tell you about the wonderful excursion we made on Pentecost, namely to Goslar, where we arrived just as the procession was getting under way. The day was wonderful with so many lasting impressions, and above all we admired our young man [Eberhard], the standard bearer, who to Mutti's great joy we were able to provision with plenty of bread since it is not so easy to cater to 20,000 men. Eberhard has been put up in a big room at an estate with 200 other men from Braunschweig. He slept only 1½ hours the first night, and 4 hours the second, and his feet are pretty sore. He comes back tomorrow.

All the young people in Goslar from across Germany made me think of you. Almost every city was represented [at the annual "All-German" gathering of the "Association for German Culture Abroad"].

Irmgard Gebensleben to her mother Elisabeth Gebensleben, Utrecht, 15 June 1927

[. . .] [August] has decided to take a little trip abroad for his last week of vacation and would like nothing better than to go to Berlin for several days. Thereupon, I decided for myself to invite him to come to Braunschweig for a few days at the tail end and he accepted this "invitation" happily. Of course, this depends on whether it is alright with you. [. . .] It would be best if you could send a telegram to let us know one way or the other. I know this is all a little sudden.

Jan Brester to his foster daughter Irmgard Gebensleben, Utrecht, 26 July 1927

[. . .] There's nothing very interesting happening here. Carel is going to Doesburg "ins Militär." He'll be commanding a squad armed with the newfangled machine gun, ideal for shooting 100 young men dead in 2 or 3 minutes. And then 40 others will be left blind and 20 paralyzed for life, while 10% will go crazy. Stupendous! They gave the inventor an award, by accident, instead of hanging him.

Irmgard Gebensleben to her parents Karl and Elisabeth Gebensleben, Utrecht, 29 December 1927

You will know from my two short postcard greetings that I am as happy as a clam. Sad as it is to say, I simply cannot make myself feel homesick. It is so wonderful to be here again! [. . .]

Yesterday afternoon I picked August up from the hospital, imagine, me alone, and with a transfer on the streetcar! On the outside calmly, but inside shaking, I asked the porter for *Doctor* Brester, which is something I still have to get used to.

Elisabeth Gebensleben to her daughter Irmgard Gebensleben, Braunschweig, 29 December 1927

[. . .] The second day of Christmas with the Rauchs was very pleasant. Uncle Otto told us a funny little story that I have to tell you about. In Semmenstedt there is this young farmer with a little farm, two horses, 4 cows, and a young wife. Now this farmer wants to buy two more cows, and at the same time see a little bit of the world, so he decides to travel to the cattle market in the big city of Lübeck. There he is immediately taken in by those Jew-Traders who liquor him up so that he underwrites one note after the other and before long, without knowing it, he has bought himself 33! cows. Now he is back in Semmenstedt, and to the surprise and amusement of the entire village, one by one, 33 cows arrive in Semmenstedt, although the good man has neither enough room nor enough money. The cows are stabled all over the village and good-natured farmers try to undo the financial injury by buying the cows off their world traveler. What a set up! We laughed so hard. [. . .]

Irmgard Gebensleben to her mother Elisabeth Gebensleben, Utrecht, 7 August 1928

[. . .] The speaking of Dutch is being strictly adhered to and is going pretty well. Practice is the main thing if I am to feel at ease. [. . .]

I still have lots to tell you. [. . .] to begin with, Sunday in Amsterdam [at the Olympic Games]. That was really a spectacle. I might never see something like that again. [. . .] When Vati comes to Amsterdam he just has to see the new stadium (capacity 40,000). He will hardly have seen such a modern design before. Our seats were just to the side of the VIP stand so we saw all the starts and finishes, most interesting. Luckily the rain stopped just as the games got under way. Since our seats were in the open air, it would have been pretty uncomfortable, even with umbrellas. I borrowed an old raincoat from Moes that stood up pretty well; I would have likely been quite cold in my coat. But in all the excitement, the cold was hardly on our minds. It was really a wonderful scene, the vast array of flags from the most diverse nations and the enormous, excited mass of people. And along the way you could make a study of languages and races. You could see just about every human type: tall Englishmen, elegant Americans, short Japanese and Chinese, black-eyed Italians, even Negroes and Indians. There is great celebration at the conclusion of every match. The results are then announced over a loudspeaker usually in French, but also frequently in Dutch and English. Then, to the sounds of the national anthem of the victorious nation, the flags of the 3 main winners soar into the sky, while everybody stands and the respective countrymen sing along. I was delighted to see the German flag after the three relay races, once for second place, twice for third place. It was especially exciting when the first marathon runners entered the stadium, in first place a Frenchman, in second, a Chilean, in third, a Finn. At the end of the games, the traffic control in this large area was also amazing. It is no easy thing to get 40,000 people on their way in automobiles and streetcars.

Jan Brester to the Gebensleben family, Utrecht, 28 December 1928

Dear Herr Vati, Frau Mutti, and Frau Ohmchen!

At approximately half past nine Wednesday night, my wife began to tell me and as of today she has yet to stop, although she patters on uninterruptedly, pausing only for a few hours at night! [...] And the more I hear, the more reason I have to thank you from the bottom of my heart for all your love and attention. It is becoming more and more clear to us that we can't be grateful enough that August has been embraced as a son by such a lovely family and that we gain a daughter such as our Irmy! We have often thought to ourselves: "Who could ever have known this from the beginning!?" [...]

Jan Brester to his future daughter-in-law Irmgard Gebensleben, Utrecht, 29 December 1928

[...] What a lovely welcome you have given Moes! Really, she can't stop talking about it. [...]

And the visit to Hedeper, with all its beauty and riches. Moes was very taken with that side of the family too, especially with Uncle Rauch, whom she liked very much. [...] Boy oh boy, the amount you people can eat, it's no wonder you're getting so fat. [...]

Henriette Brester to her future daughter-in-law Irmgard Brester, Utrecht, 29 December 1928

[...] How I enjoyed seeing you in your own environment, dear child, and to meet the two members of your family I hadn't yet met, Vati and Ohmchen. [...] How your dear mother spoiled me! How lovely of her to offer me "Dutch tea," to go to all that extra effort. [...] I very much appreciated it, please tell them that; it's easier to write it in Dutch than in German. [...]

Jan Brester to his future daughter-in-law Irmgard Gebensleben, Utrecht, 14 January 1929

I am just going to write to you about your translations for now; I'll answer your sweet letter later. But I want to have a word with you about your translation. Please understand that what I am about to write is only intended for your own good. I don't have a personal stake in it. I have often told you that when someone goes to live in another country, the inhabitants of that land take it for granted that you will learn to understand their language, to speak it fluently, and to write it well enough. If you don't, you'll never really be considered one of them, you'll always be a stranger. That is so in any country, and even though in our country we have a more international outlook than in most countries, and although strangers in general are better understood here than anywhere else, even here it is still generally so. I have had many German acquaintances and, as soon as they come to live in the Netherlands, they always make sure to be sufficiently familiar with the Dutch language. [. . .] Just remember that the opinion of that man in the tram (the Number 4 tram) who spouted such nonsense is, in fact, the opinion of most people. When I found out that you were going to marry August, I offered to help you. I first asked the opinion of Mr. v.d.H.—a high school teacher—who confirmed that the method we have been following can definitely result in a pupil learning to write a passable Dutch. You may not learn the fine points that way, but that is not so important right now. The student does have to keep practicing, however, and do her *very best*, and have the brains for it too. You certainly possess the latter, but the former is sadly lacking. I don't want to go into your last excuse, because of course you had to help Mutti. But then what? See, this is what you're telling yourself: "First I have to practice my music, then English, then I have to go out, and if there's any time left for translating, so much the better. If there isn't, I'll just postpone it again." That's not right. You know how strongly I have insisted that you continue your music and also study some English and French. But right now, in your present circumstances, the *most important* thing is to learn *Dutch*. That is number one, and not number last! So here is my advice: buy yourself a good dictionary and practice *every day* without fail! I am ready to correct everything you do, no matter how much there is.

There, my sermon is done. Amen. A kiss from your loving Papa.

THE PARENTS (1929–1937)

The stock market crash in New York on 24 October 1929 aggravated the already difficult economic conditions prevailing in many European countries. Unemployment, especially in winter, rose steadily so that by 1932 nearly six million Germans were without work. Falling tax revenues and rising social welfare expenses burdened governments; after 1930, no workable parliamentary coalition could be formed in the Reichstag, and the Weimar Republic became more authoritarian under Chancellors Brüning, Papen, and finally Schleicher, who were propped up by the executive powers of the presidency, held since 1925 by Paul von Hindenburg, the former Chief of the General Staff in World War I.

In these years, Karl Gebensleben served as Braunschweig's deputy Oberbürgermeister. The Oberbürgermeister led the city council, which was elected for a six-year term by the municipal parliament. Since 1915, Gebensleben had been voted unanimously into the council as Stadtbaurat, or chief city engineer, a paid position. He later assumed the title of deputy Oberbürgermeister as well. In this capacity, his job became much more challenging in December 1929 when the Social Democratic mayor of Magdeburg, Ernst Böhme (1892–1968), was elected to the office of Oberbürgermeister, which he held until he was deposed by the Nazis in 1933. Writing in 1964, Böhme recalled his encounter with Braunschweig on the eve of Weimar Germany's economic and political crisis: "When at the end of 1929, I came to Braunschweig and assumed my post as the youngest big-city mayor at the age of thirty-seven, I found a host of unsolved problems. [. . .] Thanks to the can-do spirit of youth and especially to the confidence I had in my education in municipal affairs that I received during my years in Magdeburg, I was able to accomplish a great deal, despite the few years I had until 1933. Among other things, we stabilized municipal finances, reorganized the city bureaucracy, battled against poverty with productive unemployment support, also the housing projects, the construction of the swimming pool. One of the greatest challenges was building the harbor." Böhme was supported by Social Democrats and Communists, while the conservative block made up of the German National People's Party, the German People's Party, and the "business parties" (interest groups) stood in the opposition.

While August and Immo were on their honeymoon, Elisabeth Gebensleben organized their household in Utrecht. In the meantime, Eberhard studied for a semester in Grenoble and visited the new couple in Chamonix. Prominently displayed in the home of Immo's parents was a portrait of Otto von Bismarck, who founded the second

German Reich in 1871 and remained its first chancellor until 1890. Immo's mother and grandmother in particular continued to look back wistfully on Germany's old military glories, and they regarded Versailles as a deep humiliation. The family had subscribed to the Braunschweigische Landeszeitung, *the daily newspaper that conservatives read; the* Volksfreund *was the Social Democratic paper. As a result of Karl's position in city government, Elisabeth and Karl regularly mingled with important statesmen, including Hjalmar Schacht (1877–1950), President of the Reichsbank and Reich Currency Commissar who in 1923 and 1924 contributed decisively to the stabilization of the German mark after a period of rampant inflation.*

Minna von Alten to her daughter Elisabeth Gebensleben [in Utrecht], Braunschweig, 11 September 1929

[. . .] I wish I could just take a peek at you, but I am delighted if the Dutch admire German goods as well as our cleanliness and meticulousness. [. . .]

Elisabeth Gebensleben to her (married) daughter Irmgard Brester (in Chamonix), Utrecht, 13 September 1929

Well, I am curious if Hardus [Eberhard] will make it to Chamonix. However, in my last letter, and already in Braunschweig, I advised him against making a long trip through the south of France, Marseille, Genoa, etc. He is still too young and he is *simply too inexperienced* for Genoa where the dregs of the earth end up. Frankly, I find the city itself questionable. Anyway it is not good for such a young fellow to gain too many foreign impressions. He might be tempted to waver when he has to remain spiritually strong. With as much influence as you have, Immeken, and August too, suggest to him to see the region around Grenoble, and Avignon, etc., but not to go so far as Genoa. *I would have no peace of mind.* What are the stratagems of the agents of the French foreign legion, I wonder. They would immediately see how inexperienced such a fellow is, and he can't fend for himself.

[. . .] My trip went well. [. . .] When I arrived in the evening in Utrecht, I stood at the window of my compartment; the sky was completely clear with a great many stars and the moon was rising over the spire of the cathedral. And I thought: how beautifully Immo's new home extends its welcome.

Elisabeth Gebensleben to her daughter Irmgard Brester, Braunschweig, 8 October 1929

It is so good to know that you are now reading our newspaper. When I read something interesting, I will always be thinking: Immeken is reading this as well. It was so nice of August to give you this pleasure. [. . .] Today Vati is at the Braunschweiger Club for a few hours. His name is frequently mentioned in connection to the election for Oberbürgermeister, but Vati has not yet registered himself. There are no mayors of larger cities among the candidates, only city councilmen and mayors of smaller cities such as Erfurt. Since that is the case, local councilmen should have put themselves up. [. . .]

Vati has an enormous amount to do; he is barely here for half an hour at lunchtime. Yesterday a conference that lasted a full six hours. When he does come home, he is so exhausted that he can barely eat. M. could not believe that Vati has been going at this pace for years without receiving any financial compensation.

Elisabeth Gebensleben to her daughter Irmgard Brester, Braunschweig, 7 December 1929

[. . .] I am a bit tired. It is not so easy to train the new "Frieda" who moved in yesterday. But I don't think I am mistaken to predict, she will "work out!" [. . .] She is meticulous by nature, puts in a lot of effort—she works like Minna K. [Minna von Alten's maid]. You see right away that she gets it. Of course, the training period is tedious, but I am of the opinion that the effort will be worth it. Her father is in the Stahlhelm. And "he," whom she went "out" with yesterday, is in the army. Religion Lutheran. So there is no fear that we have anything to do with "dissidents" or "Reds."

Elisabeth Gebensleben to her daughter Irmgard Brester, Braunschweig, 18 December 1929

[. . .] There is lots to tell about the new Oberbürgermeister. I happened to sit next to him in the theater during the Colonial Evening, and later at Café Lück, I was between him and Finance Councilor P. The evening was very interesting, particularly with the presence of Reich Bank Director Dr. Schacht, whom everyone is talking about. We too were introduced to him, and Vati had a long conversation with him. The new chief dances fabulously; I also danced with him, indeed the first round that he danced. [. . .] You will certainly have read that the new Oberbürgermeister has instituted a consultation hour on Wednesdays between 12:00 and 1:00 when anyone can come in without an appointment. I feared the worse about this reform and lo and behold: today between 12:00 and 1:00 more than 100 people were standing outside the door. 3 newspapermen were in attendance and even the editor at the *Volksfreund* was shaking his head. Just people off the street, many of them familiar faces in city hall because they are never satisfied. But you have to make the people love you, just like in the days of the monarchs who granted the ordinary plebs an audience. [. . .]

Karl and Elisabeth Gebensleben attended a performance of "The Threepenny Opera," which had premiered in Berlin in September 1928. Based on John Gay's "The Beggar's Opera" (1728), which is set in the seedy world of London crime, "The Threepenny Opera" featured biting satire written by Bertolt Brecht and jazzed up ballads, including the now classic "Mack the Knife," by Kurt Weill.

In February 1930, the Gebensleben were invited to a dinner to which prominent politicians had been invited, including Carl Severing (1875–1952), who served intermittently as the Social Democratic Interior Minister of Prussia and as Reich Interior Minister from 1928 to 1930; Hans Sievers (1893–1965), Braunschweig's Social Democratic Justice Minister who in 1933 fled to Denmark; and Gustav Steinbrecher (1876–1940), a former Social Democratic Labor Minister who died while imprisoned in Mauthausen.

On 25 July 1930, Karl Gebensleben boarded the Deutschland *to undertake a study trip to the United States.*

Elisabeth Gebensleben to her daughter Irmgard Brester, Braunschweig, 21 January 1930

[. . .] We went to see "The Threepenny Opera." I just cannot come to terms with it and I am seriously thinking of writing to the director. That we have to put up with seeing a piece, with correspondingly squalid jazz music, which depicts the most miserable and mean-spirited elements that you can imagine, is simply unheard-of. Once again, the work of Jews who want to pull our people further and further down. There were also lots of Jews in the theater. The usher said that even at the premiere people left, on Sunday some as well. But the Jews applauded in approval. As I looked down on the small jazz band, I just had to think: poor court theater! Where [Karl] Pohlig [former court music director] directed and we were edified by the finest and most pure art, there is now miserable tootling and the glorification of criminals. Originally opera had a completely different purpose. It was supposed to satirize the "elegant, refined world" and its fancy, affected Italian music. It wasn't about anything like that today. What we get to see is only the display of everything base that unfortunately exists on this earth. Is it really necessary that those who are lucky enough not to come in direct contact with this baseness have to be violently confronted with it after all? I really am angry. Please forgive me this outpouring, dear Immo. The M.'s sent their daughter to the performance. I told them: My most sincere condolences. [. . .]

Elisabeth Gebensleben to her daughter Irmgard Brester, Braunschweig, 12 February 1930

[. . .] You will have surely read the newspaper about the various quarrels among the parties. Vati is dreading tomorrow's city council meeting. Things will really come to a head. The bourgeois parties are up in arms against the Oberbürgermeister; the housing question has kicked up a great deal of dust. You certainly must have read the article: *Our new mayor, we don't like him!* Vati is a calming influence, as it were, on these troubled waters. His quiet nature has a compromising effect. Of course, so much is messed up, the housing affair in particular. That a childless couple can live in a house with 14 rooms in a time of housing shortages is just not in order. Even if the first floor is used for official business, that is the case maybe only twice a year, and it is a shame that the lovely rooms just sit there empty. [. . .] In the past, I didn't have the time to concern myself with politics and municipal affairs. But now I have a real taste for politics, and in the newspaper politics comes *before* the serialized novel. And this winter I have become personally acquainted with several people who play important roles such as Schacht and Severing.

Elisabeth Gebensleben to her daughter Irmgard Brester, Braunschweig, 16 April 1930

[. . .] My trip went well and was in part very amusing. At customs, you have the funniest experiences. This time I was traveling with an elderly lady, a Berliner, dressed old-fashionedly with a long skirt, who was returning home. She was sitting so oddly stiff, and when we crossed the border she triumphantly showed us (4 ladies, all Germans!) her legs: in each stocking a package of coffee. She also had sewn a pocket into her underwear in which she had also hidden coffee. She was lugging around 4 lbs of coffee by herself. "Indeed," she said very proudly, "*I* can pull this off, *you* with your short skirts could not." How I laughed—really straight from the heart.

Eberhard Gebensleben to his sister Irmgard Brester, Berlin, 3 June 1930

[. . .] I am certainly not overworking myself at the university, and out here in Grunewald it is very pleasant. [. . .] Zettel, that little dreamer, is seriously thinking that we should paddle to Holland during the vacations. For a start, he is learning Dutch at the university. He is up for anything. But his lectures in law, which is officially his main subject, he attends only once in a while. When I am with you, I will hopefully easily catch up with his head start in Dutch. [. . .]

Irmgard Brester to her mother Elisabeth Gebensleben, Utrecht, 14 June 1930

[. . .] Wednesday we had a small celebration for an anniversary that you will surely not have thought of, namely June 11, 1920 when I came to Holland for the first time. August and I have known each other for ten years now. Do you still remember the trip, Muttilein? We refreshed so many old memories and agreed how strange it was that fate prevailed as it did. No one then could have imagined that one day I would come to Holland forever as Frau Brester. [. . .]

Karl Gebensleben to his wife Elisabeth Gebensleben, on board the *Deutschland*, 26 July 1930

[. . .] Lots of people were standing on the dock and waving as we sailed out of Cuxhaven yesterday at 11:30 in the morning. A band played "Muss i' denn, muss i' denn" and "Leb' wohl, du mein lieb' Heimatland!" The melancholy of departure registered on many faces. For us that wasn't in order. I met a very nice group of travelers. [. . .] We stick together for meals, and the ship's doctor is next to us so we dine under medical supervision. And goodness, the meals. Early in the morning, from 6:00 to 7:00; tea or coffee is served; 8 to 9 o'clock a fabulous breakfast with warm and cold meat and egg dishes, wonderful fruits; around 11 o'clock snacks; 12:30 lunch with any number of courses; 4 o'clock tea or coffee and pastries; 7 o'clock a grand dinner (smoking); 10 o'clock a cold buffet. So there you have it. The land of milk and honey is nothing compared to this. [. . .] The service is unbelievably attentive; at night, exquisite fruits are placed in the cabins.

In preparation for the 14 September 1930 Reichstag elections, the NSDAP under Hitler's leadership launched an enormous propaganda campaign. Along with the other right-wing parties, it tried to take advantage of the widening economic turmoil. The Nazis fulminated against reparation payments and urged Germans to resist both Versailles and Bolshevism. In a stunning upset, the NSDAP received more than 18.3 percent of the vote, whereas the party had garnered only 2.6 percent two years earlier.

The Nazis had completely overrun the traditional nationalist parties such as the German National People's Party; they now constituted the second-largest party in the Reichstag after the Social Democrats. Landtag elections in Braunschweig on the same day actually put Nazis in power; they acquired two important ministerial posts. Social Democrats ministers Gustav Steinbrecher, Hans Sievers, and Heinrich Jasper, who had been minister president since 1927 (and who in 1945 would die in Bergen-Belsen), all lost their jobs. At the same time, the party's paramilitary wing, the storm troopers or SA, intensified its campaign of terror against Social Democrats and Communists; the pitched street battles in working-class districts in which both sides counted wounded and dead dominated the city's newspaper headlines. Street fights regularly broke out in front of the local unemployment office where partisans of all parties gathered to stand in line.

How much had changed over the course of a single lifetime became clear on 18 January 1931, the sixtieth anniversary of the founding of the German Kaiserreich in Versailles at the end of the Franco-Prussian War. To celebrate the day, many of the soldiers who had served in the old imperial regiments marched through the streets of Braunschweig for the first time since the Revolution. Major General Alfred Streccius, commander of the 17th Infantry Regiment, addressed the crowds with "hard, clear words," in which each sentence, the Braunschweigische Landeszeitung *wrote the next day, was a "slap in the face of those who with their dirty hands wanted to destroy what had been forged in Versailles with blood and iron and to trample it underneath their muddy boots." Thereafter, the Communists organized a protest march against the new right-wing government on 22 February 1931, which the Nazi Interior Minister summarily banned, at least in the old city. On 21 February, SA troops from across Germany gathered in Braunschweig. In the city as elsewhere, they marched provocatively through working-class districts, which led again and again to skirmishes. A Communist demonstration that took place despite the ban was violently broken up.*

Returning from Holland in March 1931, Elisabeth Gebensleben witnessed how a painting, supposedly a Rembrandt, was brought into Germany. In the thirties, the "discovery" of long lost Rembrandts had become something of a fad and there was considerable demand for the paintings in Germany as well as the United States. The traffic in art also included objects that had been made in Saxony's porcelain factories established by August the Strong (1670–1733), King of Poland and Elector of Saxony.

Elisabeth Gebensleben to her daughter Irmgard Brester, Braunschweig, 14 September 1930

[. . .] Today was Election Day; a very excitable atmosphere in the city! This evening we accompanied the M.'s and K.'s to the Hagenschenke [café] and then came back over the Steinweg. We could hardly get through. A policeman every three paces! Apparently the right-wing parties will make gains! That would be wonderful. No final results until tomorrow. [. . .]

MONDAY EVENING, 15 SEPTEMBER 1930

So the bourgeois parties emerged victorious; there will be a bourgeois majority in the Landtag and the red ministers Steinbrecher, Sievers, and Dr. Jasper will soon be "packing their bags," as the *Landeszeitung* remarked today. Well I am really happy, Vati as well. On the national level, the vote was also nothing to complain about. The

National Socialists achieved a fabulous boost. The newspapers here bitterly attacked each other. [. . .]

Minna von Alten to her granddaughter Irmgard Brester, Braunschweig, 6 November 1930

[. . .] It is really good to know that you are reading the *Landeszeitung* so that you will always be informed about political matters. Things are really on the upswing for us.

Elisabeth Gebensleben to her daughter Irmgard Brester, Braunschweig, 11 November 1930

[. . .] We have already arranged for Eberhard to go to Freiburg again for the summer semester. He is too distracted in Berlin. Freiburg is calmer. And so beautiful! He can afford to skip a semester of Russian.

Elisabeth Gebensleben to her daughter Irmgard Brester, Braunschweig, 22 January 1931

[. . .] After Vati and I had leisurely drunk our coffee, while reading the letters from Holland and Berlin, we went out at noon to the "parade" on the Schlossplatz, for which we had tickets. You must have read about it in the newspaper: the first parade in many years on the Schlossplatz, and for the first time the old flags, which had been stored in the local heritage museum since the war, were flown. It was splendid; the General is a marvelous man; what a pithy, articulate speech! A soldier would certainly follow that kind of a leader; that sort of fabulous martial bearing is the only way to conduct a parade in Germany. But here's the difference: before, a grand army; today, soldiers in much fewer numbers. How powerfully the memories of the good old days grabbed us. There was many an eye that did not remain dry. [. . .]

Elisabeth Gebensleben to her daughter Irmgard Brester, Braunschweig, 21 February 1931

[. . .] The situation in Braunschweig is critical. Hitler is coming on Sunday. The Oberbürgermeister is ill. In city hall, crisis conditions as well. [. . .]

Karl Gebensleben to his daughter Irmgard Brester, Braunschweig, 5 March 1931

[. . .] The first meeting of the city parliament with the *newly elected* members will probably take place next week (on the 12th). In the future it will get pretty gay around here. 14 *Sozis* and 4 Communists together constitute the majority; in the opposition, 10 *Nazis* and 7 bourgeois. Too bad that there is not one less Socialist because then they would not have a majority with the Communists. So the Socialists will govern with the Communists—as radically as possible! Well, I will await events calmly. The council will also have a new look, at least as far as those working in an honorary capacity are concerned. Right now there are 4 Sozis and 3 bourgeois. In the future, 3 Sozis, 1 Communist, 2 Nazis, and 1 bourgeois! The council too will soon see *stormy* times. We'll have to wait and see!

**Minna von Alten to her daughter Elisabeth Gebensleben [in Utrecht],
Braunschweig, 8 March 1931**

[. . .] Aunt Bertha did so well renting out during the trade fair that she could pay all her back taxes. Her long-standing boarder from Argentina arrived over Paris and London; the world economic crisis is everywhere, worst of all in England, the middle class is disappearing and he is afraid that Bolshevism is coming. His goods are all in stock, nobody is buying. Either Bolshevism or Nazi! Then better the latter. [. . .]

**Eberhard Gebensleben to his mother Elisabeth Gebensleben, Berlin,
9 March 1931**

[. . .] I was *very* interested in what you had to say about the National Socialists. I believe we first have to see what they are going to *do*. If it were really so, this idealism. . . ! Actually, it is too good to be true.

**Elisabeth Gebensleben to her daughter Irmgard Brester, Braunschweig,
16 March 1931**

[. . .] First I have to tell you about my trip, which for me was again exquisitely interesting. This trip certainly takes the cake. I really have to publish my travel adventures. After changing trains in Amersfoort, I was sitting in a compartment with three men. I am right in the corner, by the door. On the right by the window, a German gentleman who had made himself a second-class seat with his thick camel-hair blanket and was busily reading. When we reached Deventer, I ordered a cup of coffee from the waiter. Immediately, the gentleman jumped up and went into the corridor, offering me his window seat with its little table and soft upholstery. He had somewhat odd-looking luggage. A long thin finely wrapped packet with leather straps, presumably a painting. Shortly before Bentheim, he said he had more luggage and had to go through customs. Would I be so friendly and watch over his painting while he was gone. I had no reason to refuse. The German custom officials came by, curt and very strict. Each of the three gentlemen had to open their suitcases; I was once again spared. "And I also have a painting here," said the self-conscious gentleman by the window. The customs official: "Paintings are free. Now let me take a look." With great ado the picture was hauled down, a side loosened. Enough; put it back up. The train came to a halt and everyone got off. I was alone with the painting that had been entrusted in my care. Then one of the passengers turned around and asked me: "Do you even know what it is that you are looking after? The gentleman insinuated that the painting was worth more than the entire train." I was relieved when the owner returned. When we successfully crossed the border, he said to me: "Now I can tell you what you were looking after. The painting is a genuine Rembrandt."—"And you got it over the border just like that?" My heart was ready to start throbbing. "I can't get it out of Europe," he answered. Whereupon all I could say was that in that case it was a true blessing, since I could not assert that I would care to see the Americans with our Rembrandts. The painting was purchased from private hands; the gentleman, an art dealer on his way to Berlin, showed me a photograph because unpacking it would be too dangerous. It was a portrait of a young man. A young man is laying his hand on a skull. So the customs officials are anxiously on the look out for a ½ lb of tea in order to collect duties, and something like that goes duty-free over the border, or rather was smuggled over, since I cannot believe that the customs officials would have simply allowed it in if they had recognized it for what it was. The large amounts of luggage on which the art dealer had to pay customs duties consisted of a crate of porcelain; three immensely valuable vases, a gift from Augustus the Strong. Stimulating discussions followed especially about art and paintings; the man was a real expert in this field. The trip to Hanover went very quickly. [. . .]

The world economic crisis threw international commerce into turmoil. In May 1931, the largest bank in Austria failed, which prompted a run on banks throughout central Europe. The financial panic reached its climax on 13 July 1931 when the Danatbank (or Darmstädter National Bank), one of the three largest in Germany, was forced to close its doors due to a lack of cash reserves. The government subsequently ordered other banks to do the same in order to keep panicked depositors from withdrawing their savings. Chancellor Heinrich Brüning (1885–1970) also used emergency decrees to stabilize the government from attacks by the Right (NSDAP) and the Left (the Communists); Article 48 of the Weimar constitution gave the Reich President the power to alter or even suspend laws without the approval of parliament. The article allowed Brüning as well as the chancellors who followed him—Papen, Schleicher, and finally Hitler—to govern without building majorities in the Reichstag, which had become so politically divided as to be incapable of constructive action. Although the use of Article 48 was envisioned as an emergency measure, in fact, its promiscuous use after 1930 spelled the beginning of the end of Germany's parliamentary system.

In the meantime, clashes between the SA and organized workers became more frequent. On 13 July 1931, the Nazis organized a propaganda march through the city. Thereupon the Communists called upon its members to retaliate, which led to massive brawls on Braunschweig's Steinweg.

Politics dominated family discussions as well, and on one of his visits to Utrecht Eberhard got involved in long conversations with friends of August and Immo. He thereupon sent them a copy of Thomas Mann's speech, "An Appeal to Reason," which Mann had given in Berlin on 17 October 1930. Mann had warned of the dangers represented by the Nazis and argued that the bourgeoisie belonged at the side of the Social Democrats. Right-wing radicals and Nazis tried without success to disrupt the speech, but few heeded the words of the Nobel prize–winning novelist who left Germany for exile in 1933.

Eberhard continued his studies with Professor Walter Jellinek (1885–1955), a professor for constitutional law at the University of Heidelberg who a few years later was dismissed by the Nazis on account of his Jewish grandparents. Karl and Elisabeth visited Eberhard in Heidelberg in June 1931.

Eberhard Gebensleben to his sister Irmgard Brester, Berlin, 18 March 1931

This morning I had a little pamphlet with a speech by Thomas Mann regarding National Socialism sent to Dutch politicians. Although the argument is surprising and a little unconvincing, he makes some very excellent observations about our spiritual condition today and that of our wartime enemies from a more lofty perspective than daily politics. A good sampling of the convictions of a dignified, spiritual person. That said, he takes a position that is about as left as someone who wants to remain bourgeois can take. [. . .]

Elisabeth Gebensleben to her daughter Irmgard Brester, Braunschweig, 15 April 1931

[. . .] At the moment, I am completely busy. You will get the picture if I tell you that since Monday two friends are visiting Hardus, Zettel and Gerhard Nicolai. That makes three students in the house so you can more or less imagine what is going on here. Actually, you can't imagine it. For instance, what did the three just do? When Ursel wanted to go home at 11:15, all three said that they wanted to take her home and look at her room, which she has been living in for two days, next door in the building in the rear. By the way, it is a lovely room. Ohmchen was very upset! They are not about to do that: going up so late at night! But really, that's what they did. According to Zettel: "From the basement to the attic, the whole house was woken up. Actually, I felt sorry for Ursel, but we had to be firm, and even if she stood in front of her door like a lioness, eventually she had to open it up." They were doubled over with laughter! Yet Ursel lives with two very old ladies in their seventies! What were they thinking. Well tomorrow Hardus will receive his stern lecture from Ohmchen! In the meantime, I will console Ohmchen. Since it was the three of them, the whole thing was really not so dangerous; it would have been different, if only one had gone up. On the other hand, just one doesn't come up with the idea for such a dumb prank. You need several more to come up with that. [. . .] But I am having so much fun; it is such a pleasure to have the boys. Nicolai (the canoe companion) is a capital fellow. Rather serious, the opposite of Zettel; he appears to be quite a bit older. Zettel has become more calm and responsible, but with his vitality and good cheer, he is really great to have around.

[. . .] Paris! It seems like a long time ago now. I can't believe that we were there for just eight days. I thought it was weeks. That is because we saw and experienced so much in those eight days. It was really a wonderful vacation, and there is something special about the Paris air. Of course, not all our impressions were positive, and in a way it was a relief to return to our clean, meticulous Germany. I was taken most of all by the art monuments. I am pretty sure that a couple of tears rolled down my face when I looked at the Venus de Milo for the last time in the Louvre. It seemed so animated among the other dead marble figures. And more tears when I stood in front of Chopin's grave at Père Lachaise. And then there was the overwhelming view of the city of Paris from the platform on top of the Arc de Triomphe! We took many photographs. Also Versailles and the Petit Trianon, where you are so swept up by the past that you expect to see Marie Antoinette and her ladies in waiting bustling about. [. . .]

Elisabeth Gebensleben to her daughter Irmgard Brester, Braunschweig, 25 April 1931

[. . .] The 1½ weeks with our three students, who were frequently joined by a 4th fellow, a friend from Braunschweig, went very well. Especially when Zettel is around the trees grow into the skies out of sheer idealism. For him, the world is sweet violin music. That little guy will really have to trim his sails when the gray winds of reality hit him. But the whole disposition of his character certainly has a good influence on our all too serious and melancholy Eberhard, and I hope that some good will rub off on Eberhard when they spend a semester together in Heidelberg. The two departed in good cheer. [. . .]

Elisabeth Gebensleben to her daughter Irmgard Brester, Heidelberg, 22 June 1931

Ohmchen withstood the trip splendidly, but the evening in the theater after our arrival [back in Braunschweig] was really not to my liking. My thoughts persistently wandered off. I kept thinking of you all and our wonderful get-together, and not even the most beautiful Mozart arias helped. A surprising sight awaited us when we left the theater: the whole Steinweg was lit up by torches, lively music, and marching Brownshirts. The procession went on forever! At least three times the length of the Steinweg itself! Underneath the trees in front of Lück's [café] stood a vehicle with at least 20 armed policemen; policemen all along the streets, and at the end of the procession a brand new car with 30 more police. As we stood there, I pinched Vati in the arm: there, at the end of the procession where the women and girls had gathered, I saw—Gerda walking arm in arm with a girlfriend and holding a torch! There was a big National Socialist rally in the Hofjäger [Braunschweig's largest hall]. You must have read about it in the paper, Immo. It was followed by the torchlight procession, in which many members of the audience enthusiastically took part, including Gerda and her friend. After coming from peaceful Holland, the procession and the armed policemen had a strange effect on me.

[. . .] Here [in Heidelberg] we have seen many beautiful and interesting sights. On Saturday night, the castle was lit up like in a fairy tale in honor of a big Nazi meeting. August, I know, I know! Big and little boats with lamps crowded the waters of the Neckar around Heidelberg. In addition, thousands of spectators stood in dense rows along the shore. All of a sudden, a cannon shot, and out of the darkness emerged the lit-up castle in all its romantic glory. It looked as if it were in flames. And a splendid fire works display as well. Everything proceeded in good order. The Nazis maintain a strict discipline. and around here there are not so many Communists who might disrupt the peace and quiet. On Sunday morning, Eberhard was invited to have a meal with a law professor who is supposed to be very important. He was invited along with one other student. and he good-naturedly explained: "This is an invitation without favor." He didn't know how he came to be selected since so many students attend the professor's lectures. However, when I looked over the papers on Eberhard's desk, for which he received good grades, the invitation made sense to me. The essays must have made the professor take notice. However, Eberhard's appearance concerns me. He looks somewhat tired and doesn't sufficiently attend to his physical needs. And I think I know the reason for his somewhat sleepy nature. Zettel is too restless. Just today he told me that his day begins at 11:00 in the evening and that he usually doesn't go to bed until 1:30. Naturally he disrupts Eberhard. Today I gave him my opinion about the matter, and I will also speak to Eberhard. Zettel looks terrible. The landlady, a sweet, good soul, also confided her concerns to me: Herr Gebensleben is so modest and quiet and she and her husband enjoy him so, but Herr Zeitler, he is too disruptive and she doesn't know how long she can put up with him. She is renting out seven rooms and obviously the lodgers need to be considerate of one another. Yet at 2:00 in the morning Herr Zeitler is still banging in nails and in the beginning he had filled the bathtub three times a day, which is a waste of money. And so on in that vein. I think Zettel's good luck will soon run out, which pleases me on Eberhard's account. It was a good idea for us to finally visit him.

[. . .] To Eberhard I gushed on about Scheveningen and Den Haag, and Gerda as well. It was simply wonderful! And Loosdrecht. Absolutely everything!

Elisabeth Gebensleben to her daughter Irmgard Brester, Braunschweig, 15 July 1931

At the moment, Grossmutti is absolutely not in the mood to write the cheerful letter to Holland that she would so like to do. You get the German newspaper and will know our situation. I always think that it is all a bad dream from which I will soon awake. The pressure on us is terrible. Personally I think I tend to see things too darkly, and Vati and Ohmchen, who returned from Salzuflen this afternoon, agree. I try to fight it, but until now without success. This uncertainty and insecurity, which envelops the entire nation, is simply very difficult to endure. Every evening the radio broadcasts: remain calm, steady the nerves; then the explanations regarding the emergency decrees, which do in fact help educated Germans to understand and to calm themselves. But what about the simple folk? All the unemployed? They are quiet as long as they receive money, and therefore it is important that reasonable, responsible people do their part by not hoarding cash. Well, in this regard there is not much that can be done at the moment, since we can't take anything out from the banks. Savers who have bank accounts are not being paid out. Withdrawals allowed only to pay wages, unemployment, and salaries.

Just now at midnight Reich Finance Minister Dietrich gave a speech on "Projections on the Bank Holidays" and on "The New Emergency Decree." Every day brings new decrees and they are our salvation. The speech was very well delivered. And we were able to learn a great deal. In the last three months, Germany has paid back 3 to 4 billion in short-terms loans abroad. That is an impressive achievement. But to find 7 billion within a year's time is surely quite an impossibility. If the nation continues to remain calm, we will hopefully get over this difficult crisis.

CONTINUED THURSDAY AFTERNOON

Your lovely long letter really brought a bright ray of sunlight. [. . .] we so much hope to have you here and look forward to it. Luckily August's vacations are not until August when conditions will have hopefully improved. These days it is dismal to wander about the city. In the shop windows, you see goods offered at knockdown prices but the shops are empty. Scattered along the streets, especially in front of banks, groups gather in more or less agitated conversation. But there has not yet been any real disorder. Yesterday Ohmchen was still in a triumphant mood: "I am sure to get some money from the bank, at least the accumulated interest," but she did not get a penny, just as I had said. I feel sorry for the bank tellers. It is no small thing to have to deal with the public nowadays. One gentleman, a doctor from the college, started reprimanding in the most terrible way: "My salary is deposited directly into the bank; my laboratory costs money every single day; I have no cash at home. Workers get unemployment, but what about us? Should we starve?" This is typical of the mood around here. Today and tomorrow, Frau M. is coming over. Little Frau M. [the seamstress], she has suddenly become even smaller and she stepped in the door like a small bundle of misfortune. She too deposited her bitterly stitched earnings in the savings bank. "We already lost our money once, and now a second time?" I tried to calm her down, and tonight she seems a little less unhappy. We ourselves had been able to put a little money in the bank; a few thousand marks. Once in a while, we thought of sending it to Holland, but then thought better of it; we didn't seem to have any reason since we had gotten to know people from the world of finance. On our trip with the bowling club we accompanied the director of the Danat Bank in the bank's automobile. The director made a very jolly impression, and his wife was very elegant. Did they have any suspicions? Quite possibly. I also find it very cowardly, even sinful of the Fatherland to hand over to foreign countries the money that is so desperately needed here at home. We wish we had a few funds in reserve, savings for a rainy day.

I would be most sorry if Eberhard has lost his money since he saved long and hard. Just by coincidence he received 50 M at the last moment. Early last Monday, he wrote me a letter asking me to send him 50 M from his bank account so that he could buy a camera. In any case, Vati and I would have left him some money. As it was, without any sense of foreboding, I went to his bank at noon on Monday and asked for 50 M, which was paid out to me no questions asked. Little did I know that at the very same time people were storming banks in the city. Had I known about the impending catastrophe, I would, for all my love for the Fatherland, have withdrawn more, if not everything. Later on, when Vati returned home he looked completely beat and I finally realized: "The Danat Bank has suspended all withdrawals."

Little by little, we have all calmed down. Even if in the worst case the money is lost, which I don't believe, money is not the biggest problem. We are even somewhat proud that we can help the Fatherland in its time of great need with our savings. The main thing is that the situation remains calm. Perhaps it is a good thing that the German people are pulling themselves together, are closing ranks. I just can't imagine that there are still Social Democrats who swear by the International and cannot see that France is our worst enemy and continue to rattle on about international peace and understanding. Maybe August disagrees. What do you think, August: a small debate on the National Socialists? I can very well imagine friendly relations with Holland, even with England. It was a real load off my mind when I read this morning that the only bank exchanging reichsmarks was Amsterdam's. But friendship between Germany and France? I think that is as impossible as it is impossible for Peter [the dog] to get along with Sonja's cat [next door], which he attacked one more time and which Sonja has to nurse again.

[. . .] [I heard] that law professors spoke very highly of young Gebensleben at a faculty gathering. He is one of the most talented members of the new generation, and Professor Jellinek in particular, the one who had invited Hardus over for a meal, explained that it was very satisfying to watch young G. develop his legal talents. [. . .]

Irmgard Brester to her mother Elisabeth Gebensleben, Utrecht, 17 July 1931

I had a long talk with Papa and August about the difficult situation in Germany at present, something we naturally read about at great length in the newspapers. But even if we are up on the conditions in general, we can't really imagine how it works itself out on individual people. That is precisely what your letter, for which I dearly thank you, described so tellingly. What a state of anxiety you are in! We are constantly thinking of you and hope, along with you, that you will overcome these dreadful days without serious problems. I can imagine the atmosphere in Germany; I remember the difficult times a few years back. Having come to peaceful Holland, I feel a bit as though I have deserted the flag. But perhaps you can have a certain sense of security and calm, knowing that you have a personal connection to Holland. August and I want you to know if we can help you out of any difficulties you will let us know immediately. According to August, you can buy Reichsmarks anywhere here. We are of the opinion that the greatest danger is not the financial fallout from the present crisis but the prospect of civil unrest and rebellion in the future. In any case, it might be best henceforth to establish a small reserve of Dutch funds; then if there is some sort of catastrophe, you wouldn't suddenly be left without anything. But these are considerations for later, first we have to get over these critical days, which, for all the mistrust and nervousness, will pass without disruption. You are totally right, Mutti: it was right not to travel during these cheerless days. Hopefully everything will be back to normal in September when we can enjoy our get-together all the more happily. And I am so grateful that your [last] visit here went so well.

On 20 June 1931, U.S. President Herbert Hoover proposed that European states impose a one-year moratorium on the payment of international debts and reparations in order to prop up Germany's banks. France, which had consistently opposed such postponements, eventually agreed to Hoover's proposal on 6 July. Two weeks later in London, a conference on financial aid for Germany was convened. It would go on for seven months, although banks reopened for business in Germany on 5 August 1931.

The Braunschweigische Landeszeitung published the following proclamation on its front page on 22 July 1931:

"The leaders of the National Opposition have sent the following letter to Chancellor Bruening in London:

'The plan of the American President Hoover, originally conceived as relief, has been countered by the undisguised intentions of the French to force the Germans to submit permanently to their demands. As a result, what was intended as relief will become something worse.

The responsible circles in France are not ignorant of the sense of despair that has increased amidst our suffering people, especially among

*young people, so much so that the most dangerous lines of thought have
emerged.*

> *The German people, who feel exonerated from blame for the war,
> cannot and will not carry the forcibly imposed unjust burdens any longer.
> A further narrowing of Germany's sovereignty is all the more unacceptable
> and indefensible. The entire National Opposition therefore wants to make
> it clear in every way possible that in accordance with its basic principles it
> does not consider new commitments to France legally binding.'"*

*Alfred Hugenberg (1865–1951), an industrialist and newspaper magnate, was
the leader of the German National People's Party. From January to June 1933 he also
served as Reich Economics Minister under Hitler, but resigned once it became clear
that all parties except for the NSDAP would be banned. Franz Seldte (1882–1967)
founded the veterans' association, the Stahlhelm, and was Reich Labor Minister under
Hitler. Second-in-command in the Stahlhelm, Theodor Düsterberg (1875–1950) ran
unsuccessfully for the office of the Reich Presidency in March 1932. These right-wing
figures all belonged to the "National Opposition," which on 11 October 1931 organized
a large, highly publicized gathering along with the NSDAP in Bad Harzburg in order
to establish a broad political front against the Brüning government. Much of the
excitement spilled over to nearby Braunschweig.*

*While Immo and August were staying in Braunschweig in September 1931, Immo's
father asked them to attend a Nazi rally in order to learn of their opinion of the new and
dynamic political movement. Although Hitler was originally scheduled to speak, Goebbels
addressed the large audience instead. Many decades later, Immo could still remember
how Goebbels limped into the hall with his clubfoot and in just a few minutes was able to
whip the audience into a frenzy. Completely repelled by the noise and mayhem, August
and Immo left the rally before it ended. Joseph Goebbels (1897–1945) was the prominent
Nazi Gauleiter of Berlin, since 1929 the NSDAP's Reichsleiter for propaganda, and after
the Nazi seizure of power, the Reich Minister of Public Enlightenment and Propaganda.
Goebbels and his wife killed themselves and their six children on 1 May 1945.*

Eberhard Gebensleben to his sister Irmgard Brester, Heidelberg, 19 July 1931

[. . .] In recent days, visitors came round again. Last Monday evening, I am
at the university, standing around lost in thought, staring at the sky, when this
completely wild looking individual in the worn-out uniform of the German youth
movement approaches me, hops off his bicycle, and turns out to be my friend Nicolai,
you know, who once was going to accompany me to Holland. He is in Marburg now
and from one moment to the next lost interest in studying so instead he bicycled
out into the world for a week. He camped out for two nights in my flat, and you
can well imagine all trips around the world that the two of us started to plan. But
for God's sake, don't mention anything to Mutti; she will think we will want to take
the collapsible boat down the Volga. Incidentally, trips abroad have become quite a
bit more expensive: 100 M to cross the border according to the emergency decrees.
Braunschweig will have informed you of the conditions prevailing in Germany. I don't

want to make any profound observations or report on the great sympathy that France has acquired for itself!

[. . .] Many thanks for the little picture I asked for. Hopefully I can return the favor soon. In any case, not everything abroad is "hostile."

Elisabeth Gebensleben to her daughter Irmgard Brester, Braunschweig, 21 July 1931

[. . .] Of course, in these difficult days our thoughts reach out to one another, and your sweet letter reveals that they stretch from Holland to Germany as well as from Germany to Holland. Many, many thanks especially for your willingness to help. Certainly we will soon have overcome these critical tension-filled days, but will we be able to breathe easily afterward? I am not sure. The long-term foreign loans, which God willing will be approved, can eliminate the present danger, but they will not bring about a general recovery. They add up to more debt and heavier shackles. The only thing that will really help is the cancellation of war debts and the elimination of the war reparations that we pay—and this is what is so grating—without bearing the blame. I am sure that among the gentlemen conferring in London there are those who agree, but will they show the courage to say so openly? Never before has there been so much talk about money. And not just in Germany, although we are the ones who suffer the consequences. If Germany falls, the other countries will suffer as well, and that is the reason that they will come to our aid. People here are very discouraged, but so far law and order have prevailed. It is a blessing that the emergency decrees are so harsh; they restored my confidence in our government as never before. If I recount the individual cases of this financial calamity, you will get a picture of just how under pressure every single one of us feels. This afternoon Aunt M. from Salder paid a visit to Ohmchen. She had just spoken to her son-in-law Z., the mayor of Blankenburg, who mentioned that he had no idea how he was going to pay unemployment next Saturday; the money had run out. I am curious to know what we will get. Most likely we will be paid in installments. A friend of Uschi, a student, was always paid out by the bank, but now she gets nothing. Lawyer L., you know him, Immo, from the Professional Club, told Vati that he was at wit's end. On Saturday, two days before the crash, he had 80,000-M inheritance to distribute. He put the funds in the Danat Bank to transfer the allotments. Of course, it is not his fault, but you can imagine the mood of the heirs. Today at noon, the telephone rang; I asked Frieda to get it and she came back to the kitchen totally distraught. A very agitated gentleman was on the phone and refused to believe that Herr Stadtbaurat was not at home. He was a friend of Herr Stadtbaurat and demanded to speak to him. I took it. It was Herr S. I told him he should come by one evening this week and discuss matters calmly with Vati. He quieted down and simply said: "Hard times!" And hard they surely are for him. What are transport companies and truck services supposed to do nowadays! And then the story of a simple, ordinary girl who entered W.'s notions store sobbing. She had just arranged for her marriage license. For years she had saved for her wedding day, 1,000 M in the end. Now she wants to marry, needs the money for a wedding dress and a small party. She too gets nothing. I can just go on and on—there are the sick who need to travel to a spa and get just 50 M, at most 100 M, no more. [. . .]

CONTINUED WEDNESDAY EVENING

[. . .] let us be extra happy about our next get-together here, which hopefully, hopefully will take place. You are "lords of the manor" and can travel wherever you want. The only possible obstacle would be if civil disorder broke out here. I am not predicting it, but I wouldn't rule it out either. If you read the front-page article with the headline "The National Opposition," you will get a sense of the mood and the frame of mind of a large part of the nation. The German people do not exist in order to let themselves be made into slaves and to live in bondage for decades. The feelings of desperation and also the pride of Germany needs to find some outlet.

I just listened to the latest reports from London on the radio. Such a radio is very important in times like these. We are so curious that we can't wait for the next morning's newspaper. [. . .]

Elisabeth Gebensleben to her daughter Irmgard Brester, Braunschweig, 6 August 1931

[. . .] I was so happy, Immo, that you convinced Herr and Frau C. to travel to the Harz. Just thinking of the local businesses, we are happy that any guest makes the trip. It is such a shame that the region is so empty. But it is completely understandable; few people have the courage or the desire or the money to take trips. Gradually money matters are returning to normal. High time too, if we are to avoid even more hardship. It is just so stupid that we personally are so squeezed since Vati's and Eberhard's bank is still closed. It is the one that got into difficulties. But it appears that it too will pick itself up. After all, the money is all in secure mortgages, there is just a lack of ready cash. I am no longer quite so pessimistic as I was when we heard about the suspension of all withdrawals at the "Bank für Handel und Gewerbe." Vati is also optimistic. [. . .]

Irmgard Brester to her mother Elisabeth Gebensleben, Utrecht, 18 August 1931

[. . .] Last Sunday we were treated to an amazing sight. As usual, we were sitting down to a late breakfast when we suddenly heard a peculiar humming in the air. We ran to the balcony, and, really, the *Graf Zeppelin* appeared, flying quietly and majestically, and quite low too, just over the house. It was a grand sight to see, a balm for my German heart. It really is a symbol of Germany's energy and strength that, despite the present troubles, will prevail! Later we read in the paper that the Zeppelin flew to England over Holland. [. . .]

Irmgard Brester to her mother Elisabeth Gebensleben, Utrecht, 29 September 1931

[. . .] Saturday night, Floor and Nina came to sit around with us; they were especially interested in hearing about the National Socialist meeting. [. . .]

Elisabeth Gebensleben to her daughter Irmgard Brester, Braunschweig, 13 October 1931

[. . .] When Vati returns from Braunlage tomorrow, he will be happy to know that the radio has been fixed. We got a new valve today. I think it is an improvement, the sound is more distinct and clear. Now that we have the daily news reports so it doesn't take as long to read the morning newspaper. I wonder whether you read some of the speeches that were delivered in Harzburg? I read them all. You have to make the time to do so. *This* event was surely of great importance; another step forward for the national movement. What will happen now? Next Sunday a great event is taking place in Braunschweig: Hitler will speak. A huge influx of people is expected. M. told me that 25 special trains have been reserved. He has no idea where to put them all. Vati said that the city has allocated the small parade ground (up by E.) and the Leonhard Square for parking. The National Socialists hold a lot of rallies, and each time the numbers and the enthusiasm grows. [. . .]

One week after the gathering in Bad Harzburg, Hitler arrived in Braunschweig to rally the faithful. On the Franzschen Field on 17 October, he consecrated twenty-five SA Standarte with the so-called blood flag, which had accompanied the unsuccessful Beer Hall Putsch in 1923. The next day, Hitler reviewed a huge parade on the Schlossplatz. The Braunschweigische Landeszeitung *reported on 18 October:*

> "Make Way for the Brown Battalions on the March!
> *A veritable river of National Socialist fighters streamed into Braunschweig, the thousand-year-old city of Henry the Lion. Yet the thousands upon thousands of warmly welcomed guests whom we are putting up today inside the walls of our city and beyond, in surrounding communities, are only a fraction of the men and lads across the German Fatherland who, ready for battle and willing to make sacrifices, have committed themselves to the ideas of their Führer Adolf Hitler. [. . .] Thanks to the Brown Day, all of Germany and indeed the entire world is watching events in Braunschweig."*

The Volksfreund *commented on 19 October:*

> *"Blood flowed in the streets of Braunschweig on Saturday and Sunday as a result of the provocative gathering of incendiary fascist battle formations.*
> *[. . .] You can get a sense of how the 'dear guests' that the right-wing bourgeoisie welcomed behaved by taking a stroll through the working-class districts of Braunschweig: Smashed and shot-up window panes, broken down doors, torn up paving stones, demolished stores. The smirk on the grotesque face of fascism is there for everyone to see!*
> *The pure fury and malice of Hitler's hordes, who were shipped here from across Germany on the bankroll of big business, raged through working-class neighborhoods. If there was any doubt, this yellow pack, cloaked with the appellation 'workers' party' but commanded by princes, generals, and moneybags, clearly displayed their fanatic hatred of Braunschweig's working class. What these cowardly acts garnered was many rounds of applause from capitalist newspapers typified first and foremost by the anti-working-class* Landeszeitung.

> [. . .] The 'punitive raids' in the Lange Strasse, in the Klint, in the Ritterstrasse had in fact been prepared long in advance. Here the Nazis showed their true character. They wanted to intimidate and to tame the working class. The swastika men, obedient students of Mussolini's methods, believed they could test out the 'Third Reich' here without encountering any resistance.
>
> [. . .] The working class is not going to be fooled by Hitler and his followers any more. [. . .] What they cannot achieve legally, with all their Hohenzollern parades and fancy speeches, they try to compel by force. Braunschweig's proletariat has now been forewarned. The invasion of the fascists in Braunschweig is an exhortation to all Germany. This is what can happen if it is a divided working class that confronts Hitler's gangs. [. . .] The fascist rampage goes well beyond civil disorder and lawlessness; it is a dress rehearsal for civil war! [. . .] Braunschweig's working class has received an object lesson in what will happen if the 'One-Third Reich' of Herr [Dietrich] Klagges [1891–1971, Interior and Education Minister in the state of Braunschweig since 1931] becomes the 'Third Reich' of Hitler throughout Germany."

An estimated hundred thousand people participated in Braunschweig's "Brown Days" (the city itself counted about one hundred fifty thousand residents); the parade alone took between four and six hours to pass. In this age of paramilitary politics, uniformed troops displayed strength, discipline, and unity; indeed, their occupation of the city anticipated the Nazi seizure of power. The Nazis put on a propaganda show that no other Weimar-era party could, not even the Reichswehr. Whoever dared to wear a Social Democratic badge along the parade route could expect to be beaten up. Small groups of SA men repeatedly ducked out of the parade to infiltrate working-class districts, where brawls immediately broke out as workers used any means to defend themselves. Two people who were coming back from a trade union meeting fell into the hands of the SA and were murdered. They were the first victims of the Nazi terror in Braunschweig. The official explanation was that the SA men had acted in self-defense after being attacked by Communists, an explanation that nationalists accepted without question, despite many inconsistent facts. To protest the murders, workers called a general strike on 22 October. At the time, the former general, Wilhelm Groener, was Reichswehr and Interior Minister. Social Democrats still governed in Prussia.

Elisabeth Gebensleben to her daughter Irmgard Brester, Braunschweig, 18 October 1931

There is no better way to spend the last hours of this thrilling Sunday than to tell you a little bit about the last two days. The events are still so completely fresh in my mind that I simply must write straight from the heart, which I know you will find interesting. But first of all let me thank you for your lovely Sunday letter. Such a darling letter on a Sunday is so special, but on this turbulent Sunday it was like a greeting from another world. Again and again I wanted the two of you at my side. You can't imagine *what* has become of our Braunschweig, our peaceful, old city. To understand, you had to have seen it with your own eyes, and even then when you think about it afterward you say to yourself: did I dream that, or was it reality that I saw? Yes, it was reality and so inspiring that Germans once again breathed freely and proudly. Germany is truly awakening, and not even the most clever speech by the chancellor or the mean-spirited interventionism and obstructionism of Severing will change that. Even reporters for foreign newspapers were on hand; the English, for example, stayed at the Park Hotel. But I doubt that the world will really learn the truth. The stories will be manipulated to suit the tastes of readers. Even in our country, the truth is glossed over. This is what made the radio reports so interesting. The broadcast goes through Prussia. The report was brief: "Hitler consecrated twenty-four new flags on the occasion of the rally of storm troopers in Braunschweig. Clashes with political opponents were reported and one worker was killed." Was there a single word about the 104,000 Brownshirts who marched through Braunschweig today, about the military review that Hitler held on the Schlossplatz after the flag consecration on the Franzschen Field that lasted 6 hours? That is to say, Hitler reviewed a column that took 6 hours to pass. The divisions marched through the Ritterbrunnen to the Schlossplatz and then on to the Bohlweg. Of course, only a small contingent could stay on the Schlossplatz. Just think about it: 6 hours, and then you get a picture of the almost endless numbers. And did the radio say one word about the exemplary discipline that these 100,000 maintained, or about the enthusiasm with which spectators greeted them? I sat in the glassed-in foyer at Lück's [Café] for over two hours to take in the drama and then witnessed a great deal on the streets. It was a dense, packed-in wall of people. People stood on chairs, on ladders, and on iron railings. They climbed up street lanterns. Flowers simply flew from windows and balconies. I myself saw people throw apples and chocolates into the crowds. And whenever a division passed by, hands went up in salute: Heil, Heil. On top of that, the marching bands and the exuberant singing and chants of Hitler's followers. It was wonderful. Not even the Kaiser elicited this sort of enthusiasm when he visited Braunschweig. And regarding the clashes with political opponents, they were the fault of Communists who ambushed Nazis who were out alone. I witnessed one such scene. They lured out-of-town Nazis who asked for directions into dark dangerous streets. Frieda was with me when Nazis who asked for Holst's Garden were sent in the wrong direction toward Schützenstrasse. She then ran after them to warn them and show them the right way. Today, when so many Hitler loyalists are here, the Communists don't dare show their faces. There was trouble on Friday night when the first Nazis moved in; those out alone were followed. And think also of the sacrifices involved in making what was often a long trip and the difficulties Prussian harassment caused. For example, the use of freight trains to transport people was prohibited. So, Berliners called a taxi. There must have been 200 Berlin taxis here. And huge numbers of buses. Automobiles filled the parking places and lined the streets. Some of them were quite fancy with a chauffeur in brown uniform and a small Nazi flag on the hood. Along our Wall there was one car after another. Vati watched as elegant ladies in fur coats brought big pots of coffee to Hitler's men who were eating sandwiches in their trucks. There were not nearly enough rooms for all the people; many slept out in the open in their trucks. None of this was anticipated. I would have gladly housed two National Socialists. Frau W. took in two, as did Dr. P. Sonja stood with flowers at the garden gate and proudly waved a little Hitler flag.

MONDAY EVENING

I am glad that in my elation I took time to write yesterday. Today a great deal happened that wasn't so nice. In the first place, it is distressing to see how the truth is being distorted and how dirt is flung at everything beautiful and pure. You actually have to laugh out loud, and that is exactly what the citizens of Braunschweig are doing when they pick up and read the *Volksfreund* on the streets. It is snapped up—for "comic relief," as one man standing next to me put it. The bold headlines declare: "The Grotesqueries of Fascism. Hitler's Hordes in Braunschweig Prepare for Civil War. Nazis Murder Two Workers." It goes on in the same tone. The Social Democrats have pushed the limits in the most outrageous way. Yesterday they sent Reichswehr Minister Groener a telegram in which they requested him to reinforce the Sipo [security forces] in defense against the Nazis since "the Braunschweig police cannot handle the Nazis." Left-wing Berlin newspapers such as *Die Welt am Montag* published the telegram. You just have to scratch your head when you read something like that. Is it really possible to lie in this manner? We know that the Social Democrats are dishonest, but this really takes the cake. They will do anything to show the world that the Nazis are a bunch of criminals. And when foreign journalists follow the lead of the Left, they spread the lies abroad. Those of us who know the truth just have to laugh, and that is what we are doing. Still it is a nasty business. A lie is always easier to believe than the truth. It is also true that now that the Nazis have left, except for a few who did not take seriously the trickery of the Communists and were so overtrustful that they stayed here, there is more civil unrest in the city than on previous days when the Nazis were here en masse. The Communists are now creeping out of their nooks and crannies. You just have to look at the groups standing everywhere around on the streets; the Sipo is on constant alert, and all day long you hear the shrill whistles of the riot squads. Earlier today I had to go to the post office to send off a little package for Eberhard. Lots of Communist groups on the Kohlmarkt. It was all so sinister. Along comes an unsuspecting Nazi out of the Schuhstrasse. A couple of broads immediately cry out: "There goes one of them." Heaps of abuse. The man calmly went his way, looking neither left nor right. A group followed on his heels, all against one. Out of a side street, two Nazis came to the aid of their comrade. One of them shouted: "Can't one walk peacefully on the street here? Aren't you ashamed of yourselves?" The plebs cursed loudly. Then whistling and ten policemen appeared to break up the crowd. I fled to the entrance of Blumenschulz. Frau S. pulled me inside. She was wiped out and I was close to tears. Frau S. asked about you and made me a gift of wonderfully fragrant violets so I would have something beautiful after this horrible scene. It is supposed to get even worse in the city tonight. L. had his show windows smashed, as did a number of other right-wing merchants. The Jews are spared. We will find out what really happened. Frieda is always in the know thanks to her contacts with the Sipo, and "by chance" an acquaintance just came by the house: the Sipo is on alert across the city, especially near Holst's Garden, where a few Nazis have remained and where the Communists have surrounded the entire hotel. Lots of Communists are supposed to have come from Hamburg. The Nazis are the ones who have to make the sacrifices. They do so without thinking of themselves, happy to serve the national cause and their Führer, for whom they would go through fire. I doubt that Brüning can count on even one hundred such loyalists willing to lay down their lives for him. The chancellor's speech did not make much of an impression on us patriots. We see the facts on the ground, we know the national cause is on the march and will become more and more powerful until a final victory. And it is high time because events today have shown to what degree the Communists have managed to contaminate the people. I have gone on too long and you can read more about it in the newspaper. What the *Landeszeitung* reports is quite true and accurate. [. . .]

Irmgard Brester to her mother Elisabeth Gebensleben, Utrecht, 23 October 1931

[. . .] Of course, we have already read a lot about Braunschweig's big Hitler days in the newspaper, but it is much more striking and telling to get a personal report. Great that you can give us so much detail. I can imagine the enthusiasm in Braunschweig. No one predicted that the Nazi rally would take on such awesome proportions. The parade for Hitler lasted 6 hours—that is fabulous. Our old, cozy Braunschweig must have been hard to recognize. It is too bad that the Communists always undertake these disgraceful attacks. Unfortunately it strikes such a jarring note in the harmonious course of events. Incidentally, the reports in our newspaper were very matter-of-fact and objective. Even so, people here cannot get an accurate picture of the dimensions of this movement. [. . .]

Elisabeth Gebensleben to her daughter Irmgard Brester, Braunschweig, 6 November 1931

[. . .] Did the *Nationalsozialistische illustrierte Zeitung* arrive? I just had to send it to you. They are all photographic images, it was really like that, only more thrilling than pictures can ever show. It is very indicative that the Ufa newsreels did not show a *single* image of the event. If the Prussians think they can wish it away, they are very much mistaken. The opposite is the case.

Irmgard Brester to her mother Elisabeth Gebensleben, Utrecht, 6 November 1931

[. . .] I haven't yet thanked Mutti for sending the sheet music and also for the illustrateds, the lovely card and the *Illustrierte Beobachter*, which we found especially interesting. The photographs of what is usually such a peaceful, quiet Braunschweig gives us at least an idea of the powerful Nazi demonstration. [. . .]

Under the auspices of the League of Nations, a major disarmament conference opened in Geneva in February 1932. In the meantime, Japan launched a war of aggression in Asia, occupying Manchuria in 1931. The League of Nations condemned Japan, but failed to apply sanctions.

Beginning on 28 January 1932, the Braunschweigische Landeszeitung *was banned. Since 1930, the newspaper had increasingly become a mouthpiece for the NSDAP, and after its attacks on Chancellor Brüning on 13 January 1932, the Reich*

Interior Minister felt compelled to prohibit the newspaper from publishing for one week.
A similar ban was imposed on the largest Nazi newspaper, the Völkischer Beobachter.

On 22 January 1932, the SA attacked workers preparing to strike Braunschweig's
Mühlenbau- und Industrie A.G. One worker was shot and killed. After the funeral,
workers clashed with police in the old city; three people were wounded and twenty
arrested.

During these months, Eberhard was once again in Berlin, studying for his
Referendar examination.

Elisabeth Gebensleben to her daughter Irmgard Brester, Braunschweig, 10 November 1931

[. . .] This birthday [Karl Gebensleben's sixtieth] and its aftermath stand in
complete contrast with the present-day mood, but we are very grateful and also a little
proud. Everything is usually so serious around here, so I hope the bright glow of the
celebrations will last a long time.

The memorial service to the fallen National Socialists [who were killed during
the 1923 Beerhall Putsch in Munich] in the state theater was the most moving and
exhilarating event I experienced in the last several days. Did you read about it in the
paper? Of course, tickets were completely sold out days before, and I got a seat by
sheer chance. What a speech that was, so poignant in the awful truths it told and so
animated by the spirit of self-sacrifice. I shiver with pride to know that these people
are willing to lay down their lives and sacrifice themselves for their cause: Germany's
freedom! Genuine German valor and bravery still exist just as they did in the time of
the Wars of Liberation [1813–1815]. The speaker said quite rightly that if it were not
for the National Socialists we wouldn't be sitting peacefully in the theater. We would
all have fallen victim to the Bolsheviks. I am afraid he is right. It is terrifying to see
the Communists gain the upper hand and wreak so much havoc.

To my great pleasure I just listened to the speeches of [James Ramsay]
MacDonald [1866–1937, British Prime Minister] and [Otto] Landsberg [1869–1957,
Social Democratic Reichstag member] on the radio and I heard them say that
the world economic crisis will not be overcome until war reparations have been
cancelled. The peace treaty was dictated in a spirit of revenge, and the German war
guilt clause is no longer morally defensible. These are the words of an Englishman, yet
the German chancellor does not have the courage to say them. [. . .]

Karl Gebensleben to his daughter Irmgard Brester, Braunschweig, 15 November 1931

[. . .] Yes, and my office in city hall was wonderfully decorated with palms and
blooming flowers; a long row of alpine violets stood on the window sill. The council
appeared in procession, led by the Oberbürgermeister. Böhme gave a really nice
speech in my honor, which you will have read (at least in part) in the *Landeszeitung*.
Then the valet brought up 2 bottles of port, glasses, cigars and cigarettes, and they
drank to my health. It really was well intentioned and well arranged. And now it is all
over; too bad you couldn't be here. [. . .]

Elisabeth Gebensleben to her daughter Irmgard Brester, Braunschweig, 27 November 1931

[. . .] In the city, the shop windows look very Christmassy, but the shops themselves are empty and the hopes of businessmen will once again be terribly disappointed. Almost no one can buy anything, only the bare necessities. And all around, foreclosures and bankruptcy sales! Some of our oldest and most solid businesses can no longer hold out. For example, Herbst (furs), Seidenschade, and others. It is dismal, all the more so when you see that we are sinking deeper in the morass on account of the emergency decrees, which tear things further apart without making the slightest effort to build back up. If things don't change, I really don't know what will happen. But Christmas is not the time for these dreary observations. We are not ready to hang our heads in despair. Instead we will sing on like old soldiers, perhaps with "Wenn die Hoffnung nicht wär', ja, dann lebt' ich nicht mehr" ("If hope were not, I should exist no more"). There is still a great deal to be happy about! [. . .]

Elisabeth Gebensleben to her daughter Irmgard Brester, Braunschweig, 11 December 1931

[. . .] The thought of accepting the sweet invitation you extended to Vati either the moment I arrive or else when I leave is so tempting that Vati, as much as I, wants to commit himself. But, Immeken, you've read the 4th emergency decree. It might seem right, especially when considered from outside Germany. Yet it brings so much new hardship, so much despair, and so many tears that I am simply astonished by Brüning. How can he coldheartedly destroy one existence after another with a stroke of the pen? The 9% salary reduction equals, with what I use for the household, the outlay for three 20-day periods. On top of that higher taxes, the head tax, for example, Vati and I 108 M (even Frieda 9 M). How prices are supposed to stabilize when a value-added tax, which Brüning himself said two years ago would be a last option, has been introduced leaves us all mystified. The appointment of a commissar for price stability is a ray of hope that something will happen. What good does it do the middle classes when freight charges are reduced or the streetcar costs 5 pf less. In any case, people ride the streetcar as little as possible. Or when bread costs 5 pf less. None of that stands in proportion to the salary reductions. Nonetheless, we keep up our hopes and won't hang our heads. As it is, I have to hold my head up high as a counterweight to Vati and Ohmchen. They are gradually getting back on their feet. And we constantly tell each other how good we have it compared to so many who have nothing: no work, no money.

[. . .] Full of pride, [Ursel] told me that she and a friend, also a student, both ate for 20 pf. It was reportedly quite good: mutton with cabbage, 10 pf per person. There is certainly more effort to make allowances and to budget in our circles, where the children are studying, than among workers on the "dole." A friend of Frieda gets 36 M dole every month. She eats schnitzel in cream sauce at Frank's for 75 pf. Frieda ends up splitting her meals with her when the money runs out at the end of the month. It is touching to see how Frieda saves part of her meal; she always uses a different excuse. Her friend often eats here in the evening; I've gotten used to calculating her in when I prepare dinner.

There is so much hardship. Times were much more spartan during the war, but at least we knew why we were sacrificing, we wanted to lend a hand and did so. But what is the point now? Everything is just dumped in this bottomless pit and sinks out of sight. Yet the greater the hardship, the closer at hand salvation must be. In any case, I think to myself: things can't stay the way they are. A way out must and will be found. Besides we have so many joys! When a letter arrives from Holland, Immeken, or from my boy, well, then all the emergency decrees just fade away and mean absolutely nothing! [. . .]

Elisabeth Gebensleben to her daughter Irmgard Brester, Braunschweig, 18 January 1932

[. . .] The trains were pretty empty; that would actually have made the trip quite pleasant if the few people traveling were also pleasant. At the Dutch border, they seized a Russian Jew from my compartment. He looked very disagreeable and suspicious to me and to my traveling companion, a young German woman married for two years to a Dutchman who is a sailor on ships to the East Indies. He maintained that he had spent three days in Amsterdam but did not have the least bit of luggage and, most importantly, did not have a visa for Holland as became clear at passport control in Oldenzaal. As a Russian, he needs a visa to enter Holland. So how did he cross the border without a visa? In any case, the officials must have considered him very suspicious. We were delighted to get rid of him, although he had not actually bothered us. [. . .]

Elisabeth Gebensleben to her daughter Irmgard Brester, Braunschweig, 1 February 1932

[. . .] Vati and I just heard the latest on the radio. The Japanese have attacked Nanking, well, well! The League of Nations has met for years and years, mountains of documents have accumulated, the league continues to hold meetings, yet the Japanese and Chinese are killing each other. One can see: reality and illusion, theory and praxis. Might makes right. The Chinese-Japanese conflict, let's be clear and say that war is hardly an encouraging prelude to the disarmament conference. These times are so eventful, and most especially for us Germans. You really have to keep your nerve in order to find the good in each and every day, as I do, and hold on to it; otherwise, we wouldn't make it.

Are you getting the *Allgemeiner Anzeiger* as a substitute for the *Landeszeitung*? It is the newspaper for undemanding readers; the K.'s read it. On the whole, it survives on advertisements; but it has the largest circulation in Braunschweig. Vati maintains that it is actually accomplishing more than usual, undoubtedly under the influence of the editorial board of the *Landeszeitung*. It is unprecedented for the *Landeszeitung* to be banned. The *Völkischer Beobachter*, the newspaper of the largest party in

Germany, has also been banned. Don't we live in a Germany that is "free," the great accomplishment of the Revolution! Germany's "freedom."

Well, things are not going to continue as they have for long. If good times can come to an end, so can bad times. After unruly days, an outward calm now prevails in our dear city. When the Nazis congregated here and 100,000 men marched in the streets, the order and discipline were such that you could let your children alone onto the streets. The [Communist] hordes were recently acting up. The ruckus they made at the funeral for a comrade whom they themselves shot was just terrible. That sort of turmoil on the streets is bad enough, but afterward it is depressing to walk the streets and see all the show windows smashed and the glass splinters lying on the ground. But order has now been restored: I was in the city in the afternoon looking astonished at the shop windows and the low prices. Immeken, it would be something for the two of us, to go out and shop together! [. . .]

Karl Gebensleben to his daughter Irmgard Brester, Braunschweig, 3 February 1932

[. . .] Let me start with Hardus, whom I visited in Berlin while I was there on a business trip. [. . .] [He] reported that he is busy meeting with a coach so that in 11 or 12 months he can get a Referendariat, but he also remarked that an acquaintance of his (a doctor) went to Greece for an assistantship and that he himself had no intention of remaining forever in the narrow confines of a prescribed career—he mentioned the word "Russia" in this context. Of course, a total fantasy, for which we—and Mutti especially—have no understanding! Well, Friday in 8 days, Mutti will be in Berlin and will undoubtedly get that little head straightened out. [. . .]

Tomorrow brings evening tea at the Oberbürgermeister's. We are curious.

Despite all the work, I am doing quite well. Yesterday evening we held a council meeting (until 12:00 at night); at great length, budget issues were discussed. Are you keeping up with the news in Braunschweig. As a substitute for the banned *Landeszeitung*, we get the *Allg. Anzeiger*; hopefully you do as well. As of Friday, the paper will appear again. All this angry politics, *party* politics that have brought so much harm to Germany. Where will it end! The antagonisms are becoming more intense, and foolish government measures aggravate the tensions. In addition, there is the terrible specter of unemployment and the associated costs for the municipalities; for example, the city of Braunschweig has to reckon with an outlay of 10–11 million marks for the coming year. We don't have the tax base to raise that sort of money. Only the gods know what will become of us. What is necessary is for the city (as well as the state and the Reich) to increase revenues (i.e., taxes) and reduce expenditures (i.e., wages and salaries). Only a reduction in prices can achieve some sort of balance. To be sure, prices are lower, but not low enough! We will hope for the best. Everyone will have to cut back. There is no harm in that, in fact it is quite the right thing!

Now I have written about something I actually didn't want to write about at all. Quite a contrast to what I am just listening to on the radio: carnival in Cologne. Rhinelanders are such a different breed. [. . .]

Elisabeth Gebensleben to her daughter Irmgard Brester, Braunschweig, 7 February 1932

[. . .] *She* or *he* will certainly be very sweet with a sunny disposition. But Immo is *also* sweet, right August! I think on *this* we can agree much more easily than over the issue of National Socialism. But I will save that for later. [. . .]

Elisabeth Gebensleben to her daughter Irmgard Brester, Braunschweig, 18 February 1932

[. . .] Sonja just acquired a little doggy; he's called "Strupp." Half Pomeranian, half dachshund. Today I asked her: "What does he look like?" "Black, but he is not Jewish; he was born a Christian." And with that dead serious little face!

In order to stand as a candidate in the March 1932 presidential elections, Hitler, who was born in Austria but was now stateless, had to acquire German citizenship. Braunschweig's right-wing government made this possible when it appointed Hitler to a position in the state's legation in Berlin. The other candidates for the presidency included the incumbent Hindenburg, the Stahlhelm's Theodor Düsterberg, and the Communist leader Ernst Thälmann (who was murdered in Buchenwald in 1944). The NSDAP launched a gigantic election campaign that reached even the smallest villages. Between 22 February and 12 March, Hitler gave nineteen speeches in Berlin alone and traveled to give nine more across the country. The Nazis made good use of film and records and printed one million posters, eight million leaflets, and twelve million extra editions of the party newspaper in addition to holding three thousand campaign rallies throughout Germany every day. Several more national elections would be held before the Nazis consolidated power in January 1933, though Hitler replaced Hindenburg as president only upon Hindenburg's death in August 1934.

The Baltic territory of Memel, which had been severed from the German Empire at the end of the war and placed under a French mandate, had been occupied by the newly independent state of Lithuania in 1923.

During the Depression, street hawkers in Braunschweig dressed in red-white suits to sell red-white fortune boxes for charity. On 11 March 1932, the Braunschweigische Landeszeitung *published Elisabeth Gebensleben's essay about her encounter with an impoverished mother in a Braunschweig bakery.*

Eberhard volunteered for voluntary labor service, a government-sponsored program that emerged out of student-run labor camps in the 1920s. In the summer of 1932, ninety-seven thousand young Germans volunteered to work, usually in the countryside. In the Third Reich, Reich Labor Service was expanded, and six-month duty became compulsory for all German men between the ages of eighteen and twenty-five in 1935.

The Gebenslebens anxiously awaited the construction of their new house. In the interim they moved into a house directly across from their old home on the Friedensallee, or "Peace Boulevard," as the Kaiser-Wilhelm Strasse was renamed while the Social Democrats were in power between 1929 and 1933.

**Elisabeth Gebensleben to her daughter Irmgard Brester, Braunschweig,
25 February 1932**

[. . .] Time flies, the loveliest hours even faster. But I hope that the days ahead
do go by quickly because they will bring bitter conflicts. Tensions are so high. You just
have to look at the Reichstag. There is nothing to be achieved through parliamentary
means. This evening between eight and nine, Vati and I listened to a speech that the
chancellor had given in the morning; it had already been recorded on gramophone
records—a grand technical feat. Of course, you could hear everything, the
commotion, the cheers, the calls for order, the bell. The uproar in the house was so
great that the chancellor often couldn't get a word in edgewise. 17(!) National Socialist
meetings are taking place in Braunschweig this evening. Frieda, who wanted to
attend one, didn't get back home until 11:30. The first four she tried were all filled to
capacity and closed by police order. She was able to still get into the fifth. The rumors
that Hitler acquired German citizenship through Braunschweig seem to have a basis
in fact. First we heard that he was appointed extraordinary professor at the college,
then minister, and now the news broke that he has been assigned to Braunschweig's
legation in Berlin. He will certainly receive a great many votes, but enough? Yesterday
noon, Sonja, who was eating lunch with us, reported: "The Nazi who is living with
us asserted: the Nazis will deliver the goods." In any case, their confidence in victory
radiates great strength. Things will not calm down before the election. Domestic and
foreign politics are tension filled; everything is poised on the knife's edge.

**Irmgard Brester to her mother Elisabeth Gebensleben, Utrecht,
27 February 1932**

[. . .] I heard the various news reports with great interest. [. . .] In addition,
all the suspense regarding the presidential elections, which completely preoccupies
everyone. We are following events with the greatest of interest. The newspapers
publish long articles, yesterday naturally all about Hitler's naturalization. [. . .]

**Elisabeth Gebensleben to her daughter Irmgard Brester, Braunschweig,
4 March 1932**

[. . .] Sometimes I can't believe that another week has gone by. The reason
is that we are living in such a state of suspense, from one day to the next. All the
events taking place, at home and abroad. Hopefully we will get over the next weeks
in reasonably good shape. There are hard battles to be fought. But it can't go on as it
has. According to Frau K., Berny P., who lives near the Polish border with a wife and
child, maintains that we have no sense of what is going on. The Poles are standing
at the ready on the border armed to the teeth and are just waiting for an excuse
to march in; and when you hear France declare that it cannot do without German
reparations and that Czechoslovakia has signed off on a 600-million-franc loan then
you can put two and two together. And what the League of Nations achieves is plain
to see. Incidentally, we were talking about how big Poland was, do you remember. At

the time, I didn't know for sure. The answer: approximately 32 million inhabitants. That includes Russian Poland. With the Versailles Treaty, Germany gave up 5 million. When we are at home, we listen to the news on radio every night. Reports come in from Memel, there is news about the war in China, and then we hear: the League of Nations is convening, preparations for the disarmament conference—then it is really hard to suppress our laughter. Law and order prevail, at least outwardly, except for dozens of Communist incidents.

Thanks to the discipline and industriousness of the German people, punctuality and cleanliness still prevail in public life. But there are all sorts of reminders of how widespread the hardship is, even where you cannot see it. Never before have so many people come to the door to beg. And these are not beggars we used to have. No, these are well-dressed individuals who try anything to find some assistance. I was in the bakery on the Bohlweg yesterday afternoon and a young woman, neatly dressed, a jacket, no hat, walked in and asked the baker's wife at the counter: "Can I have a loaf of black bread? I don't have any money, but I will leave you my wedding ring." We all stood there in shock. She went on to explain: her husband is unemployed, they have two children at home. "Admittedly, I receive 18 marks dole every week. But it is not enough for rent or coal. And I can't let us starve." The baker's wife took the ring and the little woman reached for the bread in relief. "I will redeem my ring as soon as I can." The saleslady behind the counter looked at us with horror. "A wedding ring for a loaf of bread. That makes my blood run cold." I felt the same way. Back on the street, I passed by the funny man dressed in red and white who sells "Wohlfahrtskugeln," and I bought another one although I actually had decided not to buy any more. It would have been better to buy a loaf of bread for the lady in the store, but I was so shocked that I just didn't think of doing what would have been the most sensible. But I will ask Frau F. to give me the address of the woman when she redeems the ring. Then I will see what I can do.

I have recounted so many tragedies yet there is much that is beautiful to report to you. In the garden, the snowdrops are blooming. [. . .]

Minna von Alten to her granddaughter Irmgard Brester, Braunschweig, 10 March 1932

[. . .] For us the election remains paramount. Tuesday evening, I was with Mutti at a meeting of the German National People's Party; I am going to remain loyal and vote for Düsterberg, Mutti is still undecided, but I think she will vote for Hitler. Nobody knows if things will improve or if we will fall further into the abyss. [. . .] Eberhard is once again making plans for the vacations; he wanted to enlist in the voluntary labor service, doing road construction in Schleswig. We are all against it and want to enjoy him a little bit more. Presumably it will be the last time he will live at home. [. . .]

[ELISABETH GEBENSLEBEN]

[. . .] On Saturday we will be back by evening; we have theater tickets for Saturday and we have to be here to vote on Sunday. We will be glad when the elections are over and the tension breaks. [. . .]

**Elisabeth Gebensleben to her daughter Irmgard Brester, Braunschweig,
13 March 1932**

What a quick response your lovely Sunday letter gets this time. This Sunday
afternoon I have more peace and quiet to write than at the end of last week, that is
if you can speak at all about peace and quiet today, 13 March. What I mean is *inner
peace*. While I am sitting here writing, while the clock measures its tick-tock, and
each minute passes by, a great battle is being decided, one that has raged for weeks
as thousands upon thousands cast their ballots. The fate of the nation is at stake.
You are quite right to write that the time in Braunlage served to strengthen us for
the election. In pure wondrous nature, up there in the mountains, where you can
feel eternity, our petty, workaday concerns just fall by the wayside. You see clearly
what really matters, not a party or a leader, but simply Germany, which [U.S. senator
William] Borah praised to [playwright Gerhart] Hauptmann for the exemplary
composure it has shown and the cultural authority it has maintained in conditions
that can be compared to a second world war. The rest of the world does not know
how much our *Volk* is suffering. And I don't mean the suffering of the *ordinary* folk
milling about the streets. They get their handouts. I mean those who are humiliated
and silent, who used to be independent and are now ruined, who don't fit into the
category "unemployed" and who get nothing. I mean those who have to feed a
family with a dole that is not as correspondingly high as it is for those who are single;
Frieda's friend, for example, gets 38 marks a month dole, two-times hundredweight
for heating, ¼ lb coffee a week, as well as cards that allow her to shop for inexpensive
groceries. This friend recently rejected a job offer at 45 marks a month: "Why should
I? I am better off as I am; I am free, I don't need to work." The city has to give up every
last bit of revenue for these people, and enterprises that cost money but provide work
go out of business, and civil servants have to accept salary reductions. The whole
business is so wrongheaded, the system (and now I too am using this shopworn
word) is so hypocritical that everything has to be rebuilt from scratch. I would not
want to take on this responsibility, but I admire the man who does, who wants to
make a go at reconstruction.

[. . .] I was struck dumb to see my article placed so prominently; I thought
it would land unassumingly in the "Potpourri" column if not in the great big
wastepaper basket that editorial departments are known to keep. I asked the editors
not to add my name, but I think that Vati is actually a little proud of his wife; he can't
stop smiling when he tells just about everyone *who* the author is and that his wife has
now taken up with "writers." [. . .]

My big boy also wrote me a letter today. He has more to say about the labor
camp near the Bay of Lübeck in Schleswig; in the end, he enlisted after all. He asked
all of us for our advice, but since he provided very few specifics, Vati and Ohmchen
were dead set against it, while I tried to look at the positive side—the chance to be
free of all intellectual work, physical activity, comradeship, to see different aspects of
life. But I also had concerns about too much physical labor; heavy construction in all
kinds of weather; toiling in damp conditions, sleeping in barracks. Well, now we've

heard from Hardus: 4 hours' pure physical work (laying out an athletic field), sleeping in a youth hostel. Otherwise, discussions, sport, etc. I have no objections if these are the conditions. Eberhard only regrets not being able to study 2½ hours a week. I am not happy about it, but as far as I am concerned I think it is necessary. After all, you don't learn about life only out of books and through legal articles. You have to get into the thick of things. [. . .] The radio is just beginning to broadcast election results. Actually I should have voted for [Ludwig] Winter [Nazi Reichstag member for Braunschweig]. He is that strange man who wants to put the old 1,000-mark bills back in circulation—I still have three of them. I think we will be appalled at the number of votes the Communists get. But the struggle doesn't end today. Nothing is decided for four more weeks until the next election.

Elisabeth Gebensleben to her daughter Irmgard Brester, Braunschweig, 21 March 1932

In Süpplingen [where Karl's brother Otto lived], we laughed a great deal. Of course we also carried on about politics, which is unavoidable nowadays. In our circle there were 12 National Socialists, 4 for Düsterberg, and 1 for Hindenburg. The one was Aunt Agnes! She sure had to put up with us, especially once Friedel found her out. Everyone really got on her case, even the relatives in church collars. Uncle Fritz, who had so little authority as husband that he could allow his spouse to vote for *Hindenburg*, got it too.

For just one moment, we were really able to make fun out of politics, but unfortunately it is all a matter of the utmost gravity. The times we are enduring are so awful that we would not survive if we didn't constantly make an effort to pull ourselves together. The worst is that you come upon misery and want at every turn, at least if you keep your eyes open. Recently, I was with a young woman, you know, the one from the article "Die Wohlfahrtskugel." I just couldn't let the matter rest. I got her address from the baker's wife; when the woman redeemed her ring, she asked her on my behalf. The woman lives in a nice house on the Bohlweg. I arrived with a package of cookies, cocoa, and cereal. I sat with her in her small kitchen; she was just feeding her youngest child. She said to me: "You came at just the right time, I am out of everything, I don't even have the milk money for tomorrow." What gratitude she showed for the unexpected gift! Next time, I will bring stuff for the kids. [. . .]

Let us hope that things will soon get better. Fortunately, winter is over and the spring sun once again brings hope. For the time being, we very much look forward to Hardus and the Easter celebrations.

In April 1932, after being forced into a run off against Hitler, Hindenburg won a second term as Reich President. Feeling empowered, Chancellor Brüning's government thereupon banned the SA, which at the time was some four hundred thousand men strong. However, the SA continued to march in white "prohibition shirts" instead of brown shirts. For the Gebenslebens, as for many other middle-class Germans, the SA represented a force of order that stood against the Social Democratic paramilitary organization, the Reichsbanner, which had been founded in 1924 to defend the republic,

*and the Communist Rote Frontkämpferbund ("Rotfront" or Red Front). However
Hindenburg's narrow reelection ultimately weakened Chancellor Brüning's position. He
was replaced by Franz von Papen (1879–1969), who overturned the ban on the SA. In
the weeks before new Reichstag elections on 31 July 1932, nearly one hundred people
were killed and more than eleven hundred wounded in street battles between Nazis and
Communists in the state of Prussia alone.*

*In Utrecht, Immo's cousin, Elisabeth Gebensleben, helped keep house while Immo
was expecting her second child. Eberhard's friend, Carl-Heinz Zeitler ("Zettel"), switched
his studies from law to medicine.*

Irmgard Brester to her mother Elisabeth Gebensleben, Utrecht, 16 April 1932

[. . .] Like you, we will be very preoccupied with the election and its aftermath
for some time. The result was no surprise, but who could have anticipated that
emergency decrees would be drafted against the Nazis immediately afterward. This
will certainly heighten tensions and stir animosity among the people. Such violent
measures cannot be the right response, as future developments will soon enough
surely indicate. I am curious how Braunschweig is reacting, the newspapers don't
really give us a good idea. Elisabeth [a cousin staying in Utrecht] is also a fervid Hitler
supporter, and you can imagine the heated debates with August on this issue. [. . .]

Elisabeth Gebensleben to her daughter Irmgard Brester, Braunschweig, 22 April 1932

[. . .] You cannot imagine how angry people are about the banning of the SA;
even circles that had kept their distance from Hitler are becoming attracted to the
movement. It is also not comprehensible how any German could reject this true,
ideal, genuine Germandom and would want to suppress it. But suppression will
not succeed. The more trials the movement undergoes, the more it is attacked, the
stronger it will become. The plebs are beginning to take over the streets. Red Front
and Reichsbanner think they are masters, and there are now several streets through
which you cannot go. Reichsbanner members even goad their children, who are
running around in gangs and harassing passersby. They have whistles to signal to
each other, and when a pedestrian whom they suspect to be a Nazi appears, they call
on the chase. The other day I saw how a whole horde was banging loudly on the door
of a store into which a "Nazi" must have fled, I just had to speak up and I asked one
of the insolent boys: "Boys, what are you doing?" Immediately I was surrounded by
the entire horde. "You can see what we are doing. We are walking on the street. Are
we supposed to sit in it?" The youngster who answered me couldn't have been more
than ten years old. Similar incidents take place every day. It is high time for someone
else to take over the reins. It can't go on like this. At the same time, the endless misery,
which lets you see, when you take a closer look, how unemployment and money
worries undermine the sacred bonds of families. To cite Wilhelm Busch: "O, komm
herbei, du goldne Zeit, wenn alle, die jetzt bummeln, in schöner Unparteilichkeit
sich bei der Arbeit tummeln" ("Would that golden time come, when all those out
and about rustling, would together at work get bustling"). Well, Hitler already has 13

million. Eventually he will gather up the entire nation, and then there won't be parties anymore. [. . .]

Eberhard Gebensleben to his sister Irmgard Brester, Berlin, 24 April 1932

Yesterday was an absolutely noteworthy day: I devoured the last of the "eenig echte Haagsche Hopje" [Dutch candy]. [. . .]

By the way, Zettel is turning out fabulously. His optimism still knows no earthly bounds. He is just mad about spring in Heidelberg. An (illegally snapped) picture from Anatomy shows him beaming and lovingly cradling a skull.

Today we are voting for the third time. State elections in Prussia and in southern Germany. Some 25 parties are listed on the ballot. The National Socialists will emerge as the largest party. The only thing is that there are many more than 25 opinions about what they represent and what they intend to do. Every book states something different. There is only agreement on their honesty and passion, at least in general. My dear, dear Holland. The now banned SA estimates 200 dead in the last years in Prussia alone.

Karl Gebensleben to his daughter Irmgard Brester, Braunschweig, 3 May 1932

[. . .] I spent a few hours with the Kreutzmann's this afternoon to thoroughly inform myself about "the lay of the land." I had to laugh so hard I cried. During the last elections, someone from across the street noticed that only Uncle August and Martha had gone out to vote (Aunt Minna had already been there). Pretty soon she came over to admonish Aunt Minna not to forget to go out and "vote." A few days later, the same *lady* returned to say that Uncle August (whom she could observe from "over there") was not yet reading the "right" Nazi newspaper! Well, what of it: the *Landeszeitung* has pretty much become a Nazi newspaper!

Such are the amusing stories of small-town life.

Elisabeth Gebensleben to her daughter Irmgard Brester, Braunschweig, 22 June 1932

[. . .] I do believe that I am also needed here [back from Holland after the birth of the second grandchild]. As Vati and I sat down at the table to eat, Vati commented: "How nice it is! I have been eating by myself for seven weeks." [. . .]

The news is on the radio just now. Braunschweig was mentioned as well. The Communist clashes with the police that took place here. It is terrible. The Communists have received orders from Moscow to plunder and murder where they can. The order is openly published in their newspapers and pamphlets. The police don't have a moment's rest. Riot squads are on alert all day long. This afternoon I was walking along the Steinweg when two more large vehicles turned into the Communist Mauernstrasse where crowds had gathered. Poor misguided human beings! And every day, National Socialists who are out alone are attacked and beaten senselessly or murdered. It is necessary to deal with the Communists much more severely. They are deliberately attacking the police. Not that I am worried that they will gain the upper hand and somehow get rid of us. Thankfully the National Socialists are too strong for that, and it is a wonderful sight once again to see the Brownshirts in whom I and thousands and millions of others have such faith. [. . .]

Elisabeth Gebensleben to her daughter Irmgard Brester, Braunschweig, 30 June 1932

[. . .] Early today I received a card from Eberhard that I later will copy down for you. Things look bad in Berlin. Vati was really quite appalled when he was recently there. Communists have erected barricades in north Berlin so that the armored trucks of the Sipo can't get through. More politics next time.

[. . .] Eberhard witnessed—and that is what he wrote—how the police in Berlin, which lean to the left, just ripped into National Socialists without any good reason. [. . .]

Irmgard Brester to her mother Elisabeth Gebensleben, Utrecht, 2 July 1932

The civil unrest across Germany is terrible. You don't even want to open the newspaper, with all the gruesome reports about Communist attacks and assassinations. The other day, I saw photographs of the barricades in Berlin. It is dreadful, and I am sure Hardus will have lots to tell.

Between 16 June and 9 July 1932 a conference took place in Lausanne, Switzerland, the aim of which was to come up with a permanent solution to the question of war reparations. One of the participants was Dino Grandi, the Italian Foreign Minister under Mussolini.

On 29 June 1932, the Braunschweigische Landeszeitung *published an article attacking the police president of Berlin under the headline "Out with Grzesinski!" It accused Albert Grzesinski (1879–1947, an SPD trade unionist and former Interior Minister who emigrated in 1933) of making common cause with the Communists in order to combat fascism.*

Political violence preceding the 31 July Reichstag elections continued unabated. The worst incident occurred on 17 July when the Nazis marched through the "red" working-class districts of Altona, near Hamburg. Shots were fired from rooftops and windows, and the Nazis immediately fired back. Altona's "Bloody Sunday" claimed 19 lives; 285 other people were wounded. A few days later, on 20 July, Chancellor von Papen used the violence as a pretext to remove the Social Democratic government in Prussia and to install himself as Reich Commissar, allegedly in order to main public order. The Prussian Interior Minister Carl Severing (1875–1952) relented only when threatened with violence, while Prime Minister Otto Braun (1872–1955) fled to Switzerland. The Nazis launched a vigorous propaganda campaign; Hitler campaigned by plane, visiting and holding speeches in more than fifty cities in the last two weeks of July. The assembled crowds often sang the old Dutch hymn, "We gather together to ask the Lord's blessing" ("Wilt heden nu treden, voor God den Heere"), which was written during the Dutch war of liberation against Spanish rule in the sixteenth century. With 37 percent of the vote, the Nazis became the largest party in Germany, but failed to achieve an absolute majority, so the Reichstag remained ungovernable and Chancellor von Papen continued to rule through the emergency powers granted to him by President Hindenburg.

On 21 July, Elisabeth wanted to attend a Hitler rally of the Gau Süd-Hannover-Braunschweig, but instead was brought to the hospital with head wounds after a traffic accident with their car Amor.

Elisabeth Gebensleben to her daughter Irmgard Brester, Braunschweig, 7 July 1932

[. . .] actually there are reasons to refrain from erecting these castles in the air. Just think of Lausanne! I can't even imagine what it is that they are doing there. As he took up the paper this morning, Vati said: "It's best not even to pay attention," and yesterday Elisabeth's father had said the same: "What is it that they think they have to do in Lausanne?" It would be another thing if the negotiations took place four weeks from now, after the Reichstag elections. Then the *new* Germany could send its representatives and Germany would learn to speak in a new voice. Grandi is the only sensible one; he doesn't grovel before big, crazy France. He certainly puts Papen to shame.

The stories in the German newspapers are accurate so you can read for yourself what else is happening here. It takes courage to appear on the streets in a brown uniform, particularly for someone walking alone. However, the National Socialists are serious, fearless men, just the sort we need. Aside from the newspaper, whose reports are not always believed(!), it is the incidents we personally witness that really give an accurate picture. So that you can see that reality is even worse than what the newspaper reports, I am copying out Eberhard's card, which we received a few days after our return from the Harz. The letter is dated 28 June 1932:

"I just came back from the city, and if this card is to do justice to what I saw I have to write straight from the heart. This afternoon a demonstration against Versailles took place in the Lustgarten with the entire student body, National Socialists, Stahlhelm, and fraternities in full regalia. As the march got underway, the police dived (witness!!) into the closed and disciplined singing ranks of Nazis and ripped the swastika-emblazoned flags off their poles. It was only thanks to the magnificent discipline of the Nazis that the demonstration was not dispersed. Marching in front of the university hoisting a rescued banner and bearing it down the Linden. Then at the corner of Linden/Friedrichstrasse the most unbelievable scenes that you would otherwise see only in an American movie. 2 meters in front of me, 4 policemen armed with rubber truncheons were beating a defenseless Nazi who just stood there with his head down while a 5th policeman held us in check with a drawn revolver. About half the police squads completely lost their nerves. 3 m away from me an officer gave the order to let them really have it, for no reason at all. Chaos at the corner of Linden and Friedrichstrasse: people being chased, beaten, shouting 'Germany awake!' Smashing women with *unlocked* rifles. Totally unbelievable. I couldn't avoid being hit twice with a rubber truncheon. Now spare me the inevitable letter of admonition. I went there on purpose and took part in the game of hide-and-seek between taxis and buses in order to finally verify for myself if the police really are losing their nerves."

The card arrived on the morning of the day that Peter [the dog] was run over. You can imagine my mood after I read it. The enclosed notice appeared in the newspaper the same day. Without Eberhard's card you would perhaps think and rightly so, well that is just the *Landeszeitung*! But the paper got it right. Yesterday I read that the Nazis in the Prussian Landtag submitted a petition to call Grzesinski to account; across Berlin yesterday, Social Democrats and Communists marched *together* against the Nazis, that is to say, against a patriotic Germany. In their desperation, the Marxists are doing anything to save themselves. But it won't help them. Thanks to [Interior] Minister [Dietrich] Klagges, the police here in Braunschweig have been thoroughly vetted and the Communists put out to pasture, although the Marxist press raised a huge fuss about Klagges's assault on the "nonpartisan" police force. Yes, the struggle is ongoing, and may get worse. But we certainly don't want to make that assumption. Ultimately even these conditions have to come to an end.

But I have more to report than these horrible matters; there are also many good things to tell you about, first and foremost our wonderful weekend with Eberhard. Hardus was very cheerful when he arrived; very tanned, all jauntily dressed, and when I commented that he looked a little skinny, he just laughed. He has just the right athletic figure. He looks like he has been working hard; he says he usually goes to sleep at 12:00 and wakes up at 6:00. Nicolai comes by a few times a week early in the morning at 6:00, and they go to the Grunewald to throw javelins or what have you. [. . .]

Irmgard Brester to her mother Elisabeth Gebensleben, Utrecht, 9 July 1932

[. . .] What you told me about Eberhard's experiences in Berlin is just terrible. Mutti, where are we headed if we can no longer rely on the police, the guardian and protector of the state. I read about it in the newspaper at the time, but only with these details do I have a sense of what it really means. Terrible! Of course, we are also following the news from Lausanne. What will be the end result? Will Germany always have to pay, and with what means? We can only hope that better times will come soon, very soon before Germany is completely strangled. [. . .] Now I still want to tell you that Marleentje is doing marvelously.

Elisabeth Gebensleben to her daughter Irmgard Brester, Braunschweig, 14 July 1932

[. . .] Frieda's boyfriend was just telling us that he was standing around when yet another Nazi was shot in Wolfenbüttel. Several Nazis were standing peacefully on a street corner with a few policemen when suddenly a troop of Reichsbanner men appeared and without the least cause a Reichsbanner man pulled a gun and shot at the Nazis, one of whom fell to the ground. It is horrible. Every day the attacks increase and the battles become more extensive. Eberhard is totally right: if it were not for the fabulous discipline of the Nazis, we would have a major civil war instead of just a minor one. The hatred that people show just gets worse and worse. Yesterday, a little boy came to the door to sell us something. Frieda opened the door to see what he wanted. As soon as he caught sight of Frieda's Nazi pin, he shouted "Nazi lowlife!" We didn't buy anything from him! [. . .]

Elisabeth Gebensleben to her daughter Irmgard Brester, Braunschweig, 20 July 1932

Could you be thinking of us this evening? I can almost believe it since you must have gotten wind of the exciting news reports that have unnerved us these last several days. The carefully planned Communist attack in Altona puts all previous incidents in the shade and is the reason why Prussia is now being "cleaned up." Severing, Braun, Grzesinski—they've finally been removed. We can breathe more easily, but they were in power too long not to leave without a fight. The Communists were also given too much time to organize themselves and acquire weapons. Always this tolerant way of proceeding against that pack of murderers and against the many Russian agents who long ago should have been chased out of Germany. And now the Social Democrats are collaborating with them! It is simply inconceivable; the worst is that the Prussian police are no longer reliable. When he was made aware of the Communist threat five years ago, Severing replied: "They are political naifs; they will grow out of their games." Well, they have now grown into giants who do not play harmless games. I still know precisely that at the time the Communists disrupted Hindenburg's speech on the radio I had the feeling: "This is a wake-up call." But nobody took it seriously. Even old Hindenburg has been able to open his eyes one more time and is thinking for himself again. Brüning had been just stringing him along. Tonight reports emerged of heavy clashes in Berlin. Vati and I were already worried, yet the radio's news agency carried nothing. Berlin's police number around 30,000 men; if they make common cause with the Communists, it will get very ugly. On the "other" side, the Reichswehr and, if necessary, the SA as well. They will be able to handle it, but the prospect of civil war is horrible. On a limited scale, it is already playing itself out. The woman who has the flower shop outside city hall is a member of the "Königin-Luise-Association," a right-wing group that does social welfare work, and she told Vati yesterday evening that she was harassed by Communists who nearly shattered her shop windows. She finally had to call seven Nazis over for protection. On Sunday I was on the Steinweg at around two in the afternoon, a time when there is very little traffic. Suddenly loud shouts made me flinch: "Heil Red Front!" A group of Communist bicyclists were speeding down the Steinweg, shouting again and again: "Heil Red Front!" It sounded very scary and eventually the police intervened.

Hopefully things will be better and calmer after 31 July; feelings have been running so high these last days before the election. You see a lot of Brownshirts around these days. If it were not for the National Socialists, I would not be able to keep my spirits up. How they have restored faith in Germany and in the ultimate triumph of the true Germany that we have in our blood! Have you been reading about how East Prussia cheers Hitler and welcomes him as a savior. *Those* people know all about "exploitation" and "immiseration." Last week I was on the Schlossplatz to attend a National Socialist demonstration. Although I stood in the rain for almost 3 hours, to me it didn't seem at all too long. My mood turns quiet and solemn when

I consider all the good this movement has awakened in us. The spirit of sacrifice, the burning love for the Fatherland, and the idealism! On top of that its martial bearing and discipline! Of course, the entire Schlossplatz was jam-packed, with many nonpaying onlookers around the edges. Despite the pouring rain, all the men stood with their heads bared when the Dutch prayer of thanks was sung: "We come to pray to God the righteous." I got a hold of a ticket for Hitler's speech on the Schlossplatz, in the grandstands even. 3 M a seat. Hitler will speak at 6:00 in the evening. The whole city will be on its feet! That is enough politics for now. But Immeken, understand how preoccupied we are. "For out of the abundance of the heart, the mouth speaketh."

[. . .] Last Saturday we had a surprise visit from Elisabeth's brother, Bubi. I was delighted to see him. He came by bike from Gebhardshagen flying a Nazi flag, which 4 Communists in one of the villages along the way tried to tear off. He fought them off (he has the build to do that), and since the Communists didn't have bicycles, he made a clean escape. I told him he should have ridden on without the flag, but he said he would never consider doing so: he wasn't frightened. That is a real Nazi kid. [. . .]

Irmgard Brester to her mother Elisabeth Gebensleben, Utrecht, 23 July 1932

I figured that your last letter would be very political. Everyone here is also paying attention, and the newspapers publish long articles about conditions in Germany. One really wishes one didn't have to read these terrible reports in the first place. The incessant attacks and clashes are dreadful, especially when the police panic. Will peace and quiet return after the elections? We want it with all our heart, but scarcely believe it will occur. Ultimately, whatever the results, one party or the other will always be outraged and will want to fight on and not acknowledge the victory of the others. [. . .] Hitler's speech must have been quite an event. I am curious to read what you have to say about it. [. . .]

Minna von Alten to her granddaughter Irmgard Brester, Braunschweig, 29 July 1932

[. . .] The election of course dominates everything here. According to Eberhard, in Berlin one is not so sure that Hitler will come to power. Hitler flags flutter all around us, even T. in the Mauernstrasse has put one out, which enrages that overwhelmingly Communist street; yesterday 3 policemen had to protect him. [. . .]

In Braunschweig, on the night after the election on 31 July, a Communist patrol encountered an SA troop; one SA man was shot to death. The next morning, a motorcyclist threw a bomb onto the streets of a working-class neighborhood. Although the police arrested the man, three days later they delivered him to a hospital from which he escaped the first night. The killing led to more repressive state measures against the Communists while the dead SA man was quickly memorialized as a martyr to the nationalist cause.

In the second Reichstag elections held on 6 November 1932 (the fourth national elections in 1932), the National Socialists lost two million votes, gaining just over 33 percent of the vote. Hitler insisted on the post of chancellor so that his negotiations with the other parties failed. President Hindenburg thereupon appointed Kurt von Schleicher chancellor. Schleicher (1882–1934), a former general and Reichswehr Minister, had originally supported von Papen against Brüning, but he now turned against the ineffective Papen; he would be murdered by the Nazis in June 1934 on "The Night of the Long Knives." On 30 January 1933, Hindenburg finally agreed to Hitler's chancellorship, an appointment that was celebrated in jubilant rallies across Germany. On the same day, Communist protests in Braunschweig were violently broken up.

In the meantime, Immo continued to sing, sometimes as a soloist in Utrecht's women's choir under the directorship of Karin Kwant Törngren. The choir's programs were broadcast on the radio and could occasionally be heard in Braunschweig.

Minna von Alten to her granddaughter Irmgard Brester, Braunschweig, 1 August 1932

[. . .] You will have heard the election results for yourself. Yesterday ended quietly, but this morning we were startled by 3 hand grenades. There was no holding Eberhard back, and he ran out. One was thrown near the residence of the Oberbürgermeister, one in the Schöppenstedter Strasse, and the third out by the boathouse. Now everything is calm.

Minna von Alten to her granddaughter Irmgard Brester, Braunschweig, 11 August 1932

[. . .] Today Eberhard wrote me the first letter with details. He feels better than he has in a long time. It's true they sleep in barracks with straw beds, but they bathe in the lake twice a day, they put in 5 hours' labor, and they don't have to worry about anything. There are more than enough diversions. We are very happy and reassured on his account. In the afternoon, the work teams play sports and music. [. . .]

August Brester to his father-in-law Karl Gebensleben, Utrecht, 24 September 1932

My dear newly elected Stadtbaurat, we can't say how delighted *we* were to hear the excellent news. Prepared as we were thanks to the telephone conversation right before our departure, we were still a little worried whether a disappointment wouldn't still be in the offing, which thank goodness did not occur. Now that everything has turned out, the move should not be as hard as it might otherwise be. Too bad we cannot celebrate together, particularly since we shared the tense days of anticipation. [. . .]

Karl Gebensleben to his daughter Irmgard Brester, Braunschweig, 20 October 1932

[. . .] To tell you the truth, all the excitement lately—the accident, the elections [. . .] has been very stressful. But Vati is strong! [. . .]

You are getting the *Landeszeitung* regularly now, aren't you? Incidentally, the paper is no longer quite so aggressive in its promotion of the Nazis. It was really over the top, which must have had an impact on circulation. Professionally, I am also doing well; there is plenty to do, but I can take care of matters comfortably. [. . .]

Hedeper comes by the Friedensallee regularly to visit us. Only Frieda was not happy with the swap—on account of the poor view from the kitchen window and because she can't as easily slip out of the house from time to time—Grandmother holds the opposite view and considers it a plus. As always, Mutti's heart goes out to Frieda's little troubles. [. . .]

Irmgard Brester to her mother Elisabeth Gebensleben, Utrecht, 19 November 1932

[. . .] Hedda has learned a whole bunch of new words, though they are all Dutch. But she hasn't forgotten her German so that she often talks complete gobbledygook. [. . .]

Elisabeth Gebensleben to her daughter Irmgard Brester, Braunschweig, 23 November 1932

[. . .] I am often still tired and my eyes hurt. But that will pass. We are just so happy here; just to spend a quiet evening at home.

The political tensions are a strain for everyone right now. In any case, the domestic political situation is so important, so full of consequences, and so extremely grave that everything else is secondary. Hitler is a man of too much integrity; he is true to himself; he *cannot* accept conditions that clash with his convictions. Think of all the dark forces that will be at work to prevent the positive things that will come with Germany's salvation. I am sending all my good wishes Berlin's way. Not least to Hardus! [. . .]

Irmgard Brester to her mother Elisabeth Gebensleben, Utrecht, 26 November 1932

[. . .] We are awaiting further developments in the negotiations to constitute a Reich government with great anticipation. Is Hitler doing the right thing in refusing to accept any conditions? We will just have to wait and see. [. . .]

Elisabeth Gebensleben to her daughter Irmgard Brester, Braunschweig, 1 December 1932

[. . .] Our politics are so muddled! With the collapse of the Hitler-Hindenburg negotiations, the hopes of millions of Germans have been wiped out. Hitler could not have acted differently if he wanted to remain true to himself; Hindenburg with his *old*, deeply rooted views probably could not either. And therein lies the tragedy of the whole business. I still believe that Hitler will succeed. The hardships will become so great that they will call upon him and will be relieved that he accepts. According to Schacht, "the only man who can save us is Hitler," and "if Hitler does not become chancellor now, he will in four months; Hitler can wait." But in the meantime, the German nation will continue to flounder! And the Bolsheviks will become ever stronger as desperation pushes people into their camp. Although I am very *upset*, I am not in *despair* precisely because I *know* the *National* Socialists exist. They give me peace of mind and I believe deeply that they will come to our aid.

Uncle W. is a Nazi yet gives a Slav his daughter's hand in marriage. That seems wrongheaded. Theory and practice! The wedding takes place next Tuesday at 2:00 in the Paulikirche. [. . .]

Minna von Alten to her granddaughter Irmgard Brester, Braunschweig, 4 December 1932

[. . .] On the whole Christmas will be a lean time throughout Germany. I can't remember a time when money was so short, but you learn to make economies, and we have a treasure of other joys, the arrival of your letters, for example.

Elisabeth Gebensleben to her daughter Irmgard Brester, Braunschweig, 12 December 1932

[. . .] [The wedding] was organized very attentively and lovingly by the parents K. There was even music: a very small band, violin and piano. Indeed, Herr L. played the piano in a brown Nazi uniform; his partner wore one too. L. is always playing with the Nazis and shares their convictions. By the way, he played wonderfully. [. . .]

Elisabeth Gebensleben to her daughter Irmgard Brester, Braunschweig, 6 January 1933

[. . .] Eberhard left early in the morning on 2 January because he thought he could already get his assignment on the 2nd. A letter arrived today; he wanted to let us know that he is satisfied with the topic. He only received the assignment on the 3rd, a topic in constitutional law (that is just fine; he prefers it to criminal law). Questions regarding the dissolution of the Prussian parliament. "Not at all uninteresting but not much commentary available, and none of it systematic," he writes. He has about 5–6 weeks to complete the assignment and then 4 days of examinations at the university. At the end: a full day of oral examinations. [. . .]

Irmgard Brester to her mother Elisabeth Gebensleben, Utrecht, 21 January 1933

[. . .] I am delighted that you were able to hear the concert on Monday night so well, and thank you dearly for your greeting card. It is really great that the radio helps overcome these distances. While I was singing, I was constantly thinking: they are sitting there around the speaker in Braunschweig and hear everything that is being sung in this hall. Now isn't that just too curious. [. . .] I am especially happy that you were even able to make out my high notes. Yesterday I told Frau Kwant [Immo's singing teacher] all about it. [. . .]

Elisabeth Gebensleben to her daughter Irmgard Brester, Braunschweig, 27 January 1933

[. . .] By all reports our young fellow in Berlin is doing well. I am so delighted whenever I receive good news. He writes only rarely and is completely absorbed in his work. [. . .] A package with little surprises goes out to him every week; frequently, in addition to these, an extra cheerful greeting. [. . .] I am afraid he is working until late at night and then has trouble sleeping. [. . .]

Elisabeth Gebensleben to her daughter Irmgard Brester, Braunschweig, 3 February 1933

Dear, dear Immo, the times are so filled of events I want to share with you that a letter hardly suffices. And the sun outside is beckoning; watch out, it won't be long before I come to visit! [. . .] While we were eating, Frieda came in completely pale. She could barely speak: "An unemployed man is standing outside. He's my mother's youngest brother. Just the other day, my grandfather said, if he only knew where the boy was." When he looked at Frieda's face, he fell silent. Frieda didn't know what to say either and simply closed the door. So I went to the door. The young man did in fact look quite a bit like Frieda's mother, and when I asked him where he came from, he couldn't say a word. I then asked Frieda to give him some money. He didn't answer any of Frieda's questions, but Frieda believed it was definitely him, although he looked so ashamed [. . .]

So what do you say to the course of events in Germany? Immeken, I think that you read the German newspapers pretty thoroughly. Now, Hitler's appointment as chancellor came surprisingly quickly. I was firmly convinced it was going to happen, but at first it almost seemed as though the opportunity had passed. Schacht was right after all; at the time of Schleicher's election, after negotiations with Hitler had broken down, the *Landeszeitung* wrote: "According to Schacht, Hitler can wait. If he does not become chancellor now, he will in four months."

Finally, after the most fierce battles, the goal has been reached; now a beginning, and what an endlessly difficult beginning. We heard Hitler on the radio. He is completely right when he says: "Our task is the most difficult in living memory."

The news reached us Monday as follows: Frieda, who takes such a fancy looking out our windows down the Friedensallee, suddenly shouted: "Outside dozens of Hitler flags are being put out!" I had missed the news at noon, but then Vati arrived with an extra edition. His face had broken into a huge grin. I smiled as well, but as soon as the first moment of joy passed, I had to sit off to the side for a moment to shed a couple of tears. At last, at last! Now after the most unbelievable insults and defamations, this once lowborn man who fought in the trenches, is sitting where Bismarck once sat. 14 years ago he had 7 followers, now he has 13 million. This is the result of inconceivable strength, energy, and self-sacrifice that must be unprecedented in the history of the world. But the struggles still to come! The day before yesterday, when I was in the city in the afternoon, I got mixed up in a Communist disturbance on the Bohlweg; it was terrifying. Red flags, also Reichsbanner flags; loud screams: "Down with this," "Down with that!" Music, catcalls, and shouting. In between, the police in cars, on foot, and on horseback. I fled into a store; the owners let down the iron louvers. As I watched this great mass of misguided, hate-filled people, I was suddenly struck with the worrisome thought: "Too late? Did Hitler finally reach the helm when it is already too late?" After all, Bolshevism is rooted much, much deeper in the people than one thinks—in their blind helplessness, all the statesmen who have been at the helm up to now ended up abetting its rise. It was only Hitler who really understood the enormity of the danger. He will face down the Bolsheviks; if he can't do it, no one can; and now he has the Reichswehr and the police, as well as his SA and SS guards at his lawful disposal. But he has to stay on guard. The Reichsbanner (that is Black-Red-Gold) are all on high alert.

You can see the division of the nation wherever you go. I went to the movies on Wednesday afternoon. I do that very rarely—only when I am at an impasse. Newsreels of the torchlight procession on Tuesday night in honor of Hitler and Hindenburg were shown. It must have been fabulous, national enthusiasm that we haven't seen since 1914. The torches illuminated the flags of the Stahlhelm and the swastika banners; Hindenburg and Hitler appearing at the window, the cheers, the military music. Applause broke out in the cinema, interrupted at the same time by whistling and boos; in the first few rows, workers even sprang up. It was horrible. Thankfully, the images lasted only a few moments. From the balcony, shouts of "Quiet" and then came the wonderful songs by [Hermann] Löns, which calmed down tempers.

Sonja's visit on Monday afternoon, the first since she had the flu, was simply enchanting. She telephoned her mother: "Mutti, have you already heard, Hitler has become 'Reich President'! And, Mutti, now he will tell us all what to do. Mutti, aren't you just as happy?" Well, and if Mutti wasn't happy. And Aunt Stadtbaurat as well, especially over the "President" and over the little convalescent enjoying her black bread with Harz cheese with a cup of hot milk. Just as Sonja came, I was rereading Vati your wonderful letter. She listened to everything with great interest, what you reported about Heddalein and Marleentje. [. . .]

No news from Eberhard. The allotted time for his assignment is almost over. He is actively engaged in the big political events now taking shape, even with everything he has to do. [. . .]

Irmgard Brester to her mother Elisabeth Gebensleben, Utrecht, 3 February 1933

[. . .] And we really enjoyed the illustrateds. So Hitler is actually Reich Chancellor? I am so eager to hear what you have to say about that; here everyone was also totally excited about the new direction to the German government. If only everything works out, and Hitler is really able to live up to the hopes placed in him! [. . .]

Elisabeth Gebensleben to her daughter Irmgard Brester, Braunschweig, 8 February 1933

[. . .] We are expecting the Oberbürgermeister, City Councilor S., City Councilor S., with wives of course, the S.'s, Professor R., the M.'s, and Herr and Frau F. Hopefully the evening will proceed nicely. As far as I am concerned, I would rather have prepared a warm meal, which wouldn't have been in the least bit more inconvenient, on the contrary [. . .] but Vati agreed to this format with the Oberbürgermeister, unfortunately without consulting me. And it was the Oberbürgermeister who started the trouble. There was that evening with him, when Schleicher was still in power and no one thought that Hitler would become Reich Chancellor so soon. There we sat around a big round table, everyone on their best behavior, when talk did turn to politics, which we had until then anxiously avoided. Admittedly, Hitler had already been the subject of some pointed remarks on the part of several college professors, who in the aftermath of the incidents in the college had little good to say about National Socialism. Up to that point I had held myself back, waiting for the appropriate moment to give my opinion. Those in attendance were all against the Nazis. Thereupon a professor at the college commented: "Isn't it strange that in high society nobody openly admits support for National Socialism." I broke up the silence that had descended after these words: "I do." You should have seen the expressions on their faces! The wife of the Oberbürgermeister simply said: "Really, you?" and Municipal Council S. added: "And you have the courage to say that, so openly?" Actually I think my Nazi spirit impressed them a bit!

Last Sunday Hardus wrote a very contented letter: "I was out and about on the epoch-making night (torchlight parade) from 8:00 to 12:00. What might appear to be overly effusive descriptions such as the one published in the *Deutsche Allgemeine Zeitung* are not exaggerations at all."

Domestic politics, and now the dissolution of the Prussian parliament, are completely in line with the topic of Eberhard's big examinations. The most famous legal scholars are racking their brains over this question. I wonder how Eberhard is finding his way! All the material he has to read, even completely opposing views. [. . .]

The Reichstag building burned in a spectacular fire on 27 February 1933, the cause of which remains unclear to this day. However, in the run-up to new elections on 5 March 1933, the Nazis immediately held the Communists responsible, which provided the grounds for emergency legislation that suspended constitutional rights and gave the new government unprecedented police powers. Exploiting the incident to dramatize the civil war conditions in which Germany allegedly found itself, Hitler won several million more votes in the election (nearly 44 percent of the vote, a significant gain, but not a majority).

In Braunschweig on 10 and 14 February, clashes with the Nazis led to the deaths of two workers. The funerals prompted renewed battles with the police, in which protesters were wounded and arrested. On 9 March 1933, Braunschweig's Nazis attacked the offices of the local Social Democratic newspaper, Der Volksfreund. *Police cordoned off the area so that no one heard the cries of the employees, who were brutally mistreated; all the while the paper's furnishings burned on the curb outside for three days. Prominent Social Democratic politicians were subsequently hauled to the* Volksfreund *offices, which had become one of the SA's "wild" torture centers. Today a commemorative plaque pays homage to the victims.*

On 8 March 1933, a group of Nazis entered Braunschweig's city hall and under the threat of violence demanded that the swastika-emblazoned flag be raised over the building. Not a single employee resisted, except for the Social Democratic mayor, Ernst Böhme. The Nazis raised the flag and banned all socialist pennants and emblems. The Nazis continued to wage war on Communists and Social Democrats; they banned both the Communist party and the Social Democratic paramilitary auxiliary, the Reichsbanner.

A revolt on the Dutch warship De Zeven Provincien *on 4 February held the country in thrall; navy personnel had suffered the third cut in pay since the summer of 1931. On 10 February, after navy fliers bombed the ship, the crew surrendered off the coast of Sumatra, but not before twenty-three sailors were killed. Social Democrats and Communists in the Netherlands sharply condemned the action.*

Irmgard Brester to her mother Elisabeth Gebensleben, Utrecht, 11 February 1933

I am not a bit surprised that you are all enthusiastic about the new Reich Chancellor. It is just frightening to consider the animosity of the population that thinks differently. We can only hope that events take their course calmly. Did you read about the mutiny on the Dutch battleship, which has finally been captured after a suspenseful chase that lasted for days? Moscow is certainly behind it! Recently you asked about Japanese and Chinese products flooding the Dutch markets. That is so, nowadays you can buy such things very cheaply just about everywhere. For example, when I bought a pound of coffee today, I received a big inflatable rubber ball for free; Hedda is delighted. The label reads: *Made in Japan.* [. . .]

Elisabeth Gebensleben to her daughter Irmgard Brester, Braunschweig, 16 February 1933

[. . .] Monday we had a great big surprise. The doorbell rang long two times and Frieda called: "Herr Eberhard!" And really, there he was standing at the door. [. . .] Actually I was very happy that I had my son for myself first since it was clear: something was up. To begin with, I did what came naturally: I hugged him with all my heart. And then came the question: you are not sick, are you? When I scrutinized him, I could see right away that he was not physically sick; it had to be wounds on the inside. We sat together very quietly and Eberhard told me all about his big assignment on which he had worked for 6 weeks, too exhaustively and conscientiously, I am sure. The assigned topic was: the question of the dissolution of the Prussian parliament. The topic interested him a great deal, but he began to realize that he was going to have problems sticking to the deadline, which was this Tuesday. He began to work deep into the night, until 3:00, and to take up where he left off at 8:00. On Sunday he couldn't gather his thoughts anymore, and at 6:00 in the evening he realized that it would be impossible for him to complete the assignment by Tuesday. Everything still had to be put in order and tightened, then dictating to a typist, which alone would have taken two days (approximately 90 printed pages). He then took the consequences and threw all his papers in the oven. Immeken, let me tell you, when I heard that then there was just one thing to do: pull myself together. I couldn't let myself show him how much it hurt, the entire work of 6 weeks! I said: "Hardus, I am sure you had a great many good ideas." "Sure," he agreed, "I suppose it was a decent paper and I also know that I got it right." If Eberhard, who is always so self-critical, says that, it must be so. I asked about a possible extension of the deadline. That is not allowed. Berlin's rules! According to Ursel, extensions are allowed here. You know, Immo, that I allowed Hardus to leave after Christmas though I was full of worries and that I continued to worry about him. I mentioned to him what August had said about the Germans working too hard, and Eberhard agreed that that was probably right. In the end, he couldn't even get to sleep. *In order to clear any misunderstanding*, the failure to deliver this assignment has *no* effect on the results of his examinations or his candidacy in general. Eberhard can simply get himself assigned a new topic. This assignment is just to establish his candidacy for the examinations. [. . .] If Eberhard had been at home these last 6 weeks, matters would have been very different. [. . .] The situation is a clear warning sign, but nothing has been decided. Hardus is recovering well. [. . .] Vati and I are of the opinion that Hardus should take his examinations in Braunschweig; we hope that he comes around to our point of view. Yesterday Vati made inquiries with Attorney General K.; he was of the opinion that if Eberhard did well in his examinations, it would be more advantageous to take them here than in Berlin. As an assessor he could later find a place in the civil service. Vati has many contacts, and his contacts to Berlin are really the best imaginable. (Reich Chancellor Hitler is Regierungsrat for Braunschweig.) The examinations are much less difficult here than in Berlin. The big six-week assignment would cease to be a problem. [. . .]

By the way, *no one* is to hear the fate of Eberhard's assignment, although he doesn't believe there is any reason to conceal anything. But you know how people are: the whole business will be misunderstood, and in the end the bottom line will be that Eberhard failed his examinations. And there is *nothing at all* to that.

Elisabeth Gebensleben to her daughter Irmgard Brester, Braunschweig, 23 February 1933

[. . .] days in which you stand before a decision and don't know what is for the best are terrible. Hopefully we've done the right thing. Eberhard returned to Berlin yesterday morning. As we were waiting for the streetcar, goodbyes were waved from three windows. Aunt Bertha waved out of one, Ohmchen out of another, and Frieda out of the third. Vati met us at the train station. [. . .] [The president of the appellate court] advised him to take the examinations in Berlin, particularly since that is what Eberhard has been preparing for. Moreover, the examinations in Prussia are regarded more highly and offer better chances in the future than the ones in Braunschweig. During his probationary period Eberhard could still find positions (within the three years) in Braunschweig. He said he would take Eberhard on immediately. They like to take lawyers trained in Prussia, but not the other way around: Prussia would not take a lawyer trained in Braunschweig. Eberhard was relieved to hear this information. He felt it repugnant to his own sense of self-worth to take the examinations here. He thereby admitted his shortcoming, a setback. [. . .] In the next difficult weeks of work he must not feel that he has been left alone. [. . .] We will have to visit him in Berlin. [. . .] We should blame ourselves, not Eberhard. [. . .]

Frieda mentioned that her fiancé dropped by for a bit. He's working now at the airport with the Nazi aviation squad and is always in uniform. Night before last he had guard duty and didn't get to bed at all. They really have a lot to do, the SS, the SA, and the auxiliary police. The auxiliary police has been mobilized just at the right moment. Every last man is needed to hold the line against the Communists. Frieda runs to the window whenever she hears an airplane buzz overhead! Often "he" is the pilot, and then he takes delight in circling over the church spire and flying so low over our house that we all jump up in fright! [. . .]

Elisabeth Gebensleben to her daughter Irmgard Brester, Braunschweig, 2 March 1933

One event chases the next, and every day we experience so many things that a weekly letter is hardly sufficient to tell you everything. [. . .]

Yesterday, we received the long-awaited postcard from Hardus. He has already been to the court of appeals three times and still has not gotten an assignment; supposedly it was sent to him and should arrive any day now. Vati will travel to Berlin from Sunday to Monday. [. . .] What an exciting time Hardus is having in Berlin! It is simply ghastly. The immense dangers that Germany is facing. Thank God we have this resolute government. The day before yesterday, in the evening, we heard a very objective report on the radio about Communist plans to incite civil war. This matter-of-fact report probably had a more chilling effect than a passionate denunciation would have. Our hair stood on end. It is simply not imaginable what was in store for us. Now push comes to shove. We have to get rid of the Communists, and the Marxists too. Göring said in a speech yesterday evening: "If opinion around the world thinks that we are being too tough on the Communists, then it should take care of this bestial band." The editor of *Vorwärts* was arrested because he informed the foreign press that it was possible that the National Socialists themselves had set the Reichstag on fire. What are you supposed to say to that? But you shouldn't be surprised that so many false reports about the National Socialists have been circulated in the foreign press. We listen to the speeches on the radio every evening. Foreigners cannot even begin to understand just how much the German people love, celebrate, and honor Hitler. Nothing like this has ever occurred in world history. [. . .]

Irmgard Brester to her mother Elisabeth Gebensleben, Utrecht, 4 March 1933

[. . .] Many, many thanks for the illustrateds and for your lovely, informative letter. I have thought so much about you these days, and I share your excitement. Here too tempers flared over the shocking Reichstag fire; the newspapers are consumed with German politics each and every day. What a dreadfully divided and agitated time we live in! And what are we going to do about all this violent animosity, which devours humanity. This shameful deed of the Communists just about beats everything, not to mention what might still have occurred. And that it is a Dutchman who is an accomplice has also created a huge uproar here. It is hard to imagine how all this was prepared in total secrecy. Incidentally, the rumor that the Nazis were in fact the arsonists did indeed surface here, just as you wrote, but it was immediately disregarded. Yesterday we received a postcard from Eberhardus depicting the burning of the Reichstag. He must have been terribly upset. It is good that Vati is going to visit him tomorrow. [...]

Elisabeth Gebensleben to her daughter Irmgard Brester, Braunschweig, 10 March 1933

Can it be that an entire week has once again passed? The events tumble over each other; every day brings something new and flies by. Of course, you are well informed thanks to the German newspaper; the foreign press often prints the most distorted reports, thanks to the work of the Socialists and Communists, who are naturally bitter. The "Revolution from the Right" proceeds with great order and severe discipline in contrast to the "Revolution from the Left" in November 1918, which remains such a ghastly memory. The national government's uncompromising measures may appear to many somewhat off-putting, but it is necessary to start by thoroughly cleaning up and clearing out; the antinational forces have to be neutralized, otherwise the reconstruction effort will have no chance.

Just now I am hearing the loud cries "extra edition!" on the street. What has happened now? Tomorrow night from 8:30 until 10 o'clock there will be a big demonstration in Berlin, certainly the biggest one up to now, with a speech by Hitler. I wish you could listen to it; then you would get an idea of the enormous national enthusiasm in Germany. No kaiser was ever celebrated as Hitler is loved, honored, and admired. Couldn't you invite yourselves over to acquaintances who have a radio to listen to the speech?

In honor of the national renewal, Frieda and I raised the old, wonderful black-white-red flag on the balcony. It flew merrily in the breeze until Monday. I can't tell you how we celebrated! For fifteen years the banned flag lay in the cellar, the flag for which millions gave their lives for the glory of the Fatherland. As I unfurled it, I became very solemn, and in my mind's eye I saw myself fifteen years ago, when I, along with you and Eberhard (since your children's hands helped), hung out the flag whenever a victory from the front was announced or when our front soldiers were honored. What bunting there was throughout the streets of the city on Saturday and especially on Sunday, which delivered such a glorious election result. So many people rushed to the polls that they had to stand in line. We've never seen anything like this, yet this is what Hitler has achieved. It is hard to comprehend the enormous power this man possesses, not just in intellectual but also in physical terms. All the campaign speeches he held! He spared himself no effort! Indeed, Vati spent Election Day first here, then in Berlin. By 3:00 in the afternoon, he was with Eberhard. He didn't return until Monday evening, totally excited, very enthusiastic and satisfied. Sunday afternoon, he and Eberhard witnessed the Stahlhelm procession, 25,000 men in all, reviewed by Göring, Papen, and Seldte. To their great delight they coincidentally bumped into Nicolai on Unter den Linden. He was happy to join them; all three spent the evening in a Bavarian beer hall, where a heady mood prevailed. Stahlhelm, Nazis, military music, and patriotic song. Hardus and Nicolai were really in stride, singing along, and, yes, they even wrote me a postcard with a poem they composed themselves—each one taking turns writing a verse. For example, Eberhard wrote "Left on the Balcony, the brown Battalion; dressed in brown and gray, distinguished from the fray." Vati was very pleased with Eberhard's condition. He is looking very good and seems upbeat. It has been 8 days since he has gotten his new assignment, which follows thematically from the first so all the preparation will not be in vain. He now just has to bear up under all the pressure; of course, I worry about him and I don't fail to admonish him. [. . .]

Did you read the lead article in the newspaper yesterday, Thursday? The Oberbürgermeister will not be forgiven for his "Hands in His Trouser Pockets." Quite dramatic scenes accompanied the raising of the Nazi flags over city hall. Böhme knew already on Tuesday that the flags were to be raised on Wednesday, but said nothing to council members as he should have. Instead, without saying anything he took the key to the building's steeple with him home. When Vati arrived at city hall on Wednesday morning, the office manager approached him trembling: "The Nazis are here and want to raise the flag. They want me to give them the key." Vati replied: "Call the Oberbürgermeister." He was already on his way. The Nazis should bide their time until he arrived. Then Böhme showed up. Negotiations with about 8 Nazis in his office. Böhme refused to hand over the key, became angry, the Nazis as well. They told him to at least take his hands out of the pockets of his trousers as he spoke to them. Then Böhme to the Nazis: "Would you be so kind as to take off your caps." "We won't take them off; the uniform requires caps." Böhme: "Pshaw, uniforms? Not to me they aren't." Just in case, the Nazis had brought along a locksmith who forced the door open, and, accompanied by cheering crowds, the two Nazi flags were raised. Then the leader of the Nazis, hand to his cap. "Reporting as ordered, Herr Oberbürgermeister, flags raised." Over the course of the day, the black-white-red flag was raised to make a threesome. Böhme will not be working for long under the banner of the swastika. I imagine he will be "retired" one fine day, like so many of his comrades.

The city has really come to life. Yesterday I went to my beloved pottery market again. What a delightful article I acquired there! I won't say a thing. Only this: it is a toy for Heddalein.

Irmgard Brester to her mother Elisabeth Gebensleben, Utrecht, 11 March 1933

These days we always look so forward to your dear letters, and from the bottom of our hearts we thank you for describing to us in detail what we also find so interesting. We get a good sense of what is happening nowadays in Germany and I just wish I could pay a quick visit in order to form my own opinion. From a distance, it is possible to see more objectively and calmly and judge more soberly than in the thick of things as you are. First and foremost, we trust that Hitler will achieve his goals by peaceful means and that he acts in the best interests not only of Germany but of all of humanity, which everywhere you look has been hurt by the present-day crisis. Needless to say, his measures against the Communists are widely praised here, at least insofar as they do not lead to a dictatorship. However, the high import tolls, 2½ cents on Dutch eggs, for example, seem to be very shortsighted measures. Of course, he is lending German agriculture a hand, but is he thinking farther into the future? Now the Dutch will respond with countermeasures that will make it impossible to export the goods manufactured in German factories, so another blow for Germany somewhere else. You can well imagine that the Dutch will no longer buy German goods if they believe that their own economy is being ruined! Conflicts and antagonisms are festering between nations where none had existed before. As a result, world history takes a step backward instead of forward. Why do nations have to undermine their respective means of existence instead of supporting each other through trade and commerce. It is not clear where things are headed and what goals Hitler intends to pursue. Up to now he has just been laying the groundwork. The elections favored him, but it remains to be seen what he wants to accomplish. Now he has the power in his hands. Our Utrecht newspaper, which, by the way, is objective in its reporting, refers to the "Revolution from the Right," just as you did, Mutti. The Nazis just have to remember that the world does not revolve around Germany. They have to look across the border once in a while. I always have the feeling that the Nazis do not see far enough; their horizons are very narrow. Well, what will come will come, and no one is able to see the entire picture or to know what hidden forces are waiting to reveal themselves.

I can imagine the power of the enthusiasm you are experiencing now that the red regime in all its horror and ugliness has been removed. The black-white-red banner we had to conceal for so long is now flying again. My German heart beats faster, and I am grateful to the man who made that possible. Your story about the flag flying on the steeple of city hall is just exquisite! I also agree that Böhme will not long be able to "govern" with the nationalist majority in city hall. I had to keep thinking of you on Election Sunday, we heard the results already in the evening from an acquaintance who has a radio. [. . .] On Sunday we went to church for the first time since Marleentje's baptism and heard a wonderful sermon given by a champion of the progressive cause. It was really an edifying hour. [. . .]

By order of the Reich President Hindenburg, all public buildings were required to fly the old black-white-red flag of the Kaiserreich as well as the swastika-emblazoned flag of the Nazis for the period 13–15 March 1933 in order "to commemorate the triumph of the National Revolution."

On 11 March, the shop windows of Jewish shops in Braunschweig were smashed, an incident that the Braunschweigische Landeszeitung *described the next day as a "spontaneous action" by men and women who suddenly pressed into the Schuhstrasse while listening to an SA band concert on the Kohlmarkt. "It happened so quickly that it was already over by the time the riot squad arrived. Police are continuing to search for the perpetrators." In fact, the entire incident was instigated by SS men—the elite paramilitary force that would eventually staff Nazi police actions, including the "Final Solution"—in plain clothes. Braunschweig's Nazi Interior Minister, Dietrich Klagges, had warned the police that a NSDAP operation would take place and ordered them not to intervene. The riot squad arrived only after personnel from one of the department stores under attack raised the alarm. Shortly thereafter, Friedrich Alpers, a lawyer for the local NSDAP and a senior SS office who had taken part in the operation, held a speech in which he blamed the Communists for the attacks on Jewish shops. In May, Klagges was appointed Prime Minister in Braunschweig and Alpers Finance and Justice Minister.*

Two days later, on 13 March, uniformed Nazis hauled the Social Democratic Oberbürgermeister, Ernst Böhme, out of a city council meeting. A party of SS men hustled him out of city hall past rows of Nazi paramilitaries and took him to the prison in Rennelberg. Released that same day, Böhme went into hiding. A week later, he telephoned the police from his home to inquire whether there were any charges against him; the police reassured him that there were not. A few minutes later, however, members of the SA and SS climbed over the balcony and broke into his house. Böhme managed to call the police, but they were intercepted by the SS and backed off. Böhme was packed into a car and taken to the Volksfreund *building, where Alpers was already waiting for him. He forced Böhme to sign a document in which he resigned from all his offices. After Alpers left, SS men brutally attacked Böhme, dragging him on a table, ripping off his clothes, and beating him with whips until he lost consciousness. They then poured water over Böhme, allowed him to get dressed, and paraded him through the streets of Braunschweig draped with a red sash before returning him to prison. A photograph captures the moment: Böhme appears completely distraught in hat, coat, and the red sash, his face is swollen, and he is surrounded by a group of SA men laughing triumphantly into the camera. Across Germany, Social Democratic mayors were "removed from office" in similar fashion. Böhme eventually moved to Berlin and survived the Third Reich as an accountant. After the war, he returned to Braunschweig, where the US military authorities appointed him Oberbürgermeister, a post he held until 1948.*

The Braunschweigische Landeszeitung *wrote on 14 March 1933: "Stadtbaurat Gebensleben, the senior city councilor, has taken over the duties of Böhme's office [and] will assume the leadership of the council for the interim. The key words are undoubtedly 'for the interim.'*

"An eyewitness report: Lieutenant Schinkel asked the Oberbürgermeister if he was prepared to immediately leave city hall on his own. A somewhat inappropriate, but sentimental scene ensued. Herr Böhme expressed the desire to take leave of the members of the city council. 'Under no circumstances,' someone shouted, whereupon Herr Böhme said goodbye to Stadtbaurat Gebensleben, who had tears in his eyes."

Of course, the press suppressed an account of the actual events.

Immo made mention of the conductor Fritz Busch (1890–1951); he emigrated to the United States after being dismissed by the Nazis for political reasons in 1933. He was not Jewish.

Elisabeth Gebensleben to her daughter Irmgard Brester, Braunschweig, 14 March 1933

[. . .] All the excitement of the last several days, which will continue for some to come. I think that even if you had nerves of steel they would give way by now. The fact is that these are revolutionary times. We simply have to get through them. When Vati and I went into the city Sunday afternoon in order to see the film "Choral von Leuthen," we found ourselves right in front of police cordons down by the Kohlmarkt, where a big "shop window" action had taken place. Maybe you read about it in the newspaper. Nazis, Stahlhelmers, and police stood guard around the department stores that had come under attack. Sunday morning we walked along the Sack. It looks ghastly: the huge show windows at Frank's, Karstadt, Hamburger's have all been completely destroyed and are nailed up with plywood. At least thirty windows must have been taken care of. During their recent marches, the Communists had recently shoved in the windows of Karstadt and others in the Sack, but not as badly as this. Since only Jewish establishments have been hit, one might come to the conclusion that the attacks could have been instigated by crowds of National Socialists on the street (Nazis not in uniform). At least it is possible if you consider that a movement of millions will give way to excesses, which Hitler is aggressively combating. These attacks are often the work of provocateurs who, we know, have infiltrated the NSDAP in order to embarrass the patriotic movement at home and abroad. Young boneheads, Communists, and their followers are the ones to blame. That is the general view, though the investigation might clear up matters.

With its clear sunny weather and bell ringing, Remembrance Day also gave us some solemn moments. Already at 10:00 in the morning, large numbers of National Socialists passed by our house on their way to the Stadtpark, where they laid wreaths at the Colonial Memorial. Vati stayed up on our balcony to get a good view; I quickly ran after them, stood at the memorial, and heard the gripping speech that a local National Socialist gave. Then the ceremonial wreath-laying, after which the troops made their way to the War Cemetery. Vati and I then took a walk in the city. While Vati quickly took care of an errand in city hall, I stepped into the cathedral for fifteen minutes, just as the formal prayer service began. Brownshirts completely filled the two aisles of the cathedral, which made a very impressive picture. Then the powerful, solemn roar of the choirs: "Eine feste Burg ist unser Gott" ("A Mighty Fortress Is Our God"). I stood near the entrance to the cathedral since I did not have a lot of time. But I will not soon forget the festive mood. At 2:00 in the afternoon we listened to Hitler's speech to the NSDAP on the radio. First the Chancellor announced the presidential edict on the flag question and added his own explanation. I assume you've read it. It is in Monday's, that is yesterday's, *Landeszeitung*. If you haven't read it, make sure you take your time; read it through more than once: there is so much to it that you can't take it in all at once. It was *hammered in* to the German people— every two hours on the radio, also on records. To get a sense of it you also have to hear Hitler's *voice*, succinct, energetic, and firm. For example: "I *order* you to show the most severe and *unquestioning* discipline. Spontaneous actions are forbidden. Only in the event that *resistance* to our legal directives is taken up by the enemies of our national movement, should it be *smashed root and branch*. Be on guard against provocateurs and informers; we have evidence that the Communists have slipped them into our formations." Hitler's voice can also be soft, from the bottom of his heart, for example when he says: "I thank you for the *boundless* loyalty and sacrifice and discipline you have shown me." [. . .]

Before I tell you about yesterday's excitement, the removal of the Oberbürgermeister, let me first thank you with all my heart, Immeken, for your lovely letter. And our Marleentje has her first tooth! Marleentje, I think you are owed a little package from Mimi; what do you think about that? And Heddalein's streetcar trip to

Zeist! How I would have liked to have seen that little person sitting there with bright happy eyes. Her mother as well, in her "elegante Toilette" for the posh theater gala.

Well, our dear Vati has once again become acting Oberbürgermeister. What had to happen finally happened on Monday: Böhme's dismissal. The fact of the matter was predictable, but the manner in which the dismissal took place was insupportable. I would have wished that Böhme had a somewhat less disgraceful departure. You will have read the story. Böhme had been advised often enough to resign on his own. As far as I am concerned, he should have done just that, although I suppose he has his rights; above all he wanted to save his pension. And they also won't be able to take it away from him since he was not a pure party hack like so many of his colleagues who have been dismissed; he has a university education. I actually don't think he is the rabid Marxist his wife is. She was always the driving force. That became very clear at the beginning of his term, when they were looking for a residence, for example.

On Monday, Vati came home from work completely beat. He was present during the whole business. The chief police inspector had asked Vati to remain as a witness to the arrest; Böhme himself asked Vati, when he had to fetch him from the council meeting, to accompany him to his office where the police were waiting. Vati said it was terrible. The report of the "eyewitness" published in the newspaper is not completely accurate, and we all resented the sentence about "the tears in the eyes of Stadtbaurat Gebensleben." That Vati was moved is only human. After all, he worked with Böhme, just as had the other councilmen, who were also effected even if they were not personally present. It may be that at the last moment Vati got a little misty-eyed as he heard the jeers of the crowd as he helped the mayor, who started trembling, into his overcoat. But tears—out of the question. Frieda came home last night: "Frau Stadtbaurat, I heard that Herr Stadtbaurat wept when the Oberbürgermeister was arrested, the newspaper said so." So you can see how the whole business has been distorted. Vati conferred with the other municipal councilors, including the National Socialists. The National Socialists themselves sharply criticized the way Böhme was hauled away, and they maintained they would have been unsettled as well if they had witnessed the scene. Anybody who has a bit of sympathy will completely understand.

Vati had a long conversation with Klagges, who was very nice and obliging. They discussed a number of issues and got along well. Böhme has now left town for eight days, but left his wife here. I don't understand that. I would not have left my husband alone in such a state. But that depends on the mutual relations spouses have with one another. By the way, Böhme was released from jail the same evening and spent the night at home. Everybody is convinced that if he had left city hall without police protection the crowds would have certainly beaten him to death. In any case, what he experienced in the truck was not nearly as bad as what happened to our honest, unassuming Oberbürgermeister Retemeyer, who [in 1918] had been forced by the Reds to march at the head of parade holding the red flag. Those were also mean-spirited times when you didn't dare show yourself on the streets and when an overnight bag with Vati's essentials stood ready since we expected him to be arrested any day. All the things we have survived! When will Germany finally have peace and quiet! Hopefully the time has come with Hitler's strong hand at the helm. Vati has so much to do these days! Standing in for Böhme, standing in for Municipal Councilor S. who has been ill for months, not to speak of his own responsibilities.

Eberhard Gebensleben to his father Karl Gebensleben, Berlin, 15 March 1933

[. . .] According to the triumphant *Landeszeitung*, Böhme's ouster occurred in an extraordinarily dishonorable manner. For all the flying banners, you have to be blind not to see the rather large number of blemishes that have become visible. I have seen a few things myself. [. . .]

Irmgard Brester to her mother Elisabeth Gebensleben, Utrecht, 18 March 1933

[. . .] But first of all your very lovely and very detailed letter that, Muttilein, I enjoyed immensely. And do you know what? It was so great that it came on time and I could savor and "digest" it before answering. Your letters contain so much news and such interesting descriptions that you really must say they have to be "digested." After reading the sensational news about Böhme's dismissal in the newspaper, we thought a great deal about our loved ones. Well, the whole thing was foreseeable, but we really didn't wish Böhme an exit that was quite so dishonorable. After all, as a person he was not so unjust and in many ways he tried to do his best. And then all the excitement that our Vati had to witness firsthand. [. . .] Why was Böhme taken from city hall to prison rather than to his home? We are not very clear about that. And now Vati once again has so much work to do. What I would like to do is bring our two sweet little children to you for an hour or two to give you a break from all the stress and strain. And then the two of us could much more easily discuss all the questions that concern us so. [. . .] We simply want to believe with all our heart that Hitler will set things right. The whole world is now following developments in Germany with the greatest interest. Our newspapers are full of news from Germany. A great deal has been achieved, and Hitler's speeches themselves are always very striking, although ranters and ravers like Goebbels and Göring end up ruining so much. It is such a pity that they cast the entire Nazi movement in an unfavorable light. A lot of people came up to me after Goebbels's speech last Friday, which stations across Europe broadcast and in which he denounced all Jews as "scoundrels and swine." Sure there are Jews who are scoundrels, but one cannot forget all the great men among the Jews who contributed so much to the arts and sciences. No, this harassment is disgusting. I was just enraged when I read the story in one of the last *Landeszeitungen* that the Nazis simply jeered a concert in Leipzig. Fritz Busch is one of our great conductors, who is recognized at home and abroad and has certainly enhanced Germany's standing in the world. So why should he be booed? Because he is Jewish [Immo was wrong here] and has a political line that the Nazis don't support? These sorts of incidents I find catastrophic. I have to immediately think of Toscanini, who Mussolini kicked out of Italy because he didn't want to conduct a fascist song. Excesses of this kind have to be resisted because they do incredible damage to the image of the National Socialist party.

Well, that is enough about politics, which alone would fill up an entire letter. But I bet you want to hear about our two little ones who are such a delight and make us so happy. [. . .]

Minna von Alten to her granddaughter Irmgard Brester, Braunschweig, 19 March 1933

We live in such extraordinary times; may God provide Hitler the ability to control his followers. He himself is an idealist who wants only the best, who has no regard for his own interests, who lives only for his people. But ultimately in such a great movement there will always be hangers-on who focus on their own ideas and believe that anything goes. It is too bad that you can't listen to Hitler's speeches; the man is a born leader. Otherwise he would not have been able to bring about this great renewal. All eyes are focused on next Tuesday, Potsdam, the opening of the new Reichstag. Rooms with a view are supposed to have been already all rented out. Apparently, an American paid 800 marks for a room. I am relieved to know that you are reading the paper and therefore have an idea of what is happening. [. . .]

The newly elected Reichstag was sworn in on 21 March 1933, the same day that Bismarck inaugurated the first Reichstag of the Second Reich in 1871. The ceremony took place in Potsdam's Garnisonkirche since the burned-out Reichstag building in Berlin was unusable. High ranking military officials from the time of the Kaiser as well as the former Crown Prince in full-dress uniform were seated in the places of honor among leading Nazi, German Nationalist, and Catholic Center Party politicians. After greeting President Hindenburg in an uncharacteristically deferential manner, Hitler held a speech in which he celebrated "the marriage of the symbols of our ancient greatness and new strength." For many Germans, the spiritual reunion represented by this "Day of Potsdam" gave both Potsdam and the Garnisonkirche a special importance. After the ceremony, SA, SS, and Stahlhelm filed past Hitler, Hindenburg, and the Crown Prince. In the evening, tens of thousands of SA men marched in a torchlight procession through the old town while Wilhelm Furtwängler directed Richard Wagner's "Die Meistersinger" in the opera.

On 23 March, two days after the national spectacle, the Reichstag promulgated the "Law to Remedy the Distress of People and Reich," enabling legislation that gave Hitler emergency powers and suspended the constitution; only the Social Democrats, many of whom would soon find themselves in exile, voted against the law (Communist deputies had been banned, and their absence allowed the Nazis to secure the necessary two-thirds majority). In Braunschweig, interim Oberbürgermeister Karl Gebensleben held a speech in city hall in which, as the Braunschweigische Landeszeitung *reported on 24 March 1933, he said: "We are still standing under the spell of the celebration of our national renewal. I have assembled you here so that we, in the gravity of this moment, can collectively and unreservedly demonstrate our spiritual solidarity with the national movement. In this hour we want to swear our loyalty to the Reich President, the Reich government, and the German people. We want to solemnly pledge that each one of us will, to the best of our abilities, work to improve the lot of the German people and do so with a strict sense of duty and discipline. What we will have in mind are not the special interests of the individual, not the interests of party, but solely the good of the people. Whoever pursues personal interests or divides us with partisan coalitions sins against the Fatherland. Such a person is not carrying out the work of reconstruction; instead of*

building, he only destroys. However, if we loyally and conscientiously do our duty, we
will succeed in the task of national reconstruction. This should and must be our goal."

Elisabeth Gebensleben to her daughter Irmgard Brester, Braunschweig, 22 March 1933

[. . .] Vati is not yet home; rarely do we eat our evening meal before 8:30. Usually we don't sit down to lunch before 2:30. However, I am happy that Vati looks as good as he does given the many, difficult responsibilities he carries at the moment. My guess is that he is in his office right now working on the speech that he will deliver in his capacity as acting chief administrator [. . .] to all municipal civil servants in the council chambers tomorrow morning.

Today we are still completely in the shadow of yesterday's events. What a day, Immeken! I cannot even describe to you how we felt. Such a day of national celebration no doubt occurs very rarely in the history of a people; a day of tremendous national enthusiasm, the shouts of unrestrained joy; it was a day in which the greatest and most sacred parts of a nation, which had been in chains for many years, could freely express themselves and could pour out their deepest gratitude in boundless rejoicing. Vati and I savored the day to the fullest, participating in the official celebrations in Braunschweig and listening deeply moved to the radio, which broadcast the inspiring ceremonies in Berlin and Potsdam. First, in the morning, the hoisting of the flags. I so much wanted to fly the Hitler flag next to our good old German flag but on Monday there was not a single swastika flag to be found anywhere in the city. Indeed flags of any sort were sold out. I was just able to grab three little swastika pennants, which we successfully tied on. What a sea of flags surged through the streets of the city! At noon, with all the church bells tolling, Vati and I stood on the Schlossplatz where the Reichswehr's field service took place, followed by the grand parade of all the associations, the Reichswehr, the Stahlhelm, the security police, the SA and SS. It was a wonderful sight—all the more festive in the bright sunshine. Vati and I had very good seats, right behind the commander, who at the end of the ceremony reviewed the formations that marched in a proper Potsdamer goose step. Well the French would have just been overjoyed had they seen the sight. It was a delight to see the troops pass by: the Reichswehr came first, then the police, then the Stahlhelm, and at the end the National Socialists. Joy turned to enthusiasm and passion when the swastika-emblazoned flags were carried past, the band leading with the Horst-Wessel song; hats flew off heads, arms rose in salute. After the parade we sat for about an hour with several city officials and their wives in the "Glass Box" [Café Lück], watching the colorful life on the streets. Fat Councilor K. was just beside himself with joy; he was the only innkeeper who ever showed the courage to fly the old black-white-red flag, although his windows were constantly smashed in as a consequence. He refused to serve Severing when he visited Braunschweig. By the way, Vati took a number of photographs of the house all decorated with flags, inside too. If they are good, I will send them to you. Vati left again to join the torchlight parade in the evening, a grand affair. Ohmchen and I sat by the radio to take in the boundless rejoicing in Berlin and Potsdam. Today I will listen to the ceremony in the Garnisonkirche one more time on records. It must have been incredibly moving. The field marshal from the World War and the ordinary front soldier, now both the leaders of their people. What a blessing it is that Hindenburg has found his way back to the people, whom he had to some extent lost touch with. I wonder what he must be thinking when he listens to the words of Hitler, whom he mistrusted for so long, having seen only the caricature painted by his enemies. In Potsdam, even the largest police presence was not enough to hold the crowds back. The people simply broke through, and Hitler with his head bared only slowly made his way forward, step by step. The German people are living through great times, and every day I am grateful that I am alive to witness them.

The flags have now been lowered, the cries of the crowds have died down, and the difficult task of reconstruction begins. A government that so enjoys the confidence of the people will succeed, but it needs to apply an iron fist. And Hitler has to be extremely careful not to endanger his movement. Suddenly the Communists want to become National Socialists; they are already burning their red flags. Of course, that is unacceptable. First they have to undergo a three-year probation in a concentration camp. Same goes for the Social Democrats. Every day we hear about people leaving the party, as if they have suddenly discovered their National Socialist heart. Even M., who always opposed National Socialism, is now totally on fire. I said to him the other day: "It doesn't take a lot of talent to declare oneself for National Socialism now; it was different before, when the movement was scorned, maligned, and prohibited. Those who showed the courage of their convictions were the true supporters."

The slipups and excesses that you write about, Immeken, can't be endorsed, but they are understandable in a time of struggle such as this one, when the life or death of the nation is at stake. I could just write on and on. We should soon discuss all this between the two of us, right, Immeken?

[. . .] Our young man will have seen a great deal these last days. Four [of his six] weeks have already passed. Hopefully he will report that he is coming along well. I am constantly thinking about him. [. . .] Vati just called to say that he will be late. The newspapers have already asked him for the speech he will give tomorrow. So, Immeken, you will be able to read it as well. I already know what he is going to say; last night Vati brought it home to recite and we talked about it. [. . .]

THURSDAY AFTERNOON

I just heard Hitler's long speech in *today's* Reichstag session. Immo, what a man he is! The whole world complains about the so-called world economic crisis yet would be well advised to heed this outstanding man! And the *illustrated* newspapers are finally out now. Could you please save the two issues for me?

Irmgard Brester to her grandmother Minna von Alten, Utrecht, 24 March 1933

[. . .] Mutti describes everything in such detail and the newspapers bring so many enthusiastic reports that it is hard to get "through it all." [. . .] Mutti really has to come for a visit soon; you just can't discuss all the questions that concern us in letters. She would also be able to relax and recuperate. [. . .] It is already so wonderful outside, today is a beautiful bright sunny day, the crocuses and snowdrops are blooming everywhere, and picturesque flower carts filled with daffodils and tulips drive up and down the streets. [. . .]

Very quickly, anti-Semitic incidents grew in number and gravity across Germany. Hitler used the ensuing protests from abroad and scattered calls no longer to buy German goods as a justification to call for a general boycott of Jewish businesses. On Saturday, 1 April 1933, SA and SS troops stood guard in front of Jewish shops, harassing customers who attempted to cross Nazi cordons, and scrawling anti-Semitic graffiti on the windows. On 31 March 1933, the Braunschweigische Landeszeitung *announced the boycott in the following manner:* "GERMANY'S DEFENSIVE ACTION—STAND AGAINST DESECRATORS OF GERMANY'S HONOR! *Saturday morning at exactly 10 o'clock a defensive action will take place in our city, the severity of which has been determined by the despicable nature of the tirade of Jewish lies. Not a single customer will be able to enter Jewish department stores, shops, or sales agencies without first encountering the guardians of German national defense." The son-in-law of Frau M. to whom Immo referred had already been harassed several times for being a Jew.*

Elisabeth Gebensleben to her daughter Irmgard Brester, Braunschweig, 30 March 1933

[. . .] There is still quite a bit on my mind that I have to unload before I can think about something as nice as a trip to Utrecht. Aside from domestic unrest [. . .] there is the constant worry about our Eberhard.

[. . .] The Marxist poison has really contaminated people. News reports about German atrocities published in the foreign press are simply absurd. Because I know *how* absurd they are, I can't even get worked up about it. However, I certainly can get worked up about German traitors who are no longer even Germans. The Jews will feel firsthand the damage their kind has caused abroad and even here. Until now not a hair on the head of a Jew has been touched, and let us hope it stays that way. But ultimately the wrath of the nation will grow immensely, and if Hitler didn't have his iron fist, who knows if he would be able to contain his enormous following. I have great confidence in Hitler. Immeken, these political matters have no end once one gets started. I will tell you a lot more in person. [. . .]

Irmgard Brester to her mother Elisabeth Gebensleben, Utrecht, 3 April 1933

[. . .] how nice that Mimi also longs to see our dear little Schatzis; then hopefully she will come soon to visit us. Of course, you still have to digest the latest events, and Eberhard has to complete his state examinations. [. . .] People here in general all have their two cents to add when German politics are being discussed. If only you would realize how much indignation Germany arouses around the world with the horrible persecution of the Jews! Just in the last weeks a great deal of the newly won friendliness toward Germany has been spoiled. What I can tell you is that businesses no longer buy German goods; when I visited Utrecht's annual trade fair hardly a German booth could be seen. The Jews are fleeing over the border in masses, and if they haven't actually been the victims of violence, they have been fleeced of their livelihoods. There are a great many good Germans among them, who are now so outraged that they speak out against Germany. And I really can't blame them! The son-in-law of Frau M., of course a Jew himself, sought refuge here with his young wife and baby. He is a lawyer in Berlin and one day he found 2 SA men in front of his door barring any clients who wanted to consult him from entering. Isn't that scandalous? What is such a man supposed to do? He is simply being driven out of his Fatherland. I find this downright shocking, and many, many others cannot condone such "measures" either. Of course, you can't call this sort of thing an "atrocity," but what is the difference? Despite all the efforts of the Nazi press, these are facts that cannot be simply whitewashed. And there are many thousands of such cases, despite all the nice declarations about the Nazis' "desire for peace." You just can't take them seriously. The struggle against Communism was good, but this Jew-baiting is mean and ugly. There are enough nasty fellows among Christians, aren't there? Just where is this going to lead?

Now I want to finally give politics a rest; we can debate these matters for hours. I really enjoyed your lovely letter. So you approve of our vacation plans? [. . .] It is so wonderful to look forward to something as lovely as a summer trip! [. . .]

Elisabeth Gebensleben to her daughter Irmgard Brester, Braunschweig, 6 April 1933

[. . .] Did the thick package of illustrateds with the special edition, *The Day in Potsdam*, arrive yet? Do please mention it to me.

[. . .] Herr S. comes from Silesia, lives now in Breslau. He once had a wonderful large estate, but he wasn't able to hold on to it. His son now works as a *caretaker* on the old estate. 5 M. a day is what he gets, on which he has to support himself and his elderly father. As a government economist, Herr S. used to play a leading role in Silesian agriculture, and he fully understands the conditions there. According to him, of the 111 old noble estates that once existed only three remain self-sufficient. Every other one has been destroyed and wrecked. It certainly takes unbelievable strength and determination on the part of the national government to set about rebuilding the field of rubble that Social Democracy has left behind; the first order of business for Germany is a huge cleanup operation. The National Socialists are exposing everything; the degree of embezzlement and misappropriation that has now come to light is just unbelievable. No one will be spared, not even a Center Party figure such as Vice President Esser. The time we are now living through will undoubtedly be properly judged only by posterity. What we are making is world history. But world history is bigger than the fate of individuals, and that is what makes this moment, so noble and pure in its *aims*, so difficult—alongside *happiness*, compassion for *individual misfortune*. That goes for the lot of an individual Jew as well, but doesn't change our appreciation of the Jewish Question as such. The Jewish Question is as important a global issue as Communism, and if Hitler wants to take it on, just as he is doing with Communism, and he achieves his aim, then maybe Germany will again be the envy of the world. Undoubtedly the SA men stood in front of Herr M.'s door only last Saturday, the day of the Jewish boycott. This was a day to answer the smear campaign against Germany, which the Jews together with the Marxists have carried out. All the atrocity tales of ears cut off, of mutilated corpses of Jews are simply *pure fabrications*; Germany is defending itself with the only weapon it has. In any case, that some Jews are being removed from their posts in the judiciary, in medicine *also*, makes national economic sense, however hard it might effect an innocent individual. It was the German people who lost the right to exist as a result of the Versailles Treaty, and nature won't let itself be violated with impunity. A nation of 65 million, which possesses so much energy, cannot allow itself to be oppressed over the long run. It is completely understandable that Germany makes it a priority to look out for the future of its own sons. The Jews should remain in their positions according to their proportion to the total population of Germany. That is one percent of the population. And how much do they have by now! They know how to push themselves into all the professions, just as they know how to freeload all over the world. No one can deny that they are clever. Vati provided the example of the Jew K., who, before he was removed, had arranged to hold three positions simultaneously, each one of which could have fed an entire family. The Jews want to rule, not serve. Have you ever heard of a Jewish maid or a Jewish laundry woman? The proof: Frieda's former friend has long been employed by the Jew B. In Frieda's presence, he told the two girls: "Do you think that we Jews would hire *Jewish* girls as help? That would *really be a shame.* Serving is something you Christians can do. You are just cattle to us." To be sure, there are certainly many noble Jews, and I personally am not mean-spirited; the Jews in Germany are undoubtedly not being treated as badly as is suggested. What barrages of lies we are forced to endure. Just take the big war guilt question, which not a single person takes seriously anymore. Then the atrocity stories from the war, the hands of children cut off in Belgium, and all other such fairy tales. This is just a new installment. They must really fear the German people if they try again and again to cut us down to size. The *best* always meets the *most* resistance, a timeworn truth but also a consolation. We very much appreciate that we have the sympathy of Italy, a nation that through its own efforts and with determined leadership now stands firm and powerful; however, we are more than happy to do without the sympathy of France, Belgium, or Poland. As long as Germany allowed itself to be sucked dry, we enjoyed all the sympathy in the world. That we may have lost this sympathy is hardly a *bad* sign. What did Hitler say? "I want to advance the fortunes of the Germans to such an extent that other nations will think it worthwhile to stay in our good graces." Hitler has always made good on his promises.

Well, well, Immeken, politics! There is no end to it, and since we are in the thick of it, we live and breathe politics completely. Every day comes with new surprises, new events. People come up to me all the time to say: "That your husband is able to endure such difficult times!" It makes me proud. But Vati is now a cause of concern for me. The second cause of concern lives in Berlin. [. . .]

Last Sunday, Frieda and her fiancé went home to attend her brother's confirmation. Communists live in their building and threatened to disrupt the confirmation celebration. And in fact Communists suddenly pushed their way in with shotguns and two axes. Frieda's father, a Stahlhelm man, was badly wounded by an ax to his head. When Frieda grabbed the ax, she was hit on her chest and back, and her arm was injured as well. She was just here, but has gone to Thiede and is really quite shaken. Every night she wakes up and sees the same horrible scene: her father standing there covered in blood and talking like a mad man. She doesn't even know how her father is doing now. She was just here with her fiancé, then off to the doctor again; she is completely incapable of working. I saw right away that she had a temperature. The injuries are healing alright, but now she has strep throat.

All the things that I could still tell you, Immeken, but now I am really going to come to an end. [. . .]

Tonight Hitler addresses the "foreign press." I *definitely* have to hear that.

August Brester to his parents-in-law Karl and Elisabeth Gebensleben, Utrecht, 7 April 1933

[. . .] We also admired the lovely photographs of Kaiser-Wilhelm Strasse and share your happiness that the black-white-red flag ones again flies over Germany! Even if we are not at all in agreement with everything that is happening in Germany today.

[IMMO CONTINUED]

[. . .] Your dear letter gave us great joy, many, many thanks. With the Easter egg dyes you fulfilled a secret wish. [. . .] And poor Frieda! I am terribly sorry for her, and for you, Muttichen, now that you are without help. [. . .] The typewriter is too slow and cumbersome for me to prepare a detailed exposition on the Jewish Question! So enough for today and I hope we can rely on a Braunschweig [radio] audience on Thursday.

Elisabeth Gebensleben to her daughter Irmgard Brester, Braunschweig, 11 April 1933

[. . .] The Holland letter stays put until Vati and I are sitting comfortably at the coffee table on Sunday morning when we can savor it as a Sunday treat.

[. . .] I can't say whether the current situation in Germany will pose problems for a trip. Time is rushing by with such speed, brings so many changes, that you don't know today what tomorrow will bring. It is clear that these events get on your nerves. Just today Vati commented: "So much is happening, it is almost too much to take." For Vati especially. As soon as Vati comes home, the two of us spend a long time reporting, discussing, deliberating, even if it is 12 o'clock at night. Yesterday was the third Sunday that Vati spent working in city hall until 2:00 in the afternoon. How the sun tempted us to take a walk! Vati was so exhausted that he just went right to bed. [. . .]

So, Immeken, Thursday another concert from Utrecht! Vati bought a [radio] program right away, and we already found the listing for Utrecht's women's choir. And will we be in the audience? Well, Immeken, you can rely on *that*! [. . .]

Irmgard Brester to her mother Elisabeth Gebensleben, Utrecht, 12 April 1933

[. . .] I am pleased that you often go to the theater, especially for the sake of Vati, who really needs distractions once in a while. Incidentally, the young K.'s spoke about conditions in Germany very calmly and objectively, and I was pleased that they were not at all in agreement with the disgusting persecution of the Jews. Frau K. added that she found it terrible that all the little Jewish shop owners and also the elderly Jewish civil servants have to suffer while the big Jewish entrepreneurs and industrialists stashed their capital abroad long ago.

Karl Gebensleben to his wife Elisabeth Gebensleben [in Utrecht], Braunschweig, 28 April 1933

[. . .] So Thursday at noon I had to cancel the city council meeting at the request of Klagges because of new circumstances (due to the defection of the German Nationalists). Now it might take a while. Since Zörner also left on Tuesday for Berlin and came back only last night, we will be able to complete our application to the NSDAP only today (naturally yours too). I will drop you a line tonight. By now you will have read the schedule of events for Monday, 1 May. We have to be ready already at 7:00 in the morning. I am sure that we will *not* be able to get out of the torchlight parade. [. . .]

Karl Gebensleben to his daughter Irmgard Brester, Braunschweig, 28 April 1933

[. . .] Please inform Mutti that Dr. Hesse won't take care of the application until tomorrow. I had written Mutti this morning that it would already be done today.

Well, well, Immo, all the things that have changed since you were here in the fall. But isn't it wonderful, how unified the upheaval has been! Also tell Mutti that the business of 1 May will not be so strenuous after all; I heard that after 9 o'clock everyone is free to go. The evening torchlight parade will also be made easier. But *Mutti* can simply stay longer with you. She won't miss anything. Really, I am doing *very* well. [. . .]

On 31 March and 7 April 1933, laws were promulgated by which the state parliaments were organized exactly as the Reichstag; a Reichsstatthalter was appointed to every state to insure that state legislation conformed to national interests. On 29 April, Braunschweig's Landtag convened for the first time; the new government was the first in Germany to be constituted completely by National Socialists. Before the convocation, the parliamentarians marched in uniform to the cathedral so that their new strength might be blessed by a church service, which was held by Pastor Schlott.

For nearly fifty years, workers had celebrated 1 May as Labor Day (Tag der Nationalen Arbeit), although it was never recognized officially as a holiday; in 1933, the Nazis renamed 1 May as a "Day of National Labor." Goebbels organized a huge mass celebration on Berlin's Tempelhofer Feld. The day after this "commemoration," the Nazis raided trade-union offices, banned independent unions, and confiscated their property. Many trade-union leaders were arrested and sent to concentration camps; others fled the country. Thereupon the Nazis established the German Labor Front in which most workers were required to enroll.

In a speech on the occasion of the first city council meeting after the political coordination of Reich, state, and city, Karl Gebensleben, as reported by the Braunschweigische Landeszeitung *on 5 May 1933, exclaimed:*

The times of political confusion are fortunately over. After the German people clearly decided in the Reichstag elections of 5 March to put their unshakeable faith in the Reich government led by our highly esteemed Herr Reich Chancellor and People's Chancellor Adolf Hitler, it was necessary to achieve a coordination of Reich, state, and local parliaments. Only in this way is it possible to guarantee that a unity of opinion can be expressed at all levels of the state structure.

This unity will insure that useless, unproductive partisan conflicts will be banished from this hall once and for all. Time and energy will therefore be made available for fruitful work, for the work of renewing the German people.

Gentlemen! The words of Adolf Hitler should illuminate even the work of municipal agencies: "We want to build a genuine community out of Germany's tribes, out of its estates and professions, and out of its previously existing classes." The work of reconstruction must enable a just reconciliation of our vital interests, which is what the future of our entire people requires. Farmers, workers, and the bourgeoisie will once again become a single, united people.

In the meantime, Elisabeth Gebensleben joined the Movement of German Christians, which had been established in 1932. The German Christians adhered to the Führer principle and to the National Socialist worldview and sought a purified national evangelical church from which Germans of Jewish origin would be excluded.

In Utrecht, Immo continued to follow events in Braunschweig with interest, but it became more and more clear to her that her mother's obsession with political developments gave her little opportunity to learn more about what was happening to friends and family. At the same time, Immo's time was increasingly monopolized by her two children, her singing lessons, and the cultural events that also interested August whenever he could find time in his busy schedule as head of the department of internal medicine. An additional burden was the serious illness of Immo's mother-in-law, Henriette Brester, who died on 26 May 1933.

Elisabeth Gebensleben to her daughter Irmgard Brester, Braunschweig, 4 May 1933

[. . .] I am back in the thick of things: the wonderful days in Holland lie behind me like a graceful dream. My trip home went well; it was really quite beautiful. First the journey through Holland's spring and then the journey into Germany's. Everywhere the soft fresh green and the blossoming splendor of the fruit trees. In addition to that, our wonderfully adorned country. I never imagined that it was quite *so* decorated. Just take the train stations; sprigs of fir and birch on all the buildings; the little crossing keepers' cottages and signal shacks of the crossing keepers. And the small villages! Fir sprigs strung over the streets, bouquets of flags, everywhere flags and more flags; processions across the countryside and cheering crowds who greeted the train with upraised arms. What a special experience it was to ride for hours through such a festive country. Hanover was downright amazing, and then old Braunschweig! Vati and Frieda were on hand to welcome me. I hardly recognized our train station; Vati added: "M. hauled down about half the trees in the Harz." An hour later, I was sitting at home by the radio; I passed on your greetings, talked about you, and took out the photographs. Did you hear anything about the huge demonstration? It is hard to get a sense of how formidable it was from the radio. You have to watch for the photographs in the extra edition of the *Berliner Illustrierte*. I will try and lay my hands on an issue, which hopefully will not be seized at the border as a "danger to public safety." You have to show Dr. Hingst the issue; maybe then he will get a faint idea of what is happening in Germany. What nation has ever seen quite anything so huge, so inspiring. Everybody who really experienced a day like Germany's 1 May in all its grandeur stands high above all the resentful, envious, and slanderous claptrap circulating abroad. Water off a duck's back. What really is representative is probably the photograph of old Hindenburg in the "Berliner." He speaks with such glowing enthusiasm! He seems twenty years younger! It is not only the young who are thrilled by the idealistic figure of Hitler; the older generation is also completely taken by him. It is too bad that by the end of 1 May Hitler had become so hoarse. But is that so surprising? He sacrifices himself completely. Soon nature will not be able to keep up with his spirit. After the radio demonstration, Vati and I went out to the L.'s, you know who live out by Richmond on the big Jahnplatz, where the torches were thrown into huge piles. It was a grand sight! For hours, the torchbearers passed by, and for hours, the Wolfenbütteler Strasse resembled a great big wide sea of light. The torchbearers marched 16 abreast; they filled the entire width of the street. Just imagine, Immeken, the broad river of light without end advancing for hours at the same steady pace. It was an unforgettable sight. Vati and I got home around 1:30, tired but happy. It took us about 1½ hours to get home; of course we walked. The trams couldn't get through at all, and we had our difficulties as well. In the end, we had to detour around the entire Charlottenhöhe. Most of all you have to admire the incredible discipline of the masses of people. Certainly a singular achievement. Is it really true that *one* man has brought about all this, to weld together a people that had been so divided and miserable! Aunt Minna was deeply moved to see our duke [Ernst August von Braunschweig] march along with his two sons.

Well, I really have to stop writing about the great events our nation is going through. Don't be angry, Immeken, if I just go on and on. The days since my return have flown by; yesterday I was in the city council chambers, where the new council was ceremoniously inaugurated. Afterward, Vati told me again and again how happy he was that I was there. Vati acquitted his duties wonderfully, dignified and extremely well turned-out in his appearance and in his public performance and just overall. The only stately figure in the midst of so much new blood. I just had to keep looking at Vati. I was thinking about how difficult it must be for someone of his age to completely readjust himself and to get things right in utterly new circumstances; it was all I could do to hold back my tears. [. . .]

Elisabeth Gebensleben to her daughter Irmgard Brester, Braunschweig, 12 May 1933

[. . .] Today the ministerial swearing-in ceremony in the white room of the castle; Vati was officially invited. The whole affair was pretty strenuous. I stood on the same spot for 1¾ hours. It was particularly tiring for Vati because as a guest of honor he stood in the front row and really had to keep up his bearing. The new governor is supposed to be an outstanding person. That is Vati's opinion as well. Incidentally, I don't want to write about politics; otherwise, I will never come to an end. Yesterday I attended the first big conference of the "Movement of German Christians." The church is to be reformed as well. I am delighted. The association "Friends of Evangelical Freedom" dissolved itself. I just got word. [. . .]

> *On 17 May, Hitler gave a major speech in which he emphasized his commitment to a peace-loving German foreign policy (the so-called Peace Declaration). He asserted his support for disarmament as long as the other powers disarmed as well. In the meantime, however, Germany was rearming at full speed. The same day, the* Braunschweigische Landeszeitung *reprinted excerpts from an article in* Le Petit Parisien, *which appeared under the headline "Hitler's Brownshirts Constitute a Military Formation" ("Les formations hitlériennes ont un charactère militaire"). The* Landeszeitung *commented: "France has let the cat out of the bag! Forged photographs accompany the smear campaign against Germany!"*
>
> *In Austria Chancellor Engelbert Dollfuss (1892–1934) suspended parliamentary democracy in order to battle both National Socialists and Social Democrats. He was murdered during an unsuccessful Nazi putsch on 25 July 1934.*

Elisabeth Gebensleben to her daughter Irmgard Brester, Braunschweig, 17 May 1933

[. . .] I've turned the radio on very low, just heard the incredibly lovely "Invitation to the Dance" [Carl Maria von Weber] and am waiting for the program notes. Our Hitler's upcoming speech is on my mind. Originally the broadcast was scheduled for 3 o'clock, then delayed until 5 o'clock, so now I have to pay close attention! Today is a very important day. The whole world is waiting with bated breath to hear the German Chancellor. He is not simply addressing millions, but *hundreds* of millions. Do you know, Immo, that nowadays I can hardly think of that man without tears coming to my eyes? It doesn't seem possible that a single individual has so much energy! And just think, Immo, a simple man of the people, a man who fought in the trenches of the world war as an ordinary soldier! He became the leader of a nation of 65 million; he will become the leader of the world. Perhaps you are laughing now, Immo. But I always knew he would become Germany's savior and that at a time when the Marxists wanted to drive him out of the country with a bullwhip, and now I do believe he will be the savior for all the world. If only they would make the effort to listen to him and understand him! He is dauntless. I was constantly thinking of him when I recently attended *Siegfried*, who was supposed to learn how to fear but *couldn't* do so. On top of that the *farsightedness* and the most pure truthfulness! *Fearless* and *truthful*, that is how his speech today will be. And even if Germany's enemies later distort so many things, on this day all the foreigners who listen to him, who really do so without being misguided by the press, will be taken in by his *overwhelming personality*. The other day Pastor Schlott compared Hitler to Luther, emphasizing their common character. Today the comparison imposes itself once more: Luther was proscribed and banned for his truthfulness, Hitler sat imprisoned behind fortress walls. Luther appeared before the Reichstag and all his mighty enemies, princes and bishops, and explained: "Here I stand, I can do no other, so help me God." Hitler stands before the world that has resolved to oppose him, but he stands resolved to tell the *truth*. What nation can point to a figure who can even remotely be compared to him! Except Italy! Mussolini! So you can well imagine how *our* Hitler makes us *proud* and how he is loved by his people as no other previous kaiser or statesman ever was. *He* wants peace, and if France, which has become the dictator of Europe, attempts to make Germany responsible for the breakdown of negotiations, then it is France that will have to take the blame on account of its treacherous game. Germans have only contempt for the French and their pathetic cowardliness. If a nation that is armed to the teeth constantly berates a defenseless nation for imperiling its security, then one can really only laugh with contempt. Already during the war the French were known for their cowardice in contrast to the English, for example, but their behavior now is just plain preposterous. Vati had a good laugh while he was still in bed this morning flipping through the *Landeszeitung*, which carried a photograph from the French newspapers: "The German SA." The gentlemen should at least bother to come to Germany and take a look at our SA so they can at least *properly* falsify the photographs. *No* swastika flag looks like that and *no* one would hold a rifle as it is so wonderfully depicted. And really—the SA have never worn sashes. And I've never seen the SA march with *rifles* in such a way except when law and order had to be reestablished after Communist putsch attempts. Frieda, who through her fiancé frequently associates with these people, said the other day that most of them (I would tone this down to *many*) don't even know how to handle a revolver. But these men have a martial bearing: discipline and immense enthusiasm. These are great assets. But they are certainly *not* battle-ready soldiers; only a minority are trained to handle weapons. Otherwise you would have to count our forest wardens as actual soldiers!

Austria now faces the struggle that we survived. It probably won't be long before *National Socialism* gains the upper hand there as well. No Dollfuss can stop that. National Socialism is nothing for self-serving creatures; its basic principle is "the public interest *before* private interest"! That is why it faces such a difficult struggle to establish itself. But finally an end to politics, I know that I am not supposed to get started because I don't know when to stop. But, Immo, out of the abundance of the heart. . . ! [. . .]

In the meantime, we heard the *Chancellor's speech*, as did the rest of the world. Have I said too much already, Immo? This man is so overwhelming, he could become the *leader of the world*, rising out of the misery of all people, who in the end have all been sucked into our crisis. Being able to perceive the reasons why so clearly, he can show the path to recovery. Immo, you have to read the speech *twice*. It is so rich in ideas, and it provides *answers* to *so many* questions. I don't think anyone can distort this speech. Immo, in recent years, when the rest of the world was inclined to see us favorably on account of our weakness, I sometimes felt ashamed to be a German, and I was ashamed that the German people appeared to be so weak. Now I am once more proud to be German, indeed completely *uninhibitedly proud*! Mistakes will happen, but *nothing* can dent this pride of mine. Matters of secondary importance disappear in the face of the big issues at hand. [. . .]

Irmgard Brester to her mother Elisabeth Gebensleben, Utrecht, 19 May 1933

[. . .] First let me thank you many times for being so kind to write in such detail. You know how interested I am. I am finally sending along the photographs that really turned out cute, a nice remembrance of our walks together. The ones of "Mimi" turned out the best! [. . .] By the way, the vacations are really approaching quickly. Has Mimi gotten everything ready? [. . .]

First of all Hitler's big speech, which was also eagerly awaited here. It was all over the papers, which responded to Hitler's words very appreciatively. But now words have to be followed by deeds, and we can only hope that he can count on the cooperation and not the opposition of the other nations as he realizes his plans. There can be no doubt that Hitler is a very extraordinary individual with outstanding talents and deep insight into the soul of the German nation, something not even the sharpest opponents dispute—yes, an individual in public life such as Hitler makes enemies, that is par for the course. In any case, fact is that Hitler's latest speech compensated for some of the good will that Germany had lost around the world. [. . .]

Karl Gebensleben to his daughter Irmgard Brester, Braunschweig, 25 May 1933

Ascension Day is going to be a day when we can really relax. Actually we had planned it differently: we wanted to travel to Hohegeiss with Hardus. [. . .] But Hardus is on strike, he can't afford to be "out of work" for 4 days. [. . .]

We are so looking forward to your visit. The preparations are in full swing. Well, you will certainly be astonished at how much has changed. Strict discipline in public and economic life prevails in all precincts. Politically binding, the leadership principle has been enforced at all levels. There is no more parliamentarism, there are no more compromises. Everybody is duty-bound to follow the Führer and the leaders. Coordination has been accomplished down to the smallest detail, which is extremely important if radical restructuring is to be carried out. However, in time, a loyal opposition modeled on English parliamentarism might be allowed. Time will tell.

Friday last week, Mutti and I were admitted into the NSDAP along with a large number of prominent elites (ministers, directors, nobles, former leaders of the German Nationalists, etc.). A handshake made us duty-bound to show absolute allegiance to the Führer. At Monday's city council meeting every city parliamentarian as well as the entire city council showed up in a brownshirt—complete unity. Our unity is so complete that in the future some 90% of all council motions will no longer need to be discussed in parliament but will be taken care of in committee. As a result, time and energy will be available for productive work.

And so your "old" Vati had to quickly acquire brownshirt, cap and visor, belt, tie, and party pin. Mutti thinks that the uniform suits me well and makes me look decades(?) younger!!! Oh!!! Well, well, dear August, if someone would have predicted this! But it is uplifting to see the discipline that makes everyone exert themselves to serve the Fatherland—strictly according to the principle *Public Interest before Private Interest*. If today incidents of corruption cases are being uncovered here and there, that is usually because this principle is applied retroactively even for the *past* when it did not yet apply, when private interests took precedence. Where does this apply anywhere else in the world (take America, for example!)?

Well, I don't want to talk politics anymore—but you have to give me some space so you can get to know my opinions.

Strenuous weeks and months lie behind me, which have cost me *a great deal* of work and worry. One had to adjust oneself, and the older one is, the harder it is! Ultimately there was the question whether I would be allowed to continue to lead the city administration while the restructuring (revolution) was being carried out. My nerves were often heavily tested, and I am happy to say that they stood the test. But now I do want to be relieved by a permanent Oberbürgermeister, the sooner the better because in the long run it really is a load to bear. [. . .]

Irmgard Brester to her parents Karl and Elisabeth Gebensleben, Utrecht, 26 May 1933

Our poor dear Moes has now been released. [. . .] We spent as much time as possible with her over the last days, and even last night she still recognized us. [. . .] We haven't quite realized that this boundlessly generous, faithful soul is no more and that those eyes, which always looked at us with such joy and heartwarming love, are now closed forever. [. . .]

Jan Brester to his son August Brester and daughter-in-law Irmgard Brester (in Italy), Utrecht, 11 July 1933

[. . .] How wonderful that you have found a peaceful, beautiful spot where the weather is warm. It's fortunate the government allowed you to travel there. Lucky for you! It's probably because they both [Hitler and Mussolini] wear such filthy shirts as their badge of honor! [. . .]

In summer 1933 the terror in Braunschweig claimed more lives. On the night of 29 June, two SS men conducting a raid on publishers of illegal pamphlets bumped into each other. They immediately began shooting in the darkness with the result that one SS man was killed. The press claimed that he had been killed by Communists. Klagges used this incident to launch a new wave of violence. Eleven people were shot in the nearby suburb of Rieseberg in "retaliation for the murder of an SS man." Reports of torture and murder continued to pile up, prompting Reichsstatthalter Leopold to open an investigation. The death of a Polish Jew under torture also led to renewed international protests.

Karl and Elisabeth Gebensleben with their
Dutch grandchildren Hedda and Marleen
(Braunschweig, July 1933)

In the Netherlands, the NSB or Nationaal-Socialistische Beweging gained more and more supporters. At the first national convention in Utrecht on 7 January 1933, six hundred out of the movement's thousand members appeared; ten months later, at the second convention, more than six thousand showed up, which the Braunschweigische Landeszeitung *reported on closely.*

Eberhard reported to one of the SA's military sport camps in which paramilitary exercises did in fact take place. Meanwhile, Karl and Elisabeth were obligated to appear at every one of the many official functions held by the new city government, something they found increasingly wearisome.

Irmgard Brester to her mother Elisabeth Gebensleben, Utrecht, 23 August 1933

[. . .] We talk so often about you and the wonderful days we spent in Braunschweig. [. . .] Hedda fully realizes that we are now far away from Braunschweig, even if her idea of Holland is simply our home. Long after we had crossed, Hedda still kept saying she wanted to go to Holland, to the delight of the other passengers, and only when we arrived at the front door did she explain: "Now Hedda Holland." [. . .]

Ursula Meier to her grandmother Minna von Alten, Utrecht, 29 August 1933

[. . .] The canal and harbor cruise left at 2 o'clock. The man at the wheel provided explanations, but Immo and August had to translate most of it because the Amsterdam Dutch is really something else again. It was totally interesting to sail in between the old houses against which the water laps so that the foundations are all rather decayed. We passed the tower where the fishermen's wives used to watch for their men, the oldest houses in Amsterdam, the Mint Tower, under the oldest bridge—we often had fine views of the most narrow streets—and finally through the Jewish Quarter, where it was market day. It was very interesting. Our captain remarked that Hitler was now well acquainted with them. At the end we arrived in the harbor, which reminded me a great deal of Hamburg, except that when we were there it was damp and chilly. With their yellow smokestacks, the huge East Indies liners were especially interesting. However many of them are decommissioned—the overall world crisis. We saw a German ship as well—it was an especially good feeling to see the swastika flying here! The cruise lasted 1½ hours, and we were able to see a great deal of Amsterdam.

Elisabeth Gebensleben to her daughter Irmgard Brester, Braunschweig, 30 August 1933

[. . .] Vati left for Nuremberg today, envied by all those who have heard so much about it and can't go. A few days ago Vati received an invitation from the national party to attend a gathering of all the Oberbürgermeisters in Nuremberg. The big party rally follows on Saturday and Sunday. That will be a fabulous event on a scale one cannot even imagine. Fortunately Vati received a room assignment in Nuremberg, otherwise it would not have been possible to find accommodation. Vati will experience so much! After the rally in Nuremberg, he travels to Frankfurt am Main on Tuesday for a conference to promote cities. [. . .] Hardus and I wanted to take advantage of these days to make a small holiday in the moorlands. [. . .]

Elisabeth Gebensleben to her daughter Irmgard Brester, Braunschweig, 7 September 1933

[. . .] One night we ate with 6 strapping lads from the moors in the tavern of the inn. Eberhard fetched his accordion, which one of the lads played. What an evening, I wouldn't have traded it for an evening in the theater. We sat in the simple tavern on our last night as well. We sat at a table with several SA men; one of them had just returned from Nuremberg. He didn't sleep for three days, but all the same you should have just *heard* everything *he* had to say! *Our Hitler!* "They offered to put him up in Nuremberg's castle where kings used to stay, a fine hotel as well, but he said: 'I will stay with my SA.'" With his SA he slept in the tent city. These are thousands of SA men who would go through fire for their Führer. Another SA man, also a deeply tanned local fellow, told us about the Day of Potsdam: "We were standing in front of our tent washing ourselves. Suddenly Hitler is standing in our midst. 'Good morning, lads, did you sleep well?' I will never forget that for the rest of my life," the fellow added. He had tears in his eyes as he spoke. [. . .]

Elisabeth Gebensleben to her daughter Irmgard Brester, Braunschweig, 15 September 1933

[. . .] A letter arrived from the SA Office of Higher Education to which Eberhard had applied, hoping to enlist in a military training camp (after all he can't sit around without doing something); his parents wait; finally he arrived yesterday afternoon at 5:00 in awful weather. [. . .] Yesterday at 5:30, Hardus opened the letter regarding the military sport camp, and this evening—Immo, make sure you are sitting down—he is already in Camp Zossen near Berlin. Now you can imagine, Immo, the bustle of activity at our house until late at night. Packing up all his things, many of them obligatory, telephoning to Berlin, because Hardus wanted to attend the first camp session, which began today, since the second one only begins in mid-October; then telephoning a doctor who was able to give him a checkup at 8 o'clock in order to provide him a certificate of good health. In between, a friend of Eberhard's showed up. Still, we are going to make it. The last things packed, Eberhard left the station with his heavy bags at 7:15 the next morning. [. . .]

This morning, of course, we got an early start; by 11 o'clock Vati and I were sitting in Frau Geheimrat B.'s car; she had invited us for a drive to Hanover. [. . .] Frau B. is a fabulously interesting lady, extremely able and well connected to people around the world. She had just attended the Wagner Festival in Bayreuth, dined frequently with the Wagner family, and witnessed Hitler at firsthand. The drive was magnificent; everywhere you can see people working, people laughing and singing. Factory chimneys are beginning to spew smoke, Germany is once again working. Knowing that makes you really feel good. But much, much more has to be done, and everyone has to do his part. [. . .]

Irmgard Brester to her mother Elisabeth Gebensleben, Utrecht, 16 September 1933

[. . .] The days with Hilde were quite delightful, and we took full advantage of them. I think that Hilde also found Holland marvelous. [. . .] The sea was really wonderful, and I am sure that Hilde will be gushing about the sights for some time to come. [. . .] On Wednesday we even took the streetcar to Doorn to see the Kaiser's castle. We were lucky to get into the park and see the castle because at the moment a side wing has been taken over by a charity sale for German children in need; many handicrafts made by the Kaiserin are for sale there. [. . .]

I am sure that Eberhard will enjoy the military sport camp, he is such a big fan of physical activity and the cheerful life at camp. [. . .]

Elisabeth Gebensleben to her daughter Irmgard Brester, Braunschweig, 21 September 1933

[. . .] We've received two short letters from Hardus. 400 men have been mustered. He is in Barracks No. 8. The shifts are strenuous but sensibly organized. For example, a half-hour compulsory bed rest after dinner, quite necessary, I would imagine, since a lot of physical labor is required. The certificate of good health stated that he could withstand physical exertion without side effects. Eberhard will certainly enjoy the camp's comradely spirit very much. He is now on board, marching with the youth of Germany. Unfortunately there is no news from Berlin regarding his appointment as Referendar to the Court of Appeals. He does so much want to be appointed to Berlin's Court of Appeals in order to remain connected to the university. But only local Referendare, whose parents live in Berlin, seem to be recruited. There has to be a compelling reason if he is to get it. Vati already contacted Braunschweig's minister in Berlin. B. has known Vati for a long time, and

Eberhard too. We haven't heard a response yet. Happily, Eberhard doesn't have to sit at home doing nothing during this waiting period; he would find that difficult to bear. [. . .]

Vati was on hand yesterday to dedicate the new harbor. The first ship, a small steamer, entered the port. Vati received a lot of tributes. [. . .] He just told me that the first seagulls have been spotted in the harbor. Now Hardus can row directly from Braunschweig to Utrecht!

Elisabeth Gebensleben to her daughter Irmgard Brester, Braunschweig, 28 September 1933

[. . .] not one word of complaint, but reading between the lines of the letters, which we eagerly await, it is clear that the physical demands are heavy. He is on duty from 6:00 in the morning until 8:00 at night; frequently alarms and exercises late at night. 33 men to a room. A 50-km march with gear is soon to come. [. . .] Eberhard has made various requests: foot lotion, gloves, etc. At the bottom of the letter he wrote: "Do you think you could donate a not-too-expensive sausage that can be shared with my group of 10 men?" Well a package was dispatched yesterday with two of Witte's large Braunschweiger sausages. What a surprise the "crew" will have. I also packed along some nice pears, chocolate, and some sugar for the march.

[. . .] In the meantime two letters arrived regarding Eberhard's appointment as a Referendar to the Court of Appeals; not without hope, but no promises. Actually, Eberhard should now put his oar in, but he claims he has no time and isn't in the right mood to take matters in hand. [. . .]

We always have a great deal planned. Last Sunday, I was "on duty" all day: In the morning, Hitler Youth on the Schlossplatz; 3 o'clock in the afternoon, the dedication of the New Adolf Hitler House; finally a festive evening organized by the NSDAP in the Wilhelmsgarten. Much standing around and listening to speeches. Vati and I were really tired at the end of the day. We were also out by the harbor. It will be, already really is just magnificent. [. . .]

Just think: they wanted to take Uncle Ernst to a concentration camp. A foreman who had been run off pressed some sort of charges. With her low Nazi membership number, Aunt Margot sure sprung into action and sorted everything out. I wish I could have witnessed the scene! I don't have any more details. [. . .]

Vati is very busy. All the plans for the work that is to be done have landed in his office: (1) Dietrich Klagges's garden city; (2) restoration of the old town; (3) Braunschweig's big lake. We are certainly at work here, and the unemployed are vanishing into thin air.

Immeken, I miss you so much! [. . .]

Irmgard Brester to her mother Elisabeth Gebensleben, Utrecht, 7 October 1933

[. . .] I strongly endorse the plan for a new, modern Autobahn between Holland and Germany. You surely must have read about it.

Elisabeth Gebensleben to her daughter Irmgard Brester, Braunschweig, 12 October 1933

[. . .] Eberhard is back! He took us by surprise Sunday afternoon. Luckily, Ohmchen was at home; Vati and I were at the athletic field in Richmond as guests of honor in the green-wreathed stands watching the Reichswehr practice for the "Day of the Soldier." Eberhard survived the military sport camp, with its heavy physical demands, quite well, not counting a sprained ankle, which frequently bothered him. [. . .] Right now, Eberhard is writing a letter to Heidelberg; he is thinking of traveling to Heidelberg in the next few days to meet with Professor Jellinek, who is very well disposed to him, to get advice and discuss the dissertation that Eberhard would like to do with him. But first he has to get the appointment in Berlin, which is still some way off. Perhaps Professor Jellinek will be able to help; he is the only professor with whom Eberhard has personal contact, although he studied with him for *only one* semester. After 6 semesters at Berlin's gigantic university he didn't get to know a *single* professor personally. The professors at the university in Berlin do not get to know their students, which I find deplorable. To make the acquaintance of even one professor would have been very important since Eberhard wants to take up an assistantship in the faculty alongside his Referendariat in the Court of Appeals. None of this is particularly auspicious, but we shouldn't throw in the towel. If things do not work out in Berlin, he will have to try elsewhere, perhaps in Celle. It is all I can do these days to keep him from losing confidence; this is not the Eberhard I know. [. . .]

Vati is doing well. He is rightly very proud of *his* harbor; day before yesterday, at our party meeting in the Stadtpark, he gave a well-received lecture and slide show about the harbor. [. . .]

Finally we have a new Oberbürgermeister! This evening the paper reported what we had long known, or at least had expected, that he would be coming, although Dr. Hesse faced *very* many difficulties that he had to overcome, and it almost looked as though he would not make it. Apparently there were huge concerns in Munich, but in fact he was able to pull it off. Braunschweig is shaking its head, a few party members shout "Hurrah," and the newspapers of course, but now that he is in we can only hope that everything works out for the best! Vati will be relieved of his burdens, but not from one day to the next. Just yesterday someone said to Vati: "Now you have another Oberbürgermeister to break in!"

Naturally I read about the 7,000 National Socialists in Utrecht with great interest!! Yes, yes!!

On 14 October 1933, Hitler announced that Germany felt compelled to withdraw from the League of Nations as well as the Geneva disarmament conference because it claimed it was not being treated as an equal partner. At the same time, Hitler called a national referendum to ratify the decision to be held on 12 November, the same day as new Reichstag elections. The Nazis launched a huge propaganda campaign, and the nearly unanimous ratification was the result both of heavy Nazi pressure on voters but also genuine support among Germans for Hitler's foreign policy.

Karl Gebensleben (standing) welcoming Dr. Wilhelm Hesse upon his election
as Oberbürgermeister (18 October 1933)

In the meantime, Marinus van der Lubbe (1909–1934), a bricklayer and former Dutch Communist, stood trial for the Reichstag fire. The Nazis accused van der Lubbe of being an agent of the Communists, while Communists charged the Nazis with setting the fire with van der Lubbe's help. They published a "Brown Book" on the Reichstag fire and Hitler's terror, which van der Lubbe's leftist friends in Holland countered with a "Red Book" to rebut Communist charges. Van der Lubbe was executed on 10 January 1934.

In Braunschweig, Karl Gebensleben welcomed Wilhelm Hesse as the new Nazi Oberbürgermeister of the city on 18 October 1933. A month later, on 18–19 November, Braunschweig hosted a large trade convention.

Irmgard Brester to her mother Elisabeth Gebensleben, Utrecht, 14 October 1933

[. . .] So Hesse made it after all! I was quite stunned and ending up dreaming about it all night long. I understand that Vati has very mixed feelings about his new "superior," even though they have a good personal relationship, which will hopefully stay that way. But didn't the government make a mistake to place such a fanatic person, a pure party man, at the head of a large city administration? We can only hope for the best. However, I am happy that Vati was able to dedicate the harbor, which was, after all, his project, in his capacity as acting Oberbürgermeister and that a certain Dr. H. was not able to just come and take the credit for *himself.* [. . .] During my two months in Braunschweig I got to know this business pretty much firsthand and am therefore especially interested in knowing further developments.

[. . .] I am not at all sure if our dance group will work out. We actually found several pairs, but the cost (40 gulden for two people) is naturally rather steep for us, particularly if we would keep going to concerts and the theater, and as of 1 January, August's salary will be cut another 5% (now a total of 10%). We would have to deny ourselves tickets for such things, except for the Tivoli concerts, and that is also a shame. [. . .]

Elisabeth Gebensleben to her daughter Irmgard Brester, Braunschweig, 18 October 1933

[. . .] As I am sitting here, Vati is giving his welcome speech for the new Oberbürgermeister. Vati left wearing his brownshirt. He read his speech to me and Hardus; I think the speech will be published in the newspapers word-for-word. It received Eberhard's and my endorsement. No laurels in advance, but praise for what is really worthy of praise. Vati will certainly remain on good terms with Dr. Hesse. Indeed, Dr. Hesse needs Vati and is constantly asking for his advice and guidance. He wants to do a good job. Yesterday he approached Vati: "Herr Stadtbaurat, we have to really go into action; it's time for you to join the offensive!" "Of course," responded Vati, "but only *as* far as the city can bear it." The city has undertaken quite a few things in recent years: the swimming pool, the harbor, etc. At the moment there is no rest at all. It is rare for us to spend an evening *at home*. [. . .] This morning, out at 8 o'clock, back at 3:00 for lunch, as I write, again in city hall, [the formal] election of the Oberbürgermeister, Vati's speech and attendance at the procession of the torchlight parade. Today it will be a late night again. However, I will not attend *this* torchlight parade; it should have been saved for a moment when he had earned it.

What turbulent times we live in, Immeken! To live through these important turning points in world history. The German people are standing rock-solid behind their Führer; everywhere there is support for Hitler's redemptive deeds. This evening, Hitler's speech will be rebroadcast on records. We all listened the first time around, and if possible, I will listen to it once more today. Frau M. (who is visiting today) commented: "My son-in-law says that he had never heard such a powerful speech in his entire life." The old pastor from the congregation said to Frau M. "A man such as Hitler appears only once in every 500 years." The miserable situation of distrust and slander would end if only statesmen around the world were as truthful as he is and would make an effort to appreciate his far-ranging, his astute vision. Almost every evening, we listen to the radio reports about the Reichstag fire trial. Never has a trial been conducted so openly for all the world to see. And every evening, we hear how one lie after another in the notorious, anonymous "Brown Book" has gone up in smoke. Why does anyone even care about this book of Jewish lies? We are much too good for that. But I am not going to allow myself to get into politics, otherwise I'd never finish this letter. [. . .] Next Saturday [Professor Jellinek] travels back to Heidelberg over Lehrte, Hanover, and he has requested that Eberhard come to Lehrte, where he will join him in the train so they can travel together as far as Hanover and discuss matters. If there is not enough time to discuss the dissertation, there will be time to ask for Jellinek's advice and possible good word regarding Eberhard's appointment in Berlin, which at the moment is the most important thing. [. . .]

The word around here is that very soon, maybe in 3 months, our little state of Braunschweig will completely disappear, according to "the interests of the Reich." Eberhard can then go wherever he wants, stay here in Braunschweig or go to Heidelberg or wherever; there will be no more special examinations for small states and no more crazy jurisdictions. One big German Reich! That is fantastic. [. . .]

Irmgard Brester to her mother Elisabeth Gebensleben, Utrecht, 20 October 1933

[. . .] We are keen to read all the news from Braunschweig, the inauguration of the Oberbürgermeister, Vati's speech. We were especially happy to read Dr. Hesse's gracious words thanking Vati for the warm welcome he extended! That not one of the assembled guests could be found to give Vati the least bit of thanks and credit for serving as deputy Oberbürgermeister over many difficult months is really a scandal! But Dr. Hesse will certainly not dare to impose special measures such as salary reductions and "voluntary sacrifices" now that the small state of Braunschweig is to be incorporated into Prussia. That pleases me enormously. [. . .]

Elisabeth Gebensleben to her daughter Irmgard Brester, Braunschweig, 26 October 1933

[. . .] So Eberhard's meeting with Professor Jellinek proved to be a success. The two of them met in the train, in the dining car, and in Hanover. [. . .] perhaps a basis that will result in Eberhard's appointment as Referendar. We will see. Hardus is already beginning to get very impatient. He can do his dissertation with Jellinek. They have already discussed topics. [. . .]

Interesting broadcasts on the radio. We all listened to the terrific speech by Hitler; it must have been the best speech that our Chancellor has ever given, totally enthralling and overwhelming. And yet at the same time, he makes everything so clear and simple. The sarcasm in his words was especially striking and frequently made for a good laugh. Diplomacy certainly never spoke so fearlessly. There is something so immensely great about this man! At the end of the speech, I snuck out of the room and cried. I believe that 12 November will go into history! How glorious it is: a unified people gathered around a leader whom they love inordinately, all the more so if you make comparisons, with France, for example. I believe that we, a poor, disarmed people, are happier than France, rich, mightily armed, but internally divided. [. . .]

Elisabeth Gebensleben to her daughter Irmgard Brester, Braunschweig, 2 November 1933

[. . .] With regard to Eberhard's future, nothing has been decided. [. . .] There are now other important questions, Eberhard's enlistment in the SA, etc. Eberhard is busy researching family genealogy; the genealogical volume von Alten is in front of him. [. . .] The von Altens go back to A.D. 1100, the time of the Crusades, and the family tree of our branch goes back to 1600; a gap, for which we don't have an explanation. [. . .]

Preparations for the elections are in full swing here. I don't even see why they are necessary. The German people will vote the right way, they don't need so many election speeches. The first big speech by Hitler was so overwhelming that you don't want to hear the ones to follow. At the same time, he is flying around Germany, speaking and accomplishing so much, it is almost frightening. After all, he too is only mortal, although a mortal with a drive you would not find in anyone else. Dr. Hesse's inauguration is set for Monday. Vati has to speak again. Hardus helped write the speech. [. . .]

Elisabeth Gebensleben to her daughter Irmgard Brester, Braunschweig, 9 November 1933

[. . .] Eberhard left for Berlin this morning. Not a word from the professor in Berlin, so I advised him to make a personal appointment, and Professor Jellinek wrote much the same thing. You know how it is! The correspondence lies in the desk drawer, and these great scholars never think to reply. [. . .] Eberhard has a lot to do in Berlin, then the trip to Heidelberg for the dissertation, he might eventually enroll there if there is no possibility of getting his Referendariat transferred from Berlin, should he get the appointment, to Heidelberg for 1½ years. Many questions remain unanswered, and I truly hope that his discussions go well. [. . .] He had a lot on his plate here as well, most importantly: enlistment in the SA, more specifically he reported to the *Flying Corps*. He won't start learning to fly right away, but maybe it won't be too long since he has already taken part in the military sport camp and also the voluntary labor service. What comes first is six months service with the SA. Last Sunday Eberhard had to report for the first time, 8:15 in the morning on the Franzschen Field. He doesn't have a uniform yet, but will get one soon. 400 men have reported to the Flying Corps with him. Eberhard hopes that he will have enough time in Berlin to acquire high marching boots, where a good pair can be had for a decent price. [. . .] Today was a solemn day of remembrance: the 10th anniversary of 1923's 9 November, when the first National Socialists gave their lives in front of the Feldherrnhalle in Munich. Tomorrow 12 to 1 a ceremony with Hitler's address to the entire German people; and on Sunday, the people's pledge of loyalty to the Führer. Sunday in eight days Braunschweig's big trade fair; living quarters will have to be found for 60,000–100,000 people. Almost every household will have to put up guests. [. . .]

Aunt Margot is in Munich attending a meeting of "Old Fighters" in the National Socialist movement. With such a low membership number, she must have been proud to go.

[. . .] In the meantime, Vati and I went to the theater. Premiere! *Macbeth* as opera, music by Verdi! It was simply a fabulous performance. Great enthusiasm in the audience. [. . .]

Minna von Alten to her granddaughter Irmgard Brester, Braunschweig, 17 November 1933

[. . .] As of noon tomorrow, the roads into Braunschweig will be closed, so Gerda asked to be put up and is arriving by train tomorrow morning. It is already quite lively in the city, too bad that you can't see the decorated streets and houses, but at least you have the *Braunschweigische Landeszeitung*. There are about 40 m of garlands artfully attached to our house, which comes to about 40 M, a cost the residents have to share, which does not exactly please Vati. But we do it for our dear Fatherland and for our Hitler. Unfortunately, the parade with some 300 floats heads into the city at the Ring, so we won't see anything; on the other hand, we have the torchlight parade starting at the Stadtpark tomorrow evening.

[. . .] The schools have all been requisitioned, and once again it is Ursel who has to suffer. She was supposed to start her internship today, but since the schools have to be cleared out as of today, the date of her examinations has been postponed to 5 December. That is bad luck; she is pale and gaunt after having worked so hard. And since the course of study continues, her topic will already have been covered and she will have to get a new one so the cramming will start all over again.

Aunt Margot was in Munich for the 10-year anniversary, or whatever they call it. She was underway for two nights and slept for only 6 hours on the third, but was full of enthusiasm.

On 30 January 1934, a year after Hitler's seizure of power, the "Law on the Reconstruction of the Reich" dissolved the state parliaments, effectively destroying the federal nature of the German state structure and concentrating power in Berlin.

After a series of hostile measures against them, Austria's Social Democrats took up arms against the "Austro-fascist" regime in a civil war that raged from 12 to 27 February. Hundreds of people were killed in street fighting before the government put down the uprising, banned the party, and arrested leading Social Democrats.

In Braunschweig, the National Socialist Association for Culture sponsored a "Cultural Political Week," which took place from 17 to 20 January 1934. Among the speakers was the writer and Nazi party member Erwin Guido Kolbenheyer (1878–1962).

In summer 1933, Carl-Heinz Zeitler traveled down the Rhine with a friend and stayed for several days with August while Immo was in Braunschweig with the children.

In Utrecht, on 26 February 1934, Immo sang at a concert organized by the Committee for Jewish Refugees to help aid victims of the Nazi regime.

Elisabeth Gebensleben to her daughter Irmgard Brester, Braunschweig, 4 December 1933

[. . .] The Berlin Court of Appeals has notified Eberhard that he should let himself be appointed here in Braunschweig and then work in Berlin on a visiting basis. Hopefully there won't be problems at this end. In any case, the decision shows a degree of good will. [. . .]

Carl-Heinz Zeitler to August Brester, Heidelberg, 23 December 1933

[. . .] How beautiful your country is—how beautiful Utrecht is! [. . .] As far as you were concerned, we were actually complete strangers, but you treated us as if we were your best friends whom you had known for years. [. . .]

You will surely want to know what I have been doing with myself and how I found my way through this "storm-and-stress" phase. It was damned hard, I can tell you that. You know me, and I can't and don't want to rehash everything again, but the beginning of the new semester was pure agony. Bound hand and foot by unfortunate money problems, it was all I could do to take flight from myself. It was pretty bad at times, I didn't see a way out, was close to despair. Finally, I went to Munich, just to be somewhere else, to rebuild my life in new surroundings. After two days wandering aimlessly around the big city without food, or money, or a halfway decent place to stay, I was able to think clearly and rationally. All at once it became clear to me what I was about to abandon, how meaningless life was threatening to become if I no longer had a purpose or a task. I had two options, either do nothing and that would be the end, or go back and devote my efforts to self-improvement. Perhaps you can imagine the struggle, the conflict within myself. I had to be hard on myself and overcome my pride. On borrowed money, I took the train back to Heidelberg and forced myself to get my feet on the ground. Ideas and ideals really do still have some value, except today we allow them to be overshadowed by everything that is *new*. Several weeks ago I accepted a position in the Hitler Youth, Germany's state youth organization, the young, who incorporate the entire, glorious essence of the German youth movement—will my collaboration be wasted effort? Lending a hand, joining the struggle—from the outside it looks like giving in, but that is not essential, it doesn't even get at what is really human. You should go to the heart of the matter, and these boys are good at heart. "One step backward to take two steps forward," goes the French saying, and I am glad that I took this step backward. [. . .] I am not yet completely satisfied on this new path, if I am honest with myself, but we persevere and work and do our best. Maybe the myth about the will and the way is true after all. Nobody knows for sure what is good and what is bad, although everybody acts as though they do. There is work enough for everyone, and if you have a little time, you slip into the forest, alone or with one of the boys, and see before your eyes a summer evening perhaps like the one on which we were so enchanted by the miracle of colors [of the Loosdrechter Lakes]—that is compensation enough, the knowledge that we can still experience and be dazzled by such wonders, which creates new energy, new hope, and new happiness.

On top of that, the efforts to make my career. I am gradually getting the problems under control. Gritting my teeth, I am figuring out the mystery of being both a man and a physician. [. . .] I have even gotten myself accepted as a medical intern for March/April—hopefully I will catch on by then, my knowledge is still pretty feeble, and in this situation it seems unlikely that I will quickly acquire know-how of greater value. [. . .]

Elisabeth Gebensleben to her daughter Irmgard Brester, Braunschweig, 19 January 1934

[. . .] Vati and I received a printed invitation from Elsbeth and Erwin Grotrian-Steinweg for "Tea and Music" on Monday evening at 6 o'clock. I'm sure it will be nice. [. . .] I have something special planned for tomorrow evening. Another writer is coming through: Erwin Guido Kolbenheyer. On behalf of the National Socialist Association for Culture, he will be speaking in the studio theater. It will be packed, so I have to get there early to grab a seat.

The other day, Vati and I spent a very interesting evening in the theater. It was the world premiere of *The Fable of the Changeling*, with the composer [Gian Francesco] Malipiero [1882–1973] in attendance. We had two seats in the middle of the last row of the orchestra. The composer, who sat down left in the box next to the orchestra, made a very good impression. It was a fantastic performance and moved me deeply. Of course, for those people who couldn't make sense of the foreign-sounding music, it was a very difficult opera. You would not have recognized Braunschweig's theater; a completely different audience, quite a few Italians, the Italian ambassador, etc. Prominent Americans as well. Several simply fabulous outfits! Wonderful evening dresses! The directors of Germany's biggest theaters also attended the performance. [. . .]

Elisabeth Gebensleben to her daughter Irmgard Brester, Braunschweig, 6 February 1934

Immeken, I wouldn't have begrudged you and August this wedding celebration. But with all due respect for your good appetite, I don't think the two of you would have gotten through *this* feast. Roast chicken with tongue, cutlets with asparagus, sirloin along with heaps of vegetables, roast veal and salad. [. . .] Soon after the meal, we saw cake after cake placed on the coffee tables. You could hardly see the table cloth! According to Friedel's mother-in-law, everything was baked by hand. On top of that, 35 big sheet cakes were served to the village. We also took a packet of cakes home. I think that F. made a *very* good move with his young wife. With her blond hair, she looked so splendidly fresh and energetic that it is seems likely that she will be well suited for the role of a rural pastor's wife. The whole family appealed to me; excellent; real high-quality German peasant stock. They surely all must have worked their share during these difficult last years. The whole village came along to celebrate and even shed tears during the church ceremony. Uncle Otto was suddenly moved to tears as he stood in front of his boy, and when he recounted Friedel's childhood and talked about his childhood home, his voice wavered, and you could hear sniffles and sighs from the galleries and benches where the villagers sat. Friedel himself was very moved; after the marriage ceremony, he kissed his father's hand in front of the altar. The story of how Friedel and Lisa got to know each other is adorable. It was not so long ago, the 2,000-km automobile rally, when race cars and motorcycles crisscrossed Germany. As a burly SA man, Friedel was given the assignment to be a guide in Bornum, where he stood on the street corner and pointed the way with a blue flag.

Of course, the pretty girls from the village were out and about, and it turned out that Lisa ended up standing for a long time next to Friedel. A few days later, they saw each other again, and Friedel commented to his mother that he wanted to get engaged. As a symbol of love, or rather of the occasion for their love, the blue flag was presented at the wedding banquet with a few accompanying verses. [. . .]

In between, I listened to the *news*. They even mentioned Utrecht. If I understood it correctly: the Utrecht city council condemned the boycott of German goods at Utrecht's annual trade fair. One more sound decision. When you consider what is going on in France and in Austria, then our quiet Germany is really a paradise. I just heard on the radio: as of tomorrow there is only one German Reich, one big union. All the state borders have been lifted. It took a great blacksmith to forge this unity. And on top of that the domestic Volksgemeinschaft, one sacrifice after another for the nation. Nothing like this has ever occurred. There are those who are receiving alms who never imagined that it might be so. Indeed, sometimes there is too much of a good thing. Yesterday, our good old Minna received a packet of baby diapers! What a shame, but she really cannot use them!

[. . .] The same day that I read the story in the *Illustrierte Zeitung*, "Fleeing the GPU with husband and child" (a woman describes conditions in Russia based on her own experiences), I read in our newspaper the report that a German engineer who succeeded in getting out of Russia gave here in Braunschweig. The circumstances in the two stories corresponded with each other to such an extent that I really found the coincidence that both stories fell into my hands on the same day strange. The details in the *Illustrierte* are gruesome, but you have to be acquainted with horrible events if you are going to make sense of world history. [. . .]

Irmgard Brester to her mother Elisabeth Gebensleben, Utrecht, 9 February 1934

[. . .] Keep in mind that on Monday in 14 days, on 26 February, I have to sing at a big charity concert. I quickly agreed after Frau Kwant asked me to do so, but sometimes I get a little weak in the knees when I start to think about it. There will be a variety of performances, some orations, and violin pieces. [. . .] Right before intermission, after a violin concerto by Mozart, I will sing an aria from Haydn's *Seasons*, and after the intermission some songs by Mendelssohn [. . .] August has announced that his heart is already pounding! [. . .]

Minna von Alten to her granddaughter Irmgard Brester, Braunschweig, 13 February 1934

[. . .] You, my Netherlanders, are so frequently in my thoughts. As I am sitting here, I constantly see Hedda, holding Marleentje with both her hands, wandering backward through the room. [. . .]

When everything is done, around the beginning of May, Ursel will go to one of the labor camps that can be found everywhere, in East Prussia, Mecklenburg, even Wolfenbüttel. Of course, she would prefer to go someplace far away, preferably East Prussia. Gradually I am getting myself used to the forthcoming loneliness of my last years.

Elisabeth Gebensleben to her daughter Irmgard Brester, Braunschweig, 14 February 1934

[. . .] Eberhard wrote as well; he is very content in his Werder home [near Berlin] [. . .]

We often turn the radio to Vienna. It is so terrible what is happening there, my breath is taken away. War is bad enough, but this *civil* war! They are all Germans after all, they speak our language. And now machine guns and cannons! I just can't believe it. A representative of the security forces spoke twice about all that the government had "achieved." Last night he recounted how women had emerged from an apartment block that had been under fire, carrying children in their arms and waving white aprons and towels. Doesn't he have any sense of what an indictment it is if women and children are surrendering? Is *that* what the government thinks is wise policy, machine guns? Every day we have to give renewed thanks that we were spared this civil war, thanks to our government's far-seeing, calm measures, especially the Führer's, and to the calm, phenomenal discipline of his movement. Marxism along with Communism have been rooted out here; now compare the victims among our 65 million with the victims in 6-million-strong Austria. *How* heavily armed our Communists and Marxists were! And if a Marxist here received the beating he deserved, the foreign press went into a frenzy indicting us as "barbarians." Well, now look at France, look at Austria. "All guilt avenges itself on earth" [from Goethe's *Wilhelm Meister's Apprenticeship*]. The first act is almost over in Austria. But the drama continues. Lovely, amusing Vienna! The tears that will be wept these next days. And why? Immeken, I didn't want to write anything political, but the fate of our brothers is our concern as well. For out of the abundance of the heart, the mouth speaketh. [. . .]

Irmgard Brester to her mother Elisabeth Gebensleben, Utrecht, 16 February 1934

[. . .] Above all, we are very much looking forward to getting news about the blueprints. I can't tell you how wonderful it is to think that construction will begin soon. [. . .] It is just unbelievable how many people have approached me about the concert and told me that they are coming. [. . .] In fact, you really should be there as well, even though I know that you and August would have an intense debate about the charitable purpose of the performance. [. . .]

On 30 June 1934, SA Chief of Staff Ernst Röhm and other SA officials loyal to him were murdered by order of Hitler, who accused them of preparing a putsch against him. Actually, Hitler got rid of Röhm because the SA had become too powerful and threatened Hitler's consolidation of power and especially his relations with the Reichswehr. At the same time, the Nazis murdered a number of political enemies, including the former chancellor, Kurt von Schleicher. On 2 July, Hitler returned to Berlin, where Reich President Hindenburg formally thanked him for his "courageous deed, which had saved the German people from great danger." Karl and Eberhard witnessed the jubilant crowds.

President Hindenburg died at the age of eighty-six on 2 August, just a day after Germans marked the twentieth anniversary of the outbreak of the world war.

On 13 May 1934, the new harbor in Braunschweig was ceremoniously inaugurated with Reich Transport Minister Paul Freiherr vom Eltz-Rübenach in attendance. In his speech, Oberbürgermeister Hesse portrayed the construction of the harbor as an enormous achievement of National Socialism, although his predecessor, Ernst Böhme, whom he did not mention at all, had put in most of the work.

Immo's performance at the charity conference went very well. A local Dutch paper, Het Volk, wrote on 27 February 1934: "Frau Irmgard Brester-Gebensleben, accompanied by Fräulein Karin Maria Kwant, enjoyed a great and deserved success with her songs. It should be noted that Frau Brester, the wife of a prominent doctor in Utrecht, is German by birth (a genuine 'Aryan') and for the benefit of Jews who fled Germany sang songs written by the German Jew Heine and composed by the German Jew Mendelssohn-Bartholdy!"

Among those attending the concert was the Jewish physician Dr. M., who had delivered Immo's children.

Especially after the boycott of Jewish businesses on 1 April 1933, more and more Jews fled Germany by legal or illegal means. A few weeks after the concert, in mid-March 1934, the Dutch government tightened emigration rules to limit the number of refugees on the grounds that conditions in Germany had stabilized.

As a member of the NSDAP, Karl Gebensleben assumed the administrative post of local "Amtswalter." Elisabeth continued to attend meetings of the National Socialist Women's League.

Immo's father-in-law, Jan Brester, died on 27 April 1934. A month earlier, on 20 March, the Queen Mother Emma (1858–1934), a princess of Waldeck-Pyrmont, who had been born in Arolsen, near Kassel, died.

Irmgard Brester to her mother Elisabeth Gebensleben, Utrecht, 27 February 1934

I am sure you want to know right away how it went last night? Well your good wishes certainly did their part to make it a success. It went really well. Judging by the applause and the 4 wonderful big bouquets of flowers, everybody enjoyed it. We even sang an encore. [. . .] The whole evening was really lovely, the mood very pleasant, and so many acquaintances were on hand. Dr. M. [Immo's obstetrician] was full of enthusiasm when he came up to me during the intermission to say: "I didn't know that you could do anything other than bear children! I am so terribly proud!" [. . .]

Elisabeth Gebensleben to her daughter Irmgard Brester, Braunschweig, 1 March 1934

[. . .] You were so much in my thoughts Monday evening that Vati and I kept fiddling with the radio in case it was broadcast after all; in the end we just switched on Holland and listened to Dutch reports, the news, etc. Just to hear Dutch created at least some sort of *connection* to Holland. [. . .] A small tangible token of my joy has been sent to you in the form of a small package!

[. . .] Eberhard's accordion is now in Werder. Vati took it with him in the car. They stopped by the Court of Appeals. [. . .] While they were getting Eberhard, his boss, an elderly 60-year-old man approached Vati and commented that he had *never* had a Referendar like Eberhard, *so* extremely hard-working, thorough, and conscientious. The gentleman just offered his opinion, without Vati asking for it. "I don't say this to flatter you, Herr Stadtbaurat, I *really* see it this way, and I *wanted* to tell you." Well, Vati was more than a little proud. [. . .]

Elisabeth Gebensleben to her daughter Irmgard Brester, Braunschweig, 22 March 1934

[. . .] Vati is a bit tired and stressed. He has a great deal to do, especially now that he has assumed the important position of administrator in the [party's] political department. He has a lot of running around to do. It is impossible for Vati to manage everything alone. Frieda has to lend a hand, and thanks to her sense of duty and her enthusiasm for National Socialism she is wonderfully suited for the task. By now Vati has the complete uniform, down to brown britches and black leather gaiters; on the collar of his coat, the silver bar of an administrator. Herr Major K. was astonished having recently encountered Vati all dressed up, telling me: "It suits your husband magnificently." [. . .] Tomorrow evening my Women's League meeting; there is always so much to do. [. . .] Holland is now grieving for its queen [Queen Mother Emma]. She has also been in my thoughts: I think back on my time in Arolsen when I saw the queen and heard so much about her. [. . .]

Elisabeth Gebensleben to her daughter Irmgard Brester, Braunschweig, 4 April 1934

[. . .] This week, I start my course, "First Aid in Emergencies," which to Vati's and Ohmchen's horror I signed up for. They think I have enough to do! It takes place in the Invalid's Home under the direction of a hospital matron. It is sponsored by the Women's League. And I volunteered for it. It might be of use in the future. It is 14 weeks long. [. . .]

Elisabeth Gebensleben to her daughter Irmgard Brester, Braunschweig, 16 April 1934

[. . .] The few days [in Werder] did me a world of good. Nature always has such a soothing effect; nature's uplifting purity and quiet beauty allows the heart to forget all its troubles. [. . .]

Eberhard is planning a big trip for the beginning of May. He wants to motorcycle from Werder to Heidelberg, visiting Nicolai in Marburg and Zettel in Heidelberg, but most importantly, he wants to confer with his professor in Heidelberg about a topic for the dissertation. He is still confused and has not yet come to an agreement with his professor. And he still has to get himself enrolled in Heidelberg. In Werder he can get 10 days vacation. [. . .]

By the way, now we have also been all altogether in Potsdam; Hardus said that he had been there with you as well. The Garnisonkirche, which has now acquired a special meaning for our Germany, looked very festive. [. . .]

Irmgard Brester to her mother Elisabeth Gebensleben, Utrecht, 24 April 1934

[. . .] By the way, I am now conversing frequently with Hedda in German. As soon as I say a German word or sing a German tune, she immediately adds, "That's how Mimi and Olla talk!" She really understands just about everything, and she will learn to speak more over our next vacation. It is just a scream to watch Jaantje [the maid] and Heddachen speak German to each other. After all, they are about equal in their "abilities"! [. . .]

Irmgard Brester to her mother Elisabeth Gebensleben, Utrecht, 28 April 1934

[. . .] at 10:30 last night, our dear, dear Papa was released from his heavy suffering. [. . .] It is all so terribly sad! With him my first and favorite memories of Holland have passed away. [. . .]

Elisabeth Gebensleben to her daughter Irmgard Brester, Braunschweig, 7 May 1934

[. . .] Eberhard's time in Werder has pretty much come to an end; now he has to get placed again, but the question is: where? Probably for the time being at the district court in Potsdam. That would allow him to keep his nice, wholesome apartment in Werder. The next decision depends on his dissertation, on which he still has to get started. He had wanted to earn his degree with Prof. Jellinek in Heidelberg, but now he has received word from Zettel, who is studying in Heidelberg, that the rules require 2 semesters in residence before you can advance to the dissertation. Hardus has had only 1 semester in Heidelberg. He would have to reenroll and spend a semester if possible in Heidelberg, which given the delay and the cost would have to be considered very carefully. He doesn't want to do his doctorate in Berlin. Yesterday he sent off an inquiry, having heard from colleagues that in Göttingen you can advance to a degree *without* studying there. [. . .] But everything has to be decided by 15 May, the last date to enroll. [. . .] [Frieda's fiancé] was supposed to have been transferred by now, and the wedding would have then taken place. Frieda's first words were: "Well, so I will still be here when our Netherlanders arrive!" Frieda will probably stay until the end of September. Let's hope so! [. . .] Above all, Vati will miss her; apparently she is a real help to him in his administrative duties and does a very good job. [. . .]

Elisabeth Gebensleben to her daughter Irmgard Brester, Braunschweig, 25 May 1934

[. . .] So he will do the doctorate with Jellinek. On Jellinek's advice, Eberhard petitioned the university asking that the remaining semester for the doctorate be waived, and since Jellinek is the most senior professor, it can be assumed that with his intercession, the petition will be approved. The topic will be in international law, and since Hardus has access to the best material in Berlin's university library, he will try to get himself placed in Berlin after all, and not in Potsdam. He will have a busy six months: his Referendariat, getting the doctoral thesis in hand, and on top of that two or three days duty every week with the SA. [. . .]

Frieda takes care of all the running around that comes with Vati's administrative duties; that takes up several hours, and I really feel her absence. But that is the way it has to be. In the evening, we often have to attend meetings on behalf of the party. Wednesday evening was one such meeting. Tonight there is a meeting of the party cell in the "Hofjäger"; I have to be there and help represent Vati. Then there are the Women's League evenings, which Frieda attends as well; my medical course, which incidentally is quite instructive; and Frieda's gymnastic class, which is also sponsored by the Women's League.

[. . .] I hadn't been to the movies for weeks, but this week the Ufa newsreels included the opening of Braunschweig's harbor. We knew that Ufa was filming at the dedication, though of course we didn't know whether Vati, who after all played the major role in the inspection, would appear on film. I had a premonition and thought: maybe he will be filmed standing next to the Minister of Transportation from Berlin. Indeed, three images of the dedication of the harbor; pilots circling in the skies. Then: a single image of Vati up on the steps of the storage shed next to the Transport Minister to whom he is explaining various things; you can see him talking. Just on account of this picture, I saw the newsreels twice. A new program starts tomorrow, so it is a shame that Vati will not able to see himself. [. . .]

Elisabeth Gebensleben to her daughter Irmgard Brester, Werder, 16 June 1934

[. . .] Vati was passing through and stopped here on Friday to briefly speak with Eberhard, who was just on his way to the SA and had to hurry. He still looked pretty chipper, and before he left, the gentlemen from Braunschweig who accompanied him remarked to Vati that his son was really an excellent guy, who, as Vati proudly reported, looked just splendid in his brown uniform. Yet for some time he hasn't been feeling so well. On Saturday his fever climbed to over 40°. [. . .] Therefore, I begged Vati to ask Dr. Hesse for the city's official car, which Dr. Hesse, when he heard of the circumstances, immediately placed at our disposal. Oh, Immeken, what a drive! We made it here in 3½ hours. [. . .]

Minna von Alten to her granddaughter Irmgard Brester, Braunschweig, 19 June 1934

[. . .] Sunday evening we received Ursel's orders to report to a labor camp and do you know where? In Watzum near Schöppenstedt! She had asked for East Prussia or Holstein, and of all places she gets Schöppenstedt. But she took it with humor and left yesterday evening at 5:00. But any sort of answer is preferable to just waiting around to hear. I am not at all unhappy that she will have to do without intellectual activity for a ½ year; her nerves are pretty shot. [. . .]

Elisabeth Gebensleben to her daughter Irmgard Brester, Braunschweig, 6 July 1934

[. . .] In Berlin at the beginning of the week, Vati and Eberhard witnessed the huge demonstration of loyalty and the fabulous enthusiasm the German people have for their Chancellor. Our little guy is staying in Berlin after all; it is not clear for how long. He wrote today that he has rented an apartment in Grunewald since he intends to stay in Berlin for a while in order to begin preparations for the dissertation in the university library, something he can't do in Braunschweig. But to our great delight he is arriving here this evening; he has an appointment at the appellate court.

Irmgard Brester to her mother Elisabeth Gebensleben, Utrecht, 7 July 1934

[. . .] Reading all the newspapers and extra editions, we have been thinking of you a great deal these last days. Oh, Muttilein, the times we live in, so full of rebellion, disappointment, and hope. And Germany has to endure it everything. Where will all this end?

Elisabeth Gebensleben to her daughter Irmgard Brester, Braunschweig, 14 July 1934

[. . .] Yesterday at this time we were sitting right here listening to our Chancellor speak. I so much wish you had the opportunity to really *hear*, not just read his words. I feel so humbled in the face of this man's greatness, sincerity, and forthrightness. [. . .]

Elisabeth Gebensleben to her daughter Irmgard Brester, Braunschweig, 19 July 1934

[. . .] Uschi was here for a few hours this afternoon; she had a free afternoon. [. . .] The girls really have to exert themselves in the Labor Service, and despite the hearty meals, Uschi lost weight at first. However, now there is a bit of a lull, and Uschi was able to get away for several hours. Working outside, washing and drying, her arms have become deeply tanned. The girls have to do all the laundry for the boys' camp. Uschi has already had laundry duty that lasted from 5:00 in the morning to 4:00 in the afternoon for 14 straight days, every day laundry. Now Uschi is in charge of the kitchen for 6 weeks. Today she baked 100 portions of cream of wheat. They are learning the meaning of work! The comradeship among the girls is also lovely; Uschi showed us many, many delightful pictures that she took in the camp. [. . .]

Elisabeth Gebensleben to her daughter Irmgard Brester, Braunschweig, 1 August 1934

[. . .] In these difficult times, the eyes of a child allow us to get a glimpse of a distant, blissful world. We are already looking forward to being able to look into the two lovely child faces of your little darlings. [. . .]

Tomorrow evening, Vati and I will attend a religious field service on the Schlossplatz; it looks like the day will be twice as meaningful for us. [. . .]

Irmgard Brester to her mother Elisabeth Gebensleben, Utrecht, 2 August 1934

[. . .] I just heard the tragic news that our venerated Hindenburg has died. What a heavy blow for Germany! He embodied such a large part of the old traditions and former glories of our German Fatherland, to which he dedicated his whole life and all his efforts. His distinguished, awe-inspiring towering figure will be missed. But 86 years is a pretty old age, and we have infinite admiration for the loyalty and dutifulness with which he carried out his difficult tasks until the very end. [. . .]

Elisabeth Gebensleben to her daughter Irmgard Brester, Braunschweig, 6 August 1934

[. . .] Like every evening recently, the bells of our church are tolling along with all the church bells in the city. The mood these days is solemn and serious. At noon, we heard the broadcast of the ceremony in the Reichstag. It is really amazing that we can take part in all these events. Later we will switch to Bayreuth and listen to the third act of *Walküre*. Yesterday, *Das Rheingold* was incredibly beautiful, our one and only pleasure on Sunday. [. . .]

Minna von Alten to her granddaughter Ursula Meier, Braunschweig, 16 August 1934

The enclosed certificate, which the police provided no questions asked, says it all. However, the person I spoke to maintained that if you are properly registered there, you should be able to vote. I wish you the best; we all have to stand behind our Führer.

After Hindenburg's death, the Reich Chancellor Hitler assumed the posts of Reich President and Supreme Commander of the German Reichswehr. At the same time, Hitler began to prepare for the wars that would secure more "living space" for the German people. Government spending shifted from work-creation schemes to rearmament, which was pursued on a massive scale. Already on 1 October 1934, three hundred thousand men stood under arms, in contravention to the Versailles Treaty, which had limited the size of the German army to one hundred thousand.

Holland was in a state of feverish excitement when KLM entered a Douglas DC-2, the Uiver (or stork), in the MacRobertson air race between London and Melbourne in October 1934. After a flight of ninety hours and thirteen minutes over a distance of 19,877 kilometers, the plane landed in second place.

In October 1934, Karl and Elisabeth moved into their new house on the Brockenblick (today Höxterweg).

Karl Gebensleben to his daughter Irmgard Brester, Braunschweig, 15 October 1934

[. . .] Today, Hardus assumed his office in city hall for a six-month period, to be interrupted, of course, by his military service. [. . .]

Eberhard Gebensleben to his sister Irmgard Brester, Braunschweig, 21 October 1934

[. . .] You already know that I will probably soon be stationed in Ludwigslust in Mecklenburg. It is great to completely *break* all my ties and still be so full of excitement. I am especially looking forward to Christmas, and you and the family just have to come as well. [. . .]

Irmgard Brester to her mother Elisabeth Gebensleben, Utrecht, 26 October 1934

[. . .] Have you been following the amazing air race from London to Melbourne? You can't imagine the enthusiasm and excitement here in Holland. It was also a colossal achievement for the two Dutchmen, whose transport plane with 3 passengers and a load of mail flew just a few hours longer than the Englishmen in their specially built craft and without any ballast. And above all, they didn't have any breakdowns or problems with the plane, in contrast to the Englishmen, who lost two motors and covered the last stretch with only one motor. The two pilots deserve the honors they are receiving. It takes your breath away when you consider: halfway around the globe in 3 days! On Monday, the most exciting evening, we were on our way to our concert and pushed through the crowds in front of the KLM building in order to get the latest news. The concert proceeded without a hitch. [. . .]

Elisabeth Gebensleben to her daughter Irmgard Brester, Braunschweig, 1 November 1934

[. . .] Tonight Hardus is spending his first night in the barracks in Ludwigslust. Yesterday afternoon we said our goodbyes. Vati, Ohmchen, and I went to the train station, and today my boy has been in my thoughts frequently. Eberhard was very happy to go, and even if it will be a great adjustment with tough days ahead, I am certain that he will put his heart and soul to the task. We wish him the best, especially that his health holds up. [. . .] Given his relatively short time in the position, Hardus received a nice testimonial for his work in the district court. "Good legal knowledge, diligence, accuracy, etc.; all around his conduct was *without reproach*." [. . .]

Karl Gebensleben to his daughter Irmgard Brester, Braunschweig, 8 November 1934

[. . .] To our great pleasure, we also received a detailed letter from Hardus. He very much enjoys (*exzellent*, he writes) the company of his barrack mates, lots of peasant boys from Mecklenburg who speak nothing but low German. The rigorous and exhausting duties, even riding at a gallop and such, require bodily strength. Good that he always pursued sport activities. The barracks themselves are newly and nicely furnished. His address is as follows: Trooper Eberhard Gebensleben, 5th Cavalry Regiment in Ludwigslust (Mecklenburg).

[. . .] Professionally, I am doing well, with a great deal to do; but it has been a long time since I have had any major differences with Dr. H. People have already begun to move into the housing estate in Lehndorf, and in a few weeks or months

3,000 people will be living there. Despite occasional frustrations, these are marvelous tasks and very satisfying. [. . .]

Elisabeth Gebensleben to her daughter Irmgard Brester, Braunschweig, 14 November 1934

[. . .] Hardus gets around to writing only on Sundays; his rigorous duties exhaust him or don't leave him enough time to write. A trumpet reveille in the halls of the barracks wakes them up at 5:00 in the morning. He has learned how to sleep even when it is very noisy, and he can no longer conceive of a life without horses or stable chores. Apparently he has a wonderful horse. I can well imagine how he scrubs and caresses it! The first time they were on horseback, they galloped so hard they couldn't see or hear. "No harm done!" writes Hardus. He has excellent, totally decent superiors. He can even do his laundry with Persil, but he is better still at scrubbing down the horses. Monday morning, the recruits were officially sworn in, but unfortunately not in town in front of the locals as they do it here in Braunschweig. In fact, the recruits did not have a chance to leave the camp. They still had to learn how to properly comport themselves, to salute, etc. But today a very cheerful card arrived signed by many of the comrades on the occasion of their first "supervised" leave with song and beer. How I would love to be a fly on the wall; I am just so happy that Eberhard writes so contentedly! Only his feet give him some cause for concern. [. . .] Vati is working very hard. He came unexpectedly for lunch today with the Oberbürgermeister, who wanted a chance to see the house.

Minna von Alten to her granddaughter Irmgard Brester, Braunschweig, 20 November 1934

[. . .] Yesterday I got a second letter Eberhard with his passport photo enclosed. Mutti told me over the phone that he looks a little skinny, and she immediately sent him a roasted saddle of hare.

I am astonished that you are still preparing partridges; the season already ended weeks ago here. [. . .]

Elisabeth Gebensleben to her daughter Irmgard Brester, Braunschweig, 11 December 1934

[. . .] For Christmas, Eberhard wants his own uniform, and he wrote

Eberhard and Elisabeth Gebensleben
(Braunschweig, Christmas 1934)

that he even had the cheek to already order it. I was terribly happy because it shows that he firmly believes that he will "hang in there"; I wasn't always so sure; I know of several young men who were inducted after tough trials, but were nevertheless later sent home. [. . .]

Elisabeth Gebensleben to her daughter Irmgard Brester, Braunschweig, 24 January 1935

[. . .] I already miss the li'l ones. We have so much fun with them. [. . .] We are happy that the trip home went well. Hedda and Marleentje are gradually developing into real ladies about town. A trip abroad isn't anything special anymore. [. . .]

Yesterday the birthday of the 85-year-old General Litzmann. I could hear him as clearly as if he was standing in the same room. On top of that the stupendous cheers of the locals as Hitler drove up and later on appeared in front of the house leading the old general on his arm! [. . .]

Under the terms of the Treaty of Versailles, the Saar region on the French border had been administered by the League of Nations for a period of fifteen years, after which time the population would decide in a referendum on its fate. After a gigantic Nazi campaign, over 90 percent of the electorate chose to return to Germany on 13 January 1935.

On 16 March, Hitler declared that Germany would no longer abide by the provisions of the Treaty of Versailles limiting the size of the army and reinstated universal military service. To great national acclaim, Hitler introduced the new army, the Wehrmacht, the next day.

Elisabeth Gebensleben to her daughter Irmgard Brester, Braunschweig, 28 February 1935

[. . .] We haven't heard anything from Eberhard for 14 days, although his last letter sounded very cheerful. The military is joining in the Saar celebrations tomorrow, so they will have a chance to get out of the barracks. I think Vati and I will take a drive over to Ludwigslust soon. I just have to see my boy again. [. . .]

Tomorrow Vati has a long march in front of him. I hope he doesn't catch cold. Vati has a new appointment with the district staff. He showed me the Oberbürgermeister's letter of appointment, in this case, as District Leader. Vati moved up quite a bit. And on top of that, his administratorship. He will have more to do.

Karl Gebensleben to his daughter Irmgard Brester, Braunschweig, 13 March 1935

[. . .] Mutti just left—eager as she is—for her NSDAP Women's League evening in which they will learn something about career counseling. Quite rightly, she said, "What do I need that for!" but of course that didn't stop her from fulfilling her duty. [. . .]

We received *very* good news from Hardus. He signed his card: "Your completely happy soldier."

[ELISABETH GEBENSLEBEN]

You can get and learn everything you want in the Women's League from cooking and baking to tennis, gymnastics, and riding. You have to be active in sports until you are 45. It won't be long before all the wives and mothers in Germany will be slim and fit! [. . .]

One-pot Sundays were introduced in the Third Reich: one Sunday every month, families were expected to prepare a single simple dish and donate the savings to the People's Welfare. According to the Göttingen Tageblatt, *writing on 5 November 1935, "SS men will collect the savings resulting from the one-pot meal from every household. Donors have to write down the contribution they made on the applicable list. Those people's comrades who order their one-pot meal at a restaurant will receive a receipt as proof."*

In the meantime, August and Immo prepared to move to Amersfoort, where August had taken position as chief physician. Since the house was not yet ready and August was living in a nearby boarding house, Immo took the children to Braunschweig for a few weeks. During this visit Karl suffered his first serious heart attack, which prompted Immo to extend her stay. August also traveled to Braunschweig to look after his father-in-law. Eberhard's friend Zettel continued to study medicine in Heidelberg and worked for a year under the direction of Ernst Moro (1874–1951), a professor of pediatrics at the university and directory of the university's children's hospital. Moro was forced to retire in 1936 because he was married to a Jewish woman.

Irmgard Brester to her mother Elisabeth Gebensleben, Amersfoort, 11 October 1935

[. . .] These days it seems as though the whole world has gone crazy. What will happen in Abyssinia? It is horrible to have to read war news in the newspapers every day again; I just hope that it doesn't have some sort of consequences for Europe. Here, people are consumed by the fear of war and are beginning to hoard groceries. We are not quite so frightened by events and assume that the world will come to its senses. Still tensions are high; in any case, all your letters are being opened.

Elisabeth Gebensleben to her daughter Irmgard Brester, Braunschweig, 17 October 1935

[. . .] Yesterday the director of the airport came by on official business. He brought along his files and must have stayed for an hour. Afterward, Vati perked up. He remarked that the discussion was the best possible medicine for him. He wanted to get right back to work at city hall. [. . .]

And our soldier, Hardus, is now a civilian again and back here. [. . .] He arrived from the train station with all his luggage exactly when Vati and I had gone out for a 15-minute walk. At least Marie was here and our chicken soup for the first one-pot Sunday was ready to eat. This time Eberhard was especially tired, lots of work in the stables at the end since the condition of the horses had deteriorated, then farewells, etc. In any case, a break from the rigors of work was well deserved. On Monday, he will report to the president of the appellate court and present himself to the district attorney. He goes to work next Monday, and until then we have lots to do, unpacking and so on. It is quite a sight to see the thousand things in a soldier's bags. [. . .]

Irmgard Brester to her mother Elisabeth Gebensleben, Amersfoort, 25 October 1935

[. . .] We often sing our Germans songs and think of all of you in Braunschweig. This afternoon, Hedda brought "her" letter from Minna, and I had to read it to her for the umpteenth time (of course, in German, Mimi, what do you think?). [. . .] The two little ones are especially interested in German literature; in the bookshelves they discovered [Wilhelm] Busch and are absorbed by *Julchen* and *Die fromme Helene* for hours. Mama has to read a chapter every now and then. [. . .]

Minna von Alten to her granddaughter Irmgard Brester, Braunschweig, 31 October 1935

[. . .] Ursel is flourishing in her new job, and you can see that she is in demand. Recently appointed a leader in the BDM, she has become quite strict. Saturday she was in charge of rehearsing the folk dances for the harvest festival. That she has so little opportunity to get together with young people her own age is really a shame. Time passes by so quickly, and she misses out on the chance to meet other young people. [. . .]

Carl-Heinz Zeitler to Irmgard Brester, Heidelberg, 28 November 1935

[. . .] I don't hear anything at all from Eberhard anymore. But that is not his fault alone—we had become estranged after the entire changeover in Germany—to me, his attitude is completely incomprehensible. Our worldviews are simply too far apart. We each sit at our extreme and are unwilling to make any sort of concession. How much the one or the other is right is, in this case, as in so many things in life, a very relative judgment.

The fact is that I live in a world of my own making, and no one has the right to try to intervene in order to reform me—you can call it individualism or egoism or whatever, it doesn't matter to me—but I am happy to live there, and it is the precondition for what I understand by the concepts "freedom" and "life." But leave that question aside—it would be wrong to even begin to get into all that!

In these times, there are very few people who can help me forget my loneliness. Books and, above all, work do their part, and so overall I can maintain that I am not doing badly. Of course, my examinations are not very fun, and what I find important in my work is not the stupid plodding studying but the chance to realize a valuable, worthwhile goal. But the program requires that I stuff myself with all sorts of ballast, which may or may not be useful at a later date. Of course, I don't want to deny that studying medicine gives me a broad-minded outlook on things that I take very seriously. In the end, a professional career is the important thing, and I am happy and don't regret having chosen it. "Seek and ye shall find" ended up working out for me; the back and forth at the beginning was probably necessary. I have found my way and I feel fulfilled. For over a year, I have been working with Professor Moro in the children's clinic here, and I have him to thank that I have come to realize the value and beauty of a medical career.

[. . .] I've always cared a great deal for children—they still have the instinctive gratitude, sincerity, and purity of a devoted animal. The eyes of a child can express things that the long-winded ramblings of an adult never can! [. . .] Unfortunately I have had to bid the clinic adieu as long as I am studying for my examinations, which is especially painful since Moro, whom I admire and respect beyond all measure, is probably leaving, and that means my medical internship will vanish into thin air. There are all sorts of reasons why; just thinking of the future of medicine in Germany makes me anxious and fearful. [. . .]

Eberhard Gebensleben to his sister Irmgard Brester, Braunschweig, 12 December 1935

[. . .] This evening (that is to say, Friday) you will receive the surprise of having Ohm Eberhard appear on the scene (after all!) for the purpose of enjoying a weekend in Holland. When you get this card, it will be too late for me to change my plans, so you will have to make the best of it.

Karl Gebensleben was supposed to retire on 1 February 1936. A day earlier he officially took leave from city administrators. Shortly after returning home, he suddenly died. For Immo what turned out to be a big Nazi party funeral always remained a painful memory; her mother, however, was quite impressed. The Braunschweigische Landeszeitung *reported on 4 February 1936:*

> *The Stadtbaurat was deeply appreciated and beloved in circles well beyond his immediate family. Candles filled the chapel of the main cemetery. Prominent city politicians silently held a vigil by the casket, which was surrounded by many large wreaths that expressed the distress that so many felt no longer to be able to have a word with the always amiable Stadtbaurat. Representatives of the state and the city and the party and its organizations were all present. [. . .]*
> *Accompanied by the sounds of the hymns that concluded the service, the coffin was carried out of the chapel. A long procession under the banners of the new Germany made its way to the final resting place. At the open grave, Oberbürgermeister Hesse bade his conscientious collaborator farewell: "We stand at the grave of this man especially heart-stricken on account of his sudden passing. For thirty-five years Stadtbaurat and Stadtrat Gebensleben served this city. He knew good times and bad but throughout these years he was able to accomplish a great many important tasks. It was his great fortune that this work and these achievements found their culmination in the National Socialist state. He joined the ranks of the brown fighting front as district leader and carried out his duties conscientiously. In him, we found a true comrade by whom we loyally stood. Today we recognize his accomplishments. May he rest in peace."*

In 1936, Eberhard attended the Summer Olympic Games in Berlin. The regime used the occasion to improve the international standing of the Third Reich. For a time, anti-Semitic signs and posters disappeared from public view. In July, Ursel Meier enrolled in a political training camp, which was obligatory for new teachers. Immo was expecting her third child.

Karl Gebensleben to his daughter Irmgard Brester, Braunschweig, 30 January 1936

[. . .] And now on to Wednesday (yesterday): around noon, M. turned up (alone) to see how I was doing. Around 2 o'clock I was asked to go to the municipal swimming pool to answer some questions for a committee from Hanover. At least I was driven there and back by car. Later in the afternoon, Herr Director L. came by to pour out his heart, which was overflowing with his troubles with Dr. H. Finally in the evening Dr. R. invited us over for an hour's chat. [. . .] So yesterday was pretty well filled up. Today I am taking a complete day of rest since tomorrow will be quite exhausting. At 11 o'clock, an extraordinary council session will be convened at which I will be officially retired. At least that is what I gather from what I hear. In any case, I am a bit of an emotional wreck; I am not sure I can handle it all, although I don't want to forgo it either. However, Mutti will accompany me and will wait for me in my office until I have returned from the meeting. I wish I had the session behind me!

Elisabeth Gebensleben to her daughter Irmgard Brester, Braunschweig, 13 February 1936

[. . .] Well, and then all the important visitors came by to offer their condolences, the Oberbürgermeister and the deputy mayor in full uniform. I had inquired at city hall to ask when the Oberbürgermeister would be available since my son wanted to meet with him. The secretary said she would get back to me and she called the next day to say that the Oberbürgermeister and deputy mayor would come by on Tuesday afternoon at 1 o'clock and could my son be there as well. Fortunately, Eberhard was able to rearrange his service to be here. The Oberbürgermeister was very kind. He wanted to know everything that Vati had said, and he himself had had second thoughts about the ceremony in city hall, [. . .] maybe one should have conducted the ceremony here at home. They never imagined that it would do Vati any harm. [. . .] I told Dr. Hesse that I had had the same concerns, and that my only consolation was that Vati was spared a great deal of suffering and that he was released from his duties immediately after being honored and acknowledged in such a solemn fashion. Dr. Hesse agreed that Vati "died with his boots on," a completely duty-bound civil servant to the very end. Even so, he would have so much liked to have seen Vati enjoy a few more years of rest in his wonderful home while still taking part in the most important tasks. Vati was so important to the city and did not belong on the scrap heap. Yes, that was nicely put and Vati would have thought so too and appreciated it greatly.

Elisabeth Gebensleben to her daughter Irmgard Brester, Braunschweig, 20 February 1936

[. . .] Eberhard is working with a friend this afternoon. At the beginning of March he has a big presentation to give on "Rhine and Danube in cultural and economic perspective." M. received the same assignment so the two of them can research and ponder it together. It is odd that young lawyers have to busy themselves with such tasks. But in today's Germany lawyers have to be well versed in economic and business affairs. [...]

Eberhard Gebensleben to his sister Irmgard Brester, Braunschweig, 10 March 1936

Another great sensation—a letter from Eberhard. [...] I have also tracked down the source of the delay in your letters from Holland. I sent off a very official letter to the post office, two envelopes enclosed, giving expression to my "surprise" etc. The answer I got in return is that the Reich government, not the post office was at fault. In Braunschweig, *every* letter sent from abroad goes through customs, but only some are opened at random. Your last letter was also opened again. So there is no chance that letters arriving on the night train will be delivered Sunday morning.

Eberhard Gebensleben to his sister Irmgard Brester, Braunschweig, 4 April 1936

I have an odd favor to ask of you today. Did you ever think that it would be necessary to buy a ticket in Holland for a performance that takes place in Germany? So here it goes:

I would like to see some of the Olympics in Berlin. The last tickets became available on 1 April, but I couldn't get one. But only the *German* quota is sold out. Foreigners can still get tickets. Therefore would you go to your travel agency and order 2 tickets: for track and field on the Sunday that falls in the middle of the Olympics. If I remember correctly, it is the second Sunday of the games, but in any case it is the last day for track and field events. [...] I can afford only the cheapest tickets, so 2 standing-room-only tickets, which in Germany cost 3 M each. Something better only if necessary. [...]

Elisabeth Gebensleben to her daughter Irmgard Brester, Braunschweig, 1 May 1936

[...] Now I am home again on my lovely, dear Brockenblick. [...] Immeken, it was so touching how you took care of me and now you are also certainly entitled to some tender loving care. Thank you so very much and you, August, for the lovely drives. I still see all the wonderful pictures before me and imagine myself back in your fine automobile. The dazzling fields of flowers, the brilliance of the ocean waves, the colorful folk dresses of the fisherwomen are all pictures that I see in my mind's eye and will not soon forget. In between, I still hear the chatter of your little Schatzis and see their bright little eyes. [...]

Today, 1 May, Eberhard went to the big May Day celebration on the Franzschen Field. Lisbeth [the maid] had to appear as well. So I also went out to the Fr. Field. Already the drive through the decorated city was a pleasure, as was the view out on the Nussberg. However, I didn't stay for long because I wanted to listen to Hitler's speech on the radio at home. [...] Everyone enjoyed the delicacies I brought back from Holland!

Eberhard Gebensleben to his sister Irmgard Brester, Braunschweig, 5 June 1936

[. . .] Please consider carefully if you want to take the risk of making the boy my godson. If so, I do not intend to be someone who gives him a more or less appealing present every once in a while from the time of his baptism to his confirmation. Rather, I will eventually want him for myself so that we really do something as boys. Skiing and canoeing would just be the beginning! He is lying there, little Eberhard [Karel], and doesn't have any idea of the plans his uncle has for him, and the mother to whom he belongs is perhaps already a little worried! [. . .]

Minna von Alten to her granddaughter Ursula Meier [in a teachers' camp near the Polish border], Braunschweig, 20 July 1936

[. . .] How nice that you are so content and are learning new and wonderful things, and thereby expanding your horizons and sharpening your judgment. [. . .] It is great that the camp is located so close to the border so that you young people will always be able to see what our enemies took away from us and what we want to have back. [. . .]

On 30 January 1937, on the fourth anniversary of the seizure of power, Hitler addressed the Reichstag to announce that Germany no longer recognized the Treaty of Versailles.

The King of England, Edward VIII, abdicated the throne on 10 December 1936 in order to marry an American divorcée, thereby ending a constitutional crisis in Britain. In the Netherlands, Princess Juliana married Prince Bernhard of Lippe-Biesterfeld on 7 January 1937, an event the media closely covered. And in Braunschweig, Hermann Göring, the Reich Aviation Minister, was made an honorary citizen of the city on 1 November 1937.

In the meantime, Eberhard continued his preparations for his state examinations and looked for work, which he found with T., an old business friend of Karl's. But as a Referendar he first had to complete two months of political and physical education at a paramilitary training camp in Jüterbog, south of Berlin. To gain employment, receive state benefits, attend university, and otherwise advance in the Third Reich, citizens had to attest to their "Aryan" heritage by certifying that none of their four grandparents were Jewish in a so-called Aryan Passport. Genealogy therefore became an important task.

Minna von Alten to her granddaughter Irmgard Brester, Braunschweig, 23 July 1936

[. . .] yes, your trip! What I am brooding most about is how it is all going to work out. August should not judge German and Dutch streets by the same standard. When Vati and I crossed the border [in June 1931], Vati commented that it was quite different, it was not at all like at home. We also always took breaks, eating a generous breakfast in Salzuflen, and in Osnabrück Vati laid down and napped for half an hour after lunch. We left at 6 o'clock but were already in Arnhem at 7 o'clock. To take care of matters at the border also takes time. I can already hear you saying "Ohmchen, don't worry!" I know that the two of you know much more about these things, and

August is such a careful husband. That is why I just want to look forward to the moment when you get out of the automobile on the Brockenblick.

[. . .] Ursel is spending her vacation partly in a camp in the Iser Mountains in Silesia. She writes about the thrilling beauty of the region, but she is also surprised by its poverty. They are only 300 m from the border across which Germans live who are not allowed to call themselves German. [. . .]

Elisabeth Gebensleben to her daughter Irmgard Brester, Braunschweig, 10 September 1936

[. . .] Well, if all of you had been here for lunch the other day, when Hardus and I heard the radio announcement about the engagement of Princess Juliana with a German prince, then we would have opened a bottle of champagne. I was just tickled with joy. You too, right, Immeken? I am sure that there will be all sorts of celebrations and festivities in Holland! Yesterday, the newspapers published photographs, but not the most recent engagement pictures, which probably have not yet been "released." [. . .]

Elisabeth Gebensleben to her daughter Irmgard Brester, Braunschweig, 24 September 1936

[. . .] Lately, Eberhard has been very active in sports; he has all sorts of things to do with watercraft. A test is on Saturday for which he is practicing.

To our surprise, Zettel turned up in Braunschweig, and he ate dinner with us yesterday and the day before. [. . .] Zettel gives you his very best. He claimed that the days he spent in Holland at the Tolsteegsingel under August's loving care were the best he had ever experienced. He intends to write soon. [. . .]

Elisabeth Gebensleben to her daughter Irmgard Brester, Braunschweig, 28 September 1936

[. . .] Eberhard was at the athletic field yesterday morning and successfully passed the requirements in long jumping. His certification in rowing was to have taken place in the afternoon; he was gone for 4 hours and came back home chilled to the bone and rather unhappy that he had to wait in vain for the certificate. These are all challenges that are part of a huge athletic competition, the Reichssportabzeichen, that he would very much like to complete, including the 10-km race and the jumping, for which August gave him such good massages when you were here. [. . .]

Minna von Alten to her granddaughter Irmgard Brester, Braunschweig, 22 October 1936

[. . .] Ursel and I really had luck to enjoy such great weather when we were with you while since Monday it has been raining here without interruption. What wonderful tours August organized for us. This time, I really got to know Holland, and I know now what a beautiful and productive country it is, a place where you have found your second home. [. . .]

Elisabeth Gebensleben to her daughter Irmgard Brester, Braunschweig, 3 November 1936

[. . .] Eberhard is at the Hubertus celebration on the Heinberg to celebrate Göring's visit. [. . .] He had to leave at 6 o'clock this morning; we got up already at 5 o'clock. Undoubtedly he will get in late, tired after all the activity and standing around in the fresh air. But I think he will have a good time. All the other Referendare went along with him, and I am delighted that he is part of the group. [. . .]

Saturday and Sunday, Eberhard was in Hanover, attending a rally of the Hitler Youth, which he is working for. [. . .]

Eberhard Gebensleben to his sister Irmgard Brester, Braunschweig, 11 November 1936

You wrote the other day that Augustus was having a hard time finding time to go riding. Dear Immo, *if* Augustus had plenty of time, he wouldn't find it *necessary* to go riding at all! What I mean is that it is precisely those people who are intensively engaged at work who have to be farsighted enough to recognize that with a sensible lifestyle they could extend their life's work by as much as ten years. Does it *really* have to be the case that it is *precisely* the best ones who are used up prematurely? Examples we have at hand! Two hours twice weekly would be enough; [. . .] Sincerely your wise Eberhard.

Hedda Brester to her grandmother Elisabeth Gebensleben, Amersfoort, December 1936

Lieve mimi, wir haben einen schlitten oent einen kerstboom bekomen oent iech haabe einen boech bekommen ich haabe ferien, veele groetjes von Hedda ("Dear Mimi, we got a sled and a Christmas tree and I got a book I have vacations, greetings from Hedda")

Eberhard Gebensleben to his sister Irmgard Brester, Braunschweig, 29 December 1936

[. . .] In the next few days you will receive a newspaper with photographs of your royal family. In fact, Julianchen looks cuter and cuter; one could just fall in love with her just by looking at her. That asinine Edward VIII!

Minna von Alten to her granddaughter Irmgard Brester, Braunschweig, 14 January 1937

[. . .] We followed the wedding ceremonies in Holland as closely as possible. We were especially impressed with the golden coach. We determined that Juliane became more beautiful with every passing day, and we are delighted that she will go on a proper honeymoon. [. . .]

Hildegard is getting all the Aryan certificates for her parents and grandparents sent to her from Hedeper. She needs them for a work pass, so she is going to look for real work. It's about time. [. . .]

Elisabeth Gebensleben to her daughter Irmgard Brester, Braunschweig, 27 January 1937

[. . .] It is hard to believe that little clever Hedda composed a letter to me. [. . .] And I can't say how delighted I am that little Marleentje makes up and tells fairy tales. That is so like our Marleentje, and I can just see her sitting in her little bed, her hands folded in concentration, as she tells me just one more story before I leave her room.

[. . .] Sunday, [Eberhard] traveled to Berlin to see Nicolai. [. . .] The two went to *The Cabaret of the Comics* in the evening and had a good laugh. Monday, Hardus reported to camp. Apparently, it is very well outfitted, a movie theater with shows on Wednesday evenings for 20 pf; they've already heard a very good lecture. There is a big, well-stocked library. That is something for Hardus. After just two days, he didn't have much to say about athletic opportunities. 38 Referendare sleep together in one big dorm room. Well I hope, and assume, that Eberhard will cherish his time, not least because of all the young people. It is much more exciting than staying in his mother's quiet house. His address: Referendar E. Gebensleben, Community Camp Hanns Kerrl, Zug Kaschel, Neues Lager, Kreis Jüterbog. It is not only lawyers in the *big* camp; other professions as well. [. . .] By the way, Hardus now has his sports badge!

[. . .] Hardus has now taken steps so that he can spend the next three months of his Referendariat, the last before his examinations, in Berlin and therefore he has gotten in touch with T. [. . .] On Saturday, there are important broadcasts on the radio, 1 o'clock Reichstag session and a statement by Hitler. There are sure to be surprises. I will definitely switch the radio on for Hitler's speech.

Carl-Heinz Zeitler to Irmgard Brester, Zürich, 17 February 1937

My dear Immo. Can I, as a pariah and traitor, someone without a home, even address you like this? I do not even know the extent to which Eberhard has informed you about my life, or whether you have a premonition of what has happened to me and what has been destroyed in and around me over the last year. In this letter, I want to ask you to allow me to refrain from getting into specifics—it is indescribably difficult to write this letter, and I do so in great distress and only out of faith in our long-standing friendship. Maybe you will be able to understand me and at least for the moment lend me a hand.

At the end of summer, I was in Braunschweig for the last time. Both internally and externally everything had changed. I had imagined my visit to see your beautiful house on the Brockenblick quite differently. A huge chasm opened up. I spent an evening and almost the whole night with Eberhard. We both knew who we had become, and yet we could no longer understand each other. Our paths have taken almost completely opposite directions—to bridge this gap and to come closer to each other is just not possible. It is not that one of us maintained that he was totally in the right—we wouldn't allow ourselves to do that! But I could not and did not want to change my ideas and my convictions about the world and life, not one iota. In the circumstances at the end of the year, when I was in the middle of my state examinations, a catastrophe was inevitable. Now I don't want to make the mistake of feeling sorry for myself and complaining about the bitter injustice of it all—I could have drawn the consequences beforehand, but I did not. Whatever bitterness and scorn that has gathered up inside me is the fault of the time afterward, of the treatment—beyond description—that I had to experience as a German in my own country. I cannot consider a state that takes the last opportunities away from me my homeland. No other country would treat a foreigner in this manner, not to speak of a citizen. I was in Zürich over the summer. From the most varied quarters, I was accommodated in a very friendly, understanding, and helpful manner, and I was advised to enroll for the fall and prepare my medical dissertation examinations. I wouldn't have the right to practice medicine in Switzerland but I would have a diploma from a recognized European university, which is what counts, since after all I intend to go to Brazil later. All my school certificates were in good order, and not the least difficulty would have stood in my way. However, from Germany I received one letter after another, each one continuing to give me hope to try one more time, and even my professors in Heidelberg advised me to petition the ministry to see if I could at least complete my studies by taking the German state examinations. I let myself be persuaded and returned in August. The first thing that I was required to do was to send in all my papers. I still assumed that I was dealing with regular people, and so without suspecting any mischief I bundled everything up. That was in August. Then I was allowed to wait, four weeks, eight weeks, while the last day for enrolling approached. My letters and pleas were put off with ever new promises, friends and teachers wrote on my behalf, but I didn't get anywhere. What do bureaucrats care if others wait and worry. I hated this waiting around, I was condemned to do nothing, and I was really at the end of my nerves. On top of all that, an attack of kidney stones; I was stuck in Berlin for weeks in the most horrible pain. I was at the end of my rope, old beyond my time. In the meantime, autumn was almost over, and no effort had been made to decide one way or the other. The moment I was able to more or less crawl out of bed, there was nothing to keep me at home. I just couldn't go on, my impatience just ate away at me; all the valuable time that I lost infuriated me. Despite my pain, and just plain laid low physically, I put myself on the train at the beginning of December in order to give the gentlemen a piece of my mind. I hung around office hallways, had to hear the most nauseating flattery and promises, only to be excused with new optimism in the most friendly fashion. So I ended up waiting in Heidelberg—until the decision arrived the day before Christmas. It was not only totally negative but so finely worded that other possibilities elsewhere were foreclosed as well. I had run like a blind man into the lion's cave. I had passed up all my chances from the previous summer, never thinking that I would be treated so badly. On account of my parents, I gave it one more try and achieved nothing, on the contrary, I added to our troubles. I really don't know what to do next.

Dear Immo, maybe you are wondering why I am telling you all this. I am not even sure if I am doing the right thing because I really don't have words in any language to express my feelings. Just imagine: Christmas, the decision, no prospects for the future, all my hopes, my opportunities destroyed. I even went to the ministry one more time, only to wait for four hours without seeing anyone. Over Christmas, I sat at the bed of a friend who was in the hospital with a high fever—when the worst was over, and I no longer had to worry about him, I hightailed it to Zürich because I didn't know whether I would still be able to get out once the new passport regulations took effect on 1 January. Here the struggle continues, a difficult one as you can imagine, but this time on a clean and honorable foundation. I feel that I am once again around human beings, who demand respect but show it to me as well. I breathe in the pure atmosphere of this country as if someone who has been suffocating. However, to enroll *without* papers takes a bit of doing, even here. The dean, who naturally likes me, criticized me for not following his advice last summer. But there is no use in showering myself with reproaches; what is done is done, and all the "what ifs" and "should haves" in the world will not change a thing. I want and I have to persevere, there *must* be a way. I just can't throw my beliefs overboard, and I will not give up the struggle for my life here, if only to deny others satisfaction. I grit my teeth and will simply do it! The way the anatomist here helps me is really touching, and there is a shimmer of hope that I will finish up by spring.

The biggest difficulty is to keep my head above water until my enrollment when I can exchange currency. Until then I don't get anything and am literally dying of hunger. My father tries to do everything, but you know how hard it is these days. And so I hit upon an idea since I can't go back, but I also can't stay here any longer unless I get help from somewhere. My dear Immo, can I ask you for a small loan, even if it is only in the neighborhood of 100 M; it would help me get over the next few months. I eat only every other day; otherwise, I don't spend anything. Next time you are in Braunschweig, my father would immediately send you the money plus interest, and then you wouldn't have to take any more Dutch money with you. Holland is one of the few countries that still freely exchanges currency with Switzerland—perhaps this is the way out. Please don't be cross with me for asking, try to understand my bedeviled situation at the moment. I could and would want to tell you about myself for pages, but I think you have had enough for the time being—I know, it is a terrible letter.

Maybe one of these days I will be able to write a different kind of letter! Eberhard told me about your little Brester son and heir. I am happy for you with all my heart and would have liked to have sent you and your wonderful husband my congratulations, but given my situation at the time, it was impossible. Please excuse me. I would be so happy if you would occasionally write me about your children or send a snapshot.

Carl-Heinz Zeitler to Irmgard Brester, Zürich, 1 March 1937

Words are difficult to express my gratitude to you and your dear husband. It was like a dream, the day before yesterday when the postman rang and handed me almost 24 francs—and your ears must have been ringing when I finally could afford a proper meal. You cannot imagine the help and salvation your friendship means to me right now—how thankful I am from the bottom of my heart. Your wonderful letter also arrived this morning, and I do not want to wait a single minute before answering, especially with regard to your concerns about information leaking to Germany. You can be assured that as long as I have been here, my letters have not made a single direct mention of this matter. We understand the dangers and know only too well how Germany respects the privacy of correspondence these days. We never name names, but always use a circumlocution; over time, we have developed a proper secret language that remains completely incomprehensible to an outsider. It often takes me quite a bit of time to puzzle out what my father, who is doing everything to help me, is trying to say. Then it is up to me to follow up the leads, since I can move around freely without restrictions. Without much success until now, but I don't give up hope, and the knowledge that there are still real people and dear friends in the world is what helps me again and again to hold out and to trust in a new, rightful path. In this regard you don't have to worry; neither my father nor I will mention your name or your gesture of help. For that reason, he will not be able to thank you personally, but will make up for it when you are back in Germany. Maybe you would prefer that your mother get in contact with my father. In that case, explain everything to her and ask her to write to Berlin from Braunschweig. My father will certainly approve, will thank her, and will make everything right, if that is alright with you. Otherwise, I will follow your specifications, and in any case you don't have to worry about any unpleasantness that might come out of this. And for the time being, I am taken care of with your guilders—you can't believe how long they will stretch given my way of life. [. . .] Maybe there is real reason to hope that I will soon hear that I have been accepted again by the university and with that, most likely, foreign exchange. [. . .]

You can imagine how these times have tried my parents and what hardships we have all endured and still endure. Only a genuine and deep faith in the good and beautiful things in this world keep us going.

Elisabeth Gebensleben to her daughter Irmgard Brester, Braunschweig, 24 March 1937

[. . .] Do you also have such beautiful weather? If so, the little ones can play in the garden and I will see them in my mind's eye. [. . .] I am always telling Ilse [the maid] about the babies so she now takes an interest, and just yesterday she asked whether the Dutch also look like us or maybe like the Chinese. In this case, I was able to reassure her; she always looks somewhat mistrustfully at the two Chinese who live here with Frau P. [. . .]

Eberhard has lost 5 lbs which he is very happy about, but which in my opinion was not really necessary. Well, with all that exercise! He already earned a second sports badge in camp, the SA Sport Badge. He already has the Reich Sport Badge. So now he can be happy. [. . .]

Elisabeth Gebensleben to her daughter Irmgard Brester, Braunschweig, 7 April 1937

[. . .] So Ilse and Otto [Scholz] are now in Africa; they arrived today. All the formalities are settled here, but what is it like over there? The Jews are being deported there. Will the buyers even get a farm? [. . .]

Carl-Heinz Zeitler to Irmgard Brester, Zürich, 4 June 1937

I can't be a 100 percent sure, but who else would have sent the mysterious registered letter from Holland that the postman brought me for Pentecost. The only way I can explain it is that, for the reasons you mentioned in your last letter, you took the precaution to use an alias and chose Tilburg to post the letter. In any case, the contents reached me and helped me come a ways forward. I really find it very kind of you, and you can be sure that I will never forget your kind assistance in these bitter months. You know that when you are in Braunschweig you only have to contact my father and he will transfer the equivalent value in RM to you. Since my father will be visiting me here in June, I will be able to inform him personally, and you can be certain that not a word about this will be written to Germany. [. . .]

It is difficult to imagine the amount of hate that has gathered over the last years. I have been shown so much friendship here and been accommodated in a way that I would never have held for possible. I can be a person again, an equal among equals, am able to breathe deeply and, most importantly, see the path and goal ahead of me. [. . .]

The best thing is that I am once again at a children's hospital and can write my dissertation there. [. . .] The seminars and lectures are wonderful, I have been learning a great deal, and it is a great pleasure to concentrate all my energies on what I feel called upon to do. Only here does one realize all that has been lost over there. [. . .]

I thank you and your wonderful husband with all my heart; I don't know whom else I would be able to do so. Please write me occasionally and tell me about yourselves; you really can do so directly and without worries—not a word will reach Germany. Thank God Switzerland has not reached the point where spies work in the post office and snoop on their "fellow citizens."

After her most recent visit to Amersfoort in the summer of 1937, Elisabeth Gebensleben learned that she was incurably sick. Her last excursion took her to Goslar, in the Harz mountains, where on 3 October 1937 she took part in a harvest festival that the Nazis and Hitler convened every year. In mid-December, August drove to Braunschweig to pick up his ailing mother-in-law and bring her to his hospital in Amersfoort, where she died on 23 December 1937.

Marleen and Hedda with Aunt Margot Roever (Northeim, August 1937)

THE GRANDMOTHER (1938–1940)

After Hitler and local National Socialists precipitated a serious political crisis in Vienna, German troops marched unopposed into Austria on 12 March 1938 in what is known as the "Anschluss," or annexation. Thousands of Austrian Jews now joined German Jews in the flow of refugees to Holland and elsewhere. As a consequence, Holland fortified its borders and made entry into the country even more difficult.

In May 1938, Eberhard was named Assessor and began to apply for various positions. As part of the process, he applied for membership in the NSDAP. In the meantime, he looked for tenants for his parent's house on the Brockenblick.

Minna von Alten to her granddaughter Irmgard Brester, Braunschweig, 6 January 1938

The first letter since Mutti is no longer with us! I can hardly tell you how much it hurts. Everything I do is with Mutti in mind, and I often ask myself how she would have done this or that. And then when I watch the boy and see how bravely he struggles, how he takes care and makes decisions, then I feel humbled and pull myself together. [...]

I am so relieved that you had a good trip home and, also, that you could stay so long with us; how can *we* thank you for everything you did for Mutti. How much I would like to continue to live according to her spirit, and yet how soon the day will come when everything will be obliterated. [...]

Eberhard Gebensleben to his sister Irmgard Brester, Braunschweig, 15 January 1938

[...] You know, when I think of "Brockenblick," it means perhaps more to me than to you. Needless to say, the reason for that is that I have lived up here for a longer time. When I come up the road in the evening and see the moon behind the tall Harz pines and everything is still and peaceful, or when next summer *our* roses bloom, then I think that the Brockenblick will always remain as it was, because it was Mutti's heartfelt joy. [...] In the future we should write *everything* that we are thinking in our letters and not be afraid on account of a different point of view that might be disconcerting. Alright?

Minna von Alten to her granddaughter Irmgard Brester, Braunschweig, 17 January 1938

For the first time in a long time, Eberhard was at the Hitler Youth in order to get, as one says, the yellow ribbon, the qualification to Pg. [party membership]. [. . .] I've admired him, how he has considered and taken care of everything and made sure that the house remains in the family. He has set exact conditions, wanted to engage a caretaker. [. . .]

Bertha Haedicke to her niece Irmgard Brester, Leipzig, 1 February 1938

We have to extend our congratulations to our loyal royalist Hollanders for the heiress to the throne in the House of Orange. May lucky stars accompany the little princess [Beatrix], her family, and the whole country, you my dears included as well. [. . .]

Minna von Alten to her granddaughter Irmgard Brester, Braunschweig, 2 February 1938

First, most importantly, a little princess has arrived! With blue eyes and blond hair, a compatriot of your children! We can picture the jubilation, and all Germany shares in the rejoicing. [. . .] Sunday, Ursel has to leave again for 14 days to a leadership education camp in Hanover. It is all well and good, and she is happy to do it, but I am just sorry that she is constantly with her BDM group and doesn't get to be with people on equal terms. [. . .]

Minna von Alten to her granddaughter Irmgard Brester, Braunschweig, 15 March 1938

[. . .] I have just readied the latest newspapers for you, the enthusiasm was enormous, and it is really incredible that something like this [Anschluss] was accomplished without violence.

Eberhard Gebensleben to his sister Irmgard Brester, Berlin, 30 March 1938

[. . .] you can celebrate right along with me; for about an hour now I am entitled to call myself Assessor. And that with the still rather rarely awarded ranking of "commendable," which will open all sorts of doors for me. Because of my service in the judiciary, I was asked right after the examination to present myself tomorrow to the Reich Ministry of Justice, but I will play it *very* cool. I am only telling you this in such detail so that you can share my happiness just as Vati and Mutti would have done.

Eberhard Gebensleben to his sister Irmgard Brester, Berlin, 27 May 1938

[. . .] With regard to *Guusje* [August's training horse], I hold with Bismarck who said: "I have put Germany in the saddle, but riding she will have to do by herself." In my opinion, it is completely superfluous to appeal to the sportsman's honor or to the duty to accomplish undone tasks!

Minna von Alten to her granddaughter Irmgard Brester, Braunschweig, 20 June 1938

[. . .] On Friday evening, Eberhard arrived in a good mood with the news that today he would begin working in the Ministry of Economics. We made all sorts of plans on how to invest the money. Early Saturday, the jet of cold water: he had negotiated in person, but when the written contract arrived it contained conditions that had not been discussed and very much limited his freedom of movement and that he under no circumstances would agree to. That sure dampened our high spirits; nevertheless he had to take care of all sorts of things on Saturday: your currency transactions, transferring the office he had held for several years in the Hitler Youth, etc. In addition, the requirement to present the proof of Aryan birth, the papers for which, it turns out, lay in a genealogy in one of the book crates in Hedeper. He immediately left for Hedeper early on Sunday and actually came back Wednesday with the documents. He traveled back yesterday evening, did not want to get involved with negotiations, but called this morning at 7:00 and wanted to consult with T., which came as a great relief to me. He is already depressed, and now the prospect of waiting and starting over from the beginning. [. . .] Ursel was asked to participate on a hike to Breslau where the triennial Reich Sport Festival is being held this year. 4 days on foot there and the train back. She was chosen on account of the leadership abilities she had shown in the various camps. [. . .]

Minna von Alten to her granddaughter Irmgard Brester, Braunschweig, 30 June 1938

[. . .] I am *so* happy that you are coming to Northeim. [. . .] Did Eberhard write you that he is now working in the Ministry of Economics? He seemed quite happy in his last letter, and I am also grateful that he has found a steady job. [. . .] The enclosed newspaper clipping indicates that you Hollanders don't want so many visitors anymore, no one is allowed in unless you extend a written invitation.

Minna von Alten to her granddaughter Irmgard Brester, Braunschweig, 21 July 1938

[. . .] Ursel and I were just looking at the pictures again, and Ursel noted with pleasure the young boy's Nordic skull. [. . .]

On 12 September 1938 Hitler invoked the principle of national determination for the three million Germans living in the Czech border region of the Sudetenland, which he hoped to annex to the Reich. Thereupon Czechoslovakia declared a state of emergency, and Europe seemed on the verge of a new war. The British Prime Minister Neville Chamberlain flew twice to Germany, on 15 and 22 September, to meet with Hitler and offer him concessions at Czechoslovakia's expense. When on 28 September it appeared that war was imminent, many people in the Netherlands began to withdraw their money from banks and to hoard goods. Around noon, Chamberlain announced that Hitler had agreed to postpone a general mobilization and that a

Minna von Alten with her Dutch great-grandchildren Hedda, Karel, and Marleen
(Northeim, August 1938)

*four-power conference would take place the next day in Munich. An agreement
was reached between Germany, Italy, France, and Great Britain, which required
Czechoslovakia to hand over the Sudetenland to Germany. Germany and Britain also
signed a nonaggression agreement. In order to avoid a bloodbath, the Czechoslovak
government reluctantly accepted the terms. Upon his return, Chamberlain was widely
hailed as the statesman who had secured "peace for our time." On 3 October, Hitler,
acclaimed at home as the "Liberator of the Sudeten Germans," entered the border city
of Eger (Cheb).*

    *In the meantime, tenants moved into the house on the Brockenblick; the household
effects were stored in Hedeper. At the end of October, August and Immo, who was
expecting their fourth child, visited Eberhard in Berlin. There they could see the first
preparations for the ambitious (and never realized) plan to rebuild Berlin, which Albert
Speer designed on orders from Hitler. Shortly after the visit, on 9–10 November 1938,
the Nazis launched a brutal nationwide pogrom against Germany's Jews.*

Minna von Alten to her granddaughter Irmgard Brester, Braunschweig, 15 September 1938

    [. . .] Time and again, I so much want to see all of you, the dear little ones who,
as Hilde reports, still often mention Mimi, and for whom I have an indescribable
longing! And when I think that we may be facing some very hard times ahead and
that your young people have to report to battle, then I just lose my mind. May God
protect us!

Minna von Alten to her granddaughter Irmgard Brester, Braunschweig, 21 September 1938

[. . .] My dear Immo, if only the political heavens would clear; I can't even think about it. [. . .] Minna wants to go to Hedeper for the potato harvest, good that we have this fine harvest, just think of the many 1,000s coming over to us who will have to be fed. As Aunt Bertha writes as well, we live in extraordinary times, what will the Kaiser think, when he hears that Chamberlain came to Hitler! [. . .]

Immo's notebook, 28 September 1938

The awful tension weighs on everyone. It has made me completely sick, I can hardly do anything.

Minna von Alten to her granddaughter Irmgard Brester, Braunschweig, 28 September 1938

The pressure is so great that we cannot find a moment's peace to write. [. . .] We can only pray and hope. [. . .]

Immo's notebook, 29 September 1938

What a relief!

Immo's notebook, 30 September 1938

Great, great, there won't be a war!

Eberhard Gebensleben to his sister Irmgard Brester, Berlin, 30 September 1938

Today, at the end of this eventful day, when the entire world seems content with itself, we too should wish each other happiness. With all his heart your Eberhard shares your joy. So I will see you again in October!

Minna von Alten to her granddaughter Irmgard Brester, Braunschweig, 4 October 1938

[. . .] In these difficult days, I was just thinking about the past and imagined how the Kaiser bore up during these times. What extraordinary times! I put aside a few newspapers, they will interest you, although they are already out of date. The march into Eger was broadcast yesterday, totally thrilling. Yesterday toward evening, Eberhard arrived; how I worried about him since he could have been called up at moment's notice. These last weeks, he has worked harder than ever before. He said he was so stressed out that he sometimes couldn't get out of bed for 2 days. The changeover in Austria cost them a great deal of work, and now comes Egerland. He also says that steady activity is not so strenuous, but demands are constantly being made on him from all sides. He is very much looking forward to your visit, hopefully you will take the chance, my dear child, and then you will pass through here!! It is hard to imagine!

[. . .] Right now the flags are flying and everyone has a happy face. My dear Immo, how fortunes turn—in the times of the last Kaiser there were no representatives of the world powers coming to us, instead we had to go to all the states begging. For this we have to thank our Führer. [. . .]

Minna von Alten to her granddaughter Irmgard Brester, Braunschweig, 19 October 1938

[. . .] I am listening to the gala concert from Vienna and am thinking, my dear, about your own concert. I can't wait to hear how it went. It isn't too strenuous for you, is it? [. . .] Ahead lies the dull, gray winter. You can't imagine, my dear child, how it frightens me and how much I want to simply cry my heart out. But still, I have all of you and the two here, who still need me.

Along with Ursel, I was also at the old house in Hedeper and retrieved the genealogical tree. But it broke my heart to see all these things that who knows when will be used again. You should have taken much more. [. . .]

Eberhard Gebensleben to his sister Irmgard Brester [in Braunschweig], Berlin, 3 November 1938

[. . .] That you came over here to see me was really a very big present! And we were able to really discuss certain matters.

As to Berlin: I have to admit I have the feeling that I didn't show you *anything*. [. . .] When you come to Berlin the next time, I very much hope to be able to drive you around in a car. Then the big streets and large squares will be completed, and there will be no end to your astonishment. [. . .]

Minna von Alten to her granddaughter Irmgard Brester, Braunschweig, 24 November 1938

[. . .] Toward evening, Eberhard came up to the Brockenblick one more time; there were some things in the house he needed to arrange, and he wanted to see Herr T. in order to seek his help in putting his military affairs in order. [. . .]

Last night, Uncle Otto was here; Gerda then picked him up. Right now, he is in very difficult financial straits. Farmers are so burdened these days, and on top of that he has a new round of foot-and-mouth disease on account of the newly purchased cows he introduced, a loss of at least 4,000 RM. He is at the end of his rope, only wants to sit with the regulars at the bar on Saturday night, and he will leave early by train if Gerda wants to stay here. Things are really tough for him, and he even refused Gerda a fur coat she wanted to have made in Berlin, which says a lot. He just wants to sit at home and brood; I feel so sorry for him. [. . .]

Eberhard Gebensleben to his sister Irmgard Brester, Berlin, 4 December 1938

[. . .] it will be a nice, real Christmas celebration. If Hedda and Marleentje, these lovely little creatures, go so far as to ask for their Ohm Eberhard then not even an Eskimo could refuse them.

[. . .] I went in the same direction—it was the so-called Day of National Solidarity, I had the opportunity to drop a coin in Frau *Goebbels's* collection box.

Everybody who was anybody was out in public collecting, and when the military bands joined in, it turned into a genuine folk festival. For his collection box, my direct superior in the ministry received contributions from numerous associations, firms, etc. in advance, one for as much as 2,000 RM.

Minna von Alten to her granddaughter Irmgard Brester, Braunschweig, 11 January 1939

[. . .] I went to the post office this morning and came away very, very sad. I wanted to send you your birthday money, and I was told that as of 1 January the opportunity to give you even this pleasure has been taken away. We have so little foreign currency that we cannot afford the 10 RM per person. I wanted to go directly to the exchange office to make inquiries, but it was closed. As I left, I had to press back my tears, dear Immo. Well, we have to put on a brave face and hope for better times. [. . .]

Eberhard Gebensleben to his sister Irmgard Brester, Berlin, 15 January 1939

On this reflective Saturday evening, my thoughts return to the trip to Holland. It was a total Berlin week: work, obligations, invitations—diversion, restlessness, and fatigue. I am completely absorbed in work, not because there is so much of it, but because it has become absolutely intellectually interesting, and each and every day I am amazed that I find it so agreeable. Will it stay like this in the long run, or will I be thrown back into despair? Whenever I start to worry, I think about the Holland trip to *Haus Amsvorde*, where there are also many busy people, but also so many more wonderful things. So there I am! [. . .]

Minna von Alten to her granddaughter Irmgard Brester, Braunschweig, 25 January 1939

[. . .] [Aunt A.'s son] inquired about Eberhard and heard that the gentlemen in the Ministry of Economics have a colossal amount to do. Privately, I worry if Eberhard will be able to muster the strength. He really needs to have someone to take care of him; he doesn't look after himself properly. Dear Immo, give him some sound advice. I just wish he would get married! [. . .]

Minna von Alten to her granddaughter Irmgard Brester, Braunschweig, 1 February 1939

[. . .] Many thanks for the newspaper clipping with the picture of the Kaiser [on his eightieth birthday]. It pleased me greatly. Our newspapers made no mention of it, though other foreign papers allegedly reported that old Mackensen (at nearly 90 years of age) and other prominent military types were there. You can't believe how happy that makes me. [. . .]

Despite Hitler's assurance that with the annexation of the Sudetenland Germany had no further territorial ambitions, German troops marched into Czechoslovakia on 16 March 1939. Local Nazis also became increasingly active in the Lithuanian city of

Memel, which had been part of East Prussia before the war. On 22 March, Germany forced Lithuania to accept the cession of the city.

In March, Eberhard undertook a vacation trip through Austria and Yugoslavia. In the summer, Braunschweigers worked feverishly to bring in the fruit and vegetable harvest for the local canneries.

Eberhard Gebensleben to his sister Irmgard Brester, Ischgl (Tirol), 21 March 1939

[. . .] Soon we will be leaving here: final destination Dalmatia. Politics only from afar, on the radio. These are inspiring times.

Minna von Alten to her granddaughter Irmgard Brester, Braunschweig, 22 March 1939

[. . .] My dear child, I just hung out the flag for Memel, which since last night belongs to us. We live in wonderful times, hopefully it is all for the best. [. . .]

Minna von Alten to her granddaughter Irmgard Brester, Braunschweig, 18 April 1939

[. . .] On Thursday, which is a big holiday on account of Hitler's birthday, Ursel and Herr M. [her fiancé] want to go to the theater where *Die Meistersinger* is showing. [. . .]

Eberhard Gebensleben to his sister Irmgard Brester, Berlin, 23 April 1939

In the "meantime," a quick postcard greeting. How are you and little Jan August doing? And the rest of the lovely brood? I was shocked and saddened to find that the last letter I wrote to you was in my coat pocket instead of finding its way long ago to Holland! I was very angry with myself and it will not happen again "the next time"! My punishment was a bit of bad luck: Day after tomorrow I was supposed to train with the soldiers, but the other day, I sprained my ankle. If only it would soon heal! [. . .]

Minna von Alten to her granddaughter Irmgard Brester, Braunschweig, 26 April 1939

[. . .] Do you already know that Eberhard sprained his ankle, just as he was supposed to report yesterday for training in Rostock, which he was so looking forward to? Even though he was limping, he wanted to go anyway. I don't know how it turned out, but I worry. [. . .]

Minna von Alten to her granddaughter Irmgard Brester, Braunschweig, 10 May 1939

You really are my rock whenever my nerves are frayed and I am just so sad. Then I look at your card and imagine your home and the lovely little creatures; I always see you in the garden with your boys. [. . .]

Minna von Alten to her granddaughter Irmgard Brester, Braunschweig, 18 May 1939

[. . .] As much as it is tempting to visit you, my dear child, I can't imagine making the least bit of change in the rhythm of my life. I have become very much older. Let's wait and see, but don't make any plans.

Eberhard wrote a very contented letter. He is doing marvelously, lots of riding. With an officer, he completed a 53-km ride all by himself. With this service, he hopes to qualify as a reserve officer. I wish it for him; he has put his heart and soul into it. [. . .]

Minna von Alten to her granddaughter Irmgard Brester, Braunschweig, 1 June 1939

[. . .] Diethelm has been called up as of I July. [. . .]

Minna von Alten to her granddaughter Irmgard Brester, Braunschweig, 5 July 1939

[. . .] Eberhard mentioned yet another business trip, this time to Chemnitz. He is under great pressure.

[. . .] The shortage of labor is plain to see here and in Hedeper; life is becoming ever more unsettled.

Minna von Alten to her granddaughter Irmgard Brester, Braunschweig, 2 August 1939

[. . .] On Sunday, Eberhard arrived, looking *very* overworked. Yesterday he was on another business trip to the Sudetenland.

[. . .] Once again, Aunt Margot had to cook for 20 [Reich] Labor men, and on top of that the different nationalities in her crew cause all sorts of difficulties. I've often thought about how you made your way last year through all the hustle and bustle. [. . .] Students, including Herr M., have to travel to Silesia to help out with the harvest, and many women here are working over at the cannery; there are so many vegetables and so few work hands. Martha Kreutzmann went for 4 weeks as well. [. . .]

Minna von Alten to her granddaughter Irmgard Brester, Braunschweig, 17 August 1939

[. . .] My Minna is still working at the cannery. [. . .] On Sunday, I received a nice card from Eberhard, if only the political heavens would clear a bit!

Ursel was here with Herr M., who spent 4 weeks helping out with the harvest, from 4:00 in the morning to 7:00 in the evening; he looked pretty haggard. [. . .]

On 23 August 1939, Germany and the Soviet Union signed a nonaggression pact; secret clauses gave the Soviet Union a free hand in eastern Poland and in Finland in the event of a German attack on Poland. Poland, which had in part been constituted by former German territories in 1918, refused to be intimidated by German saber-rattling.

Both unofficial and official attempts to find a negotiated settlement failed. The new international crisis prompted Holland to declare a general mobilization on 28 August 1939.

Irmgard Brester to her grandmother Minna von Alten, Amersfoort, 26 August 1939

I am sitting here on our beautiful veranda, looking out at the garden in full bloom, the 3 eldest ones are horsing around on the sunny lawn while Jan crows with joy under the chestnut tree. If only the world was as peaceful as the view here! The tensions these last days have been just terrible! And who knows what is yet to come. We can only hope that negotiations can still overcome all the problems. Those responsible just *have* to be aware of the endless suffering and misery that a war would bring to all of Europe. The newspapers have just reported Germany's mobilization. I wonder how it looks at your end! And is our Hardus in the thick of it? After his last letter confirming his visit in mid-September now all of this! I am constantly thinking of you. Please drop me a line while it is still possible. I just worry so much. [. . .]

Minna von Alten to her granddaughter Irmgard Brester, Braunschweig, 28 August 1939

Your lovely letter just arrived early this morning, and I want to quickly answer it; a proper letter follows. Eberhard has been called up since Sunday. For the time being, it is not possible to write to him; we have to get him to give us his address, which can take up to 8 or 10 days. As soon as I know something, I will write you. My dear child, what will befall us! Our help needs to come from God. Stay healthy. I am still hoping for a *happy* resolution. The harvest is in, and otherwise we are taken care of. Let's hope that mail service continues to function.

Minna von Alten to her granddaughter Irmgard Brester, Braunschweig, 29 August 1939

I hope you received my hastily written card and will still be able to get this letter; it would be very distressing if our correspondence was blocked.

So what does it look like at our end? Soldiers everywhere, schools and all other large usable spaces are completely occupied, and the single thought prevails that, God willing, everything will somehow turn out alright at the last minute. We are being well cared for, everything is being rationed, despite large stock of supplies, but in such a way that we have enough.

It will be a while before we hear from Eberhard; he is my first and last thought. I was still able to send him a packet of eggs, 6 of them, which he received, but the packet of ham and sausage that I sent him a day later, was *returned* yesterday. When it came back, tears came to my eyes. He sent me a card: "The eggs arrived safely and I am taking them with me. I am happy that I can exchange so many good ideas with people in Germany and Holland." These words have stuck in my mind and as soon as we can, we have to make sure to write him frequently. If only he had a home. He handed over his household things and his apartment to Herr B. [a lawyer]; I had written him to send me his laundry, but he left everything there. You have to get little Jan baptized no matter what; don't postpone anything during this critical time, even if events, according to the latest news, look more and more turbulent. We can never know what will happen. It would be so nice if you could come here in October, but we can't count on that anymore, dear child. Even if everything turns out alright, it will be some time before things return to normal. We are completely isolated; a few trains have been freed up for the general public, but everybody just stays at home. Automobile traffic is almost completely prohibited, so I don't see or hear anything from Hedeper either, just a short telephone call once in a while. Even so, on the whole, everything proceeds on course, just waiting quietly. But my thoughts wander, and that is hard, Immo. Ursel has a great deal to do because most teachers have been drafted. She has 60 children to teach.

Whenever you write about the children it is a ray of sunshine. Good that I was able to send you the fabrics, now it would be impossible; without a coupon, you can't buy anything. [. . .] But these are trivial matters compared to the sorrows that may well lie ahead. The lives of people no longer count. [. . .]

On 1 September 1939, German troops invaded Poland. After Hitler rejected their ultimatum to withdraw, Great Britain and France declared war on Germany on 3 September. Shortly after the German invasion, as the Polish army retreated, local Poles killed as many as two thousand ethnic Germans, many in the city of Bromberg. After fierce resistance, Warsaw was bombed by the Luftwaffe into surrendering on 27 September. The Nazis immediately began to deport Polish prisoners of war to Germany, where they worked in factories or on farms to replace the local Germans who were serving in the Wehrmacht. At the beginning of October, Hitler offered the Allies a peace proposal, but he insisted on the acceptance of the status quo and the end of an independent Polish state. Britain and France refused to negotiate. At the same time, the North Sea became increasingly dangerous: Dutch freighters and fishing boats found themselves repeatedly attacked by German warplanes and jeopardized by Allied as well German mines.

At the outbreak of the war, Eberhard was working as an assessor in the Reich Ministry of Economics. He was quickly mobilized and entered Poland a few days after the invasion. He probably witnessed the aftermath of the events in Bromberg, known as "Bloody Sunday" (3 September 1939). He remained in the neighborhood of Warsaw until the end of October, when he was transferred back to Berlin.

Immo and her three-year-old son, Karel, traveled to Braunschweig for her grandmother's eightieth birthday on 2 October 1939. Blackout rules applied everywhere. Immo had to change trains four times in train stations lit by only a few blue lights and completed her journey in an almost fully darkened streetcar. Immo's sense of anxiety about traveling through a country at war was partially relieved by her grandmother's joy at the family reunion.

Immo's notebook, 1 September 1939

Unbearably tense days.

Immo's notebook, 3 September 1939

A miserable day. The children wanted to celebrate [the tenth wedding anniversary]!

Irmgard Brester to her grandmother Minna von Alten, Amersfoort, 4 September 1939

Last night, after the news, which just takes your breath away, I thought of you and, above all, of our young ones with such a heavy heart that I had to sit at my desk and in my fear and restlessness write this letter to Eberhard. My heart just aches, for I can't help him at all. So I want to ask you, my best dear Olla, if you could put these two enclosed sheets in an envelope and send them directly to Hardus as soon as you have his address. Wherever he may be! I really hope that with you as an intermediary I can always stay in contact with him. I am also thinking of you so much, dearest Ohmchen. Be brave and keep your head up, that is what all of us have to do. Don't hesitate to read my letter to Eberhard, then you will know how lovingly our children comforted us yesterday. If it gets really bad, you must go to Hedeper!

Nina Revers to her friend Irmgard Brester, Heerenveen, 5 September 1939

In these trying times, so difficult for all of us, but especially for you, I just want to write and tell you how often you are in my thoughts. How I would like to live a bit closer to you, if only so that you could speak your mind freely to someone else besides August. For all your thoughts must surely be with your poor fellow countrymen and women. And when I think of how we are bowed down with worry and fear over the fate of Europe and our children's future, I think about how you must be feeling, with your Fatherland being directly involved in the strife. We aren't yet, thank God, but it must be very difficult for you.

As soon as I heard about the treaty with Russia, I thought of you, that must have been a blow to you. It is a godsend that you have August, with whom you can talk about all of this. And remember that you have good friends here, who understand how difficult it is for you and think about you often. It's lucky the children aren't old enough yet to be aware of what is going on.

Minna von Alten to her granddaughter Irmgard Brester, Braunschweig, 6 September 1939

How I enjoyed your letter! A first sign of life. The second letter arrived last night, from Eberhard, who still has not given me his address. When I heard from him 8 days ago, he was still in the country, but he writes that he will be going to the East tomorrow. He didn't say where he is, but says he is doing well and that I should let you know. For the time being we will not be getting mail from him. Of course, we will wait; if only we knew for certain that he will continue to do well. The burdens we carry are heavy, but we do so happily if we can be of help. The schools here are closed and filled with people from the western front who have been evacuated for safety's sake. They have been moved into private homes as well, it may well be my turn soon. Ursel has been deployed into the Home Guard. The [ration] card system still has to get sorted out. Eberhard writes with confidence. Doesn't it just make your blood boil that the English have butt in again! [. . .]

Minna von Alten to her granddaughter Irmgard Brester, Braunschweig, 8 September 1939

Last night your lovely letter arrived; it was delayed because it had been opened by customs control. I still don't have a connection to Eberhard. In his last letter of 4 September, he wrote: "I just heard that the last letters have to be posted in a few minutes, so in great haste, a greeting. For the time being, you won't hear from me. But I am doing well, the Germans here cannot believe that they belong to us once again. My warmest greetings to you and the others." That was sent from near Bromberg. Bromberg was taken on the 6th, so he was in the middle of it. In his first letter, he wrote that I should always extend his greetings to you. Now we can only pray for him, dearest Immo. [. . .]

I just read his letter one more time. He writes, "I am doing great; tomorrow we get roast pork." We should take that to heart given how poorly he takes care of himself. He also has a splendid superior officer with whom he gets along. We are dealing with shortages with courage and patience; the troops have to be provisioned first. We still have it good if you consider the refugees and migrants from the western front. At first I had difficulties with the blackout regulations because I can't climb up, but I have got it in hand now. [. . .] Hopefully we will stay in touch, dear Immo; if only the English would give it a rest! Karl K. got news from back home [in Silesia], where troops have been quartered in homes for weeks now. They wrote that they never imaged that we had so many soldiers; whenever some were deployed, new ones arrived. But the suffering that follows!!

My dear Immo, write me how you are doing, if only a postcard given the demands on your time. Our thoughts are with our loved ones. All 3 of Süpplingen's sons have been drafted. We must trust in God. [. . .]

Minna von Alten to her granddaughter Irmgard Brester, Braunschweig, 11 September 1939

Yesterday I received Eberhard's address, a preprinted card but one he filled out. It was his handwriting and a sign of life, *how* grateful I am. So: Private First Class Eberhard Gebensleben, 22614, Postsammelstelle Berlin," add *nothing* else. As you know, I have your two letters for Eberhard. I will send your last one to him today. All we do is think about our young men out there, and yet we can do so little for them. You had the baptism; I was there in spirit.

Diethelm is on the western front. Yesterday, Hilde Kammerer came by, her brother has also been drafted. The day before mobilization he sprained one foot and broke the other; he is unhappy to be lying in the military hospital. [. . .]

Eberhard Gebensleben to his grandmother Minna von Alten, Poland, 13 September 1939

Although strictly speaking it can only be good news if you do *not* hear from me, I do find a letter quite appropriate. I would especially like to hear from *you*, how you are doing. Yesterday evening, we received our first round of mail. Things still have to get warmed up so maybe I will have luck next time. So how are you doing! You also have important tasks to carry out, to keep up your spirits, first of all, whereby there really is good reason given our rapid advance in the East! Isn't it fabulous?

I have any number of things to say about myself; we will have to catch up later. The saddest part is the horrible murder of untold thousands of ethnic German *civilians* here; I don't know what the newspapers are reporting, but they can hardly be exaggerating, the opposite if anything. This is on the conscience of armed Polish bandits, but also on the withdrawing Polish *military*. There wasn't a single village that we marched through where 30–40 Germans were not massacred. Some we exhumed, others are still lying in the fields next to the country roads. Men, women, and children. How human beings can carry something like this out is incomprehensible. These are not human beings, and they have to be treated accordingly. The sorrow of the survivors! Again and again we hear: "If you had only arrived two days earlier." Of course, now with the military occupation, everything is quiet. But these were horrible scenes to witness, and they justify *any and all* measures on our part. Otherwise we are doing great, and our spirits are up. Soldiers forget quickly; it probably has to be that way. We are already at the former German-Russian border, very flat country, low-slung white houses with straw-thatched roofs. The real East begins here. Little sign of any culture, at least as far as the villages and the so-called small towns are concerned. And dirty, totally unbelievable! Apparently other standards apply here! Since we are quartered in the big estates, we are doing quite well. The gardens are still full of fruit and vegetables, and one shouldn't turn up one's nose at the celebrated Polish swine. I am sure I have gained considerable weight.

Please send me a bottle of Belladonna and Akonit in pellet form and a big packet of Wybert tablets or cough drops. Only as a prophylaxis since a small cold is easily taken care of. But please do not send *any* food stuffs, on the contrary I could ready a package for you. Once more my address: [. . .] Write "Feldpost" on the envelope, stamps are *not* necessary, delivery is free. My warmest greetings as well to the dear Hollanders. Did they postpone the baptism? Please send them the enclosed letter, because it is difficult to write directly. Also hello to Ursel.

Irmgard Brester to her grandmother Minna von Alten, Amersfoort, 14 September 1939

You can't imagine how happy I was to get your letter yesterday with Eberhard's address. Every sign of life is so valuable and now at least we know how to reach him. I sent him a card right away and now I have to call upon your help as an intermediary and ask you to send him the enclosed letter. I don't even know if he is able to receive letters from abroad. That is why I want to try it both ways. Since I am thinking so much of our boy, he might as well know that we are thinking about him all day long. Wherever may he be! Our good thoughts and prayers have to protect him, dearest Ohmchen, we can't do anything more. I am so grateful for any piece of news, Ollachen, and wait longingly for more. It is easy to believe that you were thinking of us on Sunday. True, we had envisioned the baptism differently, but all my dear loved ones were here in spirit, at the very sweet service in our little church. We really preferred not to postpone it; given these grave times, it was our desire to baptize our little child. [. . .]

Groceries are being rationed here too, tea, coffee, sugar, fats are in short supply and sometimes impossible to find. But what is that in comparison to you! And then all those soldiers housed everywhere. Luckily not in the children's school. [. . .]

Minna von Alten to her granddaughter Irmgard Brester, Braunschweig, 18 September 1939

[. . .] Unfortunately still no news from Eberhard. We have to assume that an enormous upheaval is taking place out there. The poor people who have to suffer. Here available space is occupied by people from the West. Everything is rationed—think of the world war and Grandfather Brester—you will experience it soon enough. The women here are being called up, if only I can hold on to Minna. Do you sometimes listen to the German radio broadcasts? Our government only wants what is best! [. . .]

Bertha Haedicke to her niece Irmgard Brester, Leipzig, 19 September 1939

[. . .] I thought of you with all my best wishes on the day of little Jan's baptism. I am sure that every day you think about your brother Eberhard, who is in God's hands, as they all are, our dear Ohmchen as well. I hope to travel to Braunschweig for her 80th birthday, and you will hear from us there. Diethelm is posted on the western front as a Medical Staff Sergeant. God be with us!

Minna von Alten to her granddaughter Irmgard Brester, Braunschweig, 20 September 1939

Just a quick note to let you know that the first news from Eberhard arrived. He is on the eastern front, the letter was dated the 13th, so it took 7 days. [. . .] I will send you the letter shortly. Our advances are just fantastic. [. . .] Heinrich A. and his son-in-law have also been called up, but they are still in Germany. [. . .]

Minna von Alten to her granddaughter Irmgard Brester, Braunschweig, 22 September 1939

I don't want to keep the enclosed letter from Eberhard from you any longer. What the boy has had to go through! Thank goodness he is still busy in the horse stables. [. . .] How things have turned out! But let it soon come to an end!

Eberhard Gebensleben to his grandmother Minna von Alten, Feldpost, 24 September 1939

Given the restrictions on mail, I have not been able to write, and I only received your letters on the 12th. What a joy that was! So many at once and all the good news, from Holland as well. [. . .] We've had some very nice days, relaxing on a big Polish estate, with beds and even a small bathroom, really the summer resort life I had been missing up to now. Presumably we have to move on today, again something new! Overall the news has been very satisfactory up to now, wouldn't you say? We know because we've acquired a radio and are completely in the loop. *Please write, write, write*, that is the best.

Minna von Alten to her granddaughter Irmgard Brester, Braunschweig, 27 September 1939

This morning a card arrived from Eberhard. I have copied it word for word and will enclose it. I cried tears of joy, worried as I was about him, but I am happy that he continues to be well. [. . .] Unfortunately we are no longer allowed to buy chocolate, but I still have two bars for him. How nice that they have acquired a radio, he never really knew what was happening. So today Warsaw surrendered, yet another huge step forward, but one asks oneself, now what? Hopefully you are not too affected, your poor fishermen!

[. . .] Gerda brought me a big basket of wonderful fruit. She is such a devoted housekeeper, they have so many people to feed, which can't be easy since they cook differently in the Saar. [. . .] Women are tram conductors again, just like in the world war.

[. . .] Friedel is in a bunker on the western front, the second son already had home leave, lived through many things, and the third, an active officer is still here in Germany. They are all scattered by the winds of fate. [. . .]

Don't let yourselves be deceived by English lies; everything here is taking its course.

Minna von Alten to her granddaughter Irmgard Brester, Braunschweig, 29 September 1939

I can try and tell you how much I am looking forward to you and Kaki. Hopefully you will arrive in good shape. Give me a call from the train station if you can't make it to the tram yourself. Cars are not available. Be sure to bring rolls for the trip.

Eberhard Gebensleben to his sister Irmgard Brester, near Warsaw, 2 October 1939

After a long lull, the Feldpost delivered 2 letters from Holland in addition to a lot of other mail. One of them, dated 26 August with 2 lovely photos, took over 5 weeks. [. . .] Well, we are all now especially bound together in our thoughts. Ohmchen will have relayed to you that there is no reason to worry on my account. Given the unit and the duties to which I was assigned I have had, as it were, "luck," at least when seen from one point of view. Naturally, I can't write in more detail. On top of that, the offensive in Poland is now over, as you know yourself from the newspapers and radio.

In one sense, the Dutch are once again especially badly off. You can feel the physical effects of the hardships and deprivations of war, experience your own mobilization, yet do not realize so clearly why all of this is necessary. After what I have seen and lived through, I now know why and also believe that in the end, when seen in terms of the big picture, it will be a step forward. In Poland the world before the war was just not "good and well." It is not just a question of the fate of the ethnic Germans; the overall social conditions are simply catastrophic, and measured against Dutch standards, incomprehensible. On the other hand, I have made several valuable connections that will perhaps outlive the war and this period of political antagonisms. You in Holland will hopefully be able to preserve your paradise. If you only knew how often I think of you, the children, the garden, and Amersfoort!

Minna von Alten to her granddaughter Irmgard Brester, Braunschweig, 8 October 1939

We have accompanied you in our thoughts, and I have pictured what little Kaki must be up to. I am so grateful that I was able to have you here, and every day I keep calling back to memory different scenes of all of you. [. . .]

Eberhard writes me quite cheerfully, that he has received so much mail at once, 13 letters, and that he is now completely in the picture with regard to what is happening here at home. He says they are well provisioned, with warm clothes, vests, underwear, etc., and whatever is lacking is ordered up. Many of them dream of returning to their homeland early, which he thinks is quite possible, but he is of the opinion that one shouldn't count on it too soon. He will surely have received your lovely package by now.

[. . .] Gerda will run the household alone for the time being, and since Uncle Otto is still waiting for his prisoners and is under such pressure, we are holding off on visits for now. Aunt Minna regrets not having seen you and Kaki. Now that the Führer has given his speech, we are sitting and waiting to see how things unfold. Today I heard that an answer from England is expected on Wednesday. Will it be another bluff, like 8 days ago, when we were cheated of a nice day with you? [. . .]

Eberhard sent along the *Soldatenzeitung* today and requested that I send it to you as well; my sense is that they are well informed about everything. Eberhard wrote a little bit more about himself, that they have plenty of cigars and cigarettes, which he mostly gives away. Polish girls have to wash their laundry, but they try to look after the horses themselves. Recently during a quiet period they threshed 400 hundredweights of oats. How inventive war makes you!

Minna von Alten to her granddaughter Irmgard Brester, Braunschweig, 16 October 1939

[. . .] One wants to help out, so I am really sad that your sugar is being rationed, and your little ones with their sweet tooth! [. . .]

Eberhard writes that he can send me butter, but I replied that in the world war Heini Roever did the same thing and got into trouble as a result and even lost his secure posting. [. . .]

Now just imagine who was at the door on Saturday evening, but Frieda and her husband! He had 10 days leave, was among the first to cross the border, and took part in the entire war. His company has now been reassigned at home, and for his part, he thinks he will be deployed in the West. He had lots of interesting things to recount and maintains that the whole misfortune is the fault of the black-coats and the Jews. His account of how they misled the poor Poles and fed them completely false reports was downright mind-boggling. These people organized all of the partisan attacks; the atrocities simply cannot be adequately described. They tied Germans up to trees, poked out their eyes, cut open their bodies, and left them to die without the so-called mercy shot. The black-coats welcomed the Germans with up-raised arms and a Hitler greeting so that they let down their guard, later they started shooting from trees and churches.

Frieda asked about you and enjoyed looking at your photographs. Riechers went on to say, how the most magnificent horses with the most up-to-date gear could be found all across Poland. [. . .]

Not knowing what will happen is so unbearable. The English won't even admit their losses. I still hope that Eberhard will come visit when he has leave; a lot of soldiers from the East have been in town on leave already. Aunt Bertha sent Diethelm an edition of *Faust*; I will do the same and send Eberhard a copy and enclose your letter and also another illustrated. Did you get the *Soldatenzeitung* I sent you?

Eberhard Gebensleben to his grandmother Minna von Alten, Poland, 16 October 1939

Instead of just telling you theoretically about Poland's culinary delicacies, I thought it would be better to send you a sample: hopefully it arrived safely. Lots of butter is being sent through the Feldpost. [. . .]

As a driver, I have been all over the place in my car, two days in Lodz, for example, and one day in Warsaw, for the most part not very pleasant. Tomorrow morning, I take off for a longer trip. [. . .] When I have time, I saddle up a horse and ride around the region. In other words: I am really doing very well.

Eberhard Gebensleben to his brother-in-law August Brester, Feldpost, 16 October 1939

Heartfelt greetings from your Eberhard after two days of big city life in Lodz and Warsaw.

Hilde Kammerer to her friend Irmgard Brester, Braunschweig, 17 October 1939

[. . .] Today I called your grandmother up on the telephone and found out that you and Kareltje got back home safely after changing trains four times. August must surely have been happy to get you back a day early. [. . .] Your grandmother told me that you've received good news from Eberhard. May he return to you safe and sound. Marie B. received good news from her husband. [. . .]

Warschau, „Jüdische Politiker"

Warszawa, „Żydowscy politycy"

Eberhard's postcard to August with the caption "Warsaw, 'Jewish Politicians'"

Minna von Alten to her granddaughter Irmgard Brester, Braunschweig, 18 October 1939

Your package arrived here yesterday morning without a hitch. You don't know how happy you have made me. [. . .] I've sent you several newspapers, although I assume that you know about our brave feats of war. [. . .] Diethelm wrote that we are aiming for a campaign around Christmas, some hope earlier. [. . .] I wish I were able to send you some sugar.

Minna von Alten to her granddaughter Irmgard Brester, Braunschweig, 24 October 1939

Enclosed I am sending you a copy of Eberhard's letter that arrived early Saturday with a portion of butter. I am really touched by how you and Eberhard are taking care of me. Eberhard had mentioned it before, and I in turn wrote to him that I was afraid that the authorities would make trouble, but that doesn't seem to be the case since Frieda's husband brought back all sorts of things. [. . .] I also sent you along newspapers; did they say anything new? You are undoubtedly listening frequently to the German broadcasts, aren't you? I am hugely interested in everything they report about Holland.

[. . .] You can't imagine with what pleasure I eat my buttered bread with Dutch cheese in the evening! I'm now well provisioned for a while. I often think of how Papa

Brester used to take care of you after the world war. Yesterday, I made up a package for Eberhard and included some of your good chocolate. [. . .]

Eberhard Gebensleben to his sister Irmgard Brester, Braunschweig, 1 November 1939

Can you imagine that a soldier on leave is sitting in Ohmchen's warm, comfortable dining room? Out in the kitchen, Minna is preparing a newly delivered Polish rabbit, and Ohmchen is sitting across from me, cutting up the required red cabbage. So everything is in the best of order; last night made for a great big surprise! Beforehand, I stopped off in Berlin to put some things in order, my room, etc., reported to the Ministry as well, and received nothing but reassurances about my good prospects.

On 4 November 1939, the Dutch government received two warnings that a German attack would take place on 12 November. It conscripted reservists and began to flood several tracts of territory. Apparently the attack was postponed due to poor weather conditions, but a general state of emergency remained in effect in areas that were militarily fortified. Again and again, the Dutch received information about new target dates and further postponements.

At the same time, an attempt on Hitler's life took place in Munich's Bürgerbraukeller; 8 people were killed and 63 others wounded. The Nazis initially blamed the English, but the assassination attempt was the work of a single man, Georg Elser, who was arrested and later murdered in Dachau in 1945, shortly before the concentration camp's liberation by the Americans.

The air war in the west was also heating up. On 18 December 1939, more than half of the English bombers attacking German warships in the German Bight (west of the Jutland Peninsula) were shot down by much faster German fighter planes. The next day, the Braunschweigischer Allgemeiner Anzeiger *featured the news in large type: 34* ENGLISH PLANES IN ONE BLOW; THAT WILL CAUSE AN UPSET STOMACH ON THE BANKS OF THE THAMES, *it went on to say.*

Eberhard continued working intermittently at the Ministry of Economics. Accompanied by his new girlfriend, Herta Euling, a pianist from Berlin, Eberhard visited his grandmother over Christmas. Otherwise, he was on duty in army barracks in Rostock and Frankfurt an der Oder.

Minna von Alten to her granddaughter Irmgard Brester, Braunschweig, 5 November 1939

[. . .] Suddenly on Tuesday Eberhard stood at the door with 2 suitcases and a pouch packed with a rabbit. His unit has now withdrawn to barracks in Frankfurt an der O. Wednesday we immediately washed his battle gear, brushed his uniform, and dried everything in front of the oven. [. . .] He commented: "You are living as if there is peace, your apartment is a paradise." Dear Immo, the impressions gained over there won't fade away so soon, they will stay for a lifetime. [. . .] Incidentally, Lawyer B. is also in the field. [. . .] You are rousing yourselves as well; yesterday I read that a state of siege had been declared in Utrecht and several other cities. Hopefully you are not affected. Herr M. has also been called up. [. . .] Uncle Otto came by for the first time in a long while; he still has so much to do and is lying in wait for prisoners who haven't arrived yet. Gerda has to cook for 8 soldiers who have been assigned there to help, but is without a housekeeper. [. . .] I so much wanted to get my hands on a goose in order to cook it in the event Eberhard might come, but Uncle Otto couldn't round one up in Hedeper. So I telephoned Aunt L., then finally Aunt Ella in Salzdahlum, who got lucky and has one picked out for me. [. . .]

Eberhard Gebensleben to his cousin Ursula Meier, Frankfurt/Oder, 9 November 1939

[. . .] This morning the news about the assassination attempt in Munich. You just want to fall to your knees in thanks.

Minna von Alten to her granddaughter Irmgard Brester, Braunschweig, 20 November 1939

[. . .] Eberhard was called to the Ministry for a few days to complete a project that he had been working on. Thereafter he returned here. You know that he is now a noncommissioned officer, and he has reported to his old unit. We will have to see if that works. [. . .] But first, he came back from the Ministry with a medal in the form of a commemorative coin presented by the Führer in recognition of the annexation of the Sudetenland and all the work done there. There were many soldiers who were considered, but Eberhard, who put in such a colossal amount of work, was officially recognized along with 3 other Assessors. Eberhard himself was pleased, and he recounted the whole business when Ursel and Herr M. were here on Saturday. [. . .]

Oh my dear, dear Immo, I often feel so down, and I have just suffered another huge loss with the sudden death of Frau S. [. . .] One after another, they go; there are only a few of us left. And who do Eberhard and Ursel have! When the war is over, at least the connection to Holland will be easier, you brave Hollanders! Kaki and Mama!! [. . .]

Gerda cooks valiantly on. Uncle Otto now has his prisoners, for the most part small farmers who feel very comfortable. A few affirmed that Germany was much more beautiful and wanted to fetch their wives. [. . .]

Eberhard's diary, 20 November 1939

Frankfurt/Oder. In the morning with a pack of civilians to the Schlesische train station in Berlin. Where is the big transport to be shipped? To Frankfurt/Oder again! My God, what a vicious circle! That is promising, but we should really move on.

Minna von Alten to her granddaughter Irmgard Brester, Braunschweig, 27 November 1939

You don't know how happy your package made me. It is something that I haven't had in a long time and, for a long time, won't be able to get again, as is the case with coffee as well. We learn to drink all sorts of things, peppermint tea and barley coffee, everything for the Fatherland and out of hate for England. [. . .]

But first I have to tell you that Eberhard was already recalled on the 3rd day. As he wrote, he is quite disappointed to be back, at least for the time being, in Frankfurt/Oder. His major was very surprised to see him. But he is with another unit, the artillery again; I will let you know his exact address. After 2 wonderful days, barracks life is hard to get used to; he will just have to adjust. [. . .] I sent on your detailed letter and the sweet photographs. [. . .] You can thank the English for the fact that you were so upset by the false alarm and even wanted to start packing. [. . .]

Eberhard Gebensleben to his sister Irmgard Brester, Frankfurt/Oder, 29 November 1939

[. . .] You are always thinking of me, dearest Immeken; that is so wonderful! I am also avidly following the latest news about Holland. I am sure you don't have it easy. If only the English wouldn't disturb your peace! [. . .] You've already heard about my promotion; it was very important to me and the daily routine is much easier. [. . .] My congratulations to Jan for his achievements in standing up. What a wonderful little brood!

Minna von Alten to her granddaughter Irmgard Brester, Braunschweig, 4 December 1939

[. . .] Now to our boy: he wrote Saturday that he has been transferred again, to a completely new unit that is being created. He thinks it will be quite interesting. [. . .]

Aunt Lisbeth sent me 10 lbs of sugar beet syrup—if only I had the energy I would bake honey cakes just as I did during the world war. I should be getting a rabbit or a hare, but all the hunters have been called up to the front.

Bertha Haedicke to her niece Irmgard Brester, Leipzig, 9 December 1939

[. . .] I look back on the 80th birthday with gratitude as well. Your Karl was a magnificent head of the family. A somewhat belated advent calendar is coming for the little ones. Ohmchen tells me that our honorable noncommissioned officer Eberhard quite suddenly arrived on leave. What a joy! Diethelm's leave has been postponed until Christmas, to the disappointment of Hanna and the children. But war is war. [. . .]

Eberhard's diary, 14 December 1939

Frankfurt/Oder. I am already getting a surprising number of Christmas packages, the Party, Zeitlers, Aunt Agnes. From 2:00 to 10:00 in the afternoon, first watch at the main train station, as duty officer with 1 private. Mostly checking leave passes, unfortunately in a very drafty passageway. A new scene for a colorful motion picture: soldiers on leave, prisoner transports, ethnic Germans, Hungarian peasant girls in buxom traditional dress, it is actually not boring, just tiring.

Eberhard's diary, 17–19 December 1939

Frankfurt/Oder. [. . .] I am currently reading Forester's *Captain Horatio Hornblower*, as exciting as any adventure story. I doubt whether our propaganda is doing the right thing when it constantly belittles the English and their achievements. It could well end in a nasty surprise for us.

The private assigned to me on gate guard duty is a real skirt-chaser: fiancé in Berlin, a "proper" girlfriend installed in Frankfurt/Oder, and many others besides, including the girls behind the counter in the 3rd class waiting room, something that provides us with many material advantages (sandwiches!). It is for these somewhat dubious reasons that he arranged for me to meet a waitress, Eva, who I've invited to the movies and a cup of coffee this evening (the 19th). Damn, I am actually too old for this sort of business!

Minna von Alten to her granddaughter Irmgard Brester, Braunschweig, 18 December 1939

I wish you a joyous and reflective Christmas celebration! [. . .]

Eberhard writes that he has guard duty at the train station, in itself not strenuous, only tiresome and boring. Always 8 hours, then 16 hours free. At the moment, 2:00 in the afternoon until 10:00 at night and next week from 6:00 in the morning to 2:00 in the afternoon. Then the night shift. [. . .]

Dearest Immo, just two years ago everything was so different!

[. . .] Diethelm is not getting leave, not Hans L. either. The war, the terrible war! [. . .] And we can't talk to each other, when Eberhard was here, we tried, but telephone calls to Holland are prohibited. [. . .]

Minna von Alten to her granddaughter Irmgard Brester, Braunschweig, 19 December 1939

What a surprise! [. . .] I just packed up Eberhard's portion. I would love to see his expression when he opens a genuine Holland package! [. . .] I am also sending you today's newspaper. I want you to stay informed about the air war—what it is really like. [. . .] We must trust in God.

Irmgard Brester to her grandmother Minna von Alten, Amersfoort, 25 December 1939

What did you say when Eberhard told you about our completely successful phone conversation! What a pleasure that was! And how good it was to know that the two of you were together on Christmas Eve. And I am delighted that you had a little tree, dear Olla! [. . .]

Eberhard Gebensleben to his sister Irmgard Brester, Braunschweig, 25 December 1939

[. . .] just a short Christmas greeting by mail. It was so good to hear your voices and, in passing, those of the dear children last night. Ohmchen was so happy for me, even though I had to use another telephone, not hers. (Besides it wasn't so easy to obtain permission.) Then we spent a very quiet and appreciative Christmas Eve together.[. . .]

We already refreshed ourselves mightily thanks to your "supply" package. With your parcels, dearest Immo, you are giving many people a great, heartfelt pleasure; the Dutch war refugee has herself now become a benefactor. That must be a great and uplifting feeling for you.

26 DECEMBER 1939

[. . .] in the meantime, we received a visit from my best and most genuine friend in Berlin, a young pianist in whose apartment I have occasionally had the pleasure of listening to private recitals. Tomorrow morning we travel back together to Berlin, and then I go on to Frankfurt/Oder. [. . .]

Eberhard's diary, 31 December 1939

Eichkamp [Berlin] in deep snow. Telephoned with Eberhard [someone else] and Herta. Lunch with Eberhard in the "vegetarian" near the Zoo. The three of us will enjoy a harmonious and contemplative New Year's Eve in Herta's well-kept apartment. What a woman! Will the two of them come together? It almost seems so! Could I imagine marrying Herta? Strange thought. One thing I do know is that she also wants to have an emotional relationship with just me.

Eberhard's diary, 8 January 1940

Berlin. In the evening with Herta Euling. The unbelievable is becoming believable. Just one remark to the decisive point in our conversation—Klott the astrologer prophesied that 8 January would be a significant day, although nothing significant has happened yet—pushes open closed doors with stunning clarity. Now we know that we love each other.

Eberhard's diary, 13 January 1940

Berlin. I take off my uniform for four weeks. My first official visit to the Ministry. I will be able to see Herta in the evening. A new, tender, more wonderful world.

Eberhard Gebensleben to his sister Irmgard Brester, Berlin, 18 January 1940

[. . .] In Berlin, I often buy a Dutch paper and practice the language and so on. You are enjoying a great ice-skating season! [. . .]

Eberhard's diary, 20 January 1940

Berlin. [. . .] Afterward a bite to eat at Herta's. An open, harmonious evening, despite the shoals of a political argument about the Nazis. Every evening together is different from earlier ones, each with a very special beauty that is hard to describe.

Eberhard's diary, 21 January 1940

Berlin. Then the afternoon and evening with Herta. Conversations about history and politics. At the end difficulties regarding our personal attitudes toward each other. She shows me old photos of her childhood and almost becomes a stranger. The foolish unapproachableness of one's beloved!

Minna von Alten to her granddaughter Irmgard Brester, Braunschweig, 21 January 1940

[. . .] I already mentioned in my card to the children that Eberhard is really spending 1 month in Berlin as *Assessor* in his own apartment. [. . .] I was able to send him ½ lb of butter and jam four days ago [. . .], and I thought that, if it was possible, you could send him a small parcel not much, perhaps some chocolate or a few grams of coffee. [. . .] He was taken care of in the barracks but is no longer there. [. . .]

Irmgard Brester to her grandmother Minna von Alten, Amersfoort, 25 January 1940

Day before yesterday I received word from Eberhard in Berlin. He writes that he has gotten leave until 12 February and will probably come to Braunschweig for a few days at the end. I thought to myself, this is a chance to see him again and right away yesterday, I sent in my application for a visa. It is now more cumbersome, takes 8–14 days, but a German gentleman I recently met will put in a good word for me, and he thought that everything will work out. So if it is alright with you, I would come to Braunschweig in early February and wait for Eberhard with you. It would just be so wonderful to be able to see him again. Please, dearest Olla, don't make any trouble on my account, I'd just feel terrible. I can procure food ration cards for the days I am in Braunschweig, at least that is what they told me. I can also take provisions with me. Give me your honest opinion!

Eberhard's diary, 29 January 1940

Berlin. Nothing new at work. Date with Herta afterward. Complicated discussions with her as well. I stay overnight.

Eberhard's diary, 4 February 1940

Sunday in Berlin. Showered and breakfasted at Herta's, tasted some of Ohmchen's goose. A walk together in the Tiergarten und a quick visit to the aquarium. In the afternoon, a concert in the Beethoven Hall: string quartet and quintet. An astonishing Schubert adagio in C Major, one of his last works as it turns out after we looked it up in Herta's library. Another evening of pure joy in her beautiful apartment, dinner and tea, a little reading. It really is an unusually happy marriage that we have been living these last 4 weeks; it is fulfilling and real, even if the last physical aspects still have to wait.

Eberhard's diary, 5 February 1940

Berlin. Monday's work in the Ministry. Ate at Bollenmüller's with Dr. S. Over coffee the three of us, from different points of view, come to the same conclusion that Germany will have to make extraordinary efforts over the coming weeks and months, first of all in the air against England. That has to succeed before our choke points become manifest. Otherwise, so help us God.

Eberhard's diary, 16 February 1940

Berlin. In the morning, I torpedo the ministry's petition of indispensability on my behalf. If Germany is at war, I *have* to be there. Have I sealed my fate? Herta is unhappy, but I wonder if she doesn't understand after all.

Eberhard's diary, 20 February 1940

With Herta in Berlin. Herta, I am sitting by the coffee table and you just scampered into the bathroom to get dressed. Herta, I believe I will come back, and I believe in our future together. If that doesn't come to pass, then remember how happy we have been these last weeks, dear Herta. It felt like a lifetime.

Irmgard Brester to her grandmother Minna von Alten, Amersfoort, 6 March 1940

Now the last ray of hope for a trip to Braunschweig has vanished. The final decision from the consulate in Amsterdam arrived yesterday morning; my application was denied. The German gentleman I am acquainted with told me that of 400 applications, 9 were approved—without a really valid reason, it is just not possible. What that means is that we have to wait patiently and hope that better times will come so that we can see each other again! [. . .]

The Soviet Union invaded Finland on 30 November 1939 after the Finns refused to allow the Russians to establish bases on their territory. Despite remarkable losses inflicted on the Soviets, Finland was forced to surrender on 12 March 1940 and accept Soviet demands.

Germany invaded Denmark and Norway on 9 April 1940.

After the German invasion of Holland, Belgium, Luxemburg, and France on 10 May 1940, postal communication between Germany and Holland was broken off for a time. The letter that Minna von Alten had written to Immo on 6 May was returned with the stamp "Zurück" ("Return to Sender").

In March 1940, Eberhard was sent to Altenkessel in the Saarland, from where he saw little action in what was known as the "Phony War" between Germany and France before taking part in Germany's invasion of France a few weeks later. In time, he was transferred to Holland, where he served briefly in the German military government before it was replaced by a civilian Reichskommissariat under Arthur Seyss-Inquart (1892–1946).

Eberhard's diary, 7 March 1940

Altenkessel. I've landed with the heavy artillery, and it is also clear that there is a lot I have to relearn! The artillery pieces are placed in enclosures right along the firing line, very nicely constructed. We are sitting here on the so-called front lines, but in a sector known to be quiet. For months, the battery hasn't fired a single shell, although there are plenty targets. A kind of tacit agreement with the French, who could easily shell our work crews. Particularly strange, even haunting, are the noises of the radio coming from the evacuated homes of the civilian population (the sets are quite fancy, not at all what we are used to!).

Eberhard's diary, 15 March 1940

Simonsschacht. In the morning, reconnaissance just in front of the tower with the scissors telescope. Then as VVB (forward field scout) with advancing infantry cover *into Forbach* and onto the Schlossberg. Supported by intelligence troops and observers of the 9th Battery, who are primarily responsible for this sector. Lying on mattresses spread out for us, took up observation from the Schlossberg tower until half past twelve. To Morsbach for better sight lines (bunkers, etc.). Then back through town alone. What a dismal place, on par with Polish conditions. There is still a lot of plundering. The infantry has now established sentries everywhere. Even so, for a time during the advance of our reconnaissance patrol I was the most forward man along the entire German front. Childish pleasure.

Eberhard's diary, 25 March 1940

Altenkessel. Easter Monday, but regular duties all day long. Reported to the lieutenant (and a little ping-pong with Sergeant S.). [. . .]

In the afternoon, an hour of gas-attack training. Built out the firing line. Then roll call, from which I unfortunately had to excuse ⅔ of my men, many of them older. [. . .]

I have been informed that my next deployment will be as platoon commander. What a busy, interesting day! It is clear to me that I have gained recognition in the battery.

Eberhard's diary, 28 March 1940

Altenkessel. Moved out at 8 o'clock. Continued constructing the side wall along the roof tops. Broke down the stairs in other houses. It is amazing how we are fortifying ourselves. It is also distressing that we have to destroy these houses. To think that would happen to our beloved Brockenblick, to simply rip out a staircase!

Eberhard's diary, 8–10 April 1940

Altenkessel. [. . .] Brilliant military campaign in Scandinavia! The conflagration is sure crackling. Now that lots of younger reinforcements have arrived, the battery will be thoroughly overhauled. In effect, back to basic training! [. . .]

Minna von Alten to her granddaughter Irmgard Brester, Braunschweig, 11 April 1940

[. . .] I received good news from Eberhard on Monday. After a busy period without a lot of sleep, he is now doing better. We are being overtaken by events.

Irmgard Brester to her grandmother Minna von Alten, Amersfoort, 16 April 1940

Yesterday I received your somewhat anxious letter, and I wanted to send you greetings right away. True, mail is now irregular. But do not let yourself get so easily worried!

Eberhard's diary, 28 April 1940

Obersalbach. Sunday. Just morning duty. Poked around in the village in the afternoon. Walked in the woods with the seventeen- and eighteen-year-old to the antitank line (second line of defense, double wire entanglement, concrete barriers, and reinforced bunkers). A little amorous, and then quite weird with both. But I will find the right way back, and the splendid, open sun-kissed landscape does its part to put me in the proper mood. But Rosel, the little tomboy, is sure nice!! In the evening, a letter from Herta touches on just these things. How she knows to take my measure.

THE BROTHER (1940–1944)

The so-called Grebbelinie, one of the Dutch lines of defense, crossed through Amersfoort. The planned attack on the city on 13 May 1940 was ultimately deflected to the south, where fewer tracts of land had been flooded and the artillery fire was less intense. On 14 May, German bombers destroyed most of Rotterdam's downtown, killing some eight hundred to nine hundred people. A day later, the Dutch army surrendered.

By June 1940, rationing had been imposed for staples such as bread, flour, coffee, tea, and various textile goods. At the same time, the Germans began sending huge amounts of fruits and vegetables back to Germany, further depleting the food stocks available to the Dutch people.

After Belgium surrendered on 28 May, German troops pushed into northern France toward the English Channel. Wilhelm, the oldest grandson of the former kaiser, was among the casualties; another grandson, Oskar, had already fallen in Poland. The former kaiser himself refused Churchill's offer of asylum in the wake of the German invasion; at the same time, he made it clear that he would never return to Germany without the restoration of the monarchy. Wilhelm II died in Doorn, Holland, on 4 June 1941. Germany launched the final offensive against France on 5 June 1940; Paris fell on 14 June, and France capitulated on the twenty-seventh.

At the same time, the Royal Air Force dropped the first bombs on Germany on the night of 10 May. Attacks on Braunschweig began on 17 August. Almost every night for the following weeks, the city's population sought the safety of air-raid shelters. Only authorized citizens were allowed in the shelters; Germans of Jewish origin and foreign workers were barred from entering.

Before the anticipated attack on Amersfoort, the city was evacuated; Immo and the wife of one of August's colleagues went to Haarlem with their children, while the two men stayed behind in the crowded hospital outside the city carrying out their duties. After Holland's surrender on 15 May, Immo immediately returned with her children to a dark and nearly deserted Amersfoort. Children went back to school on 24 May. In July, August's hospital was requisitioned by the SS and later the Wehrmacht; the patients had to be moved. In early June, Eberhard visited his sister, and until August 1943 he returned to Amersfoort regularly despite political differences of opinion with Immo and especially August. Immo would not see her grandmother again, but they continued to write each other; Minna's letters often bore the stamp "Am Schalter eingeliefert" ("Posted at the Counter").

Eberhard's diary, 10 May 1940

Obersalbach. [. . .] News of the invasion of Holland and Belgium. My dear Holland! Let it come to an end quickly against honorable but hopeless resistance. [. . .]

Eberhard's diary, 13 May 1940

In the Leischwald. [. . .] Awakened to unload a column of trucks carrying ammunition. Then fired shells, but fewer than yesterday, in general less artillery activity. Fortunately the weather is good, and our position is very scenic. Life is a combination of utmost seriousness—which I am aware of with every shot I fire—and a kind of hobo existence. When will the French start firing back in earnest?

Eberhard's diary, 14 May 1940

In the Leischwald. [. . .] Very little news about Holland. A lot of free time at the moment. Glorious weather continues. [. . .]

Eberhard's diary, 19 May 1940

In the Leischwald. [. . .] The unprecedented offensive in the north all the way to St. Quentin and Laon is announced. In the evening the bombshell: a telephone call from division headquarters that by order of the OKH [Supreme Command of the Armed Forces] I am to be put immediately on leave. I am resolved to do everything I can in Berlin to return to duty if I am not offered an especially interesting civilian task. The idea that I should take my leave from the combat troops now of all times is almost unthinkable! As a consolation prize, I am informed that I have been promoted to the rank of sergeant. [. . .]

Eberhard's diary, 22 May 1940

Berlin. [. . .] After breakfast straight away to the OKH. For an hour, the most diligent attempts in various offices to be released. I am told that I am not being posted back in the RWM [Reich Ministry of Economics] but in the military administration of the occupied territories. Reported to Ministerrat Dr. B. in Giessen. [. . .]

Minna von Alten to her granddaughter Irmgard Brester, Braunschweig, 31 May 1940

Yesterday mail traffic to Holland was unblocked. You have no idea how happy I am, and now I have some hope to receive the sign of life from you that I so long for. Just to know that you are in good health and how you lived through those terrible days. My thoughts were always with you. I am doing alright, and Eberhard, who recently passed through, has been recalled to join the administration of the occupied territories, and where!!—in Holland. A reunion is not impossible!! He will certainly get in touch with you as soon as he can. How wonderful. My thank you letter for your lovely package did not make it through and was returned; today I am sending thanks one more time. According to the newspaper reports, you are settling in with the occupation, but the children will feel the restrictions on their freedom. In those terrible days, I always imagined you on the Lichtenberg. Ursel's fiancé is in the middle of the fighting; yesterday, she heard good news from him. Was Carel called up? So many questions—if only I knew how you are doing.

Eberhard's diary, 31 May 1940

Brussels. 10 o'clock start in a Dutch tourist bus, which will deposit ca. 12 gentlemen to the various Dutch Kommandanturen; 4 gentlemen for 's Hertogenbosch (Feld- and Oberfeldkommandantur). My suggestion that we alter the route so that we arrive in 's Hertogenbosch last is gladly accepted. My main reason: Amersfoort!

The journey: Mecheln–Antwerp–Breda–Geertruidenberg–Utrecht; 2 gentlemen disembark there. Apparently less destruction in Holland than in Belgium. I am very thankful! Then I am dropped off in Amersfoort while the bus goes on to Amsterdam; it will pick me up tomorrow morning when it returns from Zwolle. The lovely house completely undamaged, Immo in the dining room. Augustus in the consulting room treating a patient. Unbelievable joy. Heddalein has tears in her eyes. So many things to tell about our personal experiences and Dutch-German affairs, for which we are all full of hope.

Nina Revers to her friend Irmgard Brester, Heerenveen, 1 June 1940

Our thoughts have also been so much with you and your family, and I asked myself how you have been handling it all; I was worried that you would be evacuated en masse. I was already picturing you with the new backpacks! Would you have gone by car? We've also had some terrible days, that is, our town was immediately occupied, and everything was quite calm and orderly, but it was more about what we had to cope with psychologically. I can't write about all of that, but how I'd love to be able to talk about all sorts of things! All the old values are overturned, the rug has been pulled out from under our feet, and I don't understand anything any more. Pentecost weekend, endlessly long and uncertain, Floor desperate, were the worst days of my life. It took me every ounce of willpower to keep everything going for the sake of the children. [. . .] I have the feeling we've aged a hundred years, don't you feel the same? [. . .] Have you received any news from Eberhard?

Eberhard's diary, 3 June 1940

's Hertogenbosch. At headquarters of the OFK [Oberfeldkommandantur] in the Palace of Justice, I realize that there is actually nothing for us to do here. There is even an official prohibition since Seyss-Inquart has formally taken over operations with his civilian administration. (In fact not the case everywhere yet.) Luncheon in the Royal, not very good since we live on army provisions from home; horrible army bread; imagine that in Holland! [. . .]

Minna von Alten to her granddaughter Irmgard Brester, Braunschweig, 4 June 1940

It was with boundless joy that I received your letter bearing good news, given the circumstances. From the very beginning, I had a feeling that Immo and the children wouldn't be able to stay at home! But where did they go? I figured that you surely could go to Prof. Hijmans van den Bergh's daughter [Nina Revers], who lives a bit off the beaten track. Well, it doesn't matter, you're back home and found Vati safe and sound; that is the main thing. In the meantime, you will have received my letter, and Aunt Minna wrote you as well. So many people wondered about you! Everybody understood the danger in which you found yourself. Maybe you have already gotten a sign of life from Eberhard. He was here one more time for several hours eight days ago Sunday, on the 26th, had to travel from here to Berlin, and then report as quickly as possible to his final destination, the military administration in Holland. He hopes to see you. But I haven't heard from him. Your wonderful package came just in time, and Eberhard got his share shortly before the advance. He was still able to write me: "What a feeling it was to open the package! Our wonderful Holland!" He will give you details—we really live as in a frenzy—who knows what will still happen! All I can say is: God protect us. Despite his workload, Eberhard looked very good. He was promoted again, to sergeant. [. . .] Until now, we have always been able to sleep without making a detour into the cellar. People who have seen the newsreels always tell me about the massive amount of destruction, but eyewitnesses give more positive reports—you are adjusting well to the military occupation. I hope it is true. How did the little ones react to artillery fire? Those little creatures are the best medicine imaginable. [. . .] People here are full of confidence; the Volk is lifted up by the Führer's spirit.

Have the schools opened again, and was Amersfoort shelled? [. . .] As soon as I hear that Eberhard has taken up his new post, I will be able to relax again. Old folks like us have to think back to the world war, and I remember the war in 70/71; it is shattering.

So take care of yourselves—I am so happy that I am able to write to you again, and hopefully I won't have to constantly be looking at an empty mailbox. The family of our former crown prince announced that they lost their eldest son; the former Kaiser is supposed to have returned as well.

Hilde Kammerer to her friend Irmgard Brester, Braunschweig, 5 June 1940

Now that we can write letters to Holland once again, I wanted to tell you right away how happy I was to hear from your grandmother that you and your family came through everything alright and are healthy. Thank God! It is a load off my mind. Your grandmother and I were a great comfort to each other! A good thing that you and the children left, but that is still an undertaking with 4 children, and even so you must have lived through a lot! And it is must have been terrible for you to leave August behind in danger. But I said right away to your grandmother that August surely has a big cross on the roof of his hospital, which our airmen would take care to spare. How nice that all of you are back at home and that your house is undamaged.

Your grandmother has amazing energy and courage, and she is really doing well. Isn't it an absolute wonder that Eberhard has been transferred to your area, at least for the time being, and as a lawyer to boot. If only I could see from this distance. When I picture Eberhard suddenly standing at your door, the reunion practically brings tears to my eyes. You didn't even know where to reach him. Now these worries have disappeared; think of all the things that the two of you will have to tell each other! [. . .] You can imagine with what burning interest I followed our actions in Holland. Hopefully our museum in Rotterdam is undamaged?

Eberhard's diary, 7 June 1940

's Hertogenbosch. I just love my room, which overlooks the bustling market, and just as in a forest, the sights and sounds put you in a contemplative mood. The most important thing these days: [Ernst] Wiechert's *The Simple Life*, which Herta gave me. War without pathos or big aims, simply a trial by fire—and not even the most difficult! Life in the woods, ordinary labor that creates a better sense of how to live. I am grateful for the book. I want to talk to Wiechert. [. . .]

Irmgard Brester to her grandmother Minna von Alten, Amersfoort, 8 June 1940

The wonderful hours, which seem like a dream now, already lie behind me. You can imagine *how* great and *what* a surprise it was the moment Eberhard suddenly stepped into the room. And wonderful as well that he brought such good news about you, dearest Olla. Hopefully you will have received my letter by now and know that we are all healthy and safe. How long it has been not to hear from each other!

Eberhard came Friday evening and was able to stay only until early on Sunday. However, we totally took advantage of Saturday. August also managed to get off work. A glorious walk in the morning and errands in the afternoon. [. . .] From here he went on to Belgium and France. Hopefully we will hear from him frequently.

Eberhard's diary, 9 June 1940

's Hertogenbosch. Probably my last day in Holland. [. . .] In the evening, a letter to Herta. Can I express to her what was so clear to me when I read Wiechert: a life together, decent

Eberhard in Amersfoort (June 1940)

and faithful to our elementary responsibilities. And as a reward, to understand even a glimmer of wisdom. Conversation in the evening with a young SS lieutenant from Braunschweig.

Eberhard's diary, 10 June 1940

's Hertogenbosch. Together with First Lieutenant S. Around noon, I was able to get a ride with a car of the secret military police, a very stately affair, like a big shot. Over to Rotterdam (like Warsaw, but the destruction is more intense, though less extensive), Utrecht, Amersfoort. Stayed a good 3 hours, played with the children in the garden. Immo sang. Then got picked up and returned by way of Utrecht.

On the way to Rotterdam the bridges that the parachutists were able to capture. [. . .] In Amersfoort, we hear about Italy's declaration of war!

Eberhard's diary, 11 June 1940

's Hertogenbosch. [. . .] The car from Arras with Oberregierungsrat Peters finally arrives toward evening. Living conditions in Arras are still on a war footing. We agree on a departure time for tomorrow. Then another page in the big picture book of the war will be turned.

Minna von Alten to her granddaughter Irmgard Brester, Braunschweig, 12 June 1940

[. . .] According to the new regulations, there are various restrictions that we have to observe. I have to show my identity card before the stamps are affixed at the counter, but what is that against the joy to be allowed to write you and to hope for news from you.

[. . .] It is such a relief to know that you can still properly feed the children. Remember the world war when Vater Brester kept you supplied with fine things. [. . .]

We are completely absorbed by our earthshaking events. We have a new lease on life! The blood of so many young people was already shed there [in France] during the world war. 8 days ago the third Süpplinger got out; God protect all our loved ones. I am pleased that you can also follow everything on the radio. What a gift of God the children are. Incidentally, when things began to look dangerous for you, Aunt Margot wrote me in all seriousness that you and your entire family could stay with her any time.

Irmgard Brester to her grandmother Minna von Alten, Amersfoort, 13 June 1940

[. . .] Yes, Ollachen, how grateful we are to be able to write each other again. The uncertainty is terrible. [. . .] So many loved ones have worried about us! I've received lovely greetings from Hilde K., Aunt Minna, and Aunt Agnes. Now things are returning to normal, at least for us here; one hardly notices that such huge upheavals ever took place. Unfortunately however, there will be no more shipments of tea and coffee! Many things are now being rationed, but it is not so bad. The main thing is that we are all healthy. And the best thing is that we have been able to see our Eberhard again and know that for the time being he is out of danger. [. . .] He even surprised us Monday evening and ate dinner with us. By now, he will have left Holland, but we will live on our memories for some time to come. Eberhard looked magnificent; he felt that he had really recuperated while in Holland. [. . .]

With all our hearts, we enjoy our beautiful garden and we are enormously thankful to still have it. So what will happen now? Events tumble over each other; we are just holding our breath. Various German officers have been over to visit us; they are all so very confident. [. . .] Correct in their behavior, German soldiers have made a very good impression here. Most of the Dutch are astonished that the Germans are not the wild barbarians they had assumed them to be. [. . .] Events have affected the children, at least the two "older" ones, but like all children they also quickly forget. The 3 days that we spent as refugees in Haarlem they actually regarded as a small holiday. Amersfoort was completely evacuated; only the Lichtenberg, which is so far out on the outskirts, stayed put. That is why August had to stay here, and we ourselves spent the first days in the hospital. In the end, though, we thought it best to grab the chance to evacuate since the city did lie in a fire zone. The surrender came at just the right time! I still have so much to tell you! [. . .]

Well, we certainly miss our car. August bicycles to the hospital and saves his ration of gas for out-of-town consultations.

Minna von Alten to J.M. [Ursula's fiancé], Braunschweig, 14 June 1940

Outside the bells are ringing and flags are flying in honor of our soldiers, who are in our thoughts and whom we ask God to protect. So much has been achieved, and our troops have defended us so well. There is nothing better than receiving news, however short, from all of you out there. I can always see by Ursel's expression, when she comes, whether you've written. Hopefully your company has been able to withdraw a bit so you can catch your breath. The Führer takes care of everything. You surely know that Eberhard was able to visit Immo? [. . .] We are living here in peace, but we often wonder, especially in this heat, how we might be able to provide our soldiers out there with some refreshment.

Lisbeth Baumgarte to her friend Irmgard Brester, Düren, 17 June 1940

My sincere thanks for your sweet letter in which you passed along the good news that all of you are doing well and are safe and sound together in your house. You can't imagine how happy I am—during the critical days I was so concerned about you.

Thanks goodness we are doing well. You in particular will understand how grateful we are to our Führer and our courageous soldiers for having kept the horrors of war from our own country! That the English frequently call on us at night can hardly unsettle us. They will soon get an accounting quickly and thoroughly.

[. . .] So, dear Immo, I will come to an end for today and will send you news only rarely as long as the war lasts, but I hope that the war will soon end in victory so that we will once again have a chance to exchange ideas in person.

Minna von Alten to her granddaughter Irmgard Brester, Braunschweig, 19 June 1940

[. . .] That Eberhard could stop by one more time is really wonderful. I've heard only once from him, but I am relieved when you say he is looking well. In the meantime so many great tasks have been accomplished, but wounds were also inflicted. You asked about Diethelm! He was heavily wounded and died after a few days in a military hospital. Poor Hanna and the two children! What a stroke of fate that Aunt Bertha is no longer alive to suffer this blow.

Minna von Alten to her granddaughter Irmgard Brester, Braunschweig, 25 June 1940

[. . .] Hopefully you are doing well and appreciate all the big "events" with the same gratitude as we do. All the things we have lived through—if only God would now command that the *very last* shot should be fired! It was also reassuring to me to know that Eberhard visited you again. I had not heard from him in a long time until a somewhat longer letter arrived on Sunday, one he wrote on the train as he reported to his unit, which cost him a great deal of effort. He couldn't say if he will keep his old Feldpost number, so I have to wait to hear from him, which hopefully will occur somewhat more quickly now that there is an armistice; during the rapid advance all of us, including Ursel, were without any news. I can understand Eberhard, but for me the worries just get bigger and bigger. God protect our boy!

Annaliese W.'s husband, whom you also know, was killed in action, so the sacrifices add up, especially when the English deliberately bomb military hospitals. They have allowed themselves to call on us in recent days, but they haven't inflicted any damage yet. [. . .]

Ursel finally got word. Thank goodness, the situation is completely calm for now so the soldiers have a chance to catch their breath!

Yesterday a suitcase arrived from Berlin with Eberhard's things, since he has now given up the apartment again. [. . .] Aunt Margot also supplied me with a package, and since I have various packets of tea from you, I thought I would send her one as a way of relaying your thanks for her hospitality. [. . .] Otherwise we eat a great many vegetables, tomatoes, cucumbers, etc. from Holland. You are making sure that we are well supplied. [. . .] We are supposed to use only one sheet of paper for letters sent abroad, but this one is in such poor condition that all my lines run into each other. [. . .]

Irmgard Brester to her grandmother Minna von Alten, Amersfoort, 27 June 1940

[. . .] All the big events completely take our thoughts hostage. [. . .] I think about you so much, and when we listen to German radio broadcasts, I imagine you sitting by your radio. I often think about my friends "out there"; I was terribly shocked to hear the sad news about Diethelm's death. Poor Hanna! [. . .] And what will happen now? So far we are doing well. The English should just leave us in peace. [. . .] We can still buy wool, but articles of clothing are rationed just as in Germany. [. . .] How touching that Aunt Margot wants to take us all in. If it were only that easy! [. . .]

Minna von Alten to her granddaughter Irmgard Brester, Braunschweig, 8 July 1940

[. . .] I just got word that Eberhard finally made it safely to his unit. For the moment, they are taking a break in a French farm village. I have the feeling that we are living through the calm before the storm; the English will be summoning up all their strength. I am troubled to read that they don't leave you alone either; here we had a few quiet nights, but on Saturday we had to seek shelter from 4:00 to 5:30 in the morning, although the raids never came. My dear child, you can't imagine how vivid the past is for me, especially the war in 70/71, when so much enthusiasm accompanied our great rise. All the names in Alsace and Lorraine come back to me; we were so proud of our Bismarck and Moltke and our old Kaiser! Bismarck, forger of the Reich! And then the subsequent fall and disgrace! I can't bear to think about it, I can only say: God save our Führer and our army! [. . .]

When by chance we are able to get a hold of some cherries, as I was this morning, we are just ticked with joy. However, we have plenty of Dutch vegetables. Our refugees from the Saar are beginning to return home; we had no less than 13,000 so there will be more fruit and other things for us.

[. . .] So now off to the post office, where I have to show my identity card to post this letter.

Irmgard Brester to her grandmother Minna von Alten, Amersfoort, 15 July 1940

[. . .] At last more news from our boy, and I have the same feelings as you, Ollachen, I would prefer him to be in the administration. But in the end he has to know what is the right posting for him, and we have to respect his decision. All our best and most loving thoughts are with him, and we have to trust in the dear Lord, Ollachen. [. . .]

This waiting period is very grueling, I agree. Let everything happen quickly so that this terrible tension comes to an end. We are sitting here right in the middle of the German army, so we have some idea of the unbelievable preparation and organization that such a large offensive requires. [. . .]

Minna von Alten to her granddaughter Irmgard Brester, Braunschweig, 21 July 1940

[. . .] Aunt Agnes and I listened to the Führer's speech together. You surely heard it as well. Once again, he offered the hand of peace, but undoubtedly without effect; the English will not take it, they will just fight on. That you have to suffer as a result is always what worries me. The English are becoming more and more shameless, and they are coming closer and closer.

I just wrote Eberhard, who gets mail irregularly. He sends his greetings to Holland.

[. . .] Herr and Frau R. just returned from their trip, and along the way they saw the many transport trains with all types of weapons in different groupings. We'll wait and see; who knows where they are headed and when Eberhard will get orders.

Basically we are doing fine. The canneries in particular are working at full speed. Minna committed herself for a 3-week stint. Ursel's J. is sitting near the coast and has sent back several packages with stockings, to Ursel's delight.

[. . .] some word about how Diethelm was wounded. He was making his way to some injured comrades when a grenade exploded 2 m in front of him. He was showered with splinters in his arms, legs, back, and one of them hit him quite deeply. The doctor immediately ordered him transferred to a military hospital, but he died before they could operate.

[. . .] Dr. B. advised me not to seek shelter in the cellar during air raids; in fact, the R.'s heard that bombs go straight through to the bottom floor. It is difficult to know the right thing to do.

Eberhard wrote that he passed by, not far from here, near the Thüringer Forest in a train crowned with wreaths headed to an unnamed destination. God protect our boy and all my grandchildren. Our harbor is supposed to be full of Dutch coal, so you are keeping us supplied. Yesterday, I got the first provisions for winter, small briquettes that I had ordered; they came from Holland too. My dear child, my very best.

On the night of 23 July 1940, the RAF targeted the railway yards in Amersfoort; the bombs fell on the nearby neighborhood of Soesterkwartier, killing four people.

In addition to Eberhard, other visitors from Germany called on Immo, including her cousin Martin Gebensleben. He did not contact her again after he heard what he believed to have been her hesitation on the telephone.

Minna von Alten to her granddaughter Irmgard Brester, Braunschweig, 27 July 1940

The radio as well as the newspapers report that the English have dropped bombs on Amersfoort. I am constantly thinking of you and want to ask you to drop me a line telling me how things are and if you are healthy. I can't bear to think about your sick children!

Thank goodness Eberhard sent me good news. He is in West Prussia among sweet-natured people who are extremely happy to belong once again to the Reich. They consider him a member of the family and so are taking good care of him.

If only we had peace and quiet at night. [. . .]

Irmgard Brester to her grandmother Minna von Alten, Amersfoort, 5 August 1940

I just got your letter of 27 July. I had no idea that your newspapers mentioned anything about bombs on Amersfoort, otherwise I would have immediately let you know that we are all, thank goodness, healthy. It was a ghastly night. We had two alarms, heard explosions as well, and saw the fires, but the bombs fell on a different part of the city so all we had was a terrible fright. Fortunately, the children no longer have fever and had already been up and about, so going downstairs did not affect them. But the fright sits in the bones. Until now we have been sleeping in the downstairs room on mattresses. But we want to try sleeping upstairs the next time; it is terrible to haul everything up and down every night. When will this awfulness come to an end? I also feel very sorry for you on account of the disrupted nights. But I am very happy that Eberhard is doing so well. [. . .]

Minna von Alten to her granddaughter Irmgard Brester, Braunschweig, 6 August 1940

Day after day I am waiting to receive some news from you, that you emerged safe and sound from the big air raid on Amersfoort. Your last two letters from the 23rd and 25th were written before, and since the raid was announced I have sent two letters of inquiry. I hope that silence is a good sign and that all of you are safe. I am very relieved that the children got over their dysentery alright. Those must have been difficult days for you.

My dear child, what dark times we live in, but we have to gather the courage to look ahead and be thankful that we remain in good health. I often think of August; the doctors here are so busy that they barely have time to make house calls. [. . .] My old nerves are getting more and more weary. On top of that my worries about all of you and Eberhard, who also had not written in a long time. Yesterday, a packet of laundry arrived and today a longer letter. He is on a farm in West Prussia. Hopefully they will stay there for a bit. Eberhard always wants to hear everything, wants to know all about our experiences, he is so interested. He is further from the war than we are, the English haven't been there yet. [. . .] Eberhard has also received confirmation that his appointment at the ministry is permanent and that he can now call himself State Assessor. [. . .]

Minna is busy canning; there are so many beans they can hardly all be canned. Everyone want to make preserves. [. . .] Stay healthy, my loved ones. Around here, people carry deck chairs down to the cellar to keep the children warm so that they go back to sleep. Thinking of you.

Irmgard Brester to her grandmother Minna von Alten, Amersfoort, 13 August 1940

[. . .] These are hard times indeed. We were up the night before yesterday. Every night, we arrange mattresses and blankets in the hallway so we can lie down and cover ourselves up. I just wish it would end! I often yearn for you; I so want to see you again and have a heart-to-heart talk. [. . .]

Eberhard Gebensleben to his sister Irmgard Brester, Feldpost, 16 August 1940

I finally received your letter in which you recounted the especially "intensive" visit of our English friends in Amersfoort. Ohmchen also told me what the newspaper had reported; I am so thankful that you were able to send me such good news! Keep your spirits up! I don't think that this phase of the fighting will last very much longer.

Today is an especially happy day because I am leaving for vacation this evening! Naturally I will first visit dear Ohmchen and then perhaps go to the Baltic Sea for a few days.

In summer 1940, Eberhard was transferred to Modlin, in Poland. At the beginning to September, Eberhard took a trip through West Prussia, where he visited the Marienburg, from which the Teutonic Knights embarked on their murderous crusades against the indigenous population in the thirteenth century.

Eberhard's girlfriend, Herta, had a Jewish grandmother, which made her a "Mischling of the second degree," or a "quarter Jew," according to the 1935 Nuremberg Race Laws. In Nazi Germany, a Jew was anyone with three or four Jewish grandparents whether or not the person considered himself or herself Jewish or had converted to Christianity.

Irmgard Brester to her grandmother Minna von Alten, Amersfoort, 29 August 1940

[. . .] Imagine, I received a letter from Martin Gebensleben, the youngest son who is stationed near Arnhem. He also recently called us and wants to visit us as soon as possible. So I am still going to get some of the visitors from Germany that I had always wanted after all.

Minna von Alten to her granddaughter Irmgard Brester, Braunschweig, 29 August 1940

[. . .] Eberhard was here for a good 8 days and left Tuesday afternoon. [. . .] His unit is still stationed in the same place; the horses need to recover fully. He is looking good, though I had the feeling that he was not so spiritually free, although he wouldn't admit it. Of course, in Berlin he saw Fräulein Euling, and he also told me that they planned to go the seaside, but then he unburdened his heart. He told me, "Ohmchen, if only the 25% didn't exist (the non-Aryan grandmother), then I would marry her immediately." You can't imagine, my dear Immo, how hard that hit me. It would have such a huge effect on his entire life, he would be thrown off the track of his professional career, would be unable to remain a civil servant, couldn't stay in the Party, and I don't know what else. I asked him if I couldn't write to you about it, and he didn't exactly say *no*, just maintained that you wouldn't completely understand the consequences. But I am so consumed with this matter that I just have to let you know, and I want to hear your honest opinion, and August's. But don't write him directly about this. Apparently the two of them have discussed the question, and Fräulein Euling assured him that she would not be able to bear it if he suffered any problems or compromises as a result. She is 33 years old; so she is 3 years older than him, and on the left and the right of her part, she has a streak of white hair about the width of a finger. Yet I find her very intelligent and talented, which means a lot to Eberhard. "Ohmchen, turn it over in your mind for a bit," he asked.

In the context of a similar discussion, my son, Hans, once told me: "Career comes first and you have to make sacrifices." Eberhard would suffer such bitter disappointments. And one can't see into the future—maybe the rules will be moderated. It is not a question of who I am or how I feel—I just want the best for him. [. . .]

We ask ourselves, where will all this lead to? I just try to get through the day, I want to can apples and the great many tomatoes that you sent us, but if the English come at night, the following day is already ruined. [. . .]

Irmgard Brester to her grandmother Minna von Alten, Amersfoort, 5 September 1940

Yesterday I received your lovely letter, the contents of which have preoccupied me ever since. Our dear, dear boy! You're right, dearest Olla, he is in a very, very difficult situation, and one wants so much to help him and advise him. But it is not easy; too much is at stake, and in the end Eberhard will have to make the decision. It is curious that he feels attracted to older, but of course also smart, intelligent girls. Ultimately, it is his affair, and age doesn't matter. Oh, Ohmchen, I feel so sorry for Eberhard and the hard battles he will have to fight. I so much wish that he had his own home, a wife, and a family, especially since his visit here, when I realized the good that a young, happy family life does him. I saw him look around a couple of times with big eyes and take a deep breath, and I thought: "Well, my boy, this is exactly what I wish for you with all my heart!" But Ohmchen, will this woman bring him the happiness we want for him? The two of us discussed your letter at length, but as far as we can judge, both of us say: no. It is too dangerous to give up your whole future and career on account of a woman; right now that sounds hard, but it frequently happens that a marriage breaks apart because of mutual recriminations. It would be so hard for Eberhard to give up the position that makes him so happy and can get him ahead. [. . .]

I hope I haven't unsettled you, dearest Ohmchen, but you asked for our honest opinion. I leave it up to you whether or not you want to let Eberhard know. From your letter I get the impression that you think as we do; it is just so sad because our hearts want the boy to have a home.

Minna von Alten to her granddaughter Irmgard Brester, Braunschweig, 9 September 1940

[. . .] Yesterday I wrote Eberhard without concealing the dangers. You can't imagine how this preoccupies me; I feel somewhat responsible, but I can't be there for him. [. . .] If the good weather lasts, I will be able to calm my nerves [in Hedeper]; we've had too many visits from the English. Last week we had only one peaceful night. We really live in a danger zone, they've even been to Hedeper from time to time. [. . .]

The risk of mines must affect your fishermen very much; they probably don't even go out. No fish from the sea for us; well, we can do without.

[. . .] Early this morning, a letter arrived from a very excited Eberhard in Marienburg. "The Marienburg is the crown jewel, a marvel of beauty overall and in every precious detail. The spirit of the Teutonic Knights continues to live on there." Today he is back with his unit.

On 13 August 1940, Nazi Germany launched a sustained air war campaign against Great Britain, the so-called Battle for Britain, which was to precede an invasion of the island nation. London suffered major bomb attacks on 7–8 September in which eight hundred people lost their lives.

On 28 October 1940, Italy invaded Greece. In 1938 the Greek Crown Prince Paul married Friederike Luise, the daughter of Duke Ernst August of Braunschweig and a granddaughter of the former kaiser, Wilhelm II.

In early November 1940, Eberhard had a serious riding accident. He recovered in Modlin and then from the end of December in Amersfoort before transferring to Rostock in April 1941.

Minna von Alten to her granddaughter Irmgard Brester, Braunschweig, 10 September 1940

[. . .] Yes, Eberhard has to decide for himself; he is the one who will bear the consequences. Yesterday a letter arrived from Marienburg—what I will try to do is tell him that it would do him well to take seriously the spirit of the memorial by upholding our true Germandom and avoiding disgracing our ancestors. [. . .] Imagine what your parents would say. He would have to break with everything! I can't bear the thought. I had the same feeling you did when I saw him all dreamy with those big eyes, and I often asked him: what is up with you, is something wrong? He always answered: "I am doing magnificently," but I still had the feeling that something wasn't quite right.

The unit has had the misfortune that the horses have been sick for weeks, and as a result the unit has been more or less compelled to be inactive. Yet, since they are still part of the occupation forces, there is little variety in their duties. He would have been better off in your neck of the woods! But you just can't tell, and we are basically powerless.

Oh, I would be so grateful if I could have the two of you around me! It is the purpose of my life, after all, to maintain your home. But how long will I be able to do so, and then what? [. . .] What will come of us! Our leaders are showing the English that there will be no more leniency! But they always have new ideas; near Hedeper they dropped small incendiary devices in which the contents had been drenched in phosphorus and ignite on contact, and also devices with potato beetles that multiply thousandfold and devastate everything. [. . .] I wish we could go back to being normal, my dear child.

Irmgard Brester to her grandmother Minna von Alten, Amersfoort, 24 September 1940

[. . .] You know what we fervently wish for you and for ourselves: that humanity might live once again in peace and quiet and that we can soon be with you in your warm, intimate home. In more than one respect, your birthday will be melancholic, but we have to hold our heads high, right, Ohmchen? Let us think back with gratitude on the 80th birthday, which we celebrated so wonderfully with all those we love. We will continue to go on our way with courage and faith in God. In my thoughts, I give you a great big hug, my dear, courageous Ohmchen! [. . .]

Minna von Alten to her granddaughter Irmgard Brester, Braunschweig, 25 September 1940

[. . .] Eberhard is now in Poland, beyond Warsaw. [. . .]

Minna von Alten to her granddaughter Irmgard Brester, Braunschweig, 29 September 1940

[. . .] Straight away, the English welcomed me with 2 very restless nights, which has greatly interfered with my recuperation. [. . .]

Working conditions are such that farmers have to struggle hard if everything is to be taken care of in an orderly fashion. Alone cooking and cutting bread for all the prisoners creates difficulties for the domestic household. Besides Gerda has incompetent household help. And Uncle Otto had a lot of trouble on account of the refugees. He had 4 families living in the Old House, all of whom made various demands and really trespassed on us. You also have had to bear some of the brunt. The downstairs pantry, where the kitchen supplies are kept, has been damaged all because the mayor ordered the room requisitioned. [. . .]

All our relatives who were on their way to Poland passed through Hedeper. [. . .] Eberhard says that his room has a pointed arch window just like in *Faust* and that Modlin lies so deep in Poland that you no longer hear a single German syllable. And the cold winter! Write him as often as you can.

I am still trying to figure out how to tell him my candid opinion about his personal affair. The longer I mull over this, the more I think that he simply should know in no uncertain terms what I think. I often wonder how it happened that the hand of fate lies so heavily on me, why your parents were taken away so early!

I have privately taken leave of Hedeper as well. I don't think that I will see it again. It was so moving to see elderly men and women come up to me in the streets and ask why I don't visit anymore. [. . .]

Minna von Alten to her granddaughter Irmgard Brester, Braunschweig, 4 October 1940

Now I have a big pile of all your greetings! Today your letter with the wonderful pictures arrived as well as a letter from Hedda. [. . .] The Ministry recalled Eberhard, but the Wehrmacht turned it down. [. . .] Almost all my acquaintances find themselves in the East. [. . .] That all of you continue to play music pleases me immensely; one has to find a counterweight in these times. In the "Hofjäger," the English came so early that the entire hall, which wasn't even sold out, had to stay put until the alarm ended at 3:00 in the morning. [. . .]

Minna von Alten to her granddaughter Irmgard Brester, Braunschweig, 17 October 1940

We constantly hear reports that the English are calling upon you again, but they never indicate which cities are affected. I end up worrying and just ask for news whether or not you have been hit. [. . .]

Irmgard Brester to her grandmother Minna von Alten, Amersfoort, 23 October 1940

Hopefully in the meantime you will have received my last long letter and can rest assured that we are doing well—thank goodness. I am so sorry that you are worrying, but the same holds true for us: we worry about you and are overjoyed whenever we hear good news. [. . .]

Minna von Alten to her granddaughter Irmgard Brester, Braunschweig, 1 November 1940

[. . .] When I think about the gray winter before me, my thoughts darken, but I pull myself together and can hear Eberhard saying in his answer to my somewhat anxious letters: "Don't think that I am in a melancholic state of mind; what we have to do now is endure, the war has to come to an end, then life will go on." [. . .] Polish girls are taking care of his laundry again. [. . .]

Greece is now the reason for the further prolongation of the war. Today I was walking by the palace, where the young crown princess Friederike was born! I had to think of you. Although the English aren't neglecting us, we are becoming more indifferent and no longer always go down to the cellar, which is now very cold. Even Aunt Minna ducks out and stays upstairs. What I do is get dressed and stay in the hallway until the bombing stops, then I lie down in my bed fully clothed until the all clear sounds. But next morning one is still a wreck all the same. [. . .]

So take care, my loved ones. Our thoughts reach out, and we find each other! Your ancient, lonely Ohmchen.

Irmgard Brester to her grandmother Minna von Alten, Amersfoort, 5 November 1940

I haven't heard anything from you for so long that I am wondering how you are doing. [. . .] No news from Eberhard for some time either, and I feel a bit disconnected. I want to assume: no news is good news!

Minna von Alten to her granddaughter Irmgard Brester, Braunschweig, 5 November 1940

[. . .] I was certainly unsettled that I did not hear anything from Eberhard after his tournament, 8 days ago last Sunday. Now I hear that he is lying in a military hospital after having the bad luck to fall from his horse while jumping. He was told that he was fortunate in his misfortune since his bones are sound and teeth are intact; only his face is very swollen so his doctor ordered 3 weeks' bed rest. Undoubtedly to make sure there are not any other complications.

Minna von Alten to her granddaughter Irmgard Brester, Braunschweig, 9 November 1940

[. . .] Eberhard writes: "Today was very strenuous. They put braces in my mouth so that it heals properly. Not so nice, but a step forward. My superiors in the battalion and the regiment are taking very good care of me. But now you have to assure me that you too are taking things as easy as I am, and are sending me your best wishes." My dear, dear Immo, my thoughts are always with the boy. God willing, everything will turn out. [. . .] All of you are my ray of sunshine, and hopefully you will remain safe and sound. We never hear where exactly the English drop their bombs on you. The last few days have been quieter. Today the postman delivered a goose that I had ordered in Hedeper. I want to preserve it for when my soldier is home on leave.

Irmgard Brester to her grandmother Minna von Alten, Amersfoort, 13 November 1940

Now we have one more reason to be unsettled and anxious. Our poor, dearest boy! [. . .] Through Frl. Euling I heard about Eberhard's accident a few days before Eberhard himself wrote about his bad luck. I was also very grateful to her for sending me the express letter because I thereby discovered that here in Amersfoort there is also a Feldpost office. That means the mail can be sent more quickly and directly; above all, I am delighted that I can also send him packages. [. . .] August reassured me that those sorts of injuries will heal. [. . .]

Minna von Alten to her granddaughter Irmgard Brester, Braunschweig, 14 November 1940

[. . .] Eberhard writes: "Please send my very very warmest greetings to Holland and let them know that there is not a day that goes by when I don't wish I were on the Lichtenberg and have them around me." [. . .] Cherished Immo, my heart aches when I know that he could have been stationed in Holland or France! But no complaints, we don't know why things happen as they do.

So yesterday evening I got a call from Frl. Euling, who, as she told me, has also written to you; I assume she wanted to find out how much I understood about the situation. [. . .] It turns out that Eberhard actually broke his jaw and suffered a concussion, although he had a great deal of luck, and that everything will turn out alright. She assured me that we don't have to worry about any harmful consequences. But he requires 6 weeks' bed rest, not 3, as he wrote me originally. We also should not push him to write because that costs him a lot of effort. [. . .]

Minna von Alten to her granddaughter Irmgard Brester, Braunschweig, 26 November 1940

[. . .] Eberhard sends his warmest greetings and said he was overjoyed to get your package; he was delighted. My letters take longer than yours. [. . .] Hopefully our Marleen is doing better. I wrote her a charming Advent letter but was not allowed to send it since there is a prohibition on letters with pictures. [. . .]

Didn't you make marzipan last year? There won't be many sweets for the celebrations this year. The ration has already been determined: 5 chocolates per person. [. . .] But send along the recipe for marzipan.

Eberhard Gebensleben to his sister Irmgard Brester, Modlin, 27 November 1940

Today I will attempt to write a greeting to you directly. After all your dear sisterly care, which reached me even out here without a problem, I really wanted to tell you that I am already much better and *how* happy you made me with everything. Those were really genuine Dutch goodies, *not at all* like wartime! [. . .] My thoughts are now turning to Christmas and whether I will get leave. You will soon be seeing *Sinterklaas*. [. . .]

Eberhard Gebensleben to his cousin Ursula Meier, Modlin, 1 December 1940

[. . .] To celebrate the first Advent I pushed myself and ventured out into the hallway in front of my room for the first time; absurd, really, that after 5 weeks something like this seems like a big expedition; I am already looking forward to repeating it tomorrow. I had no idea what it looked outside and where the military hospital was located since I regained consciousness only after I had already been put in bed. It actually was pretty bad. I have such a complicated bandage around my head and in my mouth that I could very well be a carnival attraction. [. . .]

Now that it is Christmastime, don't you have some sort of celebration or performance in your school? Preferably not too Germanic, maybe something with only the "light of the summer solstice," etc. Children at that age can make more sense of things when seeing a babe in a manger. [. . .]

Eberhard Gebensleben to his sister Irmgard Brester, Modlin, 2 December 1940

[. . .] My dear sister, I always want to say how wonderful and calming it is to know that you have been and are thinking of me! I can sense it, and surely the very worst is now over. I've made my peace with the bandage and the braces around my jaw, can pretty much get to sleep, and in exactly 14 days, the doctor will remove them. [. . .]

The fastest mail (letter and package) bore the red stamp *Deutsche Dienstpost Niederlande*. Do you have any influence there? It took only 2 days!

Immo's grandmother, Minna von Alten, died on 30 November 1940. Immo was not allowed to travel to the funeral, although she received a visa to travel to Germany with the help of an old German friend of her father-in-law Jan Brester at the beginning of March 1941. Immo was therefore able to help dissolve Minna's household. In the meantime, Herta spent a few days in Amersfoort, where Eberhard was recovering from his accident. While in Amersfoort, Eberhard had long discussions with August, including one in which they apparently disagreed about the role of the Netherlands in the future of the German Reich. Accompanied by Eberhard, Immo traveled to Braunschweig on 5 March 1941 and returned home alone on 15 March.

On 6 April 1941, Germany and Italy invaded Yugoslavia, which surrendered eleven days later. Germany, Italy, Bulgaria, and Hungary annexed parts of the former kingdom, Croatia gained nominal independence as a fascist client state aligned with the Axis powers, while an increasingly repressive German military administration ruled in Serbia.

Irmgard Brester to her cousin Ursula Meier, Amersfoort, 3 December 1940

[. . .] Our Ohmchen, our most beloved, loving Ohmchen! I simply cannot imagine that this wholly generous and caring great love is now gone forever. [. . .] There are not so many strong, loving people who for the sake of others were always able to pull themselves together and give their love and do so under the heaviest blows of fate. You know that even better yourself, Ursel. Ohmchen made sure you had a sunny childhood and adolescence and tried as much as possible to replace your mother. My thoughts constantly go back to you and our dear Eberhard. It is horrible to think that in this sad time he is still sick and weak and alone among strangers. How much I would like to be with you now, dear Ursel, and be by your side to help make arrangements and put things in order. Unfortunately, it is impossible to telephone or telegraph from here. I made inquiries yesterday as soon as I received the telegram, and even went to the local Kommandantur about permission to travel. The answers I received were quite optimistic, and I was referred to Utrecht. But in Utrecht, I was sent from one office to another without accomplishing a thing. I was told that the office in charge was in Amsterdam, but they need authorizations that I cannot provide in such a short time. I returned home very depressed; so I won't be able to attend the funeral in Braunschweig. Tomorrow will be especially difficult and sad for me. [. . .]

Please, please write me all about it, dearest Ursel. I will keep making attempts to get a visa; maybe I can come later at one point and can help with the dissolution of the household. There will undoubtedly be room for a few things in Hedeper. [. . .]

Herta Euling to Ursula Meier, Berlin, 3 December 1940

[. . .] You in particular, dear Fräulein Meier, have suffered a special loss. As much as I can remember from Eberhard's stories, Frau von Alten represented a second home to you. As it was, Eberhard wrote me today and mentioned that your fiancé has already been lying in a military hospital in Lodz for some time. All the heartache and anxiety you must have had lately!

This news makes me worry a great deal about Eberhard, and please just let me know as soon as you know that he received the news. [. . .] Just yesterday I wrote to the head doctor asking him that in the event he decides to withhold the news from Eberhard to please also find a way to control the rest of the mail so Eberhard doesn't find out from another source.

If I had known that Eberhard had told Ohmchen about his accident so soon, I would have telephoned her earlier. Eberhard and I agreed that I would tell her about any extraordinary developments. I let an extra 8 days go by because there are sometimes long intervals between Eberhard's letters. In the meantime, she got the news from him—incidentally to this day he doesn't realize how dangerous his condition really was. He did not just have, as I told Ohmchen, a crack in jaw and a concussion, but a double skull fracture (one of them at the base of the skull), a broken upper jaw, and a hairline fracture in his nasal bone as well. I want to ask you that if you have to communicate with him further about the death, to remember that he still needs a long period of recovery and he should avoid any excitement. [. . .]

Eberhard Gebensleben to his cousin Ursula Meier, Modlin, 4 December 1940

What a heartbreaking farewell. Our dear, irreplaceable Ohmchen. The doctor told me this morning and gave me the letters. You were so discreet in your attentions. [. . .] I am lying here surrounded by Ohmchen's tender loving care as I look at the things on my night table. The last cookies will arrive this morning or day after tomorrow. [. . .] If Immo was not able to come, then you and Uncle Otto really had a difficult time of it. [. . .] I am so grateful that I found out in time so that I can accompany Ohmchen and all of you in my thoughts. [. . .]

Eberhard Gebensleben to his sister Irmgard Brester, Modlin, 5 December 1940

[. . .] I am sure that you were not able to get permission to travel on such short notice, even though you felt so pulled to come to Braunschweig. So Ursel had to represent the grandchildren and great grandchildren on this last difficult journey alone. But precisely because the two of us couldn't accompany Ohmchen, we feel even more closely bound to each other, don't you agree? [. . .]

Now I am the one who will have to send you greetings and letters from Germany. No one can replace our dear loved one, and I don't even want to try. But I want to do my brotherly part and do it better than before. If only the war would fight itself to a finish!

[. . .] My dearest Immo, Ohmchen set us such an example. Not to give in to the pain but to bear it with dignity, as an old song puts it. [. . .] You don't have to worry about me. I am taking it very easy and am allowed to sit in an armchair for an hour a day. [. . .]

Ursula Meier to her cousin Irmgard Brester, Braunschweig, 5 December 1940

Yesterday we brought our dear loving Ohmchen to her final resting place. Until the very end, I kept hoping that you would be able to make it, yet I don't even know whether you received the telegram, which in the end we could send through the help of Herr Propst L., or whether a trip would even have been possible.

[. . .] I missed you and Hardus so much during these days, since only the two of you can feel the same deep pain. That you two couldn't be here is surely one of the great sacrifices that these times require us to make. You shouldn't be too sad, dear Immo, that you were not able to be with Ohmchen any more this last year. Her thoughts were so *often* with all of you. Our Ohmchen died a gentle, peaceful death. She just slipped away in her slumber one night. This is certainly what she deserved after all the suffering she bore.

[. . .] Also please write to me, and I will report about Germany and everything that concerns you here. [. . .]

Irmgard Brester to her cousin Ursula Meier, Amersfoort, 30 December 1940

[. . .] That Eberhard could come after all was a great big pleasure for all of us. Secretly, we were so full of hope, but we did not dare count on it. So in the end, we ended up having wonderful Christmas holidays. [. . .] But he has to make a complete recovery. He still looks pretty badly off and tires easily so that I had to rein in my 4 little wandering creatures as much as possible. Yet Uncle Eberhard takes so much delight in their company; it must be good for him. With regard to further treatment of his jaw, we have already taken steps; it still needs some adjustments, which hopefully can be undertaken here. [. . .] I also want to go with Eberhard to try one more time to get permission to travel. It would be very nice and, in my opinion, also extremely important for the three of us to discuss matters and decide about what to do with Ohmchen's things. [. . .]

Irmgard Brester to her cousin Ursula Meier, Amersfoort, 16 January 1941

[. . .] Eberhard has been in Utrecht's university clinic for a week now in order to get his upper jaw treated and adjusted. Eberhard must have written you that the whole business was not properly treated back in Modlin; the upper and lower jaw do not fit together. Several doctors fear that over the long run his joints would get damaged, so further procedures are necessary. I feel so sorry for the poor boy! Naturally it is all very painful and unpleasant since the break had to be reopened, but now everything is under control and will be fixed properly. He is in the best hands, in a small, very modern clinic. It is also touching to see what a grateful patient he is!

[. . .] Ohmchen would have been terribly pleased about Eberhard's promotion to lieutenant, which arrived just before he went to the hospital. With that a long-held ambition has been realized. But the big celebration will be even better when the main protagonist no longer has his jaws bound together and can join the feast! [. . .]

Eberhard Gebensleben to his cousin Ursula Meier, Amersfoort, 28 January 1941

[. . .] So much mail gets lost that it would be best to *number* our letters. What I wanted to ask you was to write to me here as soon as possible to tell me what *your time* looks like and whether you could eventually take a small vacation in the event that Immo and I came to Braunschweig. I have made several attempts already to secure permission, and it looks like they have succeeded. If at all possible we really need to be together for a few days and work. [. . .]

As you can see, I have been released from the clinic (3 days ago), and I go over to Utrecht every few days so that the doctor can check my jaw braces (not visible from the outside) and my mouth. He is quite satisfied with the healing process; no doubt, the worst and most painful period is over. It is as nice here as ever; we live with the children and their friends and . . . in politics, here where one simply *cannot* avoid the issues. All the choices that have to be made here!

If one of these days you have some time in Braunschweig, could you go to a military dress shop and buy insignia for my epaulettes and send it to me: 4 of my regiment number "12," that is 4 times the number 1 and 4 times the number 2 (in gold plate). If there are various versions, just a small, nice one.

Eberhard Gebensleben to his sister Irmgard Brester, Rostock, 3 April 1941

[. . .] How did your crate fare in Amersfoort? Did the presents meet with approval and give a little pleasure, which was ultimately their intended purpose?

As a practical matter, my short-term future is unclear. The prospects are cold and gray. In any case, I have a sympathetic commanding officer who has forbidden me to ride for another 1–2 months. The lovely time we had in Holland is still fresh in my mind. Being with you did me a world of good.

[TO HIS BROTHER-IN-LAW AUGUST BRESTER]

[. . .] It dawned on me in Berggießhübel that we must have passed through this region on our trip to Prague, and I even suspect that when we traveled to the former border we actually passed through the town itself. It is just as beautiful as ever. [. . .]

I have been in Rostock since 1 April. As always, whenever I get here the weather is atrocious, frost and driving snow. What happened to spring, which we enjoyed in Holland weeks ago? Fact is that Holland remains paradise, and after the difficulties that Immo will have told you about, you will be hard put not to agree. [. . .]

Unfortunately, the shifting in my mouth has not ceased. About a week after I stopped wearing the "elastic," a fissure about 1 mm. wide opened up. This morning, after I strapped on the rubber band overnight, it was closed again. I'd very much like to get the opinion of Herr Dr. X, at least in writing. [. . .] Maybe you could give him a call and ask him what he thinks of this matter.

Eberhard Gebensleben to his sister Irmgard Brester, Rostock, 20 April 1941

[. . .] So Jan did understand what his birthday celebration meant after all. How I underestimated him! Next year he will get the congratulations, not his mother. [. . .] There is a big military ear-nose-and-throat clinic here in Rostock, and they will take out my braces soon. [. . .] In the meantime, I moved into the "Garden City," a friendly settlement of nine houses adjacent to the barracks and right near the forest. [. . .] My duties are not very exciting, but tolerable. Meals are taken in common in the officers' club. [. . .]

As you can imagine, I paid the closest attention to events in Yugoslavia. Back then, I thought it *might* come to the German annexation of Slovenia and Croatian independence. Yet three years later, events took a completely different course, one might say, like a blind man flailing about. Or do you see the forces driving events differently?

Eberhard Gebensleben to his sister Irmgard Brester, Rostock, 28 May 1941

[. . .] About the Regierungsrat, you have been correctly informed. It must have been announced in the Berlin papers because I received congratulations from the Zeitlers (who, incidentally, want to move into our house in Braunschweig). I thought

I might get it eventually; but you will understand that given my particular personal circumstances my joy is not altogether unqualified. The grown-up nieces should write Ohm Eberhard once in a while; do they still understand German? [. . .] Herta will be in a small spa town near here over Pentecost so we will be able to see each other. As a result, the days gain some purpose and structure. May Pentecost provide a genuine celebration, despite the war and what I am sure are the constant hardships, both large and small!

> On 22 June 1941, Germany invaded the Soviet Union. In just over a week, the advancing Wehrmacht forces reached Lemberg, the capital of former Galicia, the Polish territory annexed by the Austrian Empire in 1795. Lemberg or Lwów became part of Poland in 1918, but was occupied and annexed to the Ukraine by the Soviets under the terms of the German-Soviet nonaggression pact in September 1939. Before retreating, the Soviets shot hundreds of political prisoners, an atrocity widely reported in German newspapers. Horrendous anti-Jewish pogroms took place in the following days. At the beginning of the offensive, German soldiers were more likely to be greeted as liberators from Communism than as enemies, but any illusions evaporated as soon as the SS and German civilian administrators arrived on the scene. By August, SS death squads were fully engaged in a genocide against the Jews. Over thirty thousand Jews were murdered outside Kiev at Babi Yar at the end of September 1941. In addition to capturing Kiev, German troops penetrated the outskirts of Leningrad (now Petersburg) and launched a major offensive against Moscow. Between seventeen thousand and twenty thousand Dutch volunteers or "Ostfront Freiwillige" fought with the Germans on the eastern front, either as part of the SS or as part of the "Volunteer Legion of the Netherlands" ("Vrijwilligers Legioen Nederland"). On 22 November 1941, the Wehrmacht reached the suburbs of Moscow, but a Soviet counteroffensive launched on 5 December held the Germans and managed to push them back in what was known as the "Winter War." Unprepared for winter combat, German troops were woefully undersupplied and decimated by frostbite.
>
> Eberhard belonged to Army Group South, which had overrun the Ukraine and aimed to capture the oil fields in the Caucasus. He was assigned to the Military Economics Inspectorate Russland-Süd in Lemberg, where he was responsible for supply questions, but Eberhard longed to return as a "real" soldier to his unit of the mounted artillery. At the end of August 1941, Eberhard was temporarily redeployed to his old artillery unit, but three months later he was forced to resume his administrative duties in Lemberg.

Eberhard Gebensleben to his sister Irmgard Brester, Berlin, 16 July 1941

Events have now taken me by surprise. Just as I came to you a year ago, now under similar circumstances, I am headed in the opposite direction. Naturally there is an enormous hustle and bustle as we set out to leave. All the things that I will get to live through! A thousand thanks for your *very* lovely letter enclosing the photographs of the nephews. How charming! Below my new address. Briefly back in Braunschweig again. In haste.

Eberhard Gebensleben to his sister Irmgard Brester, Feldpost, 27 July 1941

[. . .] You have to imagine me in the vicinity of Lemberg—for the time being at least—whereby, given the particulars of our part civilian, part military agency, I am not disclosing any military secrets. The god of war is raging about 100 km away from us, and only traces of his apocalyptic passing—still very serious and quite horrible—can be seen and felt.

For me as well, it appears—according to a provisional message that arrived today—that the old circuit has once again been completed: my reconversion into a proper soldier. But with this difference: this time I had nothing to do with it; rather matters took their own course—the small and personal follows in the wake of grand destiny.

Let's see how things develop. For the time being, I am in Lemberg, and I have grown accustomed enough to the "eastern" cut of everyday life (bed-bug free quarters only after moving 2x) that I am able to appreciate the splendid beauty of this city. I would call it a "little Vienna," with impressive, buoyant baroque buildings and spacious hilly surroundings, which are almost too grand and imposing. Wonderful churches and fine public buildings—really a testament to old Austria (capital of the Austrian crown territory of Galicia), but now quite dilapidated. Improvised swastika flags all around—they bear the obvious marks of the hammer and sickle against a red background—the newly constituted Ukrainian legions have shown up as well. For our part, we have installed ourselves in a former office of the Soviets amidst all the files they left behind. Lots to talk about—and be mindful of—a whole evening would not be enough if we were all together. Here splendor combines with squalor. It will be a hard winter, in the East and in the West.

Eberhard Gebensleben to his sister Irmgard Brester, in Russia, 27 August 1941

[. . .] even if you shake your heads and deny it, at least from the perspective of Russia, Holland is still "paradise." We are driven over interminably long roads, if that is what you want to call them—when it rains they are a *single* abysmal, slippery expanse of mud—only to be engulfed in blinding, towering sand storms. For a few days we established our base in a *big city* that was nothing but a miserable, shot-up dump. When the Ukrainians approach the Germans, they are very friendly and trusting. Especially striking when we were still further west were the rather touching, if improvised triumphal arches across the streets, swastika and Ukrainian flags flying side by side and crowned with Christian crosses and holy icons. The population doesn't pose any danger, more unpleasant, however, are the dysentery-like intestinal infections that almost everybody has. The end of my second attack is hopefully in sight. They leave you miserable and worn out, fasting doesn't help, only castor oil and charcoal bring relief—what you would give a horse. Or does Augustus have better ideas? It might have something to do with the damp climate (occasional swamps), but most of all with the indescribable, all-encompassing squalor.

I've taken up my new responsibilities with the best of intentions, though unusual circumstances of a more personal nature have been rather distracting. For the time being, special duties keep me away from my first Feldpost number (40735), but I assume the mail will be forwarded to me (Abteilung Wi).

Eberhard Gebensleben to his sister Irmgard Brester, Feldpost, 12 September 1941

Just a quick greeting as a sign of life and to give you my new Feldpost number. Because everything needs to be forwarded, I haven't received a lot of mail. I had a temporary posting (2 months) to a unit that was very much to my liking.

Eberhard Gebensleben to his sister Irmgard Brester, Feldpost, 19 September 1941

After quite some time, I am sending you warm greetings as a sign of life. [. . .] This country is full of mysteries and surprises. Life goes on with the unit in the best of spirits.

Eberhard Gebensleben to his sister Irmgard Brester, Feldpost, 21 September 1941

A warm loving greeting on the march through Russia. It has to be short because we are tired and we continue on early.

Eberhard Gebensleben to his sister Irmgard Brester, Feldpost, 8 October 1941

Unfortunately the Feldpost is unreliable, as the bulky mail bag shows me quite clearly whenever there is nothing for me. So I wanted to follow the short greetings I sent a few days ago with another one. Things are tolerable to good, even downright good since the weather has improved again and, what is more, I am sitting and writing in a warm Russian farmhouse. My thoughts are so often with you in Holland! Soon things will come to an end here. I read in the paper that Dutch volunteers have now joined our troops, although the two of you will undoubtedly have more and other things to say about that.

Hilde Kammerer to her friend Irmgard Brester, Braunschweig, 18 November 1941

[. . .] Despite the war, yesterday I finally succeeded in getting my hands on an Advent calendar for your children. [. . .] The carefree nature of your children will help create a proper Christmas mood for you and August. [. . .]

Eberhard Gebensleben to his sister Irmgard Brester, Feldpost, 25 November 1941

After time with "real" soldiers, I returned to my old posting where a huge surprise awaited me: ca. 40 pieces of mail, all the mail from the last 2–3 months. Among them 6 from Holland, 5 letters from 5 August to 16 September, along with the sweet package. Everything arrived safely! My wonderful, dear sister, you have been so thoughtful. I relived your whole late summer with the tandem bicycle, the holiday trips, and the farm; my heart was beating at your open-air concert as if I were there; and I avidly studied the impeccable reviews in the newspapers. And I don't want to forget the wonderful, long, error-free letter from my dear niece Hedda.

All those moments have long since become memories, and the winter poses new challenges for you.

And me? The last two months already seem unreal to me, and when in the future I get a chance to tell you about it, it will seem like a dream. But I do know one thing—I have lived fully and to the hilt during this period, and I was safe in good hands. Winter is coming with full force, right now we have already had 10° below zero. In the East, it will be a winter that will long be talked about. Although it is some 200 km from here and the difficulties seem insurmountable to me, I would like to return to my old post in order, among other things, to pick up the mail that was sent there. With the best will in the world, I cannot tell you where to write me. There are even changes coming with 40735 that are beyond my control. [. . .]

Practical matters: without records, I can't say anything about your German inheritance. B. won't be able to tell you anything either. The best thing would be to write the relevant office and tell the truth about the situation, that your brother, the trustee of the inheritance, has been called up and that they should provide you with details as soon as possible. [. . .]

Dr. X's nasty surprise can only be satisfactorily settled by the German military doctor in the university hospital, who also took care of the hospital costs and therefore has in his possession the needed documents. [. . .] I don't know if this can be worked out without me. That would be one more reason to come over and see for myself. In any case, castles in the air are free! (Incidentally there is no question that a healthy jaw is worth 510 fl.)

Eberhard, who had been transferred to Berlin in December, spent Christmas 1941 in Amersfoort. He was furious when August and Immo made it clear to him that he could no longer take walks with the family if he dressed in a German uniform or spoke German in public. He greatly resented their decision, which offended his sense of honor as a German officer. A big quarrel ensued, but Eberhard ultimately relented, borrowed August's suits, and kept quiet in public because the family sanctuary in Amersfoort was too important to him. However, Eberhard continued to press August with the question of the future of the Netherlands. The "Greater German" perspective held that the Netherlands had belonged to Germany until 1648 and therefore should be reintegrated back into the Fatherland. Eberhard tried to win his brother-in-law over to this position and even composed a study to back up his argument upon his return to Berlin. His sources included texts by Jan Wagenaar (1709–1773), who in 1758 had been appointed the official historian of Amsterdam. What follows is the introduction and conclusion to Eberhard's eight-page typescript study, which is dated 10 February 1942.

The decade-long struggle against the dictated peace of Versailles has made Germans realize more clearly than ever that this was not the first time that ancient

Reich territories were lost in a period of weakness and division. In our view, the 1648 Peace of Westphalia is the decisive factor for the ultimate loss of the western cornerstones of the Reich, the Netherlands and Switzerland. . . .

If after 300 years, the break represented by the year 1940 has opened new and even not yet anticipated avenues, let these observations conclude with a citation from Ernst Moritz Arndt who in the year 1831 contemplated the reintegration of the old Reich territories, words that provide some perspective as well as a warning: "I do not mean a compelle eos intrare *["joining by force"], for which no one has a greater revulsion than I; what I mean is that all of Germany should be put in such a rejuvenated and transformed state that they would, if not at first with great love, at least not have difficulty in realizing that they acted responsibly in accepting such an invitation." [*Die Frage über die Niederlande und die Rheinlande *(Leipzig, 1831), p. 9]*

Immo's notebook, 26 December 1941

Unfortunately, a difficult discussion with Eberhard, but happily mutual agreement. I had a long talk with him in the afternoon.

Hilde Kammerer to her friend Irmgard Brester, Braunschweig, 28 December 1941 (posted in the Netherlands)

[. . .] The entire world is in flames and is overflowing with such hate and is marked with such belligerence that the message of Christmas is particularly soothing. In this case, the peace is the one created between God and his creatures through Christ, and once that has been established we can be joyful despite worries, hardships, and war. [. . .]

How are things with your two sons? We hear a lot about cases of diphtheria. [. . .] Hopefully you finally received good news from Eberhard for Christmas! The long periods of waiting are so grueling, and in winter the mail from the East takes longer, especially if it has to go to all the way to Holland. We have to provide the soldiers in the East everything we can; hopefully Eberhard is up to the challenges.

My brother was permitted to give a Christmas sermon to the men in 5 military hospitals. A colonel and a lieutenant colonel both personally shook his hand in thanks (he is still a noncommissioned medical officer in Braunlage). [. . .]

Eberhard Gebensleben to his sister Irmgard Brester, Braunschweig, 5 January 1942

[. . .] Yesterday a Sunday visit to the Kreutzmann's. Everyone was interested, I had to recount a great deal about Holland, how it really is, of course. [. . .]

This morning I visited Herr B. in his office. His assistant told me that they certainly can assume the management of the property. Here you have their address so you can get in touch with them if necessary. [. . .]

There are 2 reasons why Ohm Eberhard wants to sit down at every meal: (1) to say, "Hedda, take off your glasses!" and (2) to say "Dear Mama, please eat one *more* slice or have *another* bite!" so that Immeken's cheeks will be pretty and full again. Despite everything!

Eberhard Gebensleben to his sister Irmgard Brester, Berlin, 25 January 1942

You will be very surprised and, at the same time, relieved to still be getting letters from Berlin. I don't have to say that I am not upset by the situation either. There were some purely formal difficulties regarding my official discharge from my duties in the Ministry of Economics. Certain documents had to be produced, so I stayed in Berlin for the time being, happy circumstances that will probably last until the beginning of February. Thereafter, I will certainly have to return to my old unit in the East. Oh the bitter cold! It is with a heavy heart that I think of the comrades out there. Even I can't really picture the conditions of their existence now. They too should be included in the prayers of your Dominee.

My dearest, bestest sister, do you think back on our New Year's Eve? It was *so* wonderful! [. . .]

In Berlin, I've begun taking—be amazed—a few violin lessons again. Art and scholarship have enriched this unexpected gift of a vacation. As far as scholarship goes, the case is as follows: to avoid having to argue in vain with my dear brother-in-law every two years, I am going to the university library to research the question of how long the Netherlands belonged to the [Holy Roman] Empire. I hope to have completed a small essay in a few days. [. . .] To my own great surprise, I was wrong about the year 1648 and so is the opinion that most people hold here! But *recent* Dutch scholars are even more wrong when they argue that the bond was already broken around 1250. With the best of will, I cannot resist the impression that a predetermined political line of argument plays a role here. The truth lies somewhere in the second half of the 16th century, when the Dutch estates (and, if I am not mistaken, William of Orange as well) asked for German military assistance against the Spaniards, which, however, given the Reich's poor state of affairs, they did not receive. Both sides clearly and self-evidently assumed an affiliation with the Empire, which was expressly called upon and referred to. I've burrowed myself into a pile of history books and old documents but realize that in the absence of German accounts, I've relied on *Dutch* historians. My Dutch is good enough to read the new accounts, and there are very good German translations of the old ones, especially of a certain Wagenaar, who wrote in the 18th century. [. . .]

Eberhard Gebensleben to his sister Irmgard Brester, Berlin-Spandau, 8 February 1942

[. . .] What horrible flooding [in the house]! It must have been dreadful! Pull through this winter for me and if necessary don't spare the cedar tree! [. . .]

My brother-in-law will receive a carbon copy as soon as I have typed out my historical opus on the typewriter. It should be kept in mind that the introduction and the conclusion are conceived as small essays, and are not "historical." I've gotten a small taste of the hard struggle the historian has to be "objective."

Herta sends many warm greetings; write her soon.

Eberhard Gebensleben to his brother-in-law August Brester, Gnesen (West Prussia), 25 February 1942

[. . .] Since we parted at the train station in Amersfoort, fate has certainly smiled on me by allowing me to remain in Germany and in the civilized world for such a long period of time! Now the expected, not exactly desired, but nonetheless endurable moment has come. I said my farewell to Herta this morning in Berlin, rode to Gnesen (incidentally located right on the edge of the civilized world), and now will begin my journey back to my old unit in Russia. It is a great mystery to me how I will manage it with all my baggage and how long it will take me. It is nothing less than a journey to an unknown country, since in two months once-familiar conditions will have changed. What I hold onto is the love that I have been shown in Germany and Holland, something I can rely on, and the responsibility to fulfill my duties. In solemn moments, there is something even higher, for which I don't find the words. We understand each other!

Enclosed my promised composition. [. . .]

Since November 1941, the Germans occupied almost all of western Russia. Throughout the winter, the Soviets remained on the offensive, pushing back the Germans one hundred kilometers to the west and, north of Moscow, two hundred fifty kilometers to the west. By spring 1942, the Germans had reinforced their lines; approximately 70 percent of all German divisions were deployed on the eastern front. On 17 May 1942, the Soviets launched a major counter offensive in the direction of Kharkov, but after ten days of combat, the Soviets found themselves surrounded, ultimately suffering great losses in men and materiel.

In the Dutch East Indies, what is now Indonesia, the Dutch colonial army surrendered to the Japanese on 9 March 1942.

Eberhard was posted again to the eastern front at the end of February 1942. The field postcards that Eberhard every now and then sent to his family bore printed warnings: "It is forbidden to identify your troop unit"; "Identify yourself by rank (soldier, private, lieutenant, etc.), not by function (sharpshooter, scout, or flier, etc.)." On 23 March 1942, Eberhard was wounded in a tank battle near Kramatorskaja. He spent May and June 1942 recovering in Goldberg in Silesia.

On the way to Goldberg, in late April, Eberhard's ambulance train stopped in Lemberg, where he convalesced at a former technical school that had been converted into a military hospital. This is precisely the place and more or less the time when Simon Wiesenthal, himself a former student at the Polytechnic, was working as a Jewish slave laborer in Lemberg and had his famous encounter with a dying SS soldier who, confessing his involvement in anti-Jewish crimes, asked Wiesenthal for forgiveness, which the prisoner did not provide. The moral dilemma haunted Wiesenthal, who recounted the incident in his book The Sunflower, which includes further commentaries by politicians, philosophers, and survivors solicited by Wiesenthal. In Lemberg, Eberhard also listened to a speech by Hitler on 26 April 1942. With much anti-Jewish invective, Hitler urged Germans to fulfill their duties without regard to the rights of others.

August had already found it awkward to convince Dr. X to operate on Eberhard's jaw, but when in June 1942 Eberhard requested him to ask the surgeon about a still outstanding receipt, August was even more shocked. Over the summer, the Brester family spent a relaxing vacation in the countryside. Eberhard, meanwhile, was posted back to Berlin in July 1942. He was able to spend considerable time in Berlin. where he and Herta saw a film about Rembrandt in which the painter was cast as a German hero who for a time was threatened by Jewish criminals.

Eberhard Gebensleben to his sister Irmgard Brester, Feldpost, 10 March 1942

[. . .] Today a sign of life with the news that I made it to my old unit. Right now I lack time and perspective, since we are very much under strain. But keep writing me; I want to know everything.

Eberhard's diary, 10 March 1942

Alisovka near Kramatorskaja. A long awaited day of rest to bathe, shave. The last 3 days were really something. Even Alisovka, which lies somewhat in the rear, has come under furious fire. [. . .]

Eberhard's diary, 11 March 1942

Alisovka. Relaxed for a few hours in our hut jam-packed with radio operators, sergeants, etc. At 2:30 sharp, with a sled to Indikowka and at 4 o'clock with an infantry reconnaissance patrol left to 1st Battalion, IR [Infantry Regiment] 169 who are as badly pinned down as we are. Well in advance of the main line without infantry support. The assignment: Reconnaissance toward Prawda without the clearance of artillery cover! Observed a tank attack on Prawda. My own carelessness attracted the hellishly well-aimed tank *fire*, the shrapnel landed between me and my radio operator, although the haystacks gave us excellent cover. Night quarter in Major M.'s kolkhoz, which is still more or less in one piece.

Eberhard's diary, 12 March 1942

Kolkhoz near Prawda. [. . .] The general opinion is that only new divisions will be able to launch the spring offensive, not our battered units—what a picture of misery all around us: frostbite, thickly wrapped feet instead of boots! Hobbling around in greasy winter vests, they are barely recognizable as soldiers. And they are still on active duty (even with amputated toes) and even now, *most of the time*, remain holed up outside in their snow forts! For the artillery the worst thing is the lack of horses. Lately, the field kitchens have occasionally been serving up Panje horse meat.

Eberhard's diary, 14 March 1942

Kolkhoz near Prawda. [. . .] I have been assigned to the 7th Battery as a reconnaissance scout. Not so nice, always back and forth! Back on the main road under heavy fire to the designated point on the map. There is absolutely *no* reconnaissance; it is actually the Russian who is better able to see us and lob precisely aimed grenades 15 m in front of your nose. Happened twice today. Who is watching over me? I make my way back. Washed up in pleasant quarters. Ordered mashed potatoes. [. . .]

When will they finally get around to cleansing this sector? Do they just want to let us bleed without providing us with any support?

Read Luther's writings.

Eberhard's diary, 15 March 1942

Shabolovka. An infernally cold day, bright sky then a furious storm with temperatures down to as low as 28°–30°. [. . .] Built snow screens; nose, fingers, and toes are constantly frozen, my head is so thickly wrapped up that I am no longer "recognizable." From a ravine, I fired off a barrage just to be on the safe side, and also shelled a Russian snow fort in the distance, most likely without any effect. This halfhearted offensive is really not fun anymore; I prefer to either leave them alone or kill them! [. . .]

Eberhard's diary, 16–17 March 1942

Two godforsaken days of fighting on "Kolkhoz No. 5" near Shabolovka. [. . .]

Today, 17 January, Russian tanks shells rips me out of sleep at 5:30, a big Russian offensive with 8 tanks. Since some had already crossed our forward positions, I can't advance at first. 8.8 cm flak, which later engulfs one of the tanks in flames, while our Pak [antitank artillery] finishes off 2 others. Because our positions were shot up yesterday, I first fire off a barrage from a halfway point (barracks) behind the Trigo [a steep rise], which is later considered to be effective. Then lay a wire in the direction of the block house under constant tank fire. The infantry was already supporting and firing over the line on its own. Things quiet down a bit in the afternoon. Nonetheless, my line of fire almost constantly under fire, just now again. Occasionally shoot back via radio. The outcome: the Russian offensive beaten back with bloody Russian losses, but also tragically our own. Among the dead, one of our V.B., a sergeant. Now just waiting for those nasty night fighters, the so-called Nähmaschine [sewing machines, on account of their nerve-rattling noise], which will constantly circle overhead and throw bombs, as they did last night. It is tough that I have such a ragtag unit and that the battery has not dug itself well enough in to support me as the other V.B.s are.

Eberhard's diary, 18 March 1942

Kolkhoz No. 5. Another Russian offensive at dawn. Collapsed before I even got to the block house. Hundreds of dead Russians here and in front of our positions. The Trigo is a mountain of dead: human body parts, blood-spattered snow. [. . .]

12 hours in the block house in damp snow. In the afternoon a second Russian attack on the Trigo (without tanks), launched with vodka-induced shouts and screams. Quickly smashed thanks to the concentrated shelling of our batteries along with flanking MG [machine gun] fire and grenade launchers from our sector. Casualties in our snow emplacements as a result of their flawless infantry barrage. Again and again, a fine chap is lightly or heavily wounded, gets an emergency bandage in the block house, and is sent to the rear by sled. In my head, I keep seeing one particular stomach

wound. In some spots, you can't even raise your head, but things happen nonetheless. Particularly tragic: 3 dead on account of our own artillery fire falling short. I know for sure it wasn't me, but I always have the terrible feeling of not being in complete control of the shelling. [. . .] Then back to desolate quarters in the kolkhoz. [. . .]

Eberhard Gebensleben to his sister Irmgard Brester, Russia, 21 March 1942

[. . .] Today is the beginning of spring. At least when this letter arrives, you will be enjoying the first flowers in the garden. Here there is only snow, snow in enormous amounts and on all sides, snowstorms, and still 25° below zero! After a period of active fighting, our sector has quieted down, the Russians did not break through. I know that I am in your hearts, and you can be sure that all of you in Holland and all the events of these past weeks are in mine. As of yesterday I once again have living quarters in which I can sit on a chair in front of a table, having progressed beyond the stage of a pure cave dweller. The snow is also our good friend. It provides us with water for all our needs, including drinking.

Eberhard's diary, 22 March 1942

Kolkhoz No. 5. The quiet interval has evidently come and gone. Timoshenko [the Soviet commander of the Kiev Military District] is on the move! Russian attacks, barrages, and other fire all day long from the kolkhoz and the block house. A battle of nerves! Toes frozen in what must be –30°; very laborious to restore circulation. On top of everything, terrible food. No peace at night either, on the contrary frequent tracer bullets, barrages, etc. My men are becoming apathetic as they troubleshoot along the repeatedly broken and in many places completely shot-up wire obstructions. Next morning orders to advance with *tanks* on special reconnaissance mission, a great "honor" for the regiment!

Eberhard's diary, 23 March 1942

Kolkhoz No. 5. The tanks arrive with a further battalion of reinforcements. We are supposed to counterattack in order to cleanse the so-called T.P. wood. As scout and commander, I climb into the turret of one of the tanks and familiarize myself with the mechanics of this well-conceived instrument of murder. Stuka attack. Then our attack after I quickly ordered the lead tank with its radio operation out of the line of fire and back to the kolkhoz—otherwise we wouldn't have radio contact. In a "rolling attack" the tank crews proudly break into song as we advance through the hollow along the edge of the wood. The moment passes quickly. The first hit smashes the MG, the next one the left tank track. We climb out into furious grenade and antitank fire. Our own infantry has taken cover a ways to the rear. I come to the aid of the badly wounded radio operator. The other tanks finally notice our nasty situation. Attempts to tow fail.

A new tank lets me hop in. Finally radio contact. My one order to aim and fire goes through: double detonation fuses for indirect firing. A direct hit also disables this tank. Back out. By now, the tanks crews are pretty demoralized, despite their war medals; only a few, among them, a sergeant, remain ice-cold, and I suppose myself.

Four tanks are now shot up in the hollow. Everyone takes off for the last tank, which has already started to back up. Climbing in, climbing on. No break in the nasty artillery fire. Just as I got at least my upper torso through the hatch, grenade shrapnel strikes my right foot; it hurts as if it has been completely smashed.

First examination at the kolkhoz. The torn-up boot is cut away: on the surface, just a lot of blood. The tank drives our small group of wounded and battered men down to the local military hospital in Kramatorskaja, not a very illustrious sight. I am alright sitting on the back. The only reason for this whole flop was that the tank crews completely underestimated the strength of the Russian position in the woods and thus overshot their targets.

In the hospital, I have to wait 1 hour in satanic pain; I am admitted only after the heavily wounded have been cared for. In all likelihood, something broken. And now I am once again lying in the familiar low-slung beds. I can only say: Lord, you have been looking out for me again.

Eberhard's diary, 24 March 1942

Field Hospital Kramatorskaja. An enormous feeling of fatigue. At least I have gotten out of this miserable Kolkhoz No. 5! [. . .]

In the ward for the badly wounded. A comrade dies. I recognize Captain W. from the kolkhoz in Prawda lying next to me. He is pretty much riddled with shrapnel. Repeated artillery shelling and bombing in the village.

Eberhard's diary, 26 March 1942

Field Hospital Kramatorskaja. After many tiresome reminders, the bookkeeper of the 6th Battery finally arrives to give me my service pay. The surgeon is satisfied, assumes there is a broken bone. Tomorrow an ambulance train should be leaving. 2 letters from Herta. [. . .]

Eberhard's diary, 27 March 1942

Field Hospital Kramatorskaja. Evacuated already at night by ambulance ("SanKW") and then loaded onto a Russian ambulance train in Konstantinovka. Very Russian! Not only half the personnel (Ivan the Good) but also the lice. [. . .] In Stalino [Donetsk] at noon. [. . .] Temperature constantly around 38°. Nervous, after the tank incident?

Eberhard's diary, 29 March 1942

Stalino [Donetsk], military hospital. I get along well with my roommates, enough points of contact. I once again realize that I do not know war in its extreme forms.

Eberhard's diary, 30–31 March 1942

Stalino, military hospital. First bad night. Apparently I shouted out tank commands. Better now, but for that 39° fever. Evacuation further down the line a dead end. Here they can bandage you up, but they don't have x-rays. Peter and Lina, an 11-year-old Ukrainian girl, look after me.

Eberhard Gebensleben to his sister Irmgard Brester, Feldpost, 2 April 1942

[. . .] I am sorry to have to tell you that I was wounded on 23 March, shortly after returning to my unit. Only lightly, so *no reason* to worry. A splinter damaged something in my foot. I go from one extreme to another: from head to toe. My foot is already in a cast, and I am in a military hospital behind the lines. Everything will be alright—we will and must be thankful that I was sufficiently protected. [. . .]

Eberhard's diary, 6–8 April 1942

Stalino. In a regular ward now. *A pigsty!!* Nothing is organized! Noise, and in return dirt and more dirt, lice too. Tiny room for 3 men, unable to air it out. Enough of it.

The Atebrin [antimalarial medicine] is effective. [. . .]

Eberhard Gebensleben to his sister Irmgard Brester, Feldpost, 10 April 1942

[. . .] First of all, I am doing just fine. My foot is in a cast, and I am lying peacefully (at least most of the time) in bed. At the time, the immediate circumstances were quite dramatic; so were the whole 2½ weeks in which I was at the front, but that is for another time.

Since I am already lying in hospital, I arranged for another unpleasant matter courtesy, in the opinion of the staff doctor, of an anopheles [mosquito], in other words a fine case of malaria (*tertiana*), probably contracted on the sandy beaches of the Dnieper last fall. The fever fit the bill, but luckily Atebrin did its job, and my temperature and my general health are almost back to normal. So much for my detailed medical report.

Dull Viennese medics and Ukrainian auxiliaries à la Modlin do the caregiving. Food is very good, I can't even finish off the chocolate, champagne, and other treats, of which there is more than enough! They are considering sending me back home in the foreseeable future, either by plane or ambulance train. Then I would be able to receive mail again. Maybe even visitors. It is the letters that I miss the most. I don't get letters addressed to 23660. I haven't gotten anything from you since the last letter you sent to Berlin. Every night my mind wanders into the two children's rooms to the dear little creatures. Are they all good and healthy, and are you *also* taking care of yourself?

Yesterday the little lice that are the only reliable company were mercilessly murdered. What could be better? For Easter we still had snow and deep snow drifts; wouldn't the first violets now be in bloom in Hedeper? [. . .]

Eberhard's diary, 22 April 1942

Temporary Ambulance Train "Vienna." 10 officers and 1 orderly to a car. [. . .] In the evening, several hours' delay on account of a broken coupler.

Eberhard's diary, 23 April 1942

Ambulance train. Made it at 4 o'clock in the morning to Dnieper and Dnipropetrovsk. We are all getting along better. [. . .]

Eberhard Gebensleben to his sister Irmgard Brester, Feldpost, 24 April 1942

It is fourteen days now, and I still haven't sent off this letter. [. . .] An ambulance train brought me to the big city in which I gained my first impressions of the East. A very comfortable transit hospital! We are supposed to be transferred to the Reich in the next few days, but nobody knows beforehand what route the train will travel. It is a bit like a lottery between Vienna, Strasbourg, and Königsberg. [. . .] Although my foot is still in a cast, I hobble around tolerably well with a cane, and I have a lust for life. I wonder what will happen in the next weeks and beyond? The spring offensive will have to wait—actually, of course, it unfortunately won't have the consideration to wait!

Eberhard's diary, 25 April 1942

Ambulance train. Over Shepetivka Zdolbuniv, we reach Lemberg already in the morning. Offloaded and brought to a quite comfortable hospital assembly point in a former technical school along with the other officers in my car. Correspondence with the Reich finally possible.

Eberhard's diary, 26 April 1942

Lemberg. The advantage of the hospital assembly point: friendly nurses and endless numbers of oranges, as much as you can eat. I am the only one who can't walk around the ward or enjoy other pleasures. "Supposedly" an ambulance train should leave "in the next several days." Well, I know all about that.

Today, Sunday and Hitler's speech, a victory for the SS.

Eberhard's diary, 29 April 1942

Ambulance Train No. 1111. Trip through the stimulating and charming foothills of the Carpathians. [. . .] In Gleiwitz and the other train stations at which we stop, the sight of an ambulance train prompts mixed feelings of sympathy and embarrassment.

Eberhard's diary, 30 April 1942

Ambulance Train No. 1111. Train unloaded twice during the night, by morning half empty. [. . .] My destination is *Goldberg.*

Eberhard Gebensleben to his sister Irmgard Brester, Goldberg (Silesia), 30 April 1942

Quickly the news that I have arrived here today around noon in good shape. A very nice military hospital, a former deaconesses' home; landscape-wise also

Ambulance train, Lemberg to Goldberg (April 1942)

very pretty at the edge of a huge mountain range. You must have certainly received my long letter from Lemberg by now.

Eberhard's diary, 1 May 1942

Goldberg in Silesia. The month of May greets us with heavy snowfall, which sticks! For me, the 8th month with snow since October! Cast is taken off, got x-rayed.

Eberhard Gebensleben to his cousin Ursula Meier, Goldberg, 5 May 1942

[. . .] As you can see, the homeland has once again very quickly taken me into her loving arms. In March I was at the front with my unit. I certainly can assure you that things had taken a turn for the worse by the time I got back. I was able to experience a bit of the winter war. Well into March on the warm southern front, icy snowstorms would drop temperatures to 30° below zero. Otherwise, it was more of the same. At the end of March we counterattacked, but luck was not with us. We lost 4 of the 5 tanks we deployed. As an artillery spotter during the attack, I rode in a tank and twice had the pleasure of firing. In these circumstances, a splinter damaged my right foot. [. . .] I slowly made my way "back" on ambulance trains, our destination the subject of more and more speculation, but I was lucky to end up in Silesia. [. . .] With a cane, I can walk small distances quite passably. Many others are much more badly off—I can't even mention it in the same breath!

Eberhard Gebensleben to his sister Irmgard Brester, Goldberg, 11 May 1942

[. . .] Aunt Agnes tells me that my entire Christmas mail is lying in Braunschweig. So maybe, hopefully I will also have some nice surprises at Pentecost, admittedly with the exception of any cakes that might come out of this production.

Now I once again have some idea of how all of you are doing, first and foremost, that everyone is alive and well. [. . .] Especially nice is the fact that Herta is now here for a week; she was able to make arrangements with her students, so I am doing really well!

[. . .] Uncle Otto wrote that Ursel broke off her engagement because she no longer can trust J.M. [. . .] Did she say anything further to you?

I know (to speak like Frau Buchholz) that the shoe pinches and I know where, dear Immo. Just stay the course. [. . .] I was wounded exactly 7 weeks ago today. What came before is already like a surreal dream, and I am writing as if it never happened. But this illusion is deceptive. What seems unreal will continue to make demands that one has to face up to.

Eberhard Gebensleben to his sister Irmgard Brester, Goldberg, 26 May 1942

[. . .] The most beautiful weather turned my birthday into an especially lovely day. We were invited to one of the families that Herta quickly became acquainted with while searching for a piano and then playing. Very refined, a big estate with a wonderful park. A horse-drawn buggy picked us up, then coffee on the terrace, etc. Later, we walked back. [. . .] Life in Silesia takes a remarkably peaceful course. It appears to be not only the Reich's air-raid shelter, but its food pantry as well! [. . .]

A retired university professor in Berlin gave me a very flattering opinion of the historical report I prepared in February and encouraged me to undertake similar studies. The idea of publishing it will come to nothing because the conclusion or rather the admonitory quote might cause offense elsewhere. Understood?

[. . .] I have a picture now of the festivities that took place for the copper wedding anniversary. That was really a very big matter, at least as big as Wilhelmina's "silver" one!

Eberhard Gebensleben to his cousin Ursula Meier, Goldberg, 27 May 1942

[. . .] The battle south of Charkhov is taking place exactly in the area where I was stationed and is the continuation and the result of our strenuous winter campaign there. Sorry not to be there. [. . .]

Eberhard's diary, 28 June 1942

Berlin. Sunday in the Kaiserallee. Daily life in Berlin has become almost unbearable. Early in the afternoon, the Rembrandt film. As far as our personal matters go, Herta and I decide that over the next days we won't force anything, but wait until we feel that the time is right. This Sunday could be considered our engagement day, festive and quiet.

Eberhard's diary, 7–8 July 1942

Amersfoort. Two wonderful days in Holland, where discussions bring some clarity: Dr. X. and the Dutch inheritance issues, and especially the important overall situation. Immo and August bring me to the train at 8:00 in the evening [. . .].

Eberhard's diary, 13 July 1942

Gnesen. Gloomy arrival in Gnesen. Nothing from the field regiment. Chances for leave not very good. So more garrison duty.

Eberhard's diary, 14 July 1942

Gnesen. [. . .] Killed the first bedbug in my barracks. [. . .]

Eberhard's diary, 23 July 1942

Gnesen. News from Herta, which will be decisive for our future. I was simply unbelievably happy when I read it! Errands in the city in the afternoon.

Eberhard's diary, 18–27 August 1942

Berlin. [. . .] Decisive days. Herta and I first have to find our way to each other. After several meetings in the ministry, an unexpectedly disadvantageous picture. I will have to resign.

From Gnesen, I hear that I have been ordered to go Russia after a new medical checkup classified me as "K.V." [fit for duty]. [. . .] Since the 19th, I have been working in my old department in the Ministry, but there is very little to do since I am not going to be working here over the long run. Testament, arrangements for the petition, very hot. [. . .]

Eberhard's diary, 13 September 1942

Berlin. [. . .] The express train is now cruelly cutting through tender ties. [. . .] My transformation into an itinerant mercenary has begun again. And I am a mercenary, not a defender of the Fatherland! I also believe that I now can see the fate that awaits us. My dearest Herta, you too should demand what is yours! [. . .]

Eberhard Gebensleben to his sister Irmgard Brester, Berlin–Warsaw Express, 16 September 1942

[. . .] The wonderful days in Berlin where I worked for almost 4 weeks—and thanks to sympathetic superiors without *over*working—are over, and my third "Mission to Ostland" began an hour ago. These departures tear apart the fabric of life and are perhaps the hardest thing to bear in this war. I will be posted with my old unit, or at least the corresponding regiment. I don't know my precise Feldpost number, but for the time being mail should reach me at 07272. You will soon find out why the leave-taking in Berlin this time was especially difficult. It was great that I was also able to spend 2 days with all of you. [. . .]

Germany launched its big offensive toward Stalingrad and the Caspian Sea on 28 June 1942, a little more than a year after the initial invasion of the Soviet Union. By 14 September, German forces had captured much of the city. Since most German observers expected a Soviet counteroffensive somewhere in the middle of the thousand-kilometer front, they were surprised when it targeted the southern sector. By mid-November 1942, the Soviets surrounded the German 6th Army in Stalingrad. Although breaching Soviet lines might have been possible, Hitler insisted that German troops hold out against the Soviets. The beleaguered, half-starved Germans ultimately surrendered on 31 January 1943. Stalingrad or "Stalingrab" ("Stalin-grave"), as soldiers called it, cost the lives of nearly one hundred fifty thousand German and over three hundred thousand Soviet soldiers; about ninety thousand Germans were captured, most of whom did not survive their captivity. Among the dead and missing was the husband of Marie B., a mutual friend of Hilde Kammerer and Immo. In retrospect, Stalingrad was the turning point of World War II, but even at the time, Germans came to realize for the first time that Germany might be defeated. Even before the conclusion of the Battle of Stalingrad, the British had launched a major counteroffensive in North Africa in October, and British and American troops landed in Morocco in November 1942—landings in Sicily and the Italian mainland followed in 1943. The Allies also began to take control of the Atlantic from German submarines. An Allied invasion of France was only a matter of time.

As a result of the defeat at Stalingrad, Goebbels declared "total war" in a spectacular propaganda speech on 18 February 1943. All possible resources were to be deployed in the war effort. Authorities closed countless bars, restaurants, theaters, and luxury stores and mobilized women in the work force.

Eberhard returned to the eastern front in September 1942 where he spent most of the time working for the military administration in South Beresovka. Passing through Kiev, he heard details about the murder of the city's Jews a year earlier; Babi Yar had already become a symbol of German barbarism. Eberhard also commented on privileged Nazis or "golden pheasants" who lived well in the safety of the homefront. At Christmas, Eberhard suffered a mental collapse. He recovered in a hospital in Wiesloch, near Heidelberg from mid-January to the beginning of April 1943.

Hilde Kammerer to her friend Irmgard Brester, Hohegeiss, 17 September 1942

[. . .] I think a lot about Marie; her husband is in the middle of the pitched battles in the East. [. . .]

Eberhard's diary, 22 September 1942

Kiev. [. . .] The glorious weather induces me to visit the Lavra Monastery. A fantastic view over the silver tear dividing the Dnieper valley. Most of the monastery is destroyed, blown up shortly after our invasion. But Rosenberg's office had already(!) taken away the most important art treasures. A German policeman took us on a tour of the desolate grounds. [. . .]

Today once again repeated conversations of a general political nature about "golden pheasants" and the murder of 35,000–40,000 Kiev Jews. According to our policeman (who had them in labor battalion), the last 300 were shot 4 weeks ago when new able-bodied Russian prisoners of war arrived to replace them.

Poor, dear Germany will pay for this.

Eberhard's diary, 27 September 1942

Sunday in Kiev. Finished preparing the packages at the antique store and—with difficulty—took them to the post office. My friend, a former white Russian officer, who is now leaving for Romania, sold me the Sèvres tea caddy. He packed it up very neatly and even built a wooden case for it. In addition, 2 enchanting candles dishes from the era of Empress Elisabeth (around 1730), for which I will later have to have two silver candlesticks made. Farewell meal with my traveling companions in the German Club; it goes on for so long that I decide to postpone my departure until tomorrow. Over the course of the tranquil afternoon, I discover the beautiful park along the steep bluffs of the Dnieper River. An almost tropical landscape. Took up Gertrud Bäumer's *The Park*, which I am reading to gain insight into several issues between Herta and me. Ordinary Ukrainians in their Sunday best. To St. Andrew's Church, where services just come to an end; aside from the 13 domes [of the St. Sophia Cathedral] it is the only baroque church in Kiev that I find appealing. Two ragged children in the church in bare feet. For the first time, I find the expression "angelic face" appropriate. I get goose bumps when I see these figures that could have been painted by Raphael. Was I right to give 5 RM? But my time is too short. On this clear day, the Dnieper River valley takes on the look of a primeval world; one is unable to fully comprehend the swirling currents of this huge body of water. A new life begins tomorrow.

Eberhard's diary, 30 September 1942

Night journey, in the morning Kursk. Inspected the 6th Battery (a training battery there). At noon on to Kastoryano in the ever widening steppes (none of it tilled!). Quarters in an assembly point near the front line. After a phone call from the major in the regiment, I am assigned to the first department! Nothing is constant except for these transfers. A sense of duty and solidarity to Hertel simply must help me. For the first time, saw and heard bomb attacks again.

Eberhard Gebensleben to his sister Irmgard Brester, Feldpost, 3 October 1942

My Feldpost address is on the next page. As you can see it is a new one, which means that I have had to adjust once again to new surroundings. [. . .] The two days I have been here have been very quiet, along with warm, summerlike weather—both not planned for. [. . .] Hopefully you received the last letter I mailed from Warsaw with all the practical information.

Eberhard Gebensleben to his cousin Ursula Meier, Feldpost, 11 October 1942

[. . .] Once again it happened all very quickly, a telegram and I was off. Along the way, I had an involuntary flu layover in Kiev; the subsequent days of recovery were very pleasant and allowed me to get to know this lovely city. At least lovely for those who know how to look beyond the damaged and abandoned facades; even the golden domes of the churches have been painted over.

For a good week now I have been with my old regiment, though a new unit; so far a quiet sector, villages in ruins, bunkers in the ground instead. I am still outfitting my castle, but I am delighted to be bunking together with people again; lots of East Prussians and Rhinelanders make for charming conversations.

Karin Kwant to her singing student Irmgard Brester, Utrecht, 18 October 1942

I just want to let you know that you have received an excellent notice from the radio critic. Here is what happened: there are two ladies who come here, who recognized your voice on the radio. [. . .] I then explained the situation to them, and asked them to not to say anything about it. However, the reviewer, who has a permanent slot on the radio, is an acquaintance of Mrs. F.'s, and she asked him what he thought of your broadcast: "Very favorable, he was struck especially by the lovely timbre of the voice."

Eberhard's diary, 29 October 1942

B-position near Lobanovka. [. . .] In the evening, the infantry launches a large stormtroop action near Ozerki, which we are to cover with artillery. Heavy shooting and the noise of combat in front of us and in the neighboring sector. Lieutenant E. and I are standing by in our bunker, listening to the radio. Climb up a few stairs and an incredible starry sky arches over us, crisscrossed by the fiery red shell trajectories. Death harvests its sacrifices, the action cost us 4 dead and 14 wounded without any particular success since the Russians are back in Ozerki the next day.

Today I find out that I am not going to take over the regimental baggage train but have been assigned to O IV at division headquarters. This is my third transfer in as many weeks. It is as if I am to be forcibly denied any rest or steady work. [. . .]

Eberhard's diary, 2 November 1942

South Beresovka. To fall from battery commander into the world of administration with dispatches, data entry, and telephone calls is horrible. I am walking around dumbstruck. [. . .]

Eberhard's diary, 4–5 November 1942

South Beresovka. [. . .] KdF [Strength through Joy] group rolls in, an evening with 3 female and 3 male functionaries, and the large evening meal together turns into a real party: red wine, rum toddies, champagne. The youngest girl, a nineteen-year-old, sits by my side. We don't break up until 3:30. It begins to snow at night.

I was very much in doubt whether I would once again be allowed to determine the course of my future in the military. Given the composition of the staff at headquarters, I do have it very good with plenty of intellectual stimulation. The two military chaplains are especially open, and I like the military judge very much. On the other hand, I am rather oppressed by how far away we are from the real world and the atmosphere of the front. And then Herta.

Eberhard Gebensleben to his sister Irmgard Brester, Feldpost, 8 November 1942

I haven't heard anything from you since your lovely first letter to 07272. [. . .] For the last three days, we have been seized by a sudden, predatory phase of winter with temperatures below zero, ice and snow, the usual, with which we will soon be on intimate terms. [. . .] Is the dear little company thinking about their Ohm Eberhard once in a while? [. . .]

Personally, I am doing very well, since I have been posted for the last week at staff headquarters. Life here is naturally incomparably more comfortable and pleasant than at the front. Otherwise, so many excellent emplacements and heated underground bunkers have been built that all the troops await the winter and the Russians without trepidation. This winter cannot in any way be compared to the last, especially with regard to personal winter gear!

You are sure to have many questions on your mind. [. . .] Herta wrote that she will be sending a package for Christmas. Yet everything will be even more difficult this year, and she has to take it easy with standing in line, etc. In case you want to send me a package, I am enclosing an authorization stamp. You have to send it by 30 November, although this letter may not even get to you in time. My dear Immo, I know how much more complicated everything has become for all of you as well. Don't deprive the children of the last treasures that may come their way! We have now received 6 of these authorization stamps for 1-kg packages, and I don't even know what to do with this somewhat dubious "blessing." We have everything here, and so it should only be a matter of a small symbolic pleasure!

Eberhard's diary, 8–12 November 1942

South Beresovka. The daily grind with some indisputably pleasant hours *after* hours. Major F. tells stories about the Führer's headquarters. Day before yesterday we heard about the Anglo-American invasion of North Africa. So the situation is changing. Here the Russians are quiet. It is a pleasure to look out my window, seeing the big marketplace and the sprightly colored village church, a beautiful winter scene.

Eberhard Gebensleben to his cousin Ursula Meier, Feldpost, 12 November 1942

[. . .] Otherwise, I can't complain about a thing. After 1 month front-line service (acting battery commander), I've once again been called to staff headquarters, which I consider deep in the rear. In physical terms, a first-rate existence, but also stimulating to sit around the table directly across from generals; there are also plenty of interesting people. But the desire to "go back" remains; I feel more comfortable with my mates. By the way, just about nothing is happening at the front—knock on wood!

Eberhard's diary, 22–23 November 1942

South Beresovka. Sunday, after the graveyard shift, worked with a massive headache, horrible heat. If only I could take a step out of this overheated office. Nonetheless, I see and hear lots of interesting things, especially regarding partisan activity! So, after the Russian breakthroughs in Stalingrad and the pincer in Africa: according to cold calculation, there is no way we can win. Even so, a people that endures in belief in itself can be redeemed! [. . .]

All our heavy artillery was redeployed to the south!

Eberhard's diary, 24–27 November 1942

South Beresovka. Almost every night the Russians sneak out like Indians to capture 1 or 2 prisoners from the infantry. We seem to be powerless to stop them. The big picture: Africa *and* the East, not so good. Today especially, I feel just miserable. Without fresh air, I feel completely cut off, nervous. [. . .] If only I had more faith.

Eberhard's diary, 28 November–10 December 1942

South Beresovka. [. . .] Snow is falling hard and fast. Numbers are the key question. Every month, several hundred men are missing, and the front steadily melts away, especially on account of sickness. Incoming recruits only delay the downward turn of the curve for a little bit, you can't even talk about "stabilizing" the situation. Infantrymen sleep on average 3–4 hours! Our army in Stalingrad is surrounded by the Russians and will be supplied by air. An entire army!! Anxious letters from Herta;

I have to be stronger and more resolved. I make my case at the IIa [section of the party chancellery that dealt with internal party matters such as Eberhard's petition] between 10:00 and 12:00 and ask what steps to take next. [. . .]

Eberhard Gebensleben to his cousin Ursula Meier, Feldpost, 14 December 1942

[. . .] There has been plenty of snow for some time with temperatures falling to 20° below zero, although today, for a change, a thaw has set in. You have to get used to Russia. This will be the first Christmas in the war that I have not celebrated at home; up to now, I have really had unheard-of good luck. But I am happy about this year and am even looking forward to it.

Eberhard Gebensleben to his sister Irmgard Brester, Feldpost, 14 December 1942

[. . .] We don't need lots of words to summon up all the things that bind us together over the holidays, especially since Christmas 1937, which is already 5 years ago. And then the last two very wonderful Christmas celebrations when I was able to be with you. On New Year's Eve, I will imagine myself sitting next to you in what is now the familiar little church listening to the words of the Dominee, which are no longer expressed in a completely foreign language. [. . .] I've written you frequently and told you already several weeks ago that Herta is expecting a child. You can understand how especially this year my thoughts wander westward, to the dearest people I have.

Hopefully a few packages have arrived from Germany; the German Christ child *must* have something for you, even if it is more symbolic in this 4th Christmas of the war. [. . .]

Eberhard's diary, 16–21 December 1942

South Beresovka. [. . .] Everything is dismal, on the military front as well. Big new breaches that will perhaps seal the fate of the army in Stalingrad. Are we about to collapse? Then farewell, dear homeland, Hertel, and child.

On the 19th, I take over a criminal defense, the case of an ethnic Russian who was stuck into a German uniform and refused to serve. Even so, the military judge hands down a death sentence. Last night I work on an appeal and a petition for clemency until 3 o'clock, the first such legal work in quite some time.

The whole issue of foreigners in our ranks affects me deeply. But does it even make sense to fight for the rights of a single individual when a general catastrophe is looming?

Hilde Kammerer to her friend Irmgard Brester, Braunschweig, 19 December 1942

[. . .] How nice it will be when the war is over and we can visit each other again and play music together. I already picture the time when your children are grown and studying in Germany; on the journeys back and forth and any time at all, they will always be welcome here and can visit us! [. . .] Is it possible to sing one time with the Hilversum I radio station because we get that very good?

[. . .] The next day, I had to comfort Marie and the children a great deal. They had hoped that Karl would come for Christmas. Now it appears that he unfortunately cannot, and naturally they are terribly disappointed. Keep her in your thoughts. She does not have it easy. [. . .]

Eberhard's diary, 25 December 1942

South Beresovka. This morning went skiing to get some fresh air. In the afternoon, which I have to endure at combat headquarters, I feel feverish. Toward evening to bed in my quarters. I want to write a letter to Hertel before the Christmas celebrations when I suddenly know: she is dead. Visions, screaming fits, nervous collapse. First Lieutenant T. and Staff Physician R., then Pastor K., who sleeps the night in my room.

Eberhard's diary, 27–30 December 1942

Naberezkno, military hospital. The doctors think it is delusion and psychosis. I struggle, at first successfully, against evacuation. Occasional fever over 39°. At one point, my nerves give way, and I become physical with the orderly. Sent Ursel pictures of Herta. No memory of the last days, like nightfall. Suddenly on an ambulance train to Kursk.

Eberhard's diary, 1–6 January 1942

Kursk. [. . .] Slowly we crawl through the countryside. The days run into each other. [. . .]

Eberhard's diary, 7 January 1943

Cracow. Onward with a new ambulance train [. . .] through Saxony, Thuringia, Hessen, in the direction of Karlsruhe. Suddenly at noon on the 9th I am offloaded in Wiesloch, near Heidelberg. At least I am permitted to make a phone call right away. Berlin 240289. "Party does not answer." An hour later, Herta's voice. She's alive. Dear, mighty God.

Eberhard Gebensleben to his sister Irmgard Brester, Wiesloch (near Heidelberg), 14 January 1943

As you can see from the return address, I was once again due for my annual trip in the ambulance train. No wound this time; rather my nerves failed me. It was too much for me after all, and I had a small breakdown. I can now see that my imagination had run away with me, and that is already the decisive step toward recovery. I don't feel unwell, I just have to get some rest.

Eberhard's diary, 15–24 January 1943

Wiesloch. [. . .] Hertel continues to spoil me with loving, calming letters. [. . .] According to the doctor in this department, many patients do not try anymore, don't cooperate, and are hard to diagnose because especially here pretending is all too easy. He thought as many as half(?).

Eberhard Gebensleben to his cousin Ursula Meier, Wiesloch, 20 January 1943

[. . .] Only now are you receiving my thanks for all the many delightful things you sent in your Christmas package. You can see why from the return address. They thought it once again necessary to ship me back to my true homeland. It wasn't a wound, but an affliction, no doubt the consequence of my earlier concerns. Obviously in the 4th year of the war, there are some defective spots. But I am doing well here, and I've already made enough progress to get up and take small walks. [. . .]

Gradually you can make the assumption that the real war is only now slowly getting started. I was just thinking back on winter '39 at Ohmchen's when all of you asked me how long the war would last.

Eberhard Gebensleben to his sister Irmgard Brester, Wiesloch, 27 January 1943

[. . .] What the war intends to do with me is very strange indeed when after barely 3 months at the front, I find myself under these conditions back home lying in a military hospital. I can rest under nice, white sheets. But in the East!!

As I wrote you, my nerves cracked up; I don't want to write anymore than that. [. . .] I am very happy to be in swift and almost daily correspondence with Herta. It is so nice to grow together again! [. . .]

She told me that you are now completely "in the picture" at last. I take it that at least one of my letters finally made it to you. There is nothing that I appreciate less in these matters than a situation of half truths or "secret insinuations"; I am *very* sorry that that is where you found yourself. It isn't necessary for either of us, isn't that right? I am so happy that the two of you are writing each other more regularly again, how good to know! Soon I will hear how you withstood the luckily rather mild winter, whether your little stoves have enough to feed on, and if everyone is healthy. [. . .]

Eberhard's diary, 25 January–3 February 1943

Wiesloch. [. . .] I am still irritable and unfocused, which is not normal and is infuriating.

Eberhard Gebensleben to his cousin Ursula Meier, Wiesloch, 14 February 1943

[. . .] The "total mobilization" of the homeland, which has been decreed since I last wrote you, was long overdue. Even so, I still have to ask myself why new films are still being shot and why, here in Heidelberg at least, girls are studying law and philology in droves. There is still some manpower that can be extracted from the theater and from various offices and organizations. Sooner rather than later, mobilization will have to be expanded even more.

[. . .] The doctor is of the opinion that I am suffering the aftereffects of my head injury in Modlin, which had been accompanied by a very high fever. I simply believe that my nerves were under great strain. The best cure: walks, rest, and friendly surroundings, which pertains here only in a limited way, however. [. . .]

Hilde Kammerer to her friend Irmgard Brester, Braunschweig, 16 February 1943

[. . .] Many thanks for your long, lovely letter. Even if it skirts the most important things, I am still always happy to hear about your circumstances and goings-on, which you describe so nicely. [. . .]

Let me tell you first about my big disappointment. Thursday evening I switched on Hilversum II as a test and confirmed that the broadcast came in loud and clear. Thereupon I reminded Marie that you were going to sing and invited her over on Friday at 10:30 to listen to your concert. And what happens, static in the broadcast! Evidently, the disruption by day is too great, which is a shame! At one point we heard some piano and a little bit of your voice, but it was more guessing than hearing. We were so looking forward to the songs by Wolf and by Strauss, and I had made a point to lay aside the sheet music. [. . .]

Do you know that Herr B. took part in the heroic battle of Stalingrad? His last letter was dated 1 January, and Marie waits and hopes! I am with her a great deal. [. . .]

Eberhard Gebensleben to his sister Irmgard Brester, Wiesloch, 21 February 1943

[. . .] You are absolutely right—being able to correspond regularly with Herta, getting answers right away to your questions and ideas, and not writing into a void is the very best thing for us. [. . .] She's made all the best preparations. The crib she had wanted was in Seesen, however, so Frau Nicolai lent her another one.

I wasn't able to hear the radio broadcast. We have only the small devices here, so I don't even know whether or not you performed. [. . .] If my vacation falls on the right dates and if I receive permission to travel, I hope that a visit—admittedly a short one—might be possible. Wouldn't that be wonderful, my dear sister? [. . .]

Eberhard Gebensleben to his sister Irmgard Brester, Wiesloch, 11 March 1943

Yet another greeting after the answer to my last letter arrived in such an astonishingly short period of time. I don't believe you know that I was sent temporarily to the Black Forest again [. . .] I returned very tanned and splendidly rested and now feel almost back to normal. When I got back, I had another pleasure, of which you are a part: all my Christmas mail had made its way back from Russia, including your lovely package. I arrayed the contents all around me and was so *very* delighted. Since they were all "timeless" things, nothing had spoiled or become useless, with the one exception of the radishes, which I could enjoy only symbolically. Indeed, I've put aside the soap for Herta, which I hope meets with your approval. [. . .]

According to the doctor's schedule, I should be released at the end of the month. I will have to wait and see what happens, especially with regards to leave. It depends on other events that cannot be determined so precisely by the calendar. Let us look forward to spring with good cheer, take our leave of stoves and colds, and allow ourselves some rest—which applies especially to you, my dear sister! Of course, what

I am worried about are the air raids; the last one in Berlin was severe and even the Kaiserallee was hit. [. . .]

Eberhard's diary, 7 April 1943

Wiesloch. In the morning, dispatched with my suitcase by horse and carriage. Final medical checkup with chief physician S. Briefly in Heidelberg, a last glance at the Neckar Valley. While I was praying in the Church of the Jesuits, it became crystal clear to me that a new period of my life is beginning. Return in wild swirling overcast weather by last light. Ordered back to the chief physician. Hertel's telegram came in the afternoon. Our little baby, a beautiful strong girl, was stillborn, most likely died for unknown reasons 1 day before delivery. (Delivery was last night.) So much is collapsing, actually: everything.

Eberhard's diary, 8 April 1943

Wiesloch. First thing, back to Berlin without a stop in Braunschweig. A journey to drive you crazy. Every last bit of meaning, the much deliberated meaning of existence, is grotesque, a joke, every thought of mine is a blasphemy against God. I broke away and will have to carry the consequences.

Telephone with my poor, dearest Hertel when I get to Berlin. Fräulein von W. and Frau M. meet me in the apartment.

Eberhard's diary, 9 April 1943

Berlin. In the morning with Frau S. and in the afternoon with Hertel in the hospital. She is so unbelievably sad and brave, so very, very brave. [. . .]

Eberhard Gebensleben to his sister Irmgard Brester, Berlin, 9 April 1943

I am writing you from Berlin where I arrived yesterday. Herta gave birth last Tuesday. She is doing fine. But the little child, a beautiful, strong 7½-pound girl, apparently died a day before the delivery. It is a mystery to the professor since it was hardly carried past term. We are devastated. Herta, who, after what had not been such an easy time and after all the loving preparations, is most affected, is being very brave. I can't say the same yet, it is all too cruel. You can't imagine how happy we were about the little child, and nothing but happy. Of course, we will come to terms with this as well.

Eberhard's diary, 10 April 1943

Berlin. Left Potsdam at 7:02 for Braunschweig. The trip is necessary among other things to bring all my forwarded baggage to Aunt Agnes. She feels for me and for us, but no one can really help. I think that this blow will become ever more destructive. Hertel says: don't let it get you too upset. But that means honor God's will as meaningful and deep and completely ignore God's senselessness. Isn't the murder of a creature in the mother's womb the most outrageous *crime*?

Hilde Kammerer to her friend Irmgard Brester, Braunschweig, 14 April 1943

[. . .] Unfortunately, I received your letter only today so once again I couldn't listen to you singing on the radio. I am very sad, particularly since I hear Hilversum I so clearly. It is as if I am not supposed to hear you sing! [. . .]

You can really be proud of your big daughter who writes such devoted and error-free German letters! [. . .]

Marie has not heard anything from her husband since 7 January, and she looks just terrible. She is amazingly strong and everyone pitches in to help her. [. . .] I am sorry to hear that Eberhard is lying in a military hospital, but in the meantime you have at least one big worry off your mind. [. . .]

Eberhard Gebensleben to his cousin Ursula Meier, Berlin-Spandau, 15 April 1943

[. . .] As you can see I am in Spandau, which is where my parents lived for a few years during the last war. There are some things that I recognize. Occasionally, I am in Berlin, where I have rented a room again.

Here we take courses to brush up on theory, some sport, swimming, etc. All quite nice. [. . .]

That is how one muddles through the good days and the bad ones and bears one's burdens, which for me are sometimes quite heavy. I've already said too much, at least for today.

At the end of April 1943, German authorities announced that all former soldiers who had served in the defeated Dutch army would be returned to prisoner-of-war camps (hundreds of thousands of French soldiers spent the entire war in German captivity). The occupiers claimed that anti-German activities proved that the trust they had placed in the former soldiers had been misplaced. The Dutch immediately responded with strikes and other forms of public resistance. Some one hundred seventy-five Netherlanders were killed and four hundred wounded when the Germans retaliated. Of the three hundred thousand former soldiers, eleven thousand were returned to prisoner-of-war camps.

At the same time, the Germans introduced obligatory labor service for all Dutch men between the ages of eighteen and thirty-five. Many young men went underground, filling the ranks of the Resistance, which had grown increasingly active as a result of the deportation of Dutch Jews, the execution of hostages, and the general deterioration of living conditions.

When a Dutch Chamber of Physicians was established in December 1941, the majority of Dutch doctors refused to join. When the Germans made membership obligatory and announced punitive measures, Dutch doctors responded with the so-called doctors' strike between 25 March and 1 April 1943. Thousands of doctors dropped the word "Doctor" from the nameplates of their offices and their prescriptions. August covered up the office sign in his front yard as well. As the conflict grew more serious at the end of June, hundreds of doctors went underground. Although the German police threatened mass arrests, most Dutch policemen wanted nothing to do with the matter. August himself was warned ahead of time, and when police came to arrest him, he was officially "at work," but in fact had gone into hiding. After negotiations, Dutch doctors sent a diplomatically worded letter to Seyss-Inquart. Thereafter, the Germans released those who had been arrested and those who had gone underground emerged from their hiding places. The doctors had won.

August worked ever more closely with the Resistance. He allowed people faced with arrest to be admitted into the hospital, from where they were taken to various safe houses. Sometimes he and Immo hid someone in their home. The last person they sheltered was Eddy Cramer (an assumed name), a nine-year-old Jewish boy who stayed with the Bresters for nine months. By this time, Immo was so rooted in Amersfoort that no one doubted where her sympathies lay, despite her German heritage.

Eberhard spent most of the rest of 1943 in Berlin and Frankfurt an der Oder, where he served as an officer for "spiritual leadership." As part of his responsibilities he attended a workshop on 22 October 1943, which included lectures by the journalist Otto Kriegk and the Nazi ideologue Arthur Rosenberg. Eberhard traveled to Holland for the last time in August 1943. In September, he commented on Italy's "betrayal" of Germany when it joined the Allied side.

Eberhard Gebensleben to his sister Irmgard Brester, Berlin-Spandau, 10 May 1943

[. . .] Once I received the letter you sent to Berlin and realized that the last one sent to Wiesloch got lost, I tried various ways to get news to you quickly. Just now another opportunity has arisen that I want to take advantage of in order to be on the safe side. [. . .]

Use this chance to write me *precisely* about whether you can rent a bank safe because I want to bring some of the things from the Braunschweig safe to you in order to distribute the risk better, which is exactly what the official recommendations are constantly urging.

Would it be alright with you if I were be able to come and visit now? I have heard some more about the circumstances there.

Eberhard's diary, 1–5 June 1943

Amersfoort. Immersed in Holland's feeling of security. This is one thing that will always be mine! Enjoyed the happiness of the children and the long evening conversations with Immo and August. [. . .] Repeated excursions with the wonderful tandem, the "double bicycle." [. . .]

Jan, Hedda, and Eberhard (out of uniform) riding a tandem bicycle (Amersfoort, June 1943)

Eberhard's diary, 6 June 1943

Amersfoort. A proper Sunday! It began with church services in the little Remonstrant church and ended with a long conversation in front of a slow burning fire in the fireplace where the three of us completely find our way to one other. The two of them understand Herta's and my entire situation.

Eberhard's diary, 7–9 June 1943

Amersfoort. Official German policies have the effect of returning the Netherlands to a "state of war." The illusion of Germanic brotherhood has come to an end. Not just on account of the savage application of martial law with mass executions, but particularly because of the reincarceration of former soldiers. Amersfoort just happens to be one of the assembly points for this action. How deceptive is the sight of this seeming unchanged, peaceful idyll with its flowery splendor! [. . .]

[. . .] I stayed on 2 days, but am now returning with German soldiers on leave. Once more, farewells that just weigh my heart down. My dearest sister!

Eberhard's diary, 22–23 June 1943

Berlin, Kaiserallee. [. . .] On the 23rd, met with Major von K. Marriage petition was sent on to the ersatz division! And this after a ½ year!! So the Wehrmacht is not an iota better, quite a bitter realization. On top of that quarrels with Herta. She just told me that I should write down that I "shouted." Evening of the 23rd, Pastor Jacoby on original sin.

Immo's notebook, 26 June 1943

Unrest among the doctors.

Immo's notebook, 1 July 1943

August did not sleep at home.

Immo's notebook, 3 July 1943

August to be arrested. Disappears from the hospital. His office cleared, locked. Package for August.

Immo's notebook, 5 July 1943

Take away the package.

Immo's notebook, 7 July 1943

With Anneke to Baarn.

Herta and Eberhard in Berlin (8 July 1943)

Immo's notebook, 8 July 1943

Office unlocked. August back home.

Eberhard's diary, 10 July 1943

Berlin, Kaiserallee. [. . .] The enemy has landed in Sicily. The pincer is closing.

August Brester to his daughter Hedda Brester (in Laren), Amersfoort, 11 July 1943

Fortunately I'm able to write this letter in my own house, sitting at my own desk. For I returned home Thursday night, after a rather exciting stay in village X, where, by the way, I was treated very well. Still, it was a funny feeling, to be running from the police. You'll understand that I often thought of you, and that I'd ask myself: how are they doing, did Hedda travel to Laren after all? [. . .] Do you sometimes still think of Uncle Eberhard?

Eberhard's diary, 14 July 1943

Frankfurt/Oder. I am now pushed into this ersatz unit, made up of convalescent and older active duty soldiers. Reported to the Kommandeur, who is considering the marriage petition. Gave suggestions regarding OKH Major von K. I also hear that the AR [artillery regiment] 168 arranged with the battery leadership to torpedo my first lieutenancy. [. . .] As of today I have been transferred! (Another one at long last!) On to the reception battery, which will undertake the hard hands-on work of training recruits in 14 days, until they are sent on to Crimea and we get new ones. Hardly a great day to receive the Ostmedaille [Russian Front Medal]. [. . .]

Eberhard Gebensleben to his sister Irmgard Brester, Frankfurt/Oder, 17 July 1943

[. . .] As you can see, I am now in Frankfurt/Oder, and since I am supposed to be fit only for barrack duties, you can use the address above for the time being. Of course, every day can still bring a new surprise. [. . .]

[. . .] I had a great deal of work to do in Braunschweig, including two visits to Hedeper. Above all in Hedeper I had to put everything on a "sound" basis; a lot had fallen into disorder. Uncle Otto mentioned that given the circumstances of the war he might eventually need more space—if not all the space!! We packed things in more tightly, took apart the beds and brought them—some in pretty bad shape—into Minna K.'s custody on the Brockenblick. [. . .]

Unfortunately, things have been stolen from one of the boxes with porcelain in the pantry. [. . .] Now all the boxes including the one packed-up laundry crate are in the New House. I couldn't relax until I got back to Berlin. The whole time I was there, I couldn't find a single summer resort; everything had been booked. But the days in Berlin have been all the more delightful with music, books, theater, and visits. [. . .] Herta has made a *splendid* recovery and—knock on wood—has come through everything. Thanks to provisions from all sides (you included) and saved up ration cards, we are well nourished each and every day. [. . .]

Eberhard's diary, 20 July 1943

Frankfurt/Oder. In the morning during artillery exercises the order: "To Potsdam for civil defense training by the end of the day" instead of First Lieutenant N., our SS officer who was taken ill. Yet another about-face, leaving behind an activity in which I was slowly making my way. I can't stand it. Herta is not even in Berlin. [. . .]

Eberhard's diary, 22 July 1943

Berlin, Kaiserallee. [. . .] 8 o'clock sharp in the barracks. With what innocence my comrades here, many of them already lieutenants, talk about defending Sicily or attacking Africa! [. . .]

Eberhard's diary, 27–28 July 1943

Berlin, Kaiserallee. We are given more exact numbers about the air raids; bombs dropped on Germany have killed some 27,000, on England 117,000! That says quite a bit about the course of events. Firefighting is the alpha and omega of civil defense!

Once again, wonderful domestic life in Berlin. But for how long?

On the 28th, news from Holland that August has been arrested, his whereabouts not known; Immo is also beset by inheritance questions. In the afternoon, coffee with Frau Major S., where I pick up my crate from Russia from the fall of 1941(!) and get a possibly valuable contact address regarding Holland. The same evening, completed my application to Frankfurt for leave. Around 1 o'clock in the morning, at the suggestion Herta, I decide to call Amersfoort immediately. To the Kommandantur Berlin and, after a short forth and back, connected to the local Kommandantur Amersfoort, where I spoke to the staff sergeant. No one answered at Immo's. Back at 3:30.

Eberhard's diary, 29 July 1943

Berlin, Kaiserallee. [. . .] To the OKH where I cleverly got permission to travel [to Holland] on the basis of the earlier approval. A great accomplishment! [. . .] Heard from Frau S.'s acquaintances that 120 prominent Dutch doctors have been arrested for organizing a strike. That is the situation. It will be difficult to get August out because he acts on principle.

Eberhard's diary, 1 August 1943

12:33 Express train to Holland from Bahnhof Zoo. Caught up on my diary. On time in Amersfoort around 10 o'clock. Hurried to Utrechtseweg 78, wondering who'd open the door? August himself! Not half as bad. He was supposed to be arrested, but went "underground" at the right time. After 5 days, the incident had been settled (a letter of agreement to the Reichskommissar) and he could reappear. Only the newspaper(!) had made reference to the seizure of inherited assets. For me, a great joy but at the same time disappointed since my ideas and efforts were all unnecessary.

Immo's notebook, 1 August 1943

Eberhard! A wonderful surprise, a shame only that he was so worried about us.

Eberhard's diary, 2 August 1943

Amersfoort. In the afternoon to the local Kommandantur to at least prophylactically give August or Immo, for that matter, some security if necessary and thus make the trip worthwhile. Received very warmly.

Thereafter, with Immo and the 4 children to the Boschbad [swimming pool], newly opened and very nice. So wonderful to be with the children in the water.

Eberhard's diary, 3 August 1943

Amersfoort. Unfortunately the weather keeps us from undertaking a second expedition to the pool. Instead "Monopoly" and "Cap the Hat," the usual games.

In the afternoon, with Immo to the local Kommandantur one more time to make introductions and contacts. Captain M. even agrees to write an attestation as a kind of letter of safe conduct. So something was accomplished after all! [. . .]

Eberhard's diary, 4 August 1943

Amersfoort. [. . .] Hedda and Els [Brester] arrange a charming evening of diverse music and entertainment as a farewell celebration for me. [. . .] Even members of the audience had to do their part; I flee to the piano with the "Jagdstück" (hunting song), Immo and August do likewise in a duet. Even Kaki and Jan have to appear on stage. It is really delightful! Furious applause!

PROGRAM: "FAREWELL EVENING WITH UNCLE EBERHARD 4 AUG. '43," AMERSFOORT

1. A word of introduction
2. "The Granny of Eemnes":   M[arleen] Brester
3. Some circus acts: E[ls] and M[arleen] Brester
4. "Evening in the Village":   K[arel] Brester
5. Singing duet (or solo):   Mr. and Mrs. Brester or Mrs. Brester
6. Mr. and Mrs. Pippel
7. "The Werewolf":   E[ls] Brester
8. Mr. Gebensleben
9. Polonaise
10. Ladies' choice

Eberhard's diary, 5 August 1943

Amersfoort. 7:51, farewell Holland. Once again, the company waving goodbye remains behind on station platform. [. . .]

To the Chancellery of the Führer of the NSDAP, Office of Pardons, 7 August 1943

Re: Lieutenant Eberhard Gebensleben's petition for clemency to marry a Jewish Mischling of the second degree and remain in the NSDAP.

The petitioner has been a member of the NSDAP since 1 May 1937 after serving in the SA from November 1933 until his voluntary enlistment in the Wehrmacht. He served 1 year in the Reichswehr. After completing his military service he belonged to the HJ [Hitler Youth]. He is a Regierungsrat in the Reich Ministry of Economics. At the moment he is completing a training course for convalescing officers in Berlin-Spandau after taking part in the campaigns in Poland, France, and Russia, where he was also wounded.

In a military hospital, the petitioner made the acquaintance of Herta Euling, a music teacher, whom he intends to marry. She is expecting a child. Herta Euling is a Jewish Mischling of the second degree. The petitioner requests that as a party comrade he be permitted to marry and to remain in the NSDAP. He declares that he has submitted this petition fully aware of the consequences and after careful consideration. He has convinced himself of Herta Euling's disposition, the reliability of her character, and her unqualified advocacy on his behalf. In particular, he has come to the conviction that she will in no way keep him from performing the duties to which the Volk, the Party, and the state call him.

The Gauleiter does not approve of this petition, and reference is made to his statement of 10 July 1943. [. . .] Moreover, given Herta Euling's strong element of Jewish blood, the highest party court considers this petition indefensible and a party member who submits such a request unworthy of further membership in the party. Heil Hitler!
on behalf of
Dr. Volkmann

Eberhard Gebensleben to his cousin Ursula Meier, Frankfurt/Oder, 21 August 1943

[. . .] On your return trip through Berlin you would not have been able to contact me since I was briefly in Amersfoort on 3 August. All of sudden, I received word from Immo that August had been arrested and quickly traveled there to make inquiries about him. Luckily, it was a more general blowup with the Dutch medical profession concerning "new organizational measures," and when I arrived, tempers had calmed down and August was back home. Incidentally, the doctors prevailed on this issue.

Barrack life goes on. I no longer have anything to do with the training of new recruits, instead I am giving general political lectures to wounded soldiers, which I find *preferable*. In addition, I am air-raid and fire-security officer for my department, which also keeps me busy. Air raids about every other night. Many things are not in good working order. [. . .]

Irmgard Brester to her cousin Ursula Meier, Amersfoort, 2 September 1943

[. . .] At the end of July, we were all together in a very nice, nourishing rural summer resort. The weather was glorious, and we could finally relax. Indeed, we really needed it after all the excitement that we personally lived through. Some day I will tell you about it, but these are bad times. [. . .]

Eberhard's diary, 9 September 1943

Frankfurt/Oder. [. . .] In the afternoon, lecture to the convalescing Reserve 101, apparently with success. Afterward in a pastry shop with Herta and Brita. [. . .]

Italy's betrayal; the form the expected fall took is reminiscent of the great intrigues and betrayals of the Renaissance. The mood in the military hospital is not satisfactory. For my part, these events give me a real boost of energy. What is now needed is to "go" at it and put in all your energy. I have never felt so close to the Führer as I do now. Came up with new ideas for my responsibility as an "officer for spiritual leadership."

Eberhard Gebensleben to his sister Irmgard Brester, Frankfurt/Oder, 3 October 1943

[. . .] I just realized that it has been exactly 2 months since I was with you, and since then I have received no news! I am still hoping that it is just a matter of delays caused by postal inspections and not something else! Under these conditions normal correspondence is just about impossible.

[. . .] Herta joined me soon after my return from Holland.

[. . .] At the moment, two of her students are staying here in Frankfurt, another comes regularly from Berlin, and she travels back for a day every ten days or so. I am a "liaison officer" for 3 local military hospitals, giving regular historical-political lectures on topics of my own choosing in order to counteract the apathy that spreads so easily in hospitals. [. . .] I am due for another medical checkup in the middle of the month, and then we will see what happens.

I heard from Aunt Agnes that Bubi from Süpplingen was killed in action in August. She was very upset. She particularly liked him.

Herta sends her greetings. Her parents' house in Hanover was completely destroyed by fire. Just a week earlier they had sold it and moved out! A few days ago, a Wehrmacht bulletin reported that Braunschweig had been attacked, but I haven't heard any details.

Eberhard's diary, 16 October 1943

Frankfurt/Oder. [. . .] I am immersing myself in my lecture on Frederick the Great. I am also reflecting on my life situation, which seems dubious and aimless after 33 years.

Eberhard's diary, 18 October 1943

Frankfurt/Oder. I am furious with the Kommandeur, whose disposition and character are completely the opposite of mine. Wants to review my suitability to be promoted to first lieutenant; I already know the outcome. Way too much officer training. Apparently the Russians have crossed the Dnieper south of Kremenshuk!! [. . .]

Eberhard's diary, 22 October 1943

Berlin, Kaiserallee. [. . .] The spiritual leadership workshop organized by the general commando on the Hohenzollerndamm starts off with an excellent lecture by Kriegk (journalist) on the political situation (in contrast to the Great War); the information on the political factors in the enemy's prosecution of the war are particularly interesting, the outcome of the Allied meetings regarding the division of Europe, thereafter questions about ethnic minorities in Crimea and Slovenia. Rosenberg's lecture on the East at 3 o'clock, an excellent rendition of the party's perspective anno '42: how do *we* shape Soviet space? [. . .]

Eberhard's diary, 25 October 1943

Frankfurt/Oder. [. . .] I am just struck dumb to hear that I have been ordered transferred as fit for active duty to France, apparently to the coastal artillery through the forwarding station in Rouen. In the afternoon, I make a casual concluding remark to the commander and find that the petition regarding my marriage has just been sitting on the desk of the department for the *last 4 months!* There is no reasonable explanation for this, and I feel myself completely released from any sense of loyalty. If Hertel were not by my side, making me see reason and showing me my true self, I would be back in Wiesloch!

Eberhard's diary, 26 October 1943

Frankfurt/Oder. Now I am going to fight. Got a doctor, have a medical examination in hand, with this sort of pressure given my totally unclarified condition, I cannot move out! Unfortunately the active regimental officer is not available. At least, they agree that I cannot leave until the day after tomorrow at the earliest. Waited in vain in the military hospital of Reserve 106 to see the psychologist Dr. M. Not until tomorrow! [. . .] In the afternoon, I hand over my duties as fire-security officer. [. . .]

Despite the situation and Russia's apparent superior position, the commander tries to improve morale. They've completely overrun the Dnieper. [. . .]

Eberhard's diary, 30 October 1943

Berlin, Kaiserallee. At 9 o'clock we go to an office of the central police headquarters at Alex [Alexanderplatz] and 1½ hours later we have Hertel's citizenship papers in our hands. Something we never imagined we would get! After that immediately to the local party office on the Kurfürstendamm and, as a matter of jurisdiction, to the Gau office on Hermann Göringstrasse in order to inquire about the "assessment" of Hertel. Herr B.'s initially warm reception cools once he understands the matter, but he remains basically helpful. In my presence, he immediately gives instructions to the local Spichern party branch. I couldn't ask for more!

And the certificate of nonobjection from the public health department is lying at home. A very successful day! The afternoon we have to ourselves.

Hilde Kammerer to her friend Irmgard Brester, Braunschweig, 30 October 1943

Although it is already late, I will answer your lovely letter of 29 September right away. It took 4 weeks to reach me! You have no idea how good it feels when people extend their sympathy and ask if you are still alive, which is the most important question these days. Yes, we came through alright, although it was our neighborhood that was hit. Nothing is damaged, broken windows at the B.'s and across the street. Nothing happened to your friends or relatives. The Klosterhof was hit harder. It was a night to remember, and we are happy just to be together. I stayed very calm; it was as though I had been lifted out of my body and yet somehow I felt protected. I well know what other people have to endure. Nowadays civilized people like us, who are encumbered with so many material things, are once again learning to be more modest/primitive and to be thankful for everything. Your own anxiety about not being able to be with us is something I can completely understand. I feel the same way.

[. . .] My brother reported for the front. With only 6 hours' notice, he can be sent off in the opposite direction taken by your brother! [. . .]

The bombing raids on German cities became more extensive and frequent over the course of 1943. Hamburg was decimated in the last week of July 1943, and Berlin suffered a major air raid on 23 November.

Assigned to the 15th Army, Eberhard was transferred west, to the area around Rouen in Normandy. The 245th Infantry Division, to which Eberhard's artillery regiment belonged, was responsible for the defense of the coast around Dieppe. Throughout this period, the Germans continued to fortify their defenses, the so-called Atlantic Wall. The Allied invasion finally came on 6 June 1944. Although Eberhard originally wanted to visit Amersfoort around 10 June on his way back to the front after leave, events kept him from doing so. The Allies liberated Brussels on 3 September 1944 and Antwerp the next day. Due to the lack of transport, most of the 15th Army remained marooned on the Belgian coast. While retreating, Eberhard's division came under fire behind the Ghent-Bruges canal. Eberhard was killed in one of the ensuing firefights on 9 September 1944. After the war, Immo and August visited the farmer who found Eberhard's body on his land and buried it in his orchard.

Allied bombers raided Braunschweig thirty-three times between 1 January 1944 and the end of the war sixteen months later. The heaviest attack took place over the night of 14 October 1944 and left over eighty thousand people homeless. The old city was very nearly destroyed. According to the press, 636 were killed, 596 Germans who had "fallen" and 37 foreign workers who "met their death."

On 11 February 1944, the Dutch Resistance raided a ration office in Amersfoort, killing one employee and wounding several others. The German Order Police thereupon stormed a house in the Bresters' neighborhood that they suspected of being a center for resistance activities. August and Piet, a student who had gone into hiding and had taken shelter with the Bresters, fled that same night, but it is not clear whether or how they were connected to the other events.

Eberhard's diary, 2 November 1943

Berlin, Kaiserallee. I decide not to leave until tomorrow. I make a phone call to the Chancellery of the Führer with a flicker of hope. A few more errands (including currency for France) while Hertel gives lessons. [. . .] May God protect our home in the Kaiserallee and especially my Hertel.

Eberhard's diary, 4 November 1943

Braunschweig. [. . .] A dismal three-hour wait in Hanover's wrecked train station, all that remains of the grand concourse are iron girders. What a reflection of the destroyed city! "Kaffee Kröpke" is just a newly improvised snack counter serving food and drink in the open air. A strange, imperturbable pessimism among the crowds. Around 3:00, the train leaves back to Paris. My travel companions give me a few tips for Paris, especially about the franchised "black" market for soldiers at the école militaire.

Eberhard's diary, 5 November 1943

We arrive at the Gare du Nord five hours late around 11 o'clock. With a baggage porter (5 RM!) right away into the Métro to St. Lazare and into the city. Opéra, Place de la Concorde, along the Seine and through the Tuileries. A German guard with band playing is crossing the Place de la Concorde, which almost swallows up the little group, though it is backed up by MG gunners. At the local Kommandantur, they assign me a room—actually without even asking me—in the Terrace Hotel at the Place de Clichy. So I don't leave this coming afternoon, but only tomorrow morning! At the soldiers' market, acquired 4 pairs of stockings (RM 9.50 a pair) for Hertel and some herbs and sweets. [. . .] According to today's Wehrmacht report, Crimea is cut off. They have penetrated as far as Cherson, catastrophic. Evening stroll up the Champs-Élysées to the Arc de Triomphe. Paris laughs, loves, and lives, even during the blackout. What a difference in looks, finery (hats!), and makeup between the Métro and the Berlin subway! Not to speak of Hanover. Who is the victor and who is the vanquished? Luckily, hot water in my bathroom, otherwise ice cold. Shopping included, the day cost some 60 RM.

Eberhard's diary, 6 November 1943

Paris. Up at 8 o'clock to St. Lazare and breakfasted at the German Red Cross. 8:45 express train to Rouen. Fog and rain veil the beauty of the Seine Valley. Become acquainted with a young Kärtner from the mountain infantry, Lieutenant S., who has lots of interesting things to say about the problems in the southeast and the errors of judgment that, in his opinion, actually caused the horrible partisan warfare (we've deployed 3 divisions). So much has been hopelessly destroyed thanks to our "civil administration"! But the picture is the same everywhere, whether Holland, Alsace, Ukraine, or Poland. [. . .] Unfortunately, I find out that I am not assigned to the coastal artillery but to a newly established stationery division responsible for the security of the channel coast. At 7:30 onward with a local train to Doudeville, 1½ hours north of Rouen, sadly in complete darkness. Directed to a school building, everybody sleeping together in one big room. Apparently we have arrived at staff headquarters of the 245th Division! Before going to sleep, a fat-rendering, ration-card-free but for that very expensive meal in a bar with a squeeze box and *fantastic wine!*

Eberhard Gebensleben to his cousin Ursula Meier, Feldpost, 9 November 1943

Let me just quickly let you know that I have arrived safely at my point of destination in Normandy.

[. . .] I stopped over in Paris for a day and refreshed old memories. What a magnificent city! At once imposing and beautiful! [. . .]

Eberhard Gebensleben to his sister Irmgard Brester, Feldpost, 15 November 1943

In the future, your thoughts will have to seek me out in the West, not in the East. [. . .]

Once again leaving Herta came and went very quickly.

[. . .] Then a short stopover and a night in Paris where I refreshed wonderful memories on the fly. Clearly, one lives and loves as before, one tries to forget. Just the bold design in hats would be unimaginable in wartime Berlin, and evidently the use of colors for "makeup" has not diminished either. And you can still dine very decently.

In the meantime, I have been plunged in completely rural stillness and solitude. A beautiful, very characteristic stretch of country, if only I can tell you about it later. You will recognize it. Wonderfully fertile land, the cows in pasture—sometimes I think that if I am not in Holland, then surely Belgium. So much seems familiar.

The German Santa Claus is not going to be able to make it this year. Just looking for and buying books was become difficult, if not impossible. Our memories of unforgettable celebrations together will help compensate!

I would be so honored to behold Hedda's new room.

Eberhard Gebensleben to his sister Irmgard Brester, Feldpost, 5 December 1943

[. . .] It is Christmastime, at least according to the calendar. Herta's apartment was completely destroyed on 23 November; nothing could be rescued from the entire building. So now the only spot for just the two of us and the modest cornerstone for a better future is gone. Of course, my losses (couch, a yellow chest from Hedeper) cannot compare to Herta's, just to think of the magnificent Bechstein grand piano. Well, that's that. In her letters, she is always completely composed and calm.

Outwardly life has been tolerable to pleasant up to now. Horses are my best company; the inhabitants are quite friendly. I have been in Paris a few times where one awkwardly tries to play peacetime. [. . .]

In the event a further greeting does not reach you in time, your dear brother Eberhard wishes you and everyone a Christmas as blissful as those we were allowed to spend together.

Eberhard Gebensleben to his brother-in-law August Brester, Gross Born, East Pomerania, 7 January 1944

When I returned to my unit after the Christmas holidays—exceptional circumstances given my constant traveling!—I was completely stunned to find 4 letters from Holland. Immo in the lead, as it should be, with 2 letters, the handwriting of my niece Hedda was also not unknown to me, only a certain yellow letter kept me in suspense until I opened it.

[. . .] I had good reason to be pleased not only because your letters have acquired a rarity value but because you know how to combine their other merits with charm as well.

[. . .] Because Herta's apartment in Berlin was destroyed, I received 14 days' leave, Christmas with her parents.

[. . .] Then a week with my unit, and immediately thereafter the order to report to the military drill grounds in Gross Born, Pomerania, where I have been able to deepen my knowledge of military matters (all in all, I have been a soldier for almost six years now). The course lasts until 3 February, followed by another course somewhere else. At the beginning of March, I should be back with my unit, which carries the Feldpost number 16266D. Otherwise, we should step bravely into the new year, as Pastor L. wrote me: "Do the immediate things that are necessary without hesitation, whether they are large or small, seem important or not, and await in trust what will come." At least that is what we will try to do.

Immo's notebook, 16 January 1944

Restless mood here. August is gone as much as possible.

Immo's notebook, 13 February 1944

For a whole week, August and Piet have been out of the house every night.

Eberhard Gebensleben to his sister Irmgard Brester, Gross Born, 3 February 1944

[. . .] Did you hear about the big air raids on Braunschweig? Aunt Agnes wrote that the Brockenblick suffered damage, but only glass and bricks. Much worse hit were Zuckerbergsweg and the houses beyond, apparently for the most part destroyed. [. . .] I myself don't yet know what happened during the raid on 30 January.

[. . .] How I would like to drop in on you, but for the time being there is little chance.

The Head of the Chancellery of the Führer of the NSDAP, Berlin, 25 February 1944

Herrn Regierungsrat Eberhard Gebensleben
In your petition you requested that as a party comrade you receive permission to marry a Mischling of the second degree.

On behalf of the Führer, I have to inform you that this request can under no circumstances be granted; your petition has thus been rejected.

In addition, it is essential that a hearing of the Party Court determine whether your continued membership in the NSDAP can be sustained.
(Reichsleiter)

Eberhard Gebensleben to his cousin Ursula Meier, Feldpost, 12 March 1944

It must have been in the gray mists of prehistory when I last wrote you. The reason: so many things went awry that I had a "falling out with the world" and simply did not want to write anymore. [. . .] Once again it has been a long time since I received any news from Braunschweig; the mail is like the lottery.

[. . .] It has been a year and a day since Hedeper replied to my occasional greetings. I found a possible reason in one of Immo's letters in which she mentions the birth of a baby boy in Hedeper. I am completely in the dark about the circumstances, and they are hardly my business. But I have to say it would be the very first time that Gerda would impress me. Such a thing can't be easy in a village like Hedeper, but would save the almost extinct name Rauch in one surprising stroke!

And our dear Braunschweig? In December, I deliberately said my farewells to the old city and our friends and those of my parents. To tell you about myself, would be a letter unto itself. The "war" (including bureaucratic battles) preceding the war is pretty hideous. Burrowing and building are being taken very seriously.

Hilde Kammerer to her friend Irmgard Brester, Braunschweig, 12 March 1944

[. . .] According to new regulations, one is allowed to send only 2 letters and cards abroad each month.

Our beautiful homeland has really changed a great deal. Almost all areas have been at least partially damaged, the neighborhood around your house as well and where your grandmother used to live. [. . .]

Fare thee well, Immo! Be grateful that you are still all together. [. . .]

Immo's notebook, 30 March 1944

Piet gone. Eddy came.

Eberhard Gebensleben to his cousin Ursula Meier, Feldpost, Easter Sunday, [9 April] 1944

[. . .] Since I have been in France, I have finally gotten to command a battery (aside from the interruption of the training course) and have gradually become a first lieutenant. It does me good to have my entire day completely filled; of course, what is "private" gets short shrift, but I am not the first person to discover that. In the past, we used to spend Easter Sunday in Hedeper, and my thoughts wandered over there today. [. . .] The Wehrmacht bulletin on the radio has just mentioned the Braunschweig region. [. . .] Is the Brockenblick still standing? Spring starts up very beautifully around here. When I find the time, my greatest pleasure is riding in the sea breezes that come across the white-blue ocean.

Eberhard Gebensleben to his sister Irmgard Brester, Feldpost, 28 April 1944

Herta forwarded me your letter from 6 April in which you quite rightly complain about my not writing. If only one wasn't so tired or didn't wonder whether it is even worth writing and receiving letters. Can you understand that?

[. . .] If you are not receiving letters from your friends and acquaintances it is probably due to the fact that you now need a special authorization stamp or some other formality to send letters abroad. Perhaps they avoid the difficulties involved or don't have any time.

There is not a lot of good to say about Braunschweig, the city. Back in December, I deliberately said my farewell. According to reports from Aunt Agnes, there is not much left of the old city. How fortunate that the parents, and especially Vati, for whom the city was his life's work, are not alive to see this. [. . .] As far as the external circumstances are concerned, I am fine. It is difficult to write about the other things. My duties at the moment are very satisfying; I happily make every effort on behalf of my troops. After almost a ½ year as commander of a battery, I have finally become first lieutenant. Don't be angry with your brother.

Eberhard Gebensleben to his sister Irmgard Brester, Feldpost, 7 May 1944

You are right to complain about my not writing. However, one letter to you was returned, "vacation trip direction Braunschweig. In 14 days perhaps back in Amersfoort. [. . .]," it didn't make it. Besides there are so few good things to tell you about. Even the Brockenblick is now destroyed. But otherwise I am doing fine. [. . .] The spring weather is just wonderful. Give my greetings to August and the dear children and stay well, you, my dear, most cherished Immo. Your brother Eberhard.

Irmgard Brester to her cousin Ursula Meier, Amersfoort, 23 May 1944

Today on the occasion of Eberhard's birthday I want to finally thank you for your lovely letters, which gave me such joy. A little chat with you gives me something from the old homeland today after all! Where might the birthday boy be today? After months of silence, I finally got a short note from him, but I still don't know where exactly he is keeping himself. [. . .] I wonder what our dear old Braunschweig looks like. How hard Vati would have taken the destruction of the city, which he spent a lifetime building and improving! When will this horrible war be over! [. . .]

Immo's notebook, 6 June 1944

France invaded! Enormous excitement and crowds at the newspaper.

Immo's notebook, 11 June 1944

Eberhard didn't come, Eddy scarlet fever.

Eberhard Gebensleben to his cousin Ursula Meier, Feldpost, 22 June 1944

[. . .] The days with Herta in Semmenstedt were wonderful.

[. . .] To come up from Semmenstedt and stand on the mountain, to look out over the deep falls and beyond to Hedeper, the Fallstein, and perhaps even to Father Brocken, makes my heart just open up, I feel so at home. [. . .]

Of course, I bicycled over to Hedeper and said hello to everyone. The little boy is good looking. [. . .] They even invited me to the baptism, but it didn't work out timewise. Uncle Otto is really "beaming," though he has gotten older.

[. . .] Today I went riding by the ocean, along the cliff line. With the rising tide, the long white-capped waves floated in a landing boat, but otherwise we have had no sign of the invasion battles. We live as peacefully as we did before, although it can't possibly go on like this. Most beautiful is the profusion of roses, a true symbol of the region in which every single one of the vine-covered houses is a sight worth seeing. I was presented with the most beautiful bouquet of roses I had ever seen, an indication that the *local commander* is not simply feared.

Eberhard Gebensleben to his niece Hedda Brester, Feldpost, 14 July 1944

[. . .] I was *very* pleased to get your letter. You told me so many things; I am no longer so good at that anymore, perhaps the war does that.

You are a big girl now and will be able to understand how good you have it with your dear parents, your little brothers, and your sister. Can you even imagine how different it would be if you were not all together? I am writing this so that you can be very thankful and very glad and happy on your birthday, that is, shout-out-loud happy over the life you have, the most wonderful birthday present. Do you understand me?

[. . .] In German I would have given you a better grade than 6+, no less than a 9! You don't believe I would?

Hedda's diary, 6 September 1944

The situation is crazy right now. Yesterday they requisitioned a whole bunch of bicycles, and you were allowed to pick them up from the barracks today. I went there to have a look. But I was quickly chased away by a *Kraut*. I felt the tip of his bayonet on my back.

Wehrmacht Support Officer to Irmgard Brester, Frankfurt/Oder, 12 October 1944

According to the communication of 11 September 44 from the Feldpost number 16266 station, your brother, First Lieutenant of the Reserves, Eberhard Gebensleben, was killed in action on 9 September 1944 around 19:00.

With regard to settling matters of the inheritance you will want to get in touch with Frl. Herta Euling, Frankfurt/Oder, Zimmerstr. 3.

Herta Euling to Irmgard Brester, Frankfurt/Oder, 10 October 1944

I have had you in my thoughts so much lately, and I would give anything to know whether all of you are healthy! I know so well all the hardships you already have endured, and now I have to bring you this terrible sadness. My dearest Immo, Eberhard is no longer alive; he fell in action, killed immediately by a bullet. For me, it is as if each and every word has withered. I am constantly thinking of you, good dear Immo. If we could just sit quietly beside each other.

Don't you think that for him this end is the high point of a life that always considered the Fatherland to be the supreme obligation in a man's existence? Shouldn't we, you and I, think about the fact that he regarded this death to be the most beautiful a man could have? And about the fact that his longing for your beloved parents, who left this earth before he did, never disappeared?

If you should get this letter, my dearest Immo, I am enclosing an official notification, which can serve as a credential in the event you want at some point to make the trip here. For the time being, I am staying in Frankfurt, where I have been deployed in the war effort as a cook in a military hospital, which gives me a great deal of satisfaction.

Dear, dear Immo, I need to take you firmly and quietly into my heart. You know and understand everything! May God protect your husband and your children.

AN OFFICER TO HERTA EULING (COPIED BY HERTA EULING)

As officer in the battery that your husband, 1st Lt. Gebensleben, my esteemed commander, led until his heroic death, I want to express today my heartfelt sympathies for your bitter loss. I think that I can wholeheartedly take the measure of your pain in losing such a principled and truly distinguished man since I believe I got to know Herr 1st Lt. Gebensleben quite well during our long months of close and fruitful collaboration. With his death, the battery lost an unceasingly energetic, considerate, and exemplary commander, and I lost a thoughtful superior and an understanding older comrade, who, thanks to his abundant life experiences and broad education, gave me so much.

On behalf of my former division commander, Herr Major T., I want to give you the detailed circumstances under which Herr 1st Lt. Gebensleben died. On 9 September we had left Brugge and set up an artillery position near Assebrouk. 1st Lt. Gebensleben was manning the B-post in Moerbrugge, in the immediate vicinity of the canal, which the enemy had already crossed at several points. The sharpshooters in Moerbrugge were inflicting heavy losses on our troops. Pointing out the extreme danger, I urged my commander by means of a telephone call to be careful; he reacted to this warning with an easygoing laugh. It was the last conversation I had with him. The B-officer gave an account of the heroic death of our commander who after putting the battery into action, wanted to more closely observe the direction of the shooting. He took a few steps from the safe cover of a house and was fatally shot in the head a few moments later. He died on the spot. A radio operator from our unit was standing nearby and ran to assist. He retrieved identification tags, a billfold, and a pay book from the corpse. However, this soldier later went missing, so these personal effects of your husband have been lost. All his other personal belongs were sent off as soon as it was possible to do so. The next day we buried the mortal remains of 1st Lt. Gebensleben by the Bruges-Assebrouk road. [. . .]

Nina Revers to her friend Irmgard Brester, Heerenveen, 6 November 1944

How we feel for you for the loss of Eberhard; how close you always were, and to think that that bond is now so rudely severed! Of course it doesn't help that you could see it coming; when you are faced with the actual fact of it, it's just as terrible. I can so sympathize how dreadful it is knowing that he was so far away, and without your loving care. It must also be almost impossible for his girlfriend to bear, and there are so many women, girls, and mothers, who have to bear it! The world is drowning in sorrow and worries. It must have been quite a shock for the children too, especially the oldest. And on top of that you have to keep yourself together in mind and spirit in the struggle to keep food on the table for your family; it isn't being made easy for us. Please do your best to carry on, your children need you, and so does August [. . .]

Ilse Scholz to her friend Irmgard Brester, Neukünkendorf, near Angermünde, 7 November 1944

Yesterday as I was reading the *Allgemeine Zeitung*, I was shocked to come across Eberhard's death notice. I still can't believe that he is no longer with us. Where did he fall? My deepest sympathies to you and August, in Otto's name as well. What a loss for you! Now you will be even more a stranger in Germany! [. . .]

Dé Hingst to her friend Irmgard Brester, Utrecht, 7 November 1944

From Clara we heard the sad news that your brother was killed in action. Our heartfelt condolences for this enormous loss. You must have been in constant fear for this eventuality, and now it has happened. What terrible times we live in, Immo, all those young lives and the unspeakable misery suffered by millions of people. Your brother too thought he had to do his duty, even if we might see things differently; he must have thought, naturally, that his way was the right way, and he has encountered death in the faithful execution of his duty. The only link you still had with your family. After all the hardships we will still have to face are behind us, I'll be happy to be able to visit you again.

Ursula Meier to her cousin Irmgard Brester, Wolfenbüttel, 7 December 1944

I don't know if this letter will ever reach you, but I hope I have found a way that it might. I feel such a need to write you and tell you how very sad I am about Eberhard's death and how much I share your sorrow. I so much want to be with you, not just in spirit, but to really hold your hands tightly. Now it is only the two of us, who share so many memories of the dear deceased.

I have your picture on the sewing table, the last photograph with Aunt Lisbeth where she has gathered her children and grandchildren (except for the smallest) around her and where Hardus still looks so young and unconcerned. In June, when he came to the Brockenblick on bombing leave, I saw him for an afternoon, he wrote me once more, but then I had no more news from him again until I read the death notice in the newspaper (at the beginning of November) and found out that he had died in action already on 9 September. Fräulein Euling wanted to inform you through

The last photograph of Elisabeth Gebensleben with her children
and grandchildren (Braunschweig, August 1937)

the Wehrmacht. At the memorial service in the Martin-Luther House, Propst L. made
mention of the letter of his major. [. . .]

Immo, the gods take those they love, who are at the height of their powers,
but will be spared so much. Given the direction of his life, he would have had many
battles to fight. He never made it easy for himself. [. . .]

Otherwise, the memorial service was disappointing. A long Protestant service
followed by the commemoration of about 10 dead men. Aunt Agnes, Fräulein Euling,
Martha Kreutzmann, and I were there. I felt much, much closer to him that day
before, when I was in Hedeper, where we so often played together, where the sheds
and barns and the garden were so familiar to us, and where we felt so at home. When
I rode back on my bicycle I had to think about his last letter in which he wrote that
his heart opened up when he looked out at Hedeper from Semmenstedt, with the falls
and Fallstein in the background, and beyond Father Brocken. When one thinks about
the family, one really regrets that he did not find a genetically suitable and for him
well-matched girl and that there are no heirs. But perhaps that was his fate.

[. . .] Immo, you have no idea how often I think about you, even dream of you at night. I am sure things are very, very difficult for you in these times. In any case, I found out from Elisabeth B., who had an acquaintance check, that the Utrechtseweg was still standing at least eight weeks ago. Would you be able to come here if you had to leave? From the Christmas letters you will know that much, very much has been destroyed in Braunschweig. But your relatives in the countryside would greet you with open arms and would so much like to see the house filled up again! I wonder how your li'l ones have grown.

[. . .] Being alone sometimes makes me very sad. It is so much nicer for a woman to be able to take care of a family.

[. . .] In Hedeper we recently celebrated the little boy's first birthday. No grandfather is more tender than Uncle Otto! And at least for now he looks very much like a "Rauch"! Like the baby pictures of Bernhard Rauch, who fell in battle so early. Did you hear that Ike A.'s husband was also killed? [. . .]

We are still holding out pretty well and believe in a good outcome for the war. But the wounds that it inflicts are heavy! It will be a quiet Christmas this year, undoubtedly for you as well. Can you still bake Ohmchen's Christmas cookies? [. . .]

Hilde Kammerer to her friend Irmgard Brester, Hohegeiss, 12 December 1944

You cannot imagine with what worries I think about you and yours since I haven't heard from you since January '44! I haven't been able to get in touch with Hedeper by telegraph and I don't know other relatives whom I could ask about you. I am sure that you took the children to Friesland in time, but to be separated from your husband will be very difficult for you. As a doctor he surely has to stay put. Will you even get this letter? [. . .]

My dear, poor Immo, I was devastated to read in the *DAZ* that your dear, talented, smart brother Eberhard fell for Germany on 9 September 1944 in the West. As a result, your entire family in Germany has been expunged. [. . .] You were certainly not able to attend the memorial service on 5 November in the Martin-Luther House, you poor dear!

Your house in Braunschweig is apparently still standing, but the loved ones are missing. You will have difficulty recognizing your hometown! We too have suffered losses: on 15 October we lost our beautiful family house in Braunschweig as a result of a direct hit that went right through into the cellar; nothing could be saved. It is not easy being homeless, but we are grateful that we can find accommodation with relatives and, especially, that my sister rescued herself from a burning house nearby. Now we have to demonstrate how much we cherish spiritual values, which no one can steal from us! With all my heart, I wish you a blissful Christmas with your loved ones, despite all the sorrows, and a healthy new year for the calendar and for our lives—1945, which hopefully bring us a favorable peace so that all the heavy losses will not have been in vain. [. . .]

THE OTHERS (1945–1949)

On 5 September 1944, "Dolle Dinsdag" or "Crazy Tuesday," thousands of Dutch Nazis and collaborators fled to the eastern part of the Netherlands as rumors that Allied troops had crossed the border spread. The Allies did indeed liberate the southern parts of the Netherlands, but after their assault on Arnhem failed at the end of September, the situation in those parts of the country still occupied by the Germans deteriorated rapidly. To support the Allied attack on Arnhem, Dutch railway workers called a general strike on 17 September. Amersfoort was the only city in the Netherlands where the Germans threatened the strikers. On several occasions, they blew up their homes in retaliation. The strike continued until the end of the war, and occupation authorities had only very limited success keeping the trains running with German personnel.

After September the Germans conscripted tens of thousands of "Spitters" (literally diggers) to excavate defensive lines along the Rhine and IJssel. Everywhere Dutch men went into hiding and Germans conducted major "Razzias" or manhunts to find them. In Amersfoort, the first German Razzia took place on 6 October 1944. The biggest one occurred in Rotterdam, where about fifty thousand men were caught. Some of them passed by the house of Immo and August, who saw neighbors slip them apples and other articles of food. August's brother Carel was also apprehended, but he was released after a sympathetic Dutch doctor wrote him a sick note. To be on the safe side, he made his way on foot to Amersfoort, where he sought refuge in his brother's house until the end of the war.

Hoping to disrupt the transportation of V-2 rockets, the Allies bombed Amersfoort's railway yards eighteen times between 3 September 1944 and 25 April 1945. At least forty-four people lost their lives. The Brester home was damaged in the most serious raid on 13 October 1944.

Both the liberation of the southern part of the country and the railway strike contributed to the near famine conditions in the rest of Holland. The winter of 1944/45 was also very severe. By January, the daily food ration available had fallen to 460 calories per person. About twenty thousand people died of malnutrition and the cold.

Since Immo and August lived on a large thoroughfare, people often stopped by to ask for a place to stay for the night. Carrying bags and suitcases, they were making their way (on foot or bicycle) north and east to try to barter their possessions for food among local farmers. Twice a week Hedda rode her bicycle into the countryside around Amersfoort to call upon patients of August who had offered to give the family a loaf of bread, a bottle of milk, or some potatoes.

On 3 January 1945, Eddy had to leave the Brester home for another hiding place after someone from his home town recognized him.

Immo's notebook, 3 January 1945

Eddy left.

Irmgard Brester to her cousin Ursula Meier, Amersfoort, 4 January 1945

What a lovely surprise that was when I was handed your dear letter. Finally a greeting from the homeland again. I am so pleased, although the reason for your letter is so endlessly sad. Dear Ursel, I too think of you a great deal and so often want to be near you so that I could talk to you about our dear Eberhard. [. . .] It is so painful to think that our dear Ohm Eberhard will never again come here. I always had the feeling that our family allowed him to relax and to revive himself. He will be missed very, very much! What provides a degree of consolation and peace is the thought that he was probably spared many difficulties. The truth is that he didn't have an easy life, and he gave his life for his ideals. It was so nice that you were able to tell me a little bit about our home and our relatives. I don't hear a thing anymore. We are the only ones left, so we have to stay even closer together; write as often as you can, alright? I am so pleased that we have had chance to connect, and I was told by the emissary that I could send along an answer tomorrow. [. . .] I think of all of you all the time, and the reports of heavy bombing worry me terribly. My poor, cherished Braunschweig! [. . .] Fortunately so far all of us are doing well, and we are still living together in our own home. Nowadays that is a very great privilege. But it is difficult, very difficult in fact. You probably cannot really get a sense of our life here, which just in material terms is hard. Food rations are constantly being cut, now only 1 kg of potatoes and 1,000 gr of bread weekly, no butter or milk at all, and also no marmalade, eggs, flour, etc. Once in a while 100 gr of low-fat cheese, 100 gr of meat, or some oil, but too little, much too little of everything so that one can already speak of famine conditions. On top of that, very little coal, no gas, no electricity (I am writing by candlelight but there are no more candles to buy), all automobile and railway traffic (except for military purposes) is out of commission; railway workers have been on strike for four months now. No one is allowed on the street after 8:00 in the evening. Those are just a few of the important matters of fact. But worse still is the pressure and the terror; not a day goes by when you don't worry about your belongings. And the men are being called up, and bicycles are being taken, and many thousands in the cities are pressed into forced labor (my brother-in-law has already been gone for months; as a doctor, thank goodness, August is still free), entire cities and villages are being evacuated and plundered, houses are being requisitioned by the Wehrmacht—the inhabitants often have to clear out with only a few hours' notice and have to leave behind most of their belongings. The result: almost everybody has strangers in their home; we ourselves have a family of four living with us. We simply can't go on living like *this*.

Also bear in mind the English planes that bomb us and shoot at us; one just wants to keep the children at home. Bombs fell quite near us and destroyed several houses; so far we have been fortunate—only shattered windows and some damage on the roof. If August didn't have various patients living in the countryside, we would be badly off. As it is, we have been lucky not to face real hardship, and we are all healthy and cheerful. Hedda is our supply sergeant, riding on her bicycle into the countryside with big bags to forage. August and our maid frequently go out foraging as well, and to this end I even brought back down the baby carriage. Everyday flocks of people descend on villages with bicycles, handcarts etc. to rustle up foodstuffs.

I would so much like to show off my 4 to you. You wouldn't recognize them. [. . .] Thanks to several generous patients, I was even able to bake some Christmas goodies. On the second day of Christmas I sang twice, here in our church and in Spakenburg, a picturesque fishing village. [. . .] The children have been out of school since summer vacation; the schools themselves are either destroyed or requisitioned.

Immo's notebook, 24 January 1945

Lodgers again.

Immo's notebook, 26 January 1945

Terribly cold, burst water pipes. Misery.

Immo's notebook, 27 January 1945

August seriously ill, dysentery, hospital.

Hedda's diary, 10 February 1945

[. . .] That crazy time when the Allies advanced. At the time, we were living out of suitcases ready to flee at a moment's notice, with our valuables buried in the ground. Yes, it was a crazy day, Tuesday, 5 September. Breaking news was constantly being announced: they are now in Breda, in Den Bosch, in the Betuwe, in Doorn. Everybody was running and carrying things, soldiers as well as civilians. It was unbelievable. People running down the street with orange-colored flowers and flags. Every now and then someone shouted: "They are already in Rotterdam; my brother-in-law saw them himself." Obviously, we lay awake all night listening to the noises on the street, quite a racket. Orders echoed throughout the night, the clacking of horse hooves, and again and again, the screeching and roaring of countless automobiles passing by.

Thereafter, things took a turn for the worse. From one moment to the next, the food was bad, everybody headed off behind the IJssel, and there was no end to the horrible firefights and bombardments. At the moment, the situation appears hopeless. It would take an entire shelf of books to describe everything exactly. I am going out to the villages frequently to get food.

Hedda's diary, 11 February 1945

It's Eddy Cramer's birthday today. Is he thinking of us?

On 20 March 1945, the Germans shot ten men in public on the Appelweg along the garden wall behind Immo's and August's house. This was in retaliation for the killing by the Resistance of a Dutch policeman who worked with the German security service. The ten prisoners had been arrested in Ede-Wageningen after being betrayed during a nighttime weapon's drop. (After the war, August donated the wall with its memorial plaque to the city of Amersfoort in order to insure that it would not be torn down.) The Resistance also attacked German automobiles. On 20 April a bomb was found on the BW Lane. The Germans gave the residents of a nearby house, who most likely had nothing to do with the incident, one hour to vacate the premises, which they then blew up. Thereafter, the Germans imposed a curfew on Amersfoort from six in the evening to six in the morning.

On the streets, German soldiers confiscated the bicycles of residents with increasing frequency. As they tried to warn cyclists about the confiscations, Hedda and Marleen were stopped by soldiers who accompanied them home. Immo tried to settle the affair by pointing to her German origins, but to no avail. "Those are the worst ones!" quipped one of the soldiers before taking Hedda's bicycle.

Immo's notebook, 15 February 1945

Private concert.

Immo's notebook, 14 March 1945

Donations from the Swedish Red Cross: 1 loaf of white bread, 125 grams of butter, groats for the children.

Immo's notebook, 20 March 1945

10 people were shot against the wall of our garden. A horrible day.

Immo's notebook, 9 April 1945

All of a sudden Carel appears on foot from Utrecht.

Hedda's diary, 12 April 1945

Are we really about to be liberated? Hellen in Dedemsvaart is already liberated, but here we unfortunate souls are still left in the lurch. Indeed, there is a great deal of hunger in the western parts of the Netherlands. Hellen and I have faithfully written to each other every Sunday. And I pack this diary with me wherever I go; I even stowed it away for a time in my emergency suitcase. I went one more time with Marleentje to Barneveld to procure some eggs for Papa's birthday. A week ago I was secretly inducted into the girl scouts. It was really impressive. Around noon today to Spakenburg on a bike with half-rotten tires, all because the shit krauts made off with my own bicycle.

Immo's notebook, 18 April 1945

The English are very near Amersfoort. We hear shooting.

Hedda's diary, 21 April 1945

We have to be at home at six o'clock and can't go out into the street until six the next morning. Punishment for attacks on a few moffen cars.

In April 1945, the front came closer and closer to Amersfoort. Putten, Ermelo, and Harderwijk were liberated on 18 April, Hoevelaken and Bunschoten on 21 April. A day later, the Resistance requested that the Canadians cease shelling the city. Their assault on Amersfoort was planned for 26 April, but to avoid heavy civilian casualties they tried to negotiate a cease-fire with the Germans. On 4 May 1945, Wehrmacht forces in Holland surrendered. But on 5 May, fighting between German occupiers and Dutch combat units broke out near the Brester house, leaving two civilians dead. Fighting spread downtown, prompting the Germans to impose a curfew from four in the afternoon until ten at night. Since the Germans had blown up most of the bridges around Amersfoort, Canadian troops had to build a temporary bridge across the Vallei canal, delaying their entry into the city until 7 May. It took several more days before all the Germans were disarmed and registered.

Once Hoevelaken and Hoogland were liberated, Hedda could no longer fetch bread and milk from August's patients, as she had regularly been able in previous weeks. But according to her diary, piano lessons continued despite the chaotic conditions.

Immo's notebook, 22 April 1945

Restless days. August for once at home tonight. Fierce shelling, some of it nearby.

Hedda's diary, 23 April 1945

Exactly six years ago I earned my swimming certificate. Boy, how the shells whistled outside the house today. Tonight all six of us are sleeping in the cellar, Papa's not here, but Janny [the maid] is. We hear that they are supposed to be near the stockyards on the Eem, which means they are establishing a bridgehead. If they keep at it, there will be plenty to hear tonight. It is hard to imagine that families in Hoevelaken and Hoogland are already liberated! The whole of Europe is holding its breath. Russian tanks are already cruising the streets of Berlin. And we're still not liberated, damn it all! If only I could finally see the royal family again. Miss Braun [the piano teacher] even said: "I can tell from your playing that you are in a defiant mood." Indeed, I am.

Immo's notebook, 26 April 1945

Suddenly a cease-fire so we can make a nice celebration for Marleen's birthday.

Immo's notebook, 1 May 1945

Nothing has changed.

Immo's notebook, 4 May 1945

Armistice!

Immo's notebook, 5 May 1945

The NSB [National Socialist Movement] withdraws at eight o'clock. Show the flag, haul in the flag. A miserable afternoon, even after a bottle of wine.

Immo's notebook, 6 May 1945

Together at church. Memorial Service. Flags, Orange.

Immo's notebook, 7 May 1945

First Canadians! What a joy. Germans still armed. It is a crazy world!

Immo's notebook, 12 May 1945

The first food rations from England. Meat, cookies, chocolate, butter.

Hedda's diary, 13 May 1945

Peace. Thank God. I attended a memorial service in our church. It was very beautiful.

In September 1944, the Nazis organized the Volkssturm into which men between the ages of sixteen and sixty not already serving in the Wehrmacht were conscripted. Not long thereafter, hundreds of thousands of Germans fled advancing Soviet troops, who launched a final offensive against Germany on 12 January 1945 and crossed the Oder River, sixty-five kilometers from Berlin, on 31 January. The Nazis circulated propaganda reports about Russian atrocities against civilians in order to stiffen the will to resist, but ended up creating panic that drove more Germans westward. As many as five million refugees were on the run; hundreds of thousands of people lost their lives in the winter cold or in the crossfire of the last firefights or in rescue boats that were torpedoed.

More than twelve thousand people were killed when Allied bombers raided Darmstadt (where Immo's cousin Else Kreutzmann lived) on 12 September 1944. Dresden was almost completely destroyed on 13–14 February 1945; some thirty thousand people, including many refugees who had swarmed into the city from the East, were killed in the ensuing firestorm.

As American troops entered Braunschweig on 12 April 1945, the interim Nazi Oberbürgermeister committed suicide. The Americans installed the Social Democrat Ernst Böhme, who had been removed in 1933, as his successor. At the end of the war, millions of forced laborers from Poland, the Soviet Union, and elsewhere sought food and shelter, which German residents in Braunschweig and Hedeper not always inaccurately described as "plundering."

After the Liberation of the Netherlands, Immo was asked to perform in memorial services, which she, as a German by birth, regarded as a great honor. When mail service with Germany resumed in 1946, Immo received letters from friends and family requesting packages of ham or tea or coffee. Immo tore these letters up, enraged at how ignorant her correspondents were of the situation that had prevailed in Holland during the war. In her view, far too many Germans thought of themselves as victims only.

Neither did Immo answer the letter of a relative who had fled the Russians and wanted to stay in Amersfoort.

Martha Kreutzmann to her cousin Irmgard Brester, Braunschweig, 15 June 1945

We have the opportunity to get this letter to Holland, a young Dutchman who has been living with us is returning home tomorrow.

So how did you make it through this whole time; we haven't heard from you for so long! Apparently things were pretty tough for you, at least what we are told is that the Hollanders didn't have much to eat. During the war, we were fine, but now the situation has gotten substantially worse. [. . .]

How are you doing? The children will be much older now. [. . .] When things finally have settled down, you will certainly come for a visit again. Eberhard's death came as a great shock to us. Thank goodness your parents and Ohmchen were not alive to have to suffer this terrible blow. Your beautiful house on the Brockenblick is unfortunately a desolate ruin, as is the rest of our dear old Braunschweig. The old town was badly hit, and whole blocks don't even exist anymore. There is nothing much left of historic Braunschweig. One can't even conceive of how it is possible that people in the 20th century can tear each other to pieces and destroy so much heritage that can never be rebuilt. We've stepped back hundreds of years.

My job at Grotrians ended when the Americans marched in since all the war factories closed. Anyway we need the time to take care of our personal affairs, and there are long lines to stand in. [. . .]

Dear Irmchen, I hope that you and your family are healthy and that you have been able to keep your home!

Immo's notebook, 19 June 1945

Electricity!

Hilde Kammerer to her friend Irmgard Brester, Hohegeiss, 5 December 1945 (posted in England)

[. . .] After 2 years, the first letter, thank you so very much! Hopefully you will also get my letter, which I ventured to give to an Englishman returning home for Christmas. At least now *you* can once again write freely, and I am very happy and relieved that all of you made it through the years of war and occupation safe and sound and that you were able to recover a bit over the summer. You are so fortunate to still have your beautiful home, and to have August be able to bring the hospital back into operation, even though it was plundered. The hunger and cold, the danger of air raids, and the terror of the occupation must have been terrible for you (especially for you as a mother and a German worried about her husband and responsible for her 4 little ones). Therefore, I can understand why Holland greeted the liberation and breathed a sigh of relief when American supplies alleviated the worst of the hardship. You have survived the worst and can make plans for the future; with patience and hard work you can regain little by little your old standard of living. At least for the time being, after the lost war, none of that can be said for us here. After all the sacrifices and deprivations of the war and terror at home we now have to suffer the hunger and cold already familiar to you and total impoverishment through reparations and humiliations. One has to accept what God provides and not lose hope that out of all these horrors and tribulations a true and God-blessed German people will once again emerge and that an independent German Reich will exist in the future.

That August was able to save the car will make reestablishing his practice much easier. [. . .] I find it so very tragic that your talented brother had to sacrifice his life; now you don't have any relatives in Germany anymore. [. . .] Couldn't you come to Braunschweig for a visit in the spring? [. . .]

I was so worried about you; during the German retreat we read so much about floodgates being opened. I thought of the dike not far from you, near the Zuiderzee. As your oldest, Hedda was so good and brave to help scrounge for food. [. . .] Not only am I unable to listen to you on the radio, I really miss my nice Philips. Is the company in Holland still in business? [. . .]

[. . .] Since the Russian zone begins beyond our village, we hear a great deal about the conditions there and see a lot of misery. My relatives in Leipzig are eating potato peels. It is incredible to hear about so much misfortune and just plain suffering nowadays. [. . .]

Irmgard Brester to her cousin Ursula Meier, Amersfoort, 8 May 1946

I was so happy to get your warmhearted and detailed letter! [. . .] Up until now, I had received only two short pieces of news, and I wanted so much to hear at least something from all the people close to me. Now to my joy several letters have arrived, and I am so happy that regular mail connections have been reestablished. [. . .]

However, for the time being, we will have to be patient when it comes to a reunion. Apparently, travel to Germany is just about impossible. [. . .] Although a return to Germany will be very wistful, many of the dear old ties have remained intact.

[. . .] I can imagine how endlessly difficult it must be to keep your spirits up. Faith in a better future is what helped us get through those 5 horrible years. Even for you, things have to eventually improve.

[. . .] We savor peace, freedom, and better food so much and are still grateful every day. Of course, conditions are far and away not as they were before the war, but that would be impossible after such chaos. [. . .]

At the Yalta Conference in February 1945, the Allies agreed on future zones of occupation. If advancing armies found themselves in a different occupation zone, they were obligated to eventually pull back. Therefore in summer 1945, Germans had the puzzling experience of seeing the British and Americans evacuate parts of eastern Germany (Mecklenburg, Thüringen, Saxony) that had been assigned to the Soviet occupation zone. At the same time, the Russians, who had liberated Berlin, made way for Americans, the British, and the French, who all occupied respective sectors in the city.

Ursula Meier, who had joined the NSDAP in 1931, was generally shunned and lived a miserable existence. After her denazification, she was not able to work in a larger secondary school. Dorothea X., who married an ethnic German from Russia, gave Immo an account of the fate of their mutual classmates. Maria B. continued to wait for news of her husband, who had gone missing in Stalingrad.

Dorothea X. to her friend Irmgard Brester, Braunschweig, 27 December 1946

I had no idea that you lived through such hard times. It was simply the case that one did not generally learn anything about all the many hardships except here and there by word of mouth. Well, our beautiful Germany. Hopefully the English are smart enough to realize that there is no good to come from Bolshevism, it is hard to believe that a confrontation with the peoples of the East can be avoided. We will just have to see. Often the most important men were born in circumstances of great humiliation, which then turned out of be a blessing for the entire world. We'll wait. Let me update you on our circle of friends.

Hilde D. lost her husband during an attack in Paris. She lives with 3 children in Gifhorn and lost everything in January.

Hilde F. lives in the countryside with 3 children; her husband, a doctor, is somewhere near the Dutch border. She lost quite a bit since he was in the SS.

Erika S., her husband was released for Christmas. They lost everything in Berlin, her newborn daughter died within days of diphtheria.

Luise H. lost everything in Berlin, fled, and lives here in the country. Her husband works as a botanist.

Lorre F. lives on the Elm, was able to save everything. Her husband is interned, was SS. She works as a photographer.

Else L. remains childless, lost everything in Berlin, and is now in Wolfenbüttel. Her husband recently returned from Norway. She is a homemaker.

Ilse S., got married near Rostock, was bombed out there, and with her husband then fled Russian-held territory and is here. She got to know the Russians and lived through a great deal. Over there, she earned her money as a seamstress, although she was never professionally trained, but she was good enough for the Russian girls.

Charlotte W., her husband is a tenant on an estate in the countryside.

Ulla G. lost everything in Beren-Folnau, that is to say the French requisitioned her house. She now lives here with the children.

Hilde L.—no one knows anything about her.

Zenta V. can't be located either.

Waltraut S., a refugee somewhere near Gifhorn.

Irene v. L., recently died. Apparently her husband was shot on 27 July 1944 [in connection with the failed plot to assassinate Hitler].

Hilde G. left for America in 1939 and never came back. [Her brother] has not heard anything from her.

Inge L., Gerda B., and Edith F. are all dead.

Alice W. is sitting homeless in Harzburg, her husband is in a prisoner-of-war camp, was SS.

Anneliese H. just recently got married.

Ursel S. works in a doctor's office.

Herta W., is a farmer's wife in the countryside.

I wrote to Anneliese Z. but haven't yet received a reply.

Your letter took exactly 14 days to reach me, and incidentally it had been opened. But nothing was noted. We have all gotten very old, my hair is almost white. [. . .] I will read your letters to those who remember you.

Over the course of the year 1947, I hope to be able to take up the fight for existence at the side of a good dear person. He has also had his experiences, lived 25 years in the Soviet Union and came to Braunschweig in 1943 as a refugee. In the event, the East should roll further over to the West, we want to go to Africa or America. If you ever should hear about the best way to get to South Africa or Brazil or Argentina, do let me know.

Hilde Kammerer to her friend Irmgard Brester, Braunschweig, 13 January 1947

[. . .] Maria learned from a comrade returning home that her husband got out of Stalingrad with only light wounds but subsequently died of dysentery in the hospital in a Russian prisoner-of-war camp, so we both spent a sad Christmas together. [. . .]

Do you have any desire to come to Germany? I would stay where you are and hold on to your memories! [. . .] Cross your fingers for me over the coming difficult months. [. . .] Think of us in our hard struggle for existence.

Dorothea X. to her friend Irmgard Brester, Braunschweig, 31 March 1947

[. . .] We were all deeply shocked to read what you had to say about the five years of continuous occupation. We had no idea that those things happened, and we were all surprised that they occurred. But perhaps it is the case that forces of good emerge out of the greatest humiliation; in the past, many peoples adopted the culture of the vanquished. The main thing is that Bolshevism stays far afield. The Americans actually realize this; one can now really follow political developments in their entirety.

It would make me very happy if, when you have a chance, you could send a little something, perhaps coffee, for a little reunion of old friends. [. . .] Enjoy your family and stay healthy. Don't forget us dear Germans, there are still some decent ones!

Gerhard Nicolai to Irmgard Brester, Rio de Janeiro, 3 April 1947

I respectfully allow myself to send this letter to the sister of my dear childhood friend Eberhard Gebensleben in order to learn something about his whereabouts. I have not heard from Eberhard since 1941 (Rostock), and your address, my gracious lady, which I have from my correspondence with your brother, is for me the only stable point of reference in the storm of events over the last years. I am very worried that Eberhard might be one of the victims of these unfortunate times. How else can

I explain his silence now that mail connections between Germany and the rest of the world have been restored already for some months now?

Gerhard Nicolai to Irmgard Brester, Rio de Janeiro, 26 April 1947

Your letter of 9 April informing me of the death of your dear brother and my only friend Eberhard left me deeply shocked and out of sorts with God and the world. To me he embodied the decent German who combined a gallant heart with a creative imagination, and he was a very significant tie to the homeland I left. That he was without guilt when he had to pay for what others did I know well from his letters. [. . .] As a central European, my character is influenced both by collectivist ("Prussian") Asia and the harmonious personality of bourgeois Europe, and Eberhard was for me a kind of guide to 1,000 years of bourgeois European culture. [. . .] You asked about my experiences in the last years. That is a long story, but I promise to tell you something of my odysseys. [. . .] From here, it is quite easy to send cigarettes and coffee, even to Germany, where I will also probably send something to Eberhard's fiancée. Although I didn't know her personally, as Eberhard's chosen one and, like me, a victim of the same injustice, she is someone I have an affinity with and feel close to and so I would like to make her a small happiness in these difficult times. [. . .]

Frieda Riechers to Irmgard Brester, Braunschweig, 7 July 1947

You will surely be astonished to once again receive a sign of life from me after all these many years. I often find myself thinking of you. How are you and your loved ones doing? Did you get through the war and all its horrors safely? Your children must all be grown up by now. Hedda must be 17 or 18 years old. I regret that I can't even get a look at her.

I was in Braunschweig today, and I always get homesick. I always think if only some of your family was still there. That would be so nice. Our city is nothing but a pile of ruins. Many people lost everything. The war was very gruesome precisely because it did not spare women and children. During the war, I worked in the post office in Braunschweig as a driver. Those were wonderful times, although I lived through every air raid. We were 4 women who drove all by ourselves across the countryside in our truck, we left at 8 o'clock in the morning, and we were already back by noon. We saw so much that was beautiful and good and also sad. So we got through 4 years of war quite well. But there were also dark sides. In 1941 I lost my favorite brother in Russia, in 1942 another brother in Africa; my oldest brother stayed home until the end, was deployed in December, and in March I heard the news that he was killed in Dresden. My 4th brother died in a military hospital after the end of the war. And my youngest brother is a prisoner of war in Russia—he is my biggest worry, especially when I see the miserable men returning home; they are no longer human beings when the Russians release them. But then I thank God that the other brothers no longer had to endure these hardships. During the collapse, I went to Thüringen to save my apartment. Those were bad days. In our village, we had two young Dutchmen who were just marvelous as they stood by our side. We shared the last pieces of bread with them. After a great deal of shelling, the Amis finally appeared. I didn't notice a thing, just went into the garden early one morning, when I suddenly bumped into black soldiers. It was not nearly as terrible as we had imagined. Our house was not requisitioned, maybe because they believed a priest lived there on account of the small cross on the house. So we were not affected by the occupation.

But the worst was still to come. My husband returned from American captivity on 23 July 1945. He had been well cared for. After a while, the Russians came to occupy our beautiful Thüringen. Many women who had hidden themselves from the Amis, although there was no need to, welcomed the Russians with flowers. I cried with rage. But these women paid a heavy price. I cannot even describe the weeks that followed. We slept for 10 days in the forest. Then one night, it was still early and we were with our neighbors—a woman who had guard duty came over, but it was too late—the Russians were already in our house, they hauled out my husband and locked all of the women in one room. While they were searching the house, we slipped out over the balcony. After that, we didn't have a moment's peace. I was such a bundle of nerves, I couldn't sleep at night. Then they started rounding up all the men. So we took the bare essentials and bicycled to Magdeburg. We stayed with my parents for a few weeks, then we came over here. I believe I can consider all my wonderful things lost forever because I will never go back there again unless the Russians leave. I have a room here, a few pieces of furniture, your dear Omi's desk, and also the large mirror. I am often very, very sad since I had my very own, very nice household. You know Herr Eberhard gave me your parents' radio set. That is my greatest pleasure now since you can really use a little music. [. . .] My only hope is that you are all still healthy and that I might receive a sign of life from you.

Margot Roever to her niece Irmgard Brester, Northeim, 21 July 1947

Finally I have gotten around to writing to you. Ursel will have told you of the many terrible things we have lived through, first and foremost dear Uncle Ernst who on 12 July was sentenced to a year in prison in Braunschweig and then Wolfenbüttel for allegedly mistreating Poles. He is now in a camp in Fallingbostel. I hope he is able to come home soon. What happened was that he was denounced by a party bigwig from the East, who in the end was directing the SS land office in Posen and served as Himmler's right hand.

Ursel kept us informed about you, and we were overjoyed to know that you are healthy and doing well again after the terrible war years, and in particular that you can pursue your art and enjoy your talented children. [. . .]

How is August doing? It is so tragic that dear Eberhard had to give his young life for that insane Hitler. I clasp both of your hands in mine. It is for the best that Ohmchen, Mutti, and Vati did not have to live through all this; they were spared a great deal. Elisabeth and Otto and the children are doing well, aside from worries about Uncle Ernst. My health is poor, my heart and my nerves are shot. [. . .] We didn't lose anything in the air raids, but we did during the plundering. Hopefully you came out of everything alright, although I know that you had to go through a lot; I always listened to the English broadcasts and knew that Amersfoort had been hit and partially damaged. [. . .] We have only the Nazis to thank for everything we had to live through: the confiscation of the monasteries, the fact that we didn't quite conform and that Uncle Ernst did not join the party until he was finally forced to, though these gentlemen continued to harass us with special judicial proceedings, etc.—well I can't tell you everything, it would take weeks.

When do you plan on coming to Germany? August was right from the beginning, and I always appreciated his foresight. [. . .] What wonderful days those were, when you were here before the outbreak of the war. [. . .]

It was two years before inheritance questions were straightened out between Amersfoort and Braunschweig. Immo and Herta Euling each inherited a half share of the property on the Brockenblick, Immo directly through her deceased parents, Herta through Eberhard. Born in Berlin in 1906, Herta died in Würzburg in 1992. Eberhard's friend, Zettel, continued to live in Switzerland until he committed suicide in 1956, when his relationship with a young German man broke apart. The fate of Gerhard Nicolai is unknown.

Carl-Heinz Zeitler to Irmgard Brester, Tesserette-Lugano, 6 October 1947

[. . .] What a pleasure it was to hear a sign of life from Amersfoort, and I am very relieved that it sounded relatively good. My thoughts wandered to Holland so very often—I constantly feared that there would be or could be conflicts in such mean and treasonous times. It has been years since we heard from each other. You won't believe the unimaginably beautiful memories I still have of my only visit to Utrecht—I hardly exaggerate when I say that I always considered your husband to be an exemplary physician and human being—and that I could not understand and was even disappointed by his opinion that he expressed in his last letter from the year 1938 (which incidentally I still possess) when he urged me to reconcile myself with the criminal world that was my country. As it was, everything happened just as I had once long ago predicted—and since I could always picture how difficult the situation must have been for you, I thought of all of you with the greatest sympathy. It is difficult to explain to you how estranged I have become from what I used to consider my homeland and how consequential my final reckoning is with the chapter entitled Germany. As long as I have been able to think politically, I made every effort to resist the plague of this gigantic insanity: I let myself be put in German prisons; I had the quite dubious pleasure of spending years as an émigré; indeed, even today I can play only a second-class role as an *individu sans nationalité*—but nothing could move me to take even one step back once I had drawn the line. Broken family ties, destroyed friendships—my parents and the family of someone who was very close to me and who was tortured to death in a concentration camp are all that I have left over there. Everything else has been erased. Maybe you think I am too fanatic about all this, but believe me, ever since I was young I had an aversion to anything related to "German character," perhaps at first without being aware of it, but later ever more loudly and clearly! Do you remember that Sunday morning—even if 100 years or more have gone by—I think it was when I was visiting all of you in the Fallerslebertorwall. Anyway: you went with Eberhard and me to that ridiculous nationalist propaganda film that dealt with population issues—on the way home, Eberhard and I got into such a fierce argument that you had to intervene—do you remember? I think it was the first time that I recognized that there were differences between us. Then there was the summer when I returned from Holland just overwhelmed with what I had seen, and when I ran into Eberhard in the Lüneberger Heide he was wearing the pin, that symbol of the nation's disgrace, and I knew everything was over—I was terribly disappointed and I felt I *had* to draw a line in the sand. Later on, I often asked myself what drew me to Eberhard when I was a kid and why I couldn't let go of him as an adult—was it perhaps an ever-present desire to be contrary that always lay just beneath the surface?

So, dear Immo, everything turned out so differently. It is not that I am basking in the triumph of having been somehow proven "right." Who knows what people, even those to whom we are close, are really thinking; in the end, we live on this world terribly alone—in any case, I had my experiences and always drew the consequences. If I seem to be unforgiving, it really is only appearances—I just don't want to have to start over only to be disappointed by everything again—keep to yourself and be done with it! I am convinced of one thing: as individuals, human beings can be saints, venerable and beloved creatures, but taken together they are worthless. From the very beginning, they have been the scum of the earth, and in a thousand years they will be as well. It is useless to try to change them! For that reason, my own aspirations to help have withered and died. I live completely on my own without goals or desires. I am not even considering becoming a citizen of a state; I find it absurd that this or that passport would make me more worthy. [. . .]

Despite everything I am not sitting around begrudging my fate. On the contrary: life has generally treated me well, and I ought be happy and thankful. At the moment, I am a staff physician at a small sanatorium in the prettiest canton in all of Switzerland. I could write you pages describing the glories of nature here and telling you in what harmony I live with the blue skies, the vineyards, and the enchanting green ground of this magical southern world.

Many years of saving up have allowed me to buy a little plot of land on the shores of Lake Maggiore, about 100 m from the Italian border. It has its own little shed, and piece by piece, I am slowly making it into a modest home. I don't know if you will be able to understand the happiness of having a roof over your head again after twenty years of homelessness. I ask for nothing, and all that is left is my love for my parents. [. . .] My parents lost everything—they're living, actually vegetating in totally primitive conditions in two rooms somewhere around the Fichtelgebirge—I have no way of helping them or bringing them here. They dream of returning to Braunschweig, or what Braunschweig once was—actually they are completely deluded. They have become very old, terribly old, and there is no way I can understand how they deserved their fate. [. . .]

There is no way that I will be able to come to Holland anytime soon. I can't even escape my condition in exile. I am not even able to visit my parents, who would so much like to see me after almost 10 years. I don't even have a passport. [. . .]

I am very, very happy that you took the first step. Let's not let this connection somehow break down. Even if we have somewhat different ideas and opinions, we don't have to belabor them, there are enough other things we can tell each other. [. . .]

Hilde Kammerer to her friend Irmgard Brester, Braunschweig, 12 December 1947

I really have to send you a great big letter of thanks for the lavish present you sent me, one that I can hardly accept much less reciprocate. Yet I feel so much love and thoughtfulness that I will happily use and revere the linens in the memory of your revered parents and your wonderful grandmother! [. . .] Your Aunt Agnes read me your letters to her so I know the problems you have regarding a trip here. It must be terribly difficult for you not to be able to travel to Germany and take care of the matters of the inheritance. [. . .] However, a trip here would have been bound up with many terribly sad things: the lonely ruin of your house, the destruction of the city generally—whatever you saw when you traveled through northern Germany was hardly the worst. That you have *only* stoves instead of central heating to us sounds almost comical and enviable [. . .]

Ursula Meier to her cousin Irmgard Brester, Wolfenbüttel, 1 May 1948

[. . .] Over the winter, I took two seminars, one on contemporary German literature. [. . .] Thomas Mann as well, although I still don't like him and consider it unbelievable how in his book *Lotte in Weimar*, he can put project all his own antagonistic views against Germany onto the elderly Goethe. [. . .] There are changes in Hedeper as well. Stefan left Germany and finally went back to Poland, to his farm, and wife and children. [. . .]

On 20 June 1948, the German mark replaced the old reichsmark in the three western occupation zones with the hope of containing inflationary pressures. Every citizen received forty new marks. At the same time, the Marshall Plan, the American reconstruction plan for western Europe, provided growing sense of economic stability.

From 1947 on, Immo had tried to get permission to visit Germany. Only after being officially invited to perform as soloist during a special church service did she get a visa. On 16 September 1949, Immo returned to Germany for the first time since the end of the war. Although she saw many old friends, she quickly realized that she had become an outsider. Her former classmates showed little interest in the difficulties she had experienced in German-occupied Holland. When she did find an opportunity to talk about life during the war, she encountered painful silence, interrupted only by the derisive comment: "You and your adopted homeland [Wahlheimat]!"

Hilde Kammerer to her friend Irmgard Brester, Braunschweig, 4 December 1948

[. . .] It makes a huge difference whether you were bombed or not bombed out, in daily life but also in understanding. You can now buy everything just as in prewar times, and if you have a good income, you are better off than before. [. . .] The city figured it would cost 10,000 M to cart away the rubble on our property and in return they will keep the bricks. It takes 6 weeks, and they are already at the cellar. I earned the workers' trust with cigarettes so I was able to retrieve odds and ends: a soup ladle, a nail brush, a door plate, bits of marble—like relics from Pompeii!

Frieda Riechers to Irmgard Brester, Thiede near Braunschweig, 15 December 1948

[. . .] Our money has run out. Now we have to start all over from scratch. But there are quite a few people who already have a lot of money. These are strange times. The shop windows are filled with goods just like before the war, but the prices. A store-bought goose costs 75 M. So you can imagine the conditions here. I walk through town without even looking at what is for sale; I would love to buy things, but would be crazy to pay those kinds of prices. What we need is foreigners to come and flood the market for our shopkeepers to get a real shock. [. . .]

Unfortunately, my husband is still unemployed, which weighs him down. But I will manage. My little brother is still in that twice-cursed Russia.

Hilde Kammerer to her friend Irmgard Brester, Braunschweig, 29 August 1949

[. . .] I really wonder how your visit will go. I can imagine with what a heavy heart you will be coming, and I only hope that you bring along some of your family. Marie and I will do everything to make your stay as pleasant as possible!

Irmgard Brester to her husband August Brester and children, Braunschweig, 17 September 1949

So here I am, finally back in the house on the Brockenblick. On the one hand I almost can't believe it yet, on the other hand it feels very normal, even though the house is very, very different now. I am now a guest of Aunt Agnes, who uses Vati's former study as a combined bedroom/living room and kitchen. Between the bed and the sofa, there are even two places to lie down, and I had a very good night's sleep. Sitting at the desk in the corner by the big windows, I am now looking at the towering trees once again in the so very familiar garden, fortunately the sun is shining, so that everything appears peaceful, as if there hasn't been a war. But that's just here, elsewhere you see traces of war everywhere. The house looks pretty dreadful from the outside, too.

But how warmly I've been welcomed here! Aunt Agnes, who really has trouble walking, was waiting for me back here, and Hilde and Marie came to greet me at the train station with flowers. Wasn't that nice! They were so very kind and welcoming that my arrival was nowhere near as awful as I'd feared. They both looked quite well, were also cheerful, on the whole I am getting the impression that people are already much more ready to face life again and that things are getting better. The train stations everywhere are still partially rubble, to be sure, but the scene is nevertheless very, very different from two years ago when we first saw it [*on the way to Denmark*].

Irmgard Brester to her husband August Brester and children, Braunschweig, 19 September 1949

[. . .] I am slowly beginning to get used to the ruined city, it really is very bad, there are just a few church steeples sticking up above the ruins, the Schloss is reduced to ashes, Steinweg and Bohlweg are gone, but there are very well stocked temporary stores where you can literally get anything. The city hall is still standing, the theater too, I've been able to see the Dom and Dankwarderode Castle only from a distance, what's left of them at least. [. . .]

The tram ride to Wolfenbüttel was wonderful and brought back many memories. The town itself is fortunately quite intact, a relief after all the ruins here. [. . .]

Irmgard Brester to her husband August Brester, Braunschweig, 21 September 1949

[. . .] It is truly moving and extraordinarily pleasant for me to see how happy everyone is to see me again. A wonderful feeling, to find so much love and friendship here in spite of everything. That, to some extent, makes up for the loss of so many beloved people and also makes staying in this ruined city somewhat bearable. On my trips through the city, usually by tram, I keep seeing more of the destruction. Simply awful! A few old buildings are still standing, so that you're at least able to orient yourself. So sad, the burnt ruins of the beautiful old churches and their toppled steeples. The Dom has already been partially restored and sufficiently fixed up to allow for services on Sundays. I want to go there this Sunday. [. . .]

Yesterday morning another good rehearsal, the organist (not a Nazi!) told me so much fascinating stuff about the battles around Braunschweig and the bombardments, that I was quite overcome. [. . .]

Irmgard Brester to her husband August Brester and children, Braunschweig, 23 September 1949

[. . .] Afterward walked past my former music school (which is still practically uninhabitable) and along the Fallerslebertor to visit Ulla G.-S. It was a very warm reunion. She immediately suggested that she would ask some of my former classmates to coffee at her house, so that I could meet them again. Isn't that nice? She is living in the house she grew up in, which is only half habitable, all the windows at the front are still bricked shut, but the garden is in beautiful shape. [. . .]

Then this afternoon our old Frieda came, with her husband, I had written to her, and she brought me a lovely bunch of carnations. She too was so friendly, kept wanting to look at the photos trying to recognize little Hedda and Marleen. [. . .]

Hilde Kammerer to August Brester, Braunschweig, 19 December 1949

Since I don't want to embarrass Immo by praising her to the sky, I want to tell you how much everybody enjoyed the church concert, the varied performances,

and Immo's recital. Not yet at peace, and unable to rest, the world is very receptive
to church music, especially in Germany, as the Dutch works indicate. I have heard
a great deal of church music and participated in the Bach festival in Leipzig, and
so I am very critical; but I've never heard such a beautiful soprano, high, clear, and
tender like the voice of an angel! Moreover, the greatest skill, singing "piano," she
did fabulously. The main thing is she did not sing for effect but with a feeling for the
piece as a whole to honor God. I very much liked Psalm 139, but for me the high
point was: "O seht, die Wahrheit steigt zu uns herab und wollet Engel mich behüten
. . . das reine Licht sei mein" ("O see how the truth takes hold of us, and may angels
protect me . . . the pure light be mine"), which sounded glorious. Of course, you know
the appreciative critics in Holland, but I thought you would like to hear a voice from
Germany. It was such a joy to see Immo looking so youthful and fresh and willing to
give her full attention to everyone and able to iron out all the rough spots! Hopefully,
both of you can come next year. That would be nice.

Eberhard's grave in the German military cemetery in Lommel, Belgium (summer 1990)

IN CLOSING

HEDDAS POESIEALBUM

Verstehst Du denn, wie's möglich ist,
Dass diese weite Welt
Soviel des Leid's, soviel der Qual
Erträgt und doch nicht fällt;

Dass jeden Morgen bricht hervor,
Aus tief dunkelster Nacht
Des hellen Tages lichter Schein,
Der Sonne Zauberpracht?

Es muss wohl über Allem sein
ein gross' hell leuchtend Licht,
Das alle Not und aller Schmerz
Vermag zu löschen nicht.

*Verse Deiner Grossmutter, Elisabeth Gebensleben geb. von Alten—von Dir
Mimi genannt—welche die kleine Hedda so lieb hatte. Am Altjahrsabend 1941 für
Dich und Dein Leben niedergeschrieben von Deinem Ohm Eberhard.*

FROM HEDDA'S FRIENDSHIP BOOK

Do you understand how
This wide world can endure
So much sorrow, so much pain,
And yet does not succumb;

How each morning breaks through
Out of night's deepest darkness
The radiance of full daylight,
The sun's magic splendour?

Over this all there must be
A great gleaming light, which
All the need and all the grief
Are unable to extinguish.

A poem by your grandmother Elisabeth Gebensleben, born von Alten—you used to call her Mimi—who loved little Hedda so dearly.

Written down for you and your life by your Ohm Eberhard on New Year's Eve 1941.

FAMILY TREES

von Alten

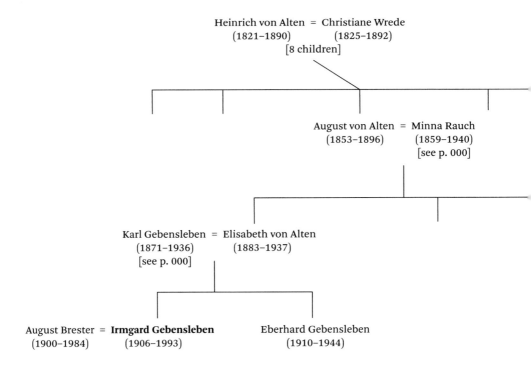

Heinrich von Alten = Christiane Wrede
(1821–1890)   (1825–1892)
[8 children]

August von Alten = Minna Rauch
(1853–1896)   (1859–1940)
[see p. 000]

Karl Gebensleben = Elisabeth von Alten
(1871–1936)   (1883–1937)
[see p. 000]

August Brester = **Irmgard Gebensleben**   Eberhard Gebensleben
(1900–1984)   (1906–1993)   (1910–1944)

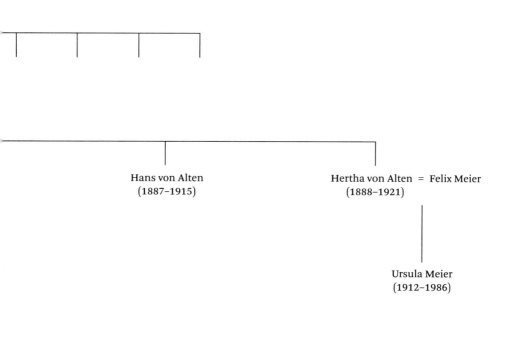

Hans von Alten
(1887–1915)

Hertha von Alten = Felix Meier
(1888–1921)

Ursula Meier
(1912–1986)

Gebensleben

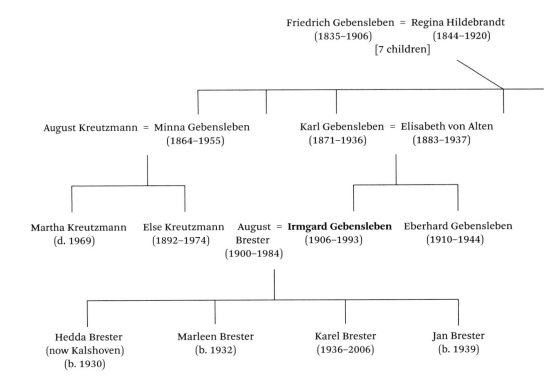

Friedrich Gebensleben = Regina Hildebrandt
(1835–1906)   (1844–1920)
[7 children]

August Kreutzmann = Minna Gebensleben   Karl Gebensleben = Elisabeth von Alten
(1864–1955)   (1871–1936)   (1883–1937)

Martha Kreutzmann   Else Kreutzmann   August = **Irmgard Gebensleben**   Eberhard Gebensleben
(d. 1969)   (1892–1974)   Brester   (1906–1993)   (1910–1944)
                                        (1900–1984)

Hedda Brester   Marleen Brester   Karel Brester   Jan Brester
(now Kalshoven)   (b. 1932)   (1936–2006)   (b. 1939)
(b. 1930)

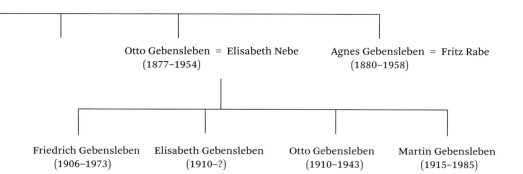

Otto Gebensleben = Elisabeth Nebe   Agnes Gebensleben = Fritz Rabe
(1877–1954)   (1880–1958)

Friedrich Gebensleben   Elisabeth Gebensleben   Otto Gebensleben   Martin Gebensleben
(1906–1973)   (1910–?)   (1910–1943)   (1915–1985)

Rauch

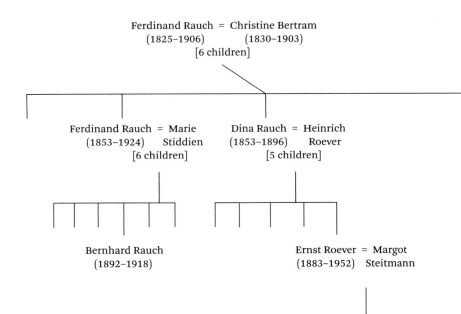

Ferdinand Rauch = Christine Bertram
(1825–1906)   (1830–1903)
[6 children]

Ferdinand Rauch = Marie   Dina Rauch = Heinrich
(1853–1924)   Stiddien   (1853–1896)   Roever
[6 children]   [5 children]

Bernhard Rauch   Ernst Roever = Margot
(1892–1918)   (1883–1952)   Steitmann

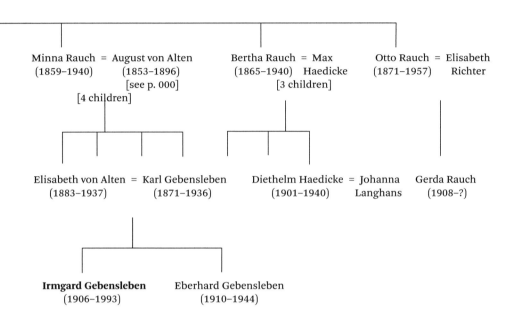

Minna Rauch = August von Alten
(1859–1940)   (1853–1896)
                [see p. 000]
        [4 children]

Bertha Rauch = Max
(1865–1940)   Haedicke
        [3 children]

Otto Rauch = Elisabeth
(1871–1957)   Richter

Elisabeth von Alten = Karl Gebensleben
(1883–1937)   (1871–1936)

Diethelm Haedicke = Johanna
(1901–1940)   Langhans

Gerda Rauch
(1908–?)

Irmgard Gebensleben
(1906–1993)

Eberhard Gebensleben
(1910–1944)

MAPS

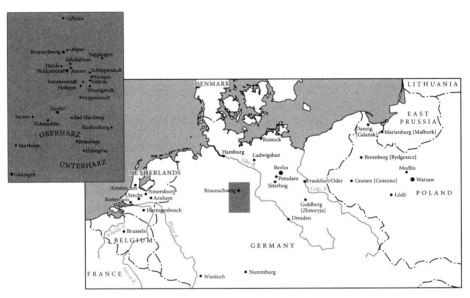

Map 1. The Netherlands, Belgium, Germany, and Poland, spring 1939

Map 2. The border region of France and Germany, March–May 1940 ("Phoney War")

Map 3. Western Russia, 1941–1942
The demarcated border between Poland and the Soviet Union is the pre–World War II border, which remained relevant to contemporaries even though neither Nazi Germany nor the Soviet Union formally recognized Poland as a geopolitical entity during the war.

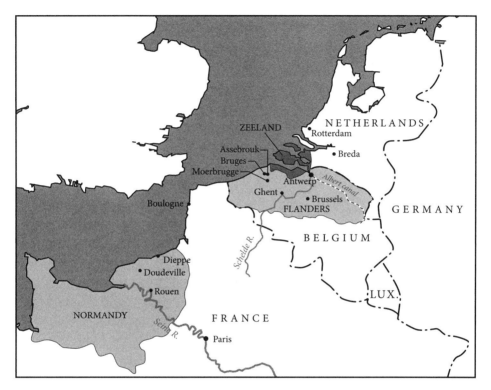

Map 4. France, Belgium, and the Netherlands, November 1943–September 1944

SUGGESTED READING

On Germany, the rise of the Nazis, and the Third Reich, see William Sheridan Allen's *The Nazi Seizure of Power: The Experience of a Single German Town, 1922–1945*, rev. ed. (New York: Franklin Watts, 1984), which discusses the town of Northeim, near Braunschweig; Richard Evans, *The Coming of the Third Reich* (New York: Penguin, 2004), *The Third Reich in Power* (New York: Penguin, 2005), and *The Third Reich at War* (New York: Penguin, 2009); as well as Peter Fritzsche, *Germans into Nazis* (Cambridge: Harvard University Press, 1998) and *Life and Death in the Third Reich* (Cambridge: Harvard University Press, 2008). The great novel of the demise of the Weimar Republic is undoubtedly Hans Fallada, *Little Man, What Now?* (Chicago: Continuum, 2001 [1933]). For World War II, see Antony Beevor, *The Second World War* (New York: Little, Brown, 2012); Stephen G. Fritz, *Frontsoldaten: The German Soldier in World War II* (Lexington: University Press of Kentucky, 1995); and Mark Mazower, *Hitler's Empire: How the Nazis Ruled Europe* (New York: Penguin, 2008). On Holland, see Gerhard Hirschfeld, *Nazi Rule and Dutch Collaboration: The Netherlands under German Occupation 1940–1945* (New York: Berg, 1988); Louis de Jong, *The Netherlands and Nazi Germany* (Cambridge: Harvard University Press, 1990); Jacob Presser, *The Destruction of the Dutch Jews* (New York: Dutton, 1969); and Henry G. Schogt, *The Curtain: Witness and Memory in Wartime Holland* (Waterloo: Wilfrid Laurier University Press, 2003).

INDEX

HEDDA KALSHOVEN is the daughter of Irmgard Gebensleben. She has been married to Albert Kalshoven since 1956.

HESTER VELMANS most recently translated Saskia Goldschmidt's *The Hormone Factory*.

PETER FRITZSCHE is W. D. and Sara E. Trowbridge Professor of History at University of Illinois at Urbana-Champaign and author of *Life and Death in the Third Reich* and many other books.

The University of Illinois Press
is a founding member of the
Association of American University Presses.

———————————————————————

Designed by Dustin Hubbart
Composed in 10/12.5 Minion Pro
by Lisa Connery
at the University of Illinois Press
Manufactured by Sheridan Books, Inc.

University of Illinois Press
1325 South Oak Street
Champaign, IL 61820-6903
www.press.uillinois.edu